Health Through Sport

...be healthy, stay healthy, enjoy and achieve!

Ronny Goodlass

Founder   Ronny Goodlass

Everton Crazy

Produced by Gwladys Street's Hall of Fame

Printed and bound by UAB Standartu Spaustuve

Cover photograph provided by Bob Thomas via Getty Images

Illustrations by Peter King

Limited edition of 1,000 copies

All royalties from this publication will be donated to

Everton Former-Players' Foundation	Registered Charity No 1080101
Health Through Sport	Registered Charity No 1113480
Everton in the Community	Registered Charity No 1099366

ISBN 978-1-909245-46-4

Preface - David France

This book begins with a confession - I'm Everton crazy. Diagnosed decades ago, my condition was confirmed recently by an American journalist. He asked for my candid thoughts on the Merseyside derby. I volunteered: 'Everton versus Liverpool is art versus porn!' He responded: 'You are effing crazy, Everton crazy!' I didn't dispute his opinion. Everton Football Club is a part of my DNA. While I don't boast an Everton badge tattoo or unduly flaunt my colours in public, always I've made sure that people are aware of my allegiance.

My convictions were fashioned during my schooldays when I relied on the goings on at Goodison to provide an escape from the chaos of illiteracy. However, I didn't formalize the club's role in my life plan until 1975. It wasn't by choice. I remember sitting in an Italian restaurant in Valletta when my bride of three days confronted me: 'Now that we're married, what are you going to do about your royal blue addiction?' Clearly, Elizabeth had failed to grasp that she had also tied an unfathomable knot with Everton Football Club. For a moment or two, I thought that I was being primed for an intervention and would be dispatched to a detox clinic somewhere in the Mediterranean.

As the tension increased, I suggested to her: 'You know that I spent my first 14 years as a slow learner and nearly as long as a fast learner, so how about I divide the rest of my time on earth into similar periods? She countered: 'Right, you can fritter away 14 years at work, then spend14 years doing something more useful and 14 years doing nothing but watch Everton. I'm not sure what you'll do after age 70 but suspect that you'll die of exhaustion rather than boredom.' With the Malta Protocol in hand, she repeated her enquiry: 'What are you going to do about your addiction in the meantime?' Bravely, I responded: 'It's a pleasurable condition. It distorts reality. I intend to feed it!'

You'll discover that my subsequent Everton journey has involved travelling in excess of two million miles to attend 1,000 or so first-team games. In addition to the breathtaking artistry exhibited by some outstanding footballers, my more vivid memories of these matches are the collective buzz on the terraces and my adventures with the truly great Blues who follow the club across the country. Always, I've been aware of the special bonds between members of the Everton family. Without question, this camaraderie has enhanced the texture of my life. It taught me about fidelity and provided an unrivalled sense of belonging. I'm aware that younger readers may struggle to recognize the lifestyle and the football club described in my journey. Hopefully, they can identify with my immense pride of being a Blue.

Now please permit me to make another confession. Even though I've earned more degrees than a thermometer and have produced 15 other Everton books, I can't write for toffee. My words don't flow fluently or effortlessly and I'm not skilled enough to indulge in the sheer joy of the English language. Despite the fact that my rear-view mirror has often doubled as a kaleidoscope, I was encouraged by fellow Evertonians who claim to know about these things that my story is worth telling. Allegedly, it chronicles what football does to an otherwise well-balanced individual.

I've taken a radical approach to penning this book; one similar to that embraced by Tom Robbins. Like him, my mind flits like a hummingbird from one thought to another. Now and then it hovers in mid-air and even flies backwards on occasions. My favourite wordsmith hones each sentence until he's satisfied. Only then, does he add a full-stop and start the next one. There is no editing by outsiders. To emulate Robbins, I acquired some voice recognition software, developed a list of 100 or more topics and dictated my story to my computer. Therefore when you read this book, you're experiencing the words not only in the order that I spoke them but almost in the order that I thought them.

I'm amazed that my laptop has ignored my chronic rhotacism - the imperfect pronunciation of the r sound - and interpreted my flat-vowelled accent when so many people have refused to do so. I'm grateful that it has never yawned excessively in my face but now and then has switched to hibernation mode. Be that as it may, the production of these memoirs has been something of a collaborative effort. I've benefited from the advice of some eloquent voices of the Everton family, namely James Corbett, Michael Kenrick, Lyndon Lloyd, Dave Prentice and Becky Tallentire. One or two of them have taken pleasure in reminding me of Mark Twain's quip that the older you get, the more clearly you remember things that never actually happened.

My career in the oil & gas industry taught me to never travel far without a lawyer and I'm beholden to Norman Jones for his friendship and wise counsel. Many other members of the Everton family served as patient sounding boards and I appreciate them - namely Anne Asquith, Ed Bottomley, Ian Maher, Linda Mann, Martin O'Boyle, Simon Paul, David Starsky and Paul Trail - not thwarting my ambitions as a royal blue raconteur. Likewise, I enjoyed working with Peter King, a non-believer, and admire his willingness to convert my ironic eye into gag cartoons. Our long friendship demonstrates that Blues and Reds can get along - from 5,000 miles apart.

Last but not least, I'm grateful to my wife Elizabeth, a genuine Toffee Lady who in the words of Alan Ball is 'another good thing to come from Farnworth', for developing my life plan and for her ongoing sufferance during its implementation.

So with these acknowledgements, confessions and apologies out of the way, I'll proceed by boasting that I'm a proud Blue - someone who prefers art to pornographic filth.

No need to gaze into my crystal ball ... I can see Everton in your eyes

Foreword - David Prentice

Evertonians of all ages recognize his name but, despite his gargantuan achievements and almost god-like status on Merseyside and much farther afield, very few know much more about my good friend - Dr David France.

Our royal blue paths crossed for the first time at the offices of the Liverpool Echo in Old Hall Street almost a quarter of a century ago. Like a long-lost older brother, he impressed me with his knowledge and deep love of Everton Football Club as well as his fascinating and somewhat ambitious plans for a series of independent initiatives to celebrate the club's strength - namely its heritage.

Given his razor-sharp intellect - cleverly disguised by an unassuming manner - it was easy to see that anything he decided to do would be executed in style. But little did I know that he was one of those rare people who have the indefatigable drive and single-mindedness to turn his visions into reality. Since then, I've been in absolute awe of his devotion towards our beloved club. In sickness and in health, he has crossed the Atlantic Ocean hundreds of times to publish his fantastic books which tell the Everton story from so many different and novel angles, founded the Hall of Fame and organized some of the most passionate football celebrations of all-time, established the EFC Heritage Society to promote the club's unparalleled history of 114 seasons in the top flight of the English game and registered the Everton Former-Players' Foundation charity to tackle the medical and other needs of old footballers as well as attend as many home and away fixtures as practical.

Also, there is the small matter of him combing the world for jewels to add to his bulging treasure trove of football antiquities. The resulting Everton Collection is truly world-class but no greater than his resolute determination to transfer it to public ownership. Around the time of the handover, Andy Burnham - former-Secretary of State for Culture, Media and Sport put it perfectly: 'Thanks to Doctor Everton the story of the heart and soul of our club has been brought together. We all owe him a huge debt of thanks for the passion and the meticulousness with which he has prepared his wonderful archives.' Bill Kenwright, the Everton chairman, added: 'Even though he has never donned a royal blue jersey, David France is just as important to Everton Football Club as those who did.'

In recognition of these trail-blazing initiatives Liverpool's Freedom of the City Panel awarded him the title of Citizen of Honour for his services to football and the local community in 2011. Later that year, he received an OBE for his services to football in the United Kingdom and Europe. But as my old friend says often: 'Such decorations are unnecessary - being a Blue is my reward.'

With no little humour, this painstakingly-crafted autobiography captures the impact that professional football has on those of us who live, sleep and breathe it. This book sparkles with the wistful intimacy of an older Blue peering through the swirling mists of his memories. The nostalgic romanticism. The exciting adventures. The blind optimism. The fading hopes. And, of course, the yearning for the School of Science and Merseyside Millionaires of his youth. More than anything, his wonderful tales and anecdotes reflect what the majestic highs and humbling lows of supporting Everton Football Club have done to such a wise and generous soul.

My good friend is a truly great Evertonian. Probably, he is one of the greatest-ever Blues. Certainly, he is one of the most enthusiastic, loyal and steadfast Blues that I've had the good fortune to meet. Always, he has shown unrelenting commitment and absolute loyalty to Everton Football Club. Throughout his childhood, schooldays and gas-fitting apprenticeship in Widnes, his further education in the United Kingdom, the USA and West Germany, his business successes in the US oil & gas industry and his lengthy retirement in some of the most beautiful places in North America - if not the entire world, he has never strayed far from his Merseyside roots nor the companionship of his Everton family.

As you'll soon discover, the author has followed our beloved club faithfully for six decades. To do so, I understand that he has travelled the equivalent of four times the distance to the moon and back. That's unimaginable. That's unrivalled. Surely, it's proof that David France is Everton crazy and the title of these memoirs is fitting.

Personally, I'm intrigued and encouraged by the fact that his hundreds of trans-Atlantic pilgrimages – poetically referred to as flights to enlightenment - never hindered him from leading a full and wonderful life with his wife. Of course, as you'll soon discover there is much more to his life story than his role as Doctor Everton. You'll be amazed by his adventures and achievements. I'll let you decide for yourself but, in my humble opinion, his personal journey is truly inspirational.

David Prentice
Sports Editor, The Liverpool Echo

Good goal Eddie ... but have you any idea of its ramifications?

1. What do you call a life-time devoted to Everton?

My name is David and I'm an Evertonian.

These words are central to a recurring dream in which I'm seated in a dark room surrounded by concentric rows of chairs. Following my verbal admission, a chorus of familiar voices responds in harmony: 'Welcome, Evertonian.' As my eyes adjust slowly to my environment, I spot many unforgettable faces. However, most seats are occupied by people whose smiles are recognizable but whose names are unknown to me and perhaps to one another.

Without any external prompting, my grandfather and my father rise to their feet to share the royal blue experiences that shaped them and me. Their fervent words are followed by those of Dave Hickson. My old pal talks quietly yet passionately about our beloved club. Next, another two old-timers, namely Gordon Watson and Wally Fielding, repeat well-honed tales from their playing days and retirement years. Their memories radiate such strong emotions that my surroundings get brighter and brighter. Almost incandescent. I fear that I've infiltrated a utopian cult. Brian Labone, my spiritual guardian and self-appointed sponsor, stands proud and smiles wryly before speaking to me: 'Doctor Everton - my old friend, I've observed your emotional hemophilia with my own eyes at Goodison and invite you to join us in royal blue heaven. But first, please answer one simple question: 'What do you call a life-time devoted to Everton Football Club?'

Had it been six decades since my very first visit to a venue that couples the thrill of the unknown with the comfort of the familiar and continues to stir something primal deep in my soul? Simultaneously, my mind is stimulated by evocative images from the terrific 1962/63 season. The capital 1969/70 campaign. The glorious 1985 crusade across the European continent. The euphoria of witnessing Alex Young - The Golden Vision, Howard Kendall, Colin Harvey & Alan Ball - The Holy Trinity and Neville Southall - The Binman in their prime. Then there are the scars. The Wembley woes. The Anfield heartaches. The inexplicable flirtations with relegation. The despair associated with big-money signings whose names I no longer speak. And how can I forget the turgid performances without which it's difficult to fully appreciate the good ones?

Gradually, these flashbacks are overwhelmed by memories of the companionship of my fellow Blues. Their unwavering faith, inseparable bonds and acts of kindness offered a sense of belonging unavailable to me elsewhere. The pride of being part of something so extra special floods my brain. My eyes bulge. My hands shake. My neck veins throb rhythmically. Brian Labone mentions the sweat trickling from my temple as I struggle to answer him. His question inspires bursts of happiness, pleasure and pure joy. So much so that my heart races as royal blue heaven awaits. I can't catch my breath and awaken disorientated, almost deranged.

With this simple question unanswered, permit me to progress to another admission – I'm proud to be a Blue but had no say in the matter. That's right, I'm a product of royal blue love. Before my mother's death, I had the opportunity to enjoy her adult friendship and raise the types of intimate questions that most sons never get around to asking. During this no-holds-barred interrogation, I learned that I was conceived as a direct repercussion of Everton's unexpected triumph at Ayresome Park in late 1947.

I'm not sure that I needed to know the specific details and, as a consequence, have had to live with the fact that I'm indebted to Eddie Wainwright for scoring the winning goal against Middlesbrough and creating the ambience for procreation. Apparently, the inside-right received a neat pass from John McIlhatton and drove the ball into the back of the net with his favorite right foot.

Nowadays, Everton Football Club defines me. I can't imagine not having it to look forward to at the weekend and to think about during the week. My earliest recollection of the club is the fuss created by the news that Dave Hickson had scored in an FA Cup tie against United, the reigning League champions, on Valentine's Day 1953. At the time I was unaware that Everton were languishing in the lower half of the Second Division and the outcome had been quite a giant-killing act.

You may recall that the bustling centre-forward had been carried off with a serious gash above his right eyebrow after he had put his head among the flailing boots and, in the manner of Roy Race of Melchester Rovers, returned after half-time to net the winner. With blood streaming profusely from the stitched wound and down his face, he controlled a cross from left-winger Tommy Eglington before beating one defender, side-stepping another and firing the ball into the back of the net.

Because my father - a life-long Evertonian from a family of life-long Evertonians - had been working that Saturday afternoon and was unable to join the sell-out crowd of some 78,000 zealots gathered at Goodison, a match-going neighbour dropped by to tell him about the epic battle and, equally as important, give me his copy of the matchday programme. I can still picture the Bovril stain on the cover of the royal blue publication as well as their faces contorted with joy.

At age 4, I wasn't quite sure what Everton Football Club was but knew that I wanted my fair share of it as soon as I was old enough.

Bad luck son ... let's make it two out of three

2. An Everton win guaranteed sunshine

My road to Everton craziness started in a small town located on the northern banks of the Mersey, a dozen miles from the centre of Liverpool. Yes, I'm talking about smelly old Widnes which is best known as the birthplace of toxic wastes. Chemicals were the town's lifeblood. Widnes didn't just welcome the chemical industry; it bent over and assumed a comfortable position. Their union was celebrated with clouds of foul odours and torrents of contaminated waters. Their legacy was mountains of solid wastes with a questionable pH called gallygu.

Despite the hazardous employment conditions which contributed to widespread wheezing, chronic bronchitis and a dearth of pensioners, the town was populated by some of the hardest-working people in the land. These included my father, a Blue by birth who laboured at ICI's Pilkington Sullivan Works, and my mother, a Blue by choice – not necessarily her own, who toiled at the Ideal Laundry.

Though my rainbows were monochromatic, I've fond memories of growing up in a two-up, two-down in the heart of the town. Those were the good old days of unlocked doors and people who talked to one another. At the top of the street was the local pub, a purveyor of Greenall Whitley ales, where my friends cadged farthings from the thirsty patrons. These consisted of chemical plant workers, dressed in their tattered overalls exhibiting the patina of life among alkalis and acids, dapper Teddy Boys and equally well-turned out US airmen from the Burtonwood base. The other end boasted bomb sites where my sister and her friends constructed homes from the debris and fields of cinders, discarded by the local foundry, where I smoked recycled Lucky Strike fag-ends with mine.

The nearest grass, a good half-mile away, was reserved for the exploits of Widnes RLFC, one of the founders of the Rugby League. Now redeveloped as Halton Stadium, Naughton Park was an eclectic mix of structures under which a rookery of young fans huddled like Emperor penguins to survive the horizontal rain. All Widnes boys were expected to spend time in a black and white hooped scarf and bobble hat at the old ground. The minimum sentence was a six-month stretch with no time off for good behaviour.

Aware of the hidden dangers from premature exposure to Everton Football Club, I remember my mother's negative response to my wishes to make my childhood complete by visiting Goodison. She declared that I was too young. Then a month later, she claimed that I was too small. It's more than likely that she just wanted me to have a peaceful and happy transit along the tightrope of life. My father reassured me that good things were worth waiting for and added that the delay would make my baptism even more memorable. Of course, he was right. And so, for that matter, was my mother and her trepidations.

Despite these pleas, petitions and prayers to see Everton, I received a Widnes season-ticket on my seventh birthday. For my parents, it was a small price to pay for the peace of mind of knowing where I was on a Saturday. For me, it was a cruel and unusual punishment. Prior to the formation of the Super League, Widnes RLFC was known nationally as the 'Chemics' and locally as the 'Comics' and it was often said that their juvenile season-tickets should have carried a health warning: 'Watching Rugby League doubles the risks of adolescent acne and adult impotence.' Wrapped in a blue and white scarf, I attended all home fixtures during the 1955/56 season. They were a mere rehearsal for going to a proper football match.

As a speck of royal blue in a small sea of black and white, the best part about those afternoons was hurrying home to listen to the classified results at five o'clock. At the first note of 'Out of the Blue', the signature tune of the BBC's Sports Report radio programme, our house came to a standstill. If my father was at work, I documented the scores for him.

Without using verbs, the lilting tones and perfect delivery of the announcer transformed names and numbers into pure drama. The slightest intonation of his voice made the Third Division South sound like a poetic and mystical land. Also his inflections told the France family what kind of weekend to expect. Some people's moods change with the weather. One of my father's virtues was his ability to change the local weather with his mood - an Everton win guaranteed sunshine.

We lived in Gerrard Street - the aorta of the Simms Cross district. It was a working-class area which had been enhanced by recent influxes of Irish, Lithuanian and Polish immigrants. Because most of the male residents were engaged in shift-work, there were curfews on certain street activities. The kicking of footballs was banned whereas tick-and-pass, a derivative of Rugby League, was encouraged. Games of 20-a-side, were common and often stretched between distant lamp-posts. The touch-lines were the curbstones which had been painted red, white and blue for the Queen's Coronation.

As a spectacle, it was not unlike the Eton Wall Game except that some of the participants had played or were to play rugby professionally. The action was frenetic and suspended only for calls of 'Pram!' and 'Woodbines!' During these tobacco breaks, a rope was stretched across the street and the young girls, with their skirts tucked under the elastic of their navy blue knickers, would skip as the grown-ups turned and reminded the nearby smokers that 'The Big Ship Sails on the Ally O.'

My mother said that we were poor yet happy. I had no reason not to believe her.

Bitter, twisted, enthusiastic ... just a touch of childhood Evertonitis

3. Why follow Everton Football Club?

Why Everton? Why not Liverpool? That's very simple. Enthusiastic references to unique fellowship, unparalleled heritage and even stubborn romanticism at Goodison Park are overshadowed by the fact that my father, two uncles and grandfather were loyal Blues. Yes, the France family has blue blood. At one time or another, I was reminded that my great-great-uncle Billy from Runcorn had owned three of the original shares of The Everton Football Club Company Limited and that I had been blessed to have entered the world as a fifth-generation Evertonian.

Given this patrimony, I was subjected to no little propaganda and, as you know, longed to exchange Naughton Park for Goodison Park to witness my favourites in action. To do so, I started a Football Fund. Savings from my modest pocket money were bolstered by the gratuities received from running errands to restock the neighbours' pantries with emergency supplies of unfiltered cigarettes, loose tea, sterilized milk and extra-dry kindling from the corner-shops.

These errands should not be confused with the Bob Run, my first-ever business venture, which involved tracking down shilling coins to satisfy the needs of thirsty electricity and gas meters when these shops were closed. It was a highly profitable initiative. Before decimalization, there were 12 pennies in a shilling and, more often than not, I received 14 pennies for every silver coin. Not a bad bit of business? To provide a speedy service to my customers, I kept an elusive coin in a woollen sock under the bed along with my Football Fund, bubble gum cards, licorice sticks and salvaged tobacco. To assist my nicotine-craving customers in their hour of need, I hid an unopened pack of Domino cigarettes - which cost 6d for four - in the sock also.

I knew that a programme cost 3d but had little idea of the price to enter Goodison. Now and then, I would empty my sock to count my pennies. I feared there would be never enough and embarked on an austerity programme. Consequently, I reduced my consumption of licorice sticks. This root is one of the greatest medicinal herbs known to mankind and was used to treat problems of the gastrointestinal and urinary tracts. I chewed it to mask the odour of cheap cigarettes.

My mother limited my clientele to the houses on the orange sides of Gerrard Street and Alfred Street where she knew the occupants. To increase my income from the Bob Run, I would stray across the religious divide. I must clarify that sectarianism didn't dominate life but it did cause tension. On the green side of the street, where all of the Coronation paints had been scrubbed from the curbstones, the Roman Catholics had the bigger terraced houses to accommodate their large families. On our side, the Church of England contingent was deluded into thinking it was better off. The Frances were Methodists and considered odd. Make that very odd.

Even though neither of my parents attended religious services, my sister and I were regulars at Milton Congregational Church. To be honest, I didn't enjoy Sunday prayers or Sunday school but looked forward to mixing with the older boys and hearing about their spiritual callings to a football temple in the Walton district of Liverpool. I longed to follow in their footsteps.

With no sports, no shops and very little public transportation, the Sunday evenings of my childhood were quiet. The highlight was raising money - one penny at a time - for even less fortunate children. The Methodist Church provided the impressionable members of its flock with books of smiling young African faces which were guaranteed to gnaw at heart strings. Each serrated page raised one penny towards the purchase of bibles. That's right, we were encouraged to solicit donations from people struggling to feed their own smiling young faces.

Walking the streets around my Simms Cross neighbourhood to the sound of my own footsteps, the door-to-door missionary work was eye-opening. With their portals locked, some residents hid behind twitching curtains. Others simply ignored me and concentrated on their heated domestic disputes.

My spirits were raised by my regulars. One frazzled mother would request: 'My usual Penny Mau Mau, please. The one with innocent eyes.' Other interactions were memorable for the wrong reasons. I remember one cold, wet and dreary evening in particular. Soaked from head to toe with only my blue and white scarf to keep out the cold, I knocked on the door of an Irish widow who lived on the green side of the street. This kind lady allowed my mother to use her bathroom facilities and piping hot water for a small fee. Her Irish lodger wasn't as accommodating. Possibly intoxicated from a lunchtime session at the Simms Cross Hotel, he coughed and spluttered throughout my sales pitch. Then just before he slammed the front-door, he mumbled: 'Sod off, you Proddy Woddy.' Then he raised his voice: 'I said bugger off, you blue bastard.'

It was the first time that I had heard anything negative about my beloved football club. I was shocked and confused. Our Catholic neighbours hadn't been reluctant to sing the praises of Peter Farrell, Tommy Eglington, Peter Corr and the other members of the Eire side which had triumphed at Goodison a few years earlier. It seemed to me that every household on the green side of Gerrard Street was related to at least one of the victors and, therefore, I had assumed that they were all loyal Blues. Indeed, I had been brainwashed to believe that everyone loved Everton.

Troup's corner hung in the air as the great man soared majestically above the Arsenal defenders ... it was sixty for Dixie

4. Play up, Everton!

My mother claimed that Hickson's famous goal in 1953 started my Everton obsession. It took decades, however, for her to accept that it wasn't going away. Née Una Baker, she was different from local women. For starters, my mother was a Geordie who sounded like a husky Paul Gascoigne when overly excited. More vexing for our neighbours was her refusal to donkey-stone the steps at the front door. They were appalled at such neglect. In her defence, my mother was too busy cooking, baking, cleaning, washing, scouring for bargains and working full-time. She was 'The Lee Carsley of Mothers'. Not that she was barracked at home. Rather that she never stopped toiling for others and every now and then would produce something spectacular.

Like Lee Carsley, she wasn't fully appreciated until after she was gone. A cocktail of Catalan eyes, Dorset innocence and Durham grit, her no-nonsense personality had been influenced by the loss of her own mother from melancholia - an innocuous term for suicide in the early Twenties - when she was aged 2. The death burdened her father with two toddlers and long-lasting bitterness which fuelled Ma Carsley's desire to leave home and join the WAAF at the earliest opportunity. Shortly afterwards, she met my father on a grass runway used by an RAF bombing and gunnery school near Dumfries. A lifetime later, she confessed that marrying such an avid Blue was a small sacrifice to make in support of the war effort.

I remember my mother working at the local laundry where her first instrument of choice was the iron. Now I'm not referring to the Fender Stratocaster models of the twenty-first century with their multi-thermostatic settings, nonstick soleplates and ergonomically designed handles. Hers was a cast-iron monster heated by a simple gas burner. It resembled a curling stone and in fact glided across Egyptian cotton as if it was ice. The side-effect of her repetitive actions was that she developed super-sized biceps, triceps and deltoids, albeit in one arm. Yes, her right belonged to Popeye, her left to Olive Oyl.

After processing a million or so shirts, she was promoted to the steam-powered press where their detachable white collars were ironed at high temperatures to attain cardboard-like rigidity. This assignment provided her with a private work-room which she shared with transient cockroaches and overwrought vermin. Apparently, the former had become immune to the poisons available to the laundry industry. They looked mean and had piercings, tattoos and bad attitudes. The mice were less smug because they had to battle with the laundry cats which patrolled the premises like Phil Jagielka on the edge of the penalty area.

Now, please permit me to digress into a somewhat delicate area. The white-collar job offered one big perk. Namely, the endless supply of paper bags with the consistency of Izal which served as toilet paper throughout the remainder of my days and nights in the Gerrard Street outhouse. The bags were cut into neat squares and threaded onto string to resolve one of the great quandaries of life — should toilet paper roll over or under? For the uninitiated who have been spoilt by super-soft quilted tissues, Izal was coarse, non-absorbent and extremely hard on the bum. It possessed an unmistakable aroma from the disinfectant added to combat typhoid fever and even worms. I can assure you that if the Andrex Puppy grabbed a mouthful of Izal, he or she would never touch another toilet roll.

When Ma Carsley ironed at home, her preferred tool was a Morphy Richards electric model. Given that she had access to only one source of electricity, the central light fixture in the living room was rigged with a crude Bakelite connector to allow both the light bulb and the iron to function. I fondly recall those Sunday evenings. The movements of the 40 Watt bulb were synchronized with those of her muscular right arm and the resulting shadows were not unlike a solar eclipse on methamphetamines.

Sunday was also nit night. While my sister and I attempted to master the art of sitting still, my mother tackled the imaginary head lice with a fine-tooth comb, a block of black Derbac soap and the vigour of Popeye. Next, an old galvanized bath was dragged in from the yard and positioned near the Dolly tub and the cold water tap in the back-kitchen. My sister was dunked, dried and dispatched to practice on the piano.

I've been told but have no recollection that, as the sickly runt of the family destined to spend my life obsessed with Everton Football Club, I was the apple of my mother's eye. If that was the case, I received no favours during the cleansing process. After the hard-water crust had been removed and an old brick had been wedged under one corner of the tub, I was immersed into the deep end. My mother took advantage of my foaming immobility to quiz me on my Sunday school homework. That's right, Sunday school homework. This involved reciting psalms, especially the one about green pastures and still waters, and learning the words of hymns.

Like most Methodists, she would announce her selections: 'No 378 - Amazing Grace' and 'No 77 - How Great Thou Art.' After an appropriate pause for reflection, we would start singing in harmony. Then without warning Ma Carsley would halt mid-verse to allow me to demonstrate my knowledge and understanding of the words. The exercise was repeated until I was proficient or, in her opinion, the bath water was too cold.

She would end the concert with a rousing verse of her all-time favourite, that is No 575, with its military theme and martial melody. All together now: 'Onward, Christian soldiers, marching as to war, with the cross of Jesus going on before ...'

It's a common problem with teenage super-stars

5. Blue beliefs

Ma Carsley's other bath-time topic was the geography of the British Isles to which she would insert a novel football theme. Every Sunday night she would challenge me to list the 48 members of the Third Divisions South and North in alphabetical order. Many of the southern clubs, such as Bournemouth & Boscombe, Brighton & Hove, Coventry, Palace, Orient, Northampton, Reading, Southampton, Swindon and Watford, aspired fleetingly to the top flight. Their northern counterparts found life far more problematic. Sadly the likes of Barrow, Bradford Park Avenue, Gateshead, Halifax, Mansfield, Stockport, Workington, Wrexham and York are no longer among the 92 League clubs. To this day, I remain convinced that football was God's preferred way of teaching geography to working-class children and that he should have shown more compassion towards local clubs with royal blue connections such as Chester, Southport and Tranmere.

In the times before televisions and telephones, old houses emitted strange noises. Some whistled, others creaked. Gerrard Street was haunted by the resonance of click-click knit one, click-click purl one – the sounds of my mother's needles. Ma Carsley could knit and talk at the same time. She could knit and read the Daily Mirror. She could knit with forensic calm in a speeding car. It's likely that she could have knitted for England. Rumours spread that she had been capped already by County Durham.

My mother took great pride in her handiwork and produced all sorts of garments including my sacred blue and white scarf; warm enough for Goodison and long enough for Dr Who. I must confess that this neck warmer was not as stylish as that sported by the likes of Roberto Mancini and Jose Mourinho. That was because I preferred to wrap it around my neck and throw it over one shoulder, rather than attempt the double loop of their designer noose. Nevertheless, I rarely left the house without it. In the decades before replica shirts, my blue and white scarf was my way of demonstrating my faith.

You'll be relieved to know that the scarf - unlike almost everything else in this book - didn't have a nickname. It had been commissioned by my paternal grandfather, the architect of my mind-bending education. Raised on the south bank of the Mersey, where football is preferred to Rugby League, he made sure that his three sons and their children grew up with Goodison in their lives. As a result, Grandad France brainwashed me with tales of William Ralph Dean.

He had seen Dixie score hundreds of times including his famous sixtieth League goal in 1928. More than anything, my grandfather believed that his one-and-only idol had been treated shabbily at the end of his Everton career. So much so that he claimed to have written to Theo Kelly and suggested that the club's secretary erect a monument in honour of the most prolific goal-scorer in the history of the English game, similar to the one in Trafalgar Square to commemorate Lord Nelson. The bronze statue of the great footballer would be much taller, with one foot in height for every goal he scored for the club in the League. His preferred site was on the old practice ground behind the Goodison Avenue Stand. Being a bit of an amateur scientist as well as a professional blacksmith, my grandfather had calculated that at 3:15 pm on the third Saturday of every August, the orientation of the sun would cast a silhouette of the 349-feet tall statue across Stanley Park, over the boating lake and across the Victorian palm-house to finish exactly at the half-way line at Anfield; thus reminding all Kopites that they would live in the shadow of Dixie Dean and Everton Football Club for another season.

Why 3.15 pm? Apparently, Saturday was a half work-day on Merseyside and the late kick off allowed workers in the docks and factories to get a quick wash before heading to Walton. Given that the pubs along Goodison Road stopped serving at 3.00 pm, the extra 15 minutes allowed for a more relaxed drinking-up time before their patrons rushed to the turnstiles.

Grandad France was the first person to refer to me as an Evertonian – or more precisely a Blue. A man of few words, he told me that Everton enjoyed a unique culture based on the Ten Blue Beliefs. There was no mention of Latin mottos. Rather, the bedrock of his ideology was that the club was peerless. Unfortunately, only eight of them come to mind:

1. Everton wear blue and white ...
2. Everton play cultured and entertaining football ...
3. Everton are leaders not followers ...
4. Everton own the finest facilities in the land ...
5. Everton maintain a high moral code ...
6. Everton develop their own ...
7. Everton reaches deep into the soul of its local community ...
8. Everton is run by Evertonians for the benefit of all Evertonians.

At that time, I was unaware of his mind control and was more interested in my reward for listening to his propaganda – an invitation to feed Sagar, his prized egg machine, and the other poultry kept at his meticulously maintained allotment.

Something else about my grandfather was special. Instead of saying hello and goodbye, I fondly remember his cigarette voice - or more accurately his Capstan Full Strength-coated larynx, bellowing: 'Play up, Everton!'

One more chorus of Johnny Todd then back to work on set-pieces

6. Being a good blue

Now it's time for a word or two about Harry France - the head of the household. My father was a process worker, which sounds like he sat all day in a control room pushing buttons and tweaking valves among the infrastructure of a chemical complex. I learnt, not from him, that process work was ICI's terminology for climbing into giant metal vats to dislodge the hardened residues with his pick and spade. I don't know if these wastes were acidic or alkali. Regardless, they scorched his skin and lungs. Back then workers were provided with little safety equipment – just overalls, gloves, goggles and muslin cloth. I understand that after my father had wrapped the latter around his face, neck and mouth, he looked like 'Chemical Harry' – an urban guerilla without the ubiquitous Kalashnikov AK-47 and the smouldering remnants of the Stars & Stripes.

Like the Ideal Laundry, ICI offered a few perks befitting its status as the UK's biggest company. These extended to seemingly endless supplies of paint, hypo and muslin cloth. Many of the doors, gutters and drain-pipes in and around Simms Cross were painted ICI blue which was not unlike the hue of our One2One era. Hypo, more formally known as hypochlorous acid, is a bleach and disinfectant. In Gerrard Street, it was used primarily to scrub dirty linoleum into submission and, in a town not noted for dental hygiene, it was diluted to clean the dentures of both young and old overnight. However, I had only strange ideas of what people did with the rolls of cloth.

Surprisingly for a Widnes native, my father wasn't a big fan of the oval ball. Without question, he was broad-shouldered enough to play rugby. Indeed, I remember him as a muscle-man with a mop of hair generally reserved for Conservative Party politicians and mood swings usually associated with former-Conservative Party leaders. Football was his passion and, from his accounts, he had been a proficient keeper who had guested for a couple of clubs during the war.

The highlight of his playing career involved an unfortunate incident at Preston. Apparently, he had run onto the pitch and received a warm welcome from his RAF pals. Then his confidence got the better of him. As he approached the penalty area my father elected to jog backwards. His journey was terminated abruptly by the metal stanchion employed to prevent the wooden cross-bar from sagging prior to kick-off. It's a part of our family lore that he was knocked unconscious. My father never discussed his war-time service during which he lost some of his hearing but wasn't shy to reminisce about the events at Deepdale.

Chemical Harry loved football. It was one of the few things he talked to me about. That said, he specialized in Everton myths. Time and time again, my father placed his hand on his heart and told me that the players wore blue stripes down their shorts to make them go faster. Also he claimed that, with the exception of Southern softies like Wally Fielding, they were required to roll up their sleeves irrespective of the weather. Most memorable of all, he swore that no-one was allowed to throw an Everton shirt onto the dressing room floor. If a player broke this law he would be fined two weeks wages. I believed him because he was my father. Even worse, if someone happened to stand on a blue shirt he would be handcuffed, blindfolded, escorted into Gwladys Street and stoned. I believed him because the punishment seemed to fit the crime.

Outwardly cheerful yet inwardly conflicted, I'll never forget the day he acquired a motor car. Gleaming with mysterious provenance, the Jowett Javelin had been the first post-war British car and discerning motoring enthusiasts have maintained their love affair with it to this day. Whatever its origin, the Javelin was a source of inconvenience for the local traffic. This consisted of a procession of horse-drawn vehicles such as milk floats, rag-and-bone men, coal wagons and bin carts that struggled to side-step around the parked car. Besides a Jaguar which belonged to the local turf accountant, it was the only private vehicle in Gerrard Street. Several neighbours speculated that, even though neither of my parents drank, smoked or gambled, they had won the Irish Hospitals' Sweepstakes.

Many others whispered that the funds could have been put to better use, I considered the high-tech vehicle to be a well-deserved reward for his graft amid hazardous residues and, because car-ownership was an indicator of economic hope, believed that my mother had earned the right not to queue at bus stops in the pouring rain with bags of heavy shopping.

Chemical Harry spent much of his free time polishing it in a ramshackled garage some 400 yards from Gerrard Street. Because this hiding place was as distant as his place of employment, he continued to go to work on his bike. The Jowett Javelin was reserved for days out to market towns in Derbyshire and pretty villages in Denbighshire where carpets of green wrapped around the rolling hills, trickling streams, mighty oaks and unpicked flowers. For me, the highlights of these trips was returning salutes to AA motorcycles and sidecars – that is the Automobile Association not the 12-step programme people – and munching sandwiches. In retrospect, the concept of eating Spam butties in front of fields of farm animals seems rather misguided.

I would love to reveal that I was conceived in the Javelin. My mother divulged, however, that I was created as well as born in the bedroom at the corner of Gerrard and Alfred Streets. It was an unheated room illuminated by the gas street-light which had been lassooed with a bicycle tyre, a popular urban decoration in 1948. The sitting-room below contained an old piano which, as you know already, my sister was required to play. At other times, it was conceded to the cockroaches which co-habited the house. On occasions, I would sneak into their room and play table-football with them. I recall that the roaches soon mastered the art of trapping a glass marble and were expert at running into space. Their passing, however, was atrocious.

Having lived in Texas for a big part of my life, I've become something of an expert at identifying dead roaches and can confirm that those domiciled with us in Gerrard Street were not the ones of my US nightmares. They boasted flailing antennae which enabled them to fly, scamper at speed, exhibit reflexes much faster than humans and, if my memory serves me well, play the piano – albeit badly. It's claimed that roaches are the only creatures likely to survive a nuclear holocaust. Their fans believe they are simply misunderstood yet rarely, if ever, mention that they eat anything and also excrete on the run. I suspect that the omnivorous shitters spent their Gerrard Street evenings hiding in inaccessible crevices after following my mother home from work. It would be a stretch of even my imagination to picture her as the Pied Piper with a trail of roaches scurrying behind her. Why you ask? Well, Ma Carsley despised them. My mother knew they were pathogens, making them suspects in the spread of cholera and dysentery. To her immense credit, she succeeded in confining the infestations to the one room and, courtesy of a Flit gun, serving them a weekly eviction notice. Eventually, the hostilities escalated - after the insects strayed across the demilitarized zone during the Roach War of 1953 - and the hand-pumped insecticide sprayer was replaced with more sophisticated chemical weapons containing a proprietary blend of boric acid and - you guessed it - hypo.

There was a kind of beauty in our despair. I shared the other bedroom and its single bed with my sister. Even though she was a loyal ally, we fought over bed space before agreeing to sleep top-to-toe. There was no heating or lighting in our room and my sister often scraped 'Everton' in the ice on the windows to make tiny snowballs and raise my spirits. Our comfort was enhanced by the soft glow of small candles and warmth from a patchwork quilt supplied by the Canadian Red Cross. Often I've imagined the women-folk of the Prairies crafting this beautiful item to keep out the bogeyman and the battle-hardened roaches of Gerrard Street. With the proliferation of candle stubs, my sister described our bedroom as 'The Sanctuary of Our Lady of Lourdes'. Wise beyond her years, she claimed we had few belongings but weren't poor. Apparently, poverty wasn't about material needs. It had more to do with loneliness and hopelessness. I believed her because she was almost three years older than me.

7. Birth of a collection

In Gerrard Street, we had lots of friends to provide love, care and peace of mind. Like most of them, we had barely enough sustenance. The early-Fifties was a time of rationing. Families grew vegetables on allotments and sought alternative ways to put food on the table. Every now and then, after completing his night shift, my father would pick potatoes to earn an extra few bob and, more important, a sack of spuds. I can picture him returning from a farm near Cuerdley Cross on the road to Warrington with his cargo balanced on the crossbar of his bike. After he had unhitched the galvanized bath to wash his prize, we panned through the muddy water in search of King Edwards to mash, boil, roast and fry. Caked in Mother Earth, the four of us sat around the weathered bath tub scrubbing the spuds and talking. This was the first time of many times that Chemical Harry told me about the incredible deeds of his hero - Tommy Lawton and his father's idol - a certain William Ralph Dean. As a sign of respect, raw potatoes were subsequently referred to as 'Dixies'.

Around that time I started my own habit of picking up things from the ground to add to my impressive collection of discarded fag ends. My most mouthwatering discoveries were the Bramley cooking apples scavenged from Widnes market. These were so badly bruised that they were deemed unfit for human consumption, even during food rationing when families were limited to buying one apple per week. In return for my initiative, I was rewarded with a dose of Scarlet Fever. Today, it's treated via a two-week course of antibiotics. But back in the Fifties, it was a life-threatening and highly contagious disease - up there with the likes of Bubonic plague and smallpox - and required immediate hospitalization.

At the first sign of my bright red tongue and body rash my mother sent for the doctor. I understand that the skin on my hands - especially at the finger-tips - and my feet had peeled by the time he arrived on his moped. Immediately, our GP arranged for me to be whisked away by ambulance to Peasley Cross Hospital in St Helens. It was no ordinary hospital, it was an isolation hospital. For a Widnes lad, it was like travelling to another world. I'm not saying that St Helens was the end of the earth but the general consensus in Gerrard Street was that you could see the end of the earth from Pilkington Brothers' glassworks.

Solitary confinement is no fun at any age. It was hell for a 7-year-old. I received few visitors but must tell you about the afternoon when my champion dropped by. Every town has its local heroes. Mine had only one famous footballer, namely Tommy Magee who had captained West Brom's FA Cup-winning side in 1931. At five feet on his tip-toes, Magee was a football star in a Rugby League town which also boasted a genuine Rugby League icon. Known as Vince Karalius in the place of his birth and simply Vinty throughout the rest of Rugby League world, the famed 'Wild Bull of the Pampas' was so hard that Australians still talk about him in whispered tones.

Born and bred in Widnes, the muscular loose-forward had joined St Helens RLFC to fulfill his ambitions and in turn won every trophy in the game. A teetotaler and a non-smoking fitness fanatic, his physique was a product of genetic blessings and brutally hard work. I had heard that he would sprint to Knowsley Road and back, a round trip of 15 miles, and dive off the Transporter Bridge to swim handcuffed across the Manchester Ship Canal and the River Mersey. Then he would discard his shackles during his jog to the General Post Office near Widnes Town Hall and dry off by ripping telephone directories in half using his front teeth. Sounds improbable? Surely, he used his molars also.

Karalius became so notorious that his photograph was included on a collector's card issued by The Victor comic. All of my friends were impressed that his intimidating mug-shot was sandwiched between those of Brazil's Pele and England's Ron Springett. Therefore, it's not surprising that I can recall his visit to Peasley Cross Hospital.

He brought wooden toys and comic books for the patients in the general ward and bottles of Lucozade for the quarantined inmates like me. I don't know, nor want to know, how or from where he had acquired the rare elixir. Wrapped in figure-hugging Cellophane, my bottle sparkled on the top shelf of my cell. Throughout my childhood, I was discouraged from asking for things. It was my mother's way of minimizing disappointment. So from my hospital bed I gawked at the unopened bottle and fantasized about its contents. The nurses claimed that the glucose syrup would make me as strong as a bull; possibly as fearsome as an infamous wild one. I stared at the bottle for 80 days and 80 nights by which time I treated it as a decoration rather than nutrition. In truth, the bottle was my secret friend. It's one of the great regrets of my childhood is that my faithful companion remained behind, with golden seal unbroken, when I was cleared to return home.

To cheer those of us in lock-down, Karalius placed his gnarled fingers against the windows of our rooms. I didn't understand that I was supposed to position mine on the other side of the glass. I simply stared at his uniquely rugged face. It would be hard to forget those craggy features that only Rugby League supporters could love, his bulging muscles and that hint of aggression common to Widnes men of his size. I was so impressed that there and then I decided that if ever I needed to nominate a combatant champion to fight my corner then it would be Karalius. After all, few heroes possess a surname that sounded like a snarl.

Other local sportsmen showed similar compassion. I've been told that Everton's Tommy Eglington and Harry Leyland, United's Bill Foulkes and Liverpool's Billy Liddell also dropped by. Many years later I had the pleasure of befriending both Tommy and Harry. They told me that their team-mates in the Fifties considered such hospital visits to be a part of their community responsibilities and never thought of informing the club or the local newspapers of their deeds.

My dose of Scarlet Fever had far-reaching consequences. Most of the items in our house were taken away and incinerated, including the Canadian quilt and my one and only Everton programme. Somehow my scarf survived. More likely, it was destroyed and Ma Carsley crafted a replica during my confinement. Simms Cross was such a friendly and close-knit neighbourhood at work and at play that upon my discharge from the isolation hospital both Catholics and Protestants gathered around the ambulance to welcome me. They didn't come empty-handed and donated an assortment of replacement household items. The working people of Merseyside are so generous. Those with so few possessions never hesitate to help the needier.

One benevolent soul - whose name remains unknown - presented me with a replacement programme - one without a Bovril stain. Little did he or I know that it would become the cornerstone of the Everton Collection.

8. Baptized in the Paddock

The Jowett Javelin has a fond place in my heart. She whisked me to Goodison for the first time. It was a match against the famous Busby Babes; the last mid-week match without floodlights. To heighten my sense of anticipation – or possibly emphasize the difference between Everton and the Funny Handshake Club – my father parked on Anfield Road. In late 1957, there was no air of smug entitlement hanging over Liverpool's home. With its corrugated metal structures, the stadium was no better than Naughton Park and had little in common with the distant sight of Mama Blue. That's how Chemical Harry often referred to the stadium and its surroundings.

I'll never forget my first glimpse of her. She was astonishingly beautiful. As we walked along Goodison Road, my chaperone and I became excited by the hustle and bustle of the fans. Through the mist of bygone years, I can picture them side-stepping the fertilizer deposited by the immaculately groomed police horses - a pre-match ritual that continues to this day. These enormous animals were employed to control the ravenous queues leading to the turnstiles and the fish & chip shop counters, as well as protect the men carrying placards which proclaimed 'The Lord is My Saviour' and other religious messages now found on the undershirts of some Premier League players. Young nuns armed with innocent voices and lustful collection boxes provided a guard of honour on either side of the turnstile doors. I felt like the luckiest boy in the world and didn't have to enter the stadium to know that it was where I wanted to watch my football.

Once inside, the enormous stadium resembled a temple of worship, pilgrimage and culture adorned with religious symbols. Floodlight pylons pierced the heavens. Cast iron balconies trapped the fervour pulsating from the terraces. Instead of incense there was the mixed aroma of Brylcreem, Higsons and Woodbines unique to football grounds in the Fifties. Then there was the noise from the 72,000 like-minded worshippers. There was no Gregorian chanting or hymn singing, just roaring synchronized with the action on the pitch. And, of course, there was the community swearing. Everyone around me was bilingual. They were proficient in English and fluent in profanity. It seemed to me that if you spent a little time at Goodison, you would be sure to emerge a different effing person.

My spiritual awakening occurred in the Paddock, now called the Lower Bullens Stand. It was so full that my father gripped my hand as he guided me down the congested gangway to the perimeter wall. He instructed me to keep away from the crush-barriers which were strategically placed to dampen the surging movements of the massive crowd. This was easier said than done. Afterwards, he confessed that his feet had not always been on the ground. Coincidentally, I had been floating on air since we left the car. The terraces were so congested that the smaller fans were passed above the sea of donkey jackets in some sort of ritual of human sacrifice. Possibly over-excited by the pandemonium, some desperate souls had to relieve themselves through rolled-up newspapers.

Knowing that I would strain to see the action at the perimeter wall, especially where it had been raised to accommodate the half-time scoreboard, Chemical Harry had carried a metal milk crate for me to stand on. I shared it with another Blue who was being baptized that evening. He was related to one of the dockers who circumnavigated the pitch carrying a huge wooden hoarding which promoted the forthcoming boxing attractions at Liverpool Stadium. My most enduring impressions were the royal blue of the shirts and the emerald, olive, bottle and jade patchwork of the manicured turf. Also, I'll never forget the screeching from the choir imprisoned in a metal cage, known officially as the Boys' Pen. It was eardrum piercing. As the excitement grew, their voices were audible only to dogs in and around Bootle. My experience involved more than sights and sounds. The air was full of unwavering faith and confirmed my father's claim that Goodison was the most evocative, intimate and atmospheric place on earth.

As for the game? It was an end-to-end cracker. Driven on by Duncan Edwards, United were 3-1 up at half-time. Everton pounded United's defence throughout the second half and Jimmy Harris netted on the hour. Then shortly after Dave Hickson's headed equalizer had been ruled offside, 18-year-old Derek Temple scored and Chemical Harry broke into a happy dance. With Mama Blue in full voice and at near perfect pitch, the noise tingled my spinal column. The final minutes were breath-taking as the home side, which included 39-year-old Wally Fielding, stretched the Busby Babes and both teams received a standing ovation at full-time. My father remarked that 3-3 was a fair outcome because the proceedings had been dominated by the most influential footballer he had ever seen, namely 'The Great Duncan Edwards'. In recent years, I've spoken to many men who played against the midfield powerhouse. They concurred that his strength and skills made other world-class players question their own abilities.

Shortly after my baptism, the Munich Disaster paralyzed the nation and football fans of all persuasions prayed as Duncan Edwards and his boss Matt Busby fought for their lives in hospital. After the greatest British footballer of all time died of his injuries, most sons of Rugby League adopted the remnants of the Manchester team as their favourites. It would have been so easy to have become a Red Devil during that period of national grief. But I was born a Blue and it had been decided, by those who adjudicate such things, that I would remain one until I die.

I treasured the matchday publication from that game. Within months it was complemented by those from the games against Bolton, Blackburn, Burnley and Preston, all founder members of the League. The attraction wasn't the celebration of football's heritage but the chance to see the likes of Nat Lofthouse, Bryan Douglas, Jimmy McIlroy and Tom Finney. Given the dearth of televised football nationally and the lack of a television set in Gerrard Street, if you wanted to see the man behind the big reputation you had to go to the match. Goodison hadn't had a national headline-maker of its own since the defection of Tommy Lawton. Without a doubt, it was home to fine players such as Peter Farrell, Tommy Eglington and Dave Hickson – men haunted by the stench of Second Division football. There was talk of a talented young defender named Brian Labone taking the place of TE Jones who played with what looked like telephone directories inside his socks. There was one other exciting prospect. Derek Temple was fulfilling his National Service obligations in Kenya.

My prayers for a hero were answered by Bobby Collins in 1958. That Christmas, his arrival was celebrated with my mother's version of an Everton shirt. In the absence of official replicas, I made do with a rugby jersey manufactured by Bukta. She had bought what looked like a blue smock with a white collar from Jack Sharp's shop in Liverpool city centre. I wasn't overly concerned by its size and was accustomed to her words of encouragement: 'Don't worry, you'll grow into it.' I was disturbed by her attempts to personalize it. She had replaced the collar with a V-neck deep enough for a Kardashian. While I had expected the No 10 worn by Collins, she went one better. With two vertical strips of white ribbon on my back, I became Eddie O'Hara. The left-winger was considered an obscure choice by the kids in Gerrard Street.

The kit made its debut against Charlton. Throughout the hard-fought FA Cup tie, I sensed my father distancing himself from me. Perhaps he was troubled by the sight of bamboo shin-pads poking out of my blue and white hooped socks. Though Everton won, Chemical Harry claimed that my No 11 shirt was jinxed and threatened to file a restraining order to keep it out of Walton. He was right. Not long afterwards, Eddie O'Hara lost form. Bobby Laverick, his replacement, never found his. Then Tommy Ring, a big money signing from Scotland, fractured his leg at Chelsea and a fortnight later Mickey Lill broke his leg at Fulham. Mysteriously, my shirt went missing. I heard several unconvincing accounts and suspect that someone had confiscated the garment to avoid serious injury to Lill's deputy - a recently de-mobbed Derek Temple.

9. Frightened and proud

Because Chemical Harry claimed that I got too excited to perch on the milk crate, we progressed to the Goodison Avenue Stand. It was a primitive structure, the first double-decker stand in the land, which had been constructed around 1906. He insisted on arriving early in order to nab what he termed the perfect vantage point in the centre of Row C. To be honest, I preferred to sit towards the back of the stand where fans of all ages stamped their feet in unison on the wooden floors. The resulting rumble was like a hurricane making landfall.

This noise was augmented by my secret weapon. When the opponents were awarded a corner I would cast my own spell to clear the danger. Under my breath I would repeat 'Get it out!' five times. It had to be exactly five times before rising to my feet and screaming 'Get it out!' Many years later I confessed my compulsive-obsessive ritual to Brian Labone. He reassured me that he had heard every one of my instructions. In the unlikely case that he was telling the truth, I'll gladly take some credit for a sequence of 39 home games without defeat. That's right, the Everton skipper and yours truly converted Goodison into a fortress. We lost only 14 of the first 126 home games played there in the Sixties. My spell, however, worked rarely beyond Merseyside and was totally ineffective during my first away game.

I recall that Chemical Harry had promised to take me to Goodison in August 1960 when we hammered United by 4-0 but was required to work a double shift. To compensate, we went to the rematch seven days later. I was thrilled by the mere sight of Old Trafford. It's always been a magnificent venue. My father was a football purist who never expressed hostility towards Northern opponents. If they had a good player, he would say so. Likewise if they scored a good goal, he would say so.

In the days when there was little mindless parochialism and crowds were good natured, it was common for visitors to mix with their hosts at Mama Blue. I grasped that a different kind of football supporter attended Old Trafford. The front cover of the United programme showed a smiling fan shaking hands with a smiling player. It was the only demonstration of friendship witnessed that night. In error, we trespassed into the Stretford End, the home of the more partisan Red Devils. My father sensed their hostility and insisted that we merge with a handful of other misplaced Blues near the white picket fence behind the goal. Sadly, our presence provoked an uncharacteristic Mancunian welcome. Some of the United fans occupying the terraces behind us spat in our direction throughout the first 45 minutes.

Even though volcanologists would have classified him as active, my father looked harmless to the casual eye. Obviously, these disgusting cowards were unaware of the price to be paid for upsetting him. At half-time, he led me to the toilets to wipe the spittle from my coat. I tagged along and held onto his coat as he carefully made his way through the packed terraces. Without warning, my father stopped to confront two men who he had identified as perpetrators. In an act of aggression choreographed by Duncan Ferguson, he grabbed one around the neck with his massive right hand and the other by the throat with his massive left hand. Then he cracked their heads together. Not once but twice. There were no raised voices, just the sickening thuds of comeuppance. After a brief pause, he recovered his composure and we continued our trip to the toilets like Moses parting a red sea of silent respect. I remember feeling both frightened and proud of him.

Though Everton lost 4-0, United suffered a deeper phlegm-stained shame that Wednesday night. As he drove home, I realized just how much I enjoyed talking football with my father. We hadn't travelled far before he asked me not to mention the spitting and head-banging incidents to my mother. I was young yet well aware that you grassed on Chemical Harry at your peril. To soften the atmosphere, he waxed lyrical about his own baptism on Christmas Day 1934, when he had accompanied Grandad France to watch Everton beat Sunderland 6-2. Dixie scored as did the other four forwards. The following day the same side was thrashed 7-0 at Roker Park. When Chemical Harry recalled key incidents from his childhood, it was as if his index fingers had been plugged into our central light fixture. Next he described his second visit to Mama Blue later that season. The opposition was The Arsenal – the famous Herbert Chapman side that earned four League titles in the Thirties. My father was disappointed that Dixie didn't play that day but recalled that the man of the match was Frank Moss, the visiting goalkeeper, who had suffered a dislocated shoulder. From the left-wing, he went on to score in Arsenal's 2-0 victory.

His enthusiasm was most intense when promoting the merits of Tommy Lawton. He reminded me that the record books ignored his hero's war-time deeds for Everton and that he had netted a grand total of 222 goals in 209 appearances - an average higher than those of Dixie Dean, Jack Southworth and even Fred 'Goal-a-Game' Geary. I regret that the nearest I got to see Lawton in action was at his 1972 testimonial which pitted an Everton XI against a Great Britain XI including the likes of Bobby Charlton and Bobby Moore. After Lawton had kicked off and retired to the stands, my father claimed that his hero - with his immaculate hair kept in place with lashings of Brylcreem - looked more sprightly than Rod Belfitt who we had been signed earlier that week. By half-time, everyone around us concurred with my father: 'Belfitt was no Tommy Lawton.'

As a schoolboy, I accompanied Chemical Harry to about 30 Everton games. I regret that it wasn't 300 games, no make that 500 games. I loved going to the match with my father. Sadly, I never ever told him.

10. Meeting Dixie

My father and my grandfather expressed conflicting opinions about the merits of Tommy Lawton and Dixie Dean. In my Chemical Harry's eyes, the former was a more complete footballer whose merits transcended statistics. Time and time again, he declared that, even as a teenager, his idol was the most inspirational forward that he had seen in action and that old photos of Lawton with his centre-parting held neatly in place thanks to a dab or two of Brylcreem only hinted at his ability to move around the pitch with frictionless ease. More than anything, he regretted that his favourite hadn't remained at Everton or any other club long enough to become a folk hero in the manner of Dixie.

The Lawton-Dean debate led to heated family rows, usually amid the quest for peace and goodwill at Christmas. On one occasion, Grandma France separated the parties by chucking a potato at them. It rebounded from the wall and struck the cage containing her beloved budgie. Peter, named after the stalwart club captain of that time, wasn't too pleased. A few weeks later, he defected through an open window in search of a friendlier environment where all of the residents knew that Dixie was without equal.

My mother swore that the half-peeled vegetable was aimed at her. Apparently, Grandma France resented the fact that Ma Carsley's voice had been marinated in coal dust rather than chemical effluents. Possibly, she was somewhat envious that my mother retained a keen sense of smell, which ironically was considered something of a luxury in the streets located downwind of the chemical plants. Perhaps more than anything, Grandma France was aware that, even though my mother considered him a big-headed youth, she sided quietly with Tommy Lawton.

My early knowledge of the club's history came from the mouths of Chemical Harry and his immediate family. They told me that Jack Sharp had been a star of football and cricket who provided secret state-of-the-art kit to both Everton and England from his shop in Whitechapel. Also Joe Mercer, a staunch Blue who had defected to win the League title and the FA Cup with Arsenal, longed to manage Everton to similar successes. I was made aware that Ted Sagar had worn two layers of comfortable thermal underwear beneath his homemade keeper's jersey and that TG Jones, a world-class defender, had left the club after throwing a hissy fit.

My father and his brothers, who had been among the 20,000 and more Blues at Boundary Park, told me that Dave Hickson gave everything and tried to give even more to clinch the Second Division title in 1954 but were united in their belief that he had betrayed them. They alleged that 'The Cannonball Kid', one of football's gentlemen, had been influenced by Billy Liddell, another of football's gentlemen, to defect to the dark side of Stanley Park. If I'm lucky enough to answer the lingering question asked by 'The Last of the Corinthians' and enter royal blue heaven, I'll reassure them that my old friend would never intentionally let down Everton. His love for the club mirrored those of say Brian Labone, Mike Lyons and Bill Kenwright. High praise indeed. Without doubt, I'm biased because, as you'll soon discover, I'm indebted to the blonde centre-forward. He helped to make an honest man of me.

By now you'll have gathered that Chemical Harry wasn't the biggest fan of Dixie Dean either. Whenever the France family visited Chester, my mother would window-shop along the timbered Rows which adorned the ancient city and he would take me for a walk around the Roman Walls. Like Centurions we hiked alongside the Roodee racecourse, River Dee and Shropshire Union Canal. Despite our route taking us past the Dublin Packet pub next to the Town Hall, where Dixie was the landlord, we never ventured inside to meet the great man or marvel at his medals and England caps on display behind the bar. I detected that my father's quarrel with the iconic centre-forward had to do with the fact that Dixie was a member of the under-performing Everton team relegated in 1930 - the first one to experience such disgrace.

To remedy the situation, a school friend and I decided to inspect these football treasures for ourselves. Before the construction of the iconic suspension bridge across the River Mersey and the Manchester Ship Canal, you had to take the Transporter Bridge to Runcorn and then catch the bus to Chester.

My travelling companion was terrified of the Transporter's gondola, which hung just feet above the contaminated waters. So much so that we paid the ha'penny toll to take the footpath on the adjacent railway bridge. This was a small price to pay for the thrill of the Liverpool to London steam locomotive thundering past only a few feet away. While we weren't knocked off our feet, the train driver must have smelt our misgivings - which I must clarify were more pungent than the atmospheric releases from the chemical plants on nearby Ditton Road.

It was a risky journey for unaccompanied 10-year-olds but not as fearsome as our meeting with the legendary footballer. After peeping through the windows of his pub and failing to spot anyone who resembled the muscular man with the trademark centre-parting portrayed on so many cigarette cards, we staked out the back-yard. Finally, an unshaven and balding figure, dressed in a collarless shirt with sleeves rolled up high to expose his muscles and trousers supported by both braces and a thick leather belt, stepped outside. We watched him stacking the crates of empty bottles. After about five minutes, he looked at us and yelled: 'Clear off, you little buggers!'

We didn't bother to ask about his medals and were half-way down Northgate Street before we realized that we had seen more of Dixie Dean than many centre-halves.

David won't be going to the match today ... he's tied up

11. Watch Everton whenever you can

Given his superior balance and hand-eye coordination, Chemical Harry excelled at all sports. He was a natural who never took any of them seriously. To his credit, he taught me how to kick and trap a tennis ball at a very early age. Much to the chagrin of the residents of Gerrard Street, I hoofed that old ball against their back-walls for hours. I kicked right-footed then left-footed. I even chalked a target and became half decent at hitting it upon his command. In fact, I would say that my ability to smash the ball against a wall from 10 yards was every bit as good as that of Mickel Arteta.

My father, however, was unimpressed and disheartened by my lack of athletic prowess. More so, after I developed a rare talent - the ability to stuff dried peas up my nose and eject them with remarkable accuracy in the direction of my sister. By general consensus, I was sickly, a bit slow and more than a bit of a disappointment to him and possibly my mother. So much so that on occasions it crossed my mind that my sister was being raised as an only child.

My playing ambitions changed one summer afternoon outside my grandparents' house in Milton Road. Seated on a child's saddle fitted to the crossbar of my father's bike, I took the opportunity to confirm my nincompoopery by dangling my right foot between the spokes of the front wheel. Unknowingly, he peddled away with my ankle mangled in his wheel. I understand that the main bones, namely the top of the talus in my foot and the bottoms of the tibia and the fibula in my leg, were crushed beyond recognition and that the pessimists at West Bank Accident Hospital feared that I would be a cripple. Their more optimistic colleagues at Whiston Hospital reconstructed my ankle joint, admittedly in a unique shape to emphasize the missing bits. I wore a plaster cast for months and limped or hobbled for decades. Looking back, I missed junior school through a conspiracy of accidents and life-threatening illness as well as the usual list of childhood diseases. Possibly, hypochondria was the only ailment I didn't catch as a youngster.

Increasingly, my father struggled to find time to spend with me. One of my rare treats was to accompany him to the barbers. Whereas my mother had to drag me towards One-Minute Harrison's at the top of the street, I enthusiastically joined Chemical Harry on his early morning trek to Gilly Potter's shop more than a mile away in Halton View. At Harrison's, the proprietor would plant an imaginary bowl on my head and remove all visible hair. Admittedly, he was fast. That said, no-one likes a barber whose idea of chit-chat is limited to 'Oops', 'Damn' and 'Don't worry, it'll grow'. At Potter's, I received a short back and sides plus an education from a variety of Blues who had witnessed the club's return to the top flight in 1954.

I'll never forget the first old-timer to share his royal blue experiences with me. Mr Mac was a workmate of Chemical Harry with no toes. Despite his protests, the Japanese had borrowed them in Burma and failed to return them. The ex-Prisoner of War likened the British Army in the Forties to Merseyside football in the early Fifties — both were guilty of monstrous betrayals. A diehard Blue who enjoyed football at Goodison one week and Anfield the next, he looked forward to his afternoons on the Kop because he didn't care about the result and just enjoyed the action. During the half-hour in which my father's luxuriant locks were being tamed, his friend re-galed me with tales of Everton's Wally Fielding and Liverpool's Albert Stubbins. I hung onto his every word. But at times, I must admit to glancing at his shoes and wondering if he used muslin cloth to pack the empty spaces.

Mr Tansey, another process worker at ICI, would wax lyrical the deeds of great Widnesians. Besides Tommy McGee and Vince Karalius, there was Charles Barkla - who received a Nobel Prize, an early Archbishop of Canterbury - whose name escapes me, and John Hutchinson - who, at age 22, established the very first chemical works in the town.

Also, there was John Brunner, another chemical industrialist. Born in Everton and allegedly a Blue, he partnered Ludwig Mond to establish the Brunner Mond & Company which became ICI in 1926. Mr Tansey told me that this paternalistic employer encouraged trade unions and welfare reforms and also donated funds for the construction of schools, libraries and village halls on the Cheshire side of the River Mersey and for research scholarships at the University of Liverpool. My favourite tale about the so-called Chemical Croesus? In addition, Brunner had provided significant financial contributions towards the completion of the state-of-the-art Transporter Bridge and, after King Edward VII had failed to show up at the grand opening in 1905, grabbed the ceremonial scissors and cut the royal ribbon himself.

Mr Tansey would wow me with his knowledge of Everton line-ups from decades earlier then bewilder me with his dexterity. I was so impressed by his ability to write with his right and left hands at the same time that I thought of him as a wizard and believed everything he told me. This included his assertion that the man who made Dinky Toys, a certain Frank Hornby, was an Evertonian and that Santa Claus, despite his red and white suit, had royal blue leanings.

I don't think that Mr Potter, the proprietor, was a Blue - not even a lapsed one. I do recall, however, that he didn't approve of young boys attending big stadiums like Goodison or Anfield and warned my father about the dangers lurking on the terraces - more precisely strangers who would press against you. Above the snip-snip of his scissors, he would caution: 'Pick-pockets and deviants have such light fingers - you'll never know a thing.'

The owner and his patrons at the barbers liked Chemical Harry. They were seduced by his easy smile and happy-go-lucky nature. Though my father wasn't my super-hero, I'm eternally grateful that he enlightened me about hard work and altruism — not in words but by example. Just as important, I'm indebted that he taught me to be a good Blue and made sure that I knew the rules of football along with the rules of life.' At least once a day he would yell nuggets of advice in my direction: 'David, good manners cost nothing' and 'Respect other people and other people's property'. His most memorable words of wisdom: 'David, learn the rules and play by them' and 'You're not on this earth for long, so you had better make the most of life and watch Everton whenever you can.'

All of my friends wanted a dad like mine. Of course, they didn't have to live with him. Because I had been bruised by the merciless weather of his moods plus the fallout from his complicated personal life, it was hard for me to see him through the eyes of the outside world. I thought of him as someone who worked tirelessly and made sacrifices so that my sister and I would have a better life. That's right, Chemical Harry was someone who would do whatever he could for his children — except spend time with them. It's lilely the mothers of my friends wanted a husband with his muscular physique and movie-star looks. No doubt with some regrets, Ma Carsley was far more appreciative of his Calvinistic work ethic and his natural generosity. As an altruistic breadwinner, every Thursday he turned over his unopened wage packet for her to distribute as she thought fit.

When it came to material things, Chemical Harry coached me about the true benefits of sharing. A modest - yet typical - display of his big heart took place in 1957 when he demonstrated his incredible reflexes by catching one of the Barker & Dobson missiles hurled into the crowded Paddock by the Toffee Lady. Effortlessly, he plucked it out of the air to the astonishment of the fans around us. I remember feeling really proud of my dad. That was until he approached me with the caramel in his outstretched hand and, to my amazement, gave it to the boy supporting Burnley next to me.

12. Never enter through the exit

What I liked most about my father is not that he took me to Goodison Park for my baptism at age 9 but that he allowed me to return by myself at age 11. Or so he thought. Having sampled the sights, sounds and smells of Goodison, I demanded more. Much more. I remained patient until one Friday night I heard Mama Blue calling my name. By candle-light, I decided to take control of my own destiny and made plans to journey to Walton the following day quite literally under my own steam.

The start to most weekends involved my sister escorting me to the matinee at either the Regal Cinema or the Premier Picture House. The latter was basic even by Widnes standards. At the first sight of her friends, she would hand over my admission money and disown me. Left to my own devices, I would search for my school-mates in the cinema auditorium which resembled a seething snake pit. When the lights went down, the rowdier kids sprinted up and down the aisles, climbed over seats and pelted the screen with missiles. The introduction of Bugs Bunny brought some order. He was followed by Laurel and Hardy. Then there was a cliff-hanger serial involving Hopalong Cassidy. Unimpressed by Cassidy's sense of fair play, the audience followed the local tradition of booing the hero and cheering the villains.

The mid-Fifties was a time when young children respected policemen, teachers and most others in authority. Cinema managers were the exception. More often than not, the head honcho at the Regal, attired in his well-worn dinner jacket, would pause the cartoons and threaten to send his patrons home if they continued to misbehave. Prior to the main feature, he would appeal for calm before conducting a sing-song of kiddy anthems, prompted by the words dancing along the screen. Finally, the cinema manager would cue the entrance of the Lone Ranger and Tonto with his own version of the William Tell Overture. Such was the influence of these two icons of American culture that after the show my more impressionable friends would ride their pretend horses down the main street towards Naughton Park.

That Saturday morning, given my increasing aversion to both masked men and Rugby League, I executed the first step of my plan by slipping away from the rear of the cinema queue. With the cash from my Football Fund in my pocket, I embarked on the two mile hike to catch the train to Liverpool. I soon discovered that God was a Blue. My first stroke of good fortune occurred when I side-stepped the ticket collector at Farnworth Station. He must have assumed that no 9-year-old runt, wearing short pants and a school mac that he had yet to grow into, would be travelling unaccompanied.

It was only after the steam locomotive pulled into Liverpool Central Station that I realized my plan was flawed. Well aware that Goodison Park was located in Walton, I had no idea how to get there. Rather than admit defeat, I wandered outside the station to find pavements overflowing with well-dressed shoppers and roads choked with modern cars. I remember thinking that Liverpool was nothing like Widnes. Even then, I was a master of understatement. Eventually, I spotted a couple of early-birds wearing Everton colours. When I asked for directions, they adopted me like a long-lost son. We chatted throughout the bus journey to Spellow Lane. My new friends assured me that it was a great time to be a Blue. Given that the club had averaged a trophy every 10 years during its history and that it had been 20 odd years since it had celebrated success, they predicted silverware was on the immediate horizon.

As expected, Mama Blue was resplendent. She towered over the rows of terraced houses in Goodison Avenue and Goodison Road. But to my amazement, these environs were quiet. There were no sellers of programmes, newspapers or rosettes in the streets, just a couple of hundred fans waiting patiently for the cash-only turnstiles to open. Disoriented and possibly overwhelmed by excitement, I entered a turnstile door to enquire about the special gate for boys and pensioners. Within seconds, a line formed behind me. Cue my second stroke of good fortune. Given my hesitancy to pay the adult price of admission, the gateman deemed that I had become a nuisance and instructed the fans behind me to unblock the entrance by lifting me over the cast iron barrier. I was thrilled by his kindness and convinced that other people knew that Mama Blue was calling me home.

As for my first impression of the empty stadium? She was both vast and ghostly. I climbed the hundreds of steps to access the rear of the Goodison Road terraces to check out the vantage points that my grandfather had talked about. He preferred the less-crowded corner near St Luke's church where he could smoke without the fear of burning someone. From the very top of the terraces, the Bullens Road Stand on the other side of the pitch looked very much like it does today – magnificently proud.

For an hour or more, I was enthralled by voices of my fellow early-birds echoing around the vast double-decker structures. Then around 2.30 pm I became bedazzled by the relentless waves of fans flooding the terraces on all four sides of the pitch. It was at that time that I realized that I was dressed for the cinema and sought temporary refuge in the warmth of the refreshment bar under the colossal grandstand. There, I sipped my first Goodison tea. Hot and sweet, it was steeped in the traditions of colonial imperialism. As I cradled the high-tech waxed paper cup, I pondered another important piece of advice provided by my grandfather: 'No matter how long the queue, never commit the sin of entering the toilets through the exit.'

There was a tremendous sense of family. The bulk of the crowd worked a five-and-a-half-day week and arrived at around 2.00 pm. They created a crush. Many of the existing fans adopted 'The Goodison Stance'. An uncle had warned me that it was common to be swept down the concrete terracing and warned me to avoid the hands in pockets pose popular at Naughton Park. He recommended that I stand with my hands raised high against my chest. Once the game started, fans leaned on the people in front of them. This caused large waves of bodies to cascade down six levels of terracing before clambering to their original positions. By half time, I was about 20 feet from where I had started and, without being able to do a thing about it, had tumbled head over heels in love with Everton Football Club.

Just before the beginning of the second-half, one Blue offered me a sip of his half-time Bovril. Tell me, who doesn't remember the first time they tasted Bovril? Another hoisted me onto the corner of the crush barrier and showed me how to lock my legs around the cast iron stanchion in order to stay there. No doubt influenced by the sights and sounds of Mick McManus tangling with his favourite television foe Jackie Pallo, he referred to my grappling hold as 'The Goodison Scissors'. Though I saw very little of the action on the pitch, I was thrilled that we defeated Tottenham by 2-1. It was modest revenge for the infamous 10-4 hammering earlier that season at White Hart Lane. At the final whistle, I was aware that I had Everton Football Club and Bovril in my life and, best of all, the Everton family to provide comfort and companionship. Of course, no-one cautioned me that my childhood was about to be stolen.

When I returned home shortly before 6.30 pm, I was greeted by the four most dreaded words in the vocabulary of a young boy: 'No tea for you!' Ma Carsley then quizzed me about where and how I had spent my afternoon. I answered: 'Watching football at Goodison Park'. In response, she raised an eyebrow, in the way that disbelieving mothers do, and clipped my ear. I could have described the poetic imagery on the manicured pitch and primal emotion on the jam-packed terraces. Later I confessed to her: 'Trainspotting at Farnworth Station'.

13. Books containing big words

My days at Simms Cross Junior School appeared normal, at least on the surface. At assembly, the teachers inspected our uniforms for smartness, necks for tidemarks, finger-nails for gallygu and ears for spuds – or in my case Dixies. Kitted out in my short grey pants, grey shirt, school tie and black blazer complete with invisible and not-so-invisible repairs, I mirrored my classmates except that my satchel –an Army surplus haversack – boasted the names of Bobby Collins and Alex Young in ink and my shiny black shoes had cardboard insoles. When it rained, my mother replaced them with pieces of linoleum cut from the back-kitchen floor to cover the cavities in their tired leather soles.

Sadly, the teachers didn't show the same diligence towards assessing the shortcomings of my education which was tainted by the shame of being someone with learning difficulties. I don't pretend to speak with authority but I didn't receive the same school books as the other students; I got the ones containing the really big words. I had few problems understanding the spoken word. The written word was a different matter. My woe stemmed from the phonetic approach to reading. I struggled to break words into component sounds and would spend so much time wrestling with individual words that I failed to comprehend the story. Despite my hippopotomonstrosesquippdaliophobia, which I've discovered is the fear of very long words, I was streamed into the top class. It wasn't by luck. In the eyes of educators, I was – wait for it – a mathematical gymnast. This may sound like hyperbole but I could process numbers like an IBM mainframe computer - which had yet to be invented. Long divisions, multiplications, square roots, even cube roots came easy to me. As a budding Sudoku black belt - the Carol Vorderman of my day, my playground specialty was calculating goal averages. By comparison, today's goal differences are for wimps.

I attended a junior school where being inquisitive was social suicide and came from a household in which there weren't any books. Besides the family copy of the 'Illustrated Methodist Hymn Book', assorted knitting patterns and an odd issue of the Daily Mirror, which was recycled to start the coal fire, I don't remember any other printed text. I suppose that my parents were preoccupied with more important matters than reading bedtime stories by candle light. Even so, how had my illiteracy gone unnoticed? To be honest, it was partly my own fault. When you agonize over words of more than one syllable you avoid situations which involve reading them. It won't surprise you to learn that I hated everything about words. I even detested alphabet soup - which also had yet to be invented. More than anything, I dreaded the classes in which I had to read aloud. My teachers knew that I was hopeless and saved my guesswork until the end of the day. My lack of fluency never failed to amuse them.

After too many years of deception, I was placed in a remedial reading group composed mainly of victims of excessive schoolyard bullying. They included stutterers, undiagnosed dyslexics, hyper-actives, big-hearted lads with low IQs and a tubby boy traumatized by St Vitus Dance. Also, there was a visiting gypsy who preferred the term 'tinker'. Nicknamed Doolally Tap, my new best friend punctuated every other sentence with profanity and claimed to be from County-effing-Wicklow where swearing was considered an effing gift. This master of obscenity, who in his own words was qualified to swear for All-effing-Ireland, shared my interest in football. I remember him challenging me: 'Name three effing clubs that contain swear words?' He didn't wait for my response before continuing: 'Arsenal, Scunthorpe United and - brace yourselves - Manchester-effing-City.' It took me years to fully understand the anatomical reference to the Lincolnshire club.

Unlike him, I even struggled to read the backs of bubble gum cards, the currency of secondary modern playgrounds in the late-Fifties. In Widnes, these humble cards were the portal to the world of football legends.

Few of my other mates had ever been to a proper football match. Nevertheless, all of us could identify the game's stars. They admired Duncan Edwards, Stanley Matthews and Tom Finney, usually in that order, plus Ferenc Puskas and Alfredo Di Stefano of all-conquering Real Madrid on the Continent. In contrast, I admired Dave Hickson, the first Evertonian to appear on a bubble gum card. Actually, I stopped collecting them after an unfortunate incident involving him.

My version of the facts is that I had found a sixpence and bought a half-dozen bubble gum cards from Bungy Parr's Tuck Shop located opposite my junior school in the hope of snagging the one featuring Hickson and his magnificent coiffure. I soon overcame the disappointment of the Everton No. 9 not appearing in my loot and sauntered home with six sticks of gum in my mouth and, by a sleight-of-hand, the sixpence in my pocket. Unfortunately, I bumped into my mother before I could dump my pickings. Without ceremony, I was frog-marched to the shop on order to return the coin and the cards and, most important, to apologize to Mr Parr.

My father decided that I should be rehabilitated at Milton Church - where one of his brothers was a Methodist lay preacher. Few ventured inside the austere building located on the main street which housed the 5th Widnes Company of the Boys' Brigade and its junior organization known as the Life Boys. Both groups mixed gymnastics, camping and knot-tying classes with religious services to keep budding delinquents off the streets. In truth, I enjoyed my evenings at the Life Boys. It was a rugby-free zone where we played football and talked football. My only problem with this refuge was the dress-code. It included a sailor's hat. Despite wearing it at a rakish angle, the hat diluted my street cred. I had learnt to take the 'kiss me quick' jibes from my friends in my stride until I met my first Kopites. It was a painful encounter.

As I waited to cross Widnes Road on my way home I was ambushed by four 15-year-olds who had been doing what teenagers did in the Fifties — smoking Domino cigarettes on the street corner. My hat or, possibly, my blue and white scarf must have made me easy prey. Three of them held me while the smallest thug stubbed his cigarette out on my face. The others followed his lead. Then the freckle-faced ringleader reloaded with a dog-end from behind his ear and repeated his abuse. Worse still, he tortured me verbally by asserting that Liverpool, then rooted in the Second Division, were better than Everton.

I returned home and said nothing about his logic or his cowardice. Chemical Harry, who was in the process of returning from work, took one look at me and erupted. Neither he nor I was a pretty sight. My father escorted me to the local pub to show my wounds to the patrons and to spread the word of the ambush. Both sides of the street were united in horror. It's a good job that I didn't finger any of the suspects because there could have been a lynching on the banks of the Mersey that night. At the police station they counted four burn marks which meant that at least one member of the gang had not joined in. Two days later I was required to confront four tearful teenagers at Kingsway Secondary Modern School. They had all confessed. I felt sorry for the blubbering bullies who were to be expelled and most likely sent to an approved school. Or so I thought. I looked them in the eye hoping to identify the one who hadn't burnt me. They all looked as guilty as sin.

I retreated to school, where I was renamed 'Ashtray', and to my old routine — that was until I ventured to the Life Boys the following week. There, at the corner of Frederick Street and Milton Road , loitered the ginger-haired Red with a brand new posse. He had escaped any real punishment. I felt betrayed and for the next couple of months was subjected to his taunts about my biological family and my football family. Of course, such torture by a Kopite was merely a sign of things to come.

14. Raised as an Evertonian by an Evertonian

One day the name-calling ceased. It was a direct result of a striking enhancement in my personal popularity. Permit me to explain. It was accepted in the grinding poverty of the Simms Cross jungle that the big kids tormented the weak ones with impunity. By far, the biggest bullies were the members of the Widneski family. I've changed their name to protect other victims. Their father was incarcerated in Walton Gaol, now known as HM Prison Liverpool, for stealing mercury - the bad boy of the periodic table. It was something he wasn't particularly adept at. In his absence, the family was headed by a nutter named Polish Johnny who wore a drape jacket, drain pipe trousers and brothel creepers to dabble, allegedly, in arson.

On the afternoon in question, his 14 year-old brother, another paranoid schizophrenic named Polish Peter, decided to pick on me. Nothing serious, he tried to twist my arm until it became detached from its socket. During the process, I lashed out with my free hand. I had intended to strike his stomach but, because he was 12 inches taller than me, my fist crashed into his most vulnerable body parts. He went down like Paul Scharner at Wigan. It was an ugly fall. His head slid down the wall, leaving a trail of skin and bright red blood, and bounced off the cobbled pavement. The only witnesses to the incident were a couple of grandmothers who, with headscarves covering their metal rollers, spent their afternoons jangling and smoking on their polished steps. I suppose not much has changed in a half-century. Mules have been replaced by Ugg boots and pinnies by cozy pyjamas, the wisdom has remained the same. By the time they reached the scene, I was standing over Polish Peter like Rocky Balboa. They warned me: 'You're a dead man!'

That evening, my father responded to loud banging on the front door and discovered two angry Widneskis. Someone had used muslin cloth to bandage the head of the younger sibling. Wrapped tightly like a boxer's fist, you could detect an egg-size bump. His face was bloodied and smelt of Germolene. Though Polish Johnny knew better than to antagonize Chemical Harry, he demanded to confront the hooligan who had savaged his brother. When the Teddy boy cast his eyes on me wearing the hand-me-down pyjamas of my older sister, he chuckled and ruffled my hair. My father remained stony-faced and announced somewhat proudly: 'Our David may be a bit slow but has been raised as an Evertonian by an Evertonian'.

Nervously, I apologized to both Widneskis: 'I'm sorry Johnny. I'm sorry Peter, I'm deeply sorry that I battered you.' My words were followed by silence. I could hear the b-word reverberating along Gerrard Street and swirling in the contaminated skies before making a near perfect crown on my head. I could've said: 'Peter, I deeply regret any misunderstanding. I apologize for defending myself. I should have known better. Please forgive me.' I didn't. I boasted that I had battered him. Polish Johnny appeared discombobulated and begged my father not to mention the incident to anyone. After they had departed, Chemical Harry clipped the back of my head. It was his way of saying 'Well done son'. Of course, I never admitted that the bully had more than likely stumbled over his own feet nor demanded a thorough explanation of 'a bit slow'.

I regret not inviting the ginger Red and the bloodied Widneski to join me at the Boys' Brigade. An organization that recognized the influences surrounding young men aren't always helpful and many stray at cost to themselves, their families and the community. Certainly, the weekly promotion of reverence, discipline and self-respect had a positive influence in my early life until the uniform became uncool. Permit me to fast-forward to the summer of 1961 when the 5th Widnes Company went to summer camp in Llandudno. It was like a para-military exercise with the captain and sergeant hogging the comfort of the cab and their BB troops huddled among the provisions in the back of the coal lorry. I was no stranger to nights under canvas and had survived several expeditions with the France family. The infamous Jowett Javelin had ventured to remote places such as the New Forest.

There, the France family wigwam - big enough for a small tribe - was literally a home from home with no electricity, no running water and no indoor toilet. The only real difference was the neighbours. The New Forest offered a different kind of wildlife – ponies, fallow deer and the type of reptiles often eaten in modern-day reality television shows. All four members of my family deserved a holiday after enduring the 12-hour journey to our summer destination. My father drove, my mother navigated the pre-motorway route and my sister and I kept quiet. From my preferred seat behind Chemical Harry and next to the week's supply of John West salmon and other groceries, I tried to escape from the tension by concentrating on the telescopic aerial which carried our family standard. It was a triangular flag shaped from heavy felt and printed with the words of my grandfather 'Play up Everton'.

Back at the BB camp in North Wales, the other occupants of my tent supported United and represented a captive audience primed for conversion to the royal blue faith. Actually, our BB unit was non-sectarian with Methodists lured from across the town, Catholics from the Simms Cross area and one boy from the Ten Lost Tribes of Israel. Because the 5th Widnes Company was skint, we practiced gymnastics rather than participate in drum and bugle parades. Some members were more athletic than others. In fact, two or three progressed to play for Widnes and even Great Britain. Our well-being was enriched by the fresh air linked with football, cross-country running and swimming. Our aptitude was tested by torchlight three-card brag and also by the funfair near Llandudno Pier. It contained the usual attractions and patter for separating young boys from their holiday money. My friends and I were drawn to a colourful stall, not unlike a coconut shy, displaying life-size cut-outs of footballers. The test of skill involved a size-5 football, the likes of which we hadn't seen before, positioned about eight yards in front of a stack of one-gallon paint cans. The pyramid was crowned by a golden can. It was obvious that this object - like the contest itself - was fixed in some way.

Undeterred we invested our thru'penny bits to capture the star prize, which from the look of its sun-scorched condition had not been replaced for many months. Encouraged by my ability to strike targets on the walls of Gerrard Street, I volunteered to go first. My attempt to remove the golden can without displacing the others mirrored the infamous efforts of Tommy Clinton in the 1953 FA Cup semi-final; except that I missed twice. My friends fared no better, much to the bemusement of the onlookers. That was until the final member of our tent sent the golden can into orbit as the other cans watched motionless. Ted MacDougall won many prizes during his professional career of over 500 games, including seven Scotland caps, but rejected the star prize. Later he admitted that his reward was watching the stall-owner chase his precious ball as it ricocheted towards the Great Orme's Head.

I told my father about Ted's skills. He doubted that they were anything special and was proven right until my pal left the ICI works team to join Liverpool Football Club. Ted didn't last long but impressed me with his determination to overcome Bill Shankly's rejection. His perseverance inspired me in a sort of Churchillian way. Ted never gave up. He conquered adversity and battled on to realize his ambitions. As an exception to the rule that a youngster must sign pro forms by age 17, my friend progressed to play League football for Manchester United, West Ham, Norwich, Southampton and others. You may recall that he topped the League's goal-scoring charts throughout the 1975/76 season and netted nine times in an FA Cup tie.

Ted was so much more talented than the rest of us at Milton that I respected his opinion on all things football except when he had the gall to compare the heading abilities of Denis Law - who hailed from the same remote part of Scotland - with those of the other blond Scotsmen who played for Everton. My friend, however, had the last word on aerial prowess when I witnessed him netting a hat-trick against Everton at Carrow Road in 1975.

15. Everton ruled my thoughts

Back in Widnes, everyone recognized that our living conditions were dire. None more than my mother who wanted to raise her offspring near the town's non-smoking schools. In fact, the name of Una France was on the council's housing list for a decade before she got her way in the late-Fifties.

We moved north to an extremely spacious three-bedroom/one-bathroom council house near Victoria Park. My first impression of Sycamore Avenue was that our immediate neighbours were posh. With an electric light and new lino in every room, I thought that we were too. It was a brave new world for all four members of my family. There was an English Electric washing machine, an Electrolux vacuum cleaner and flickering monochromatic images from the BBC via an Ekco television set with a 12-inch convex screen. Yes, we had become consumers living the Woolyback version of the American dream.

Hopefully many of you don't remember the Eleven-Plus examinations which determined the type of educational establishment that a student would attend. The exams, which consisted of an arithmetic test, an essay and a general problem-solving paper, were administered to 10- and 11-year-olds. The brighter children went to Wade Deacon - the local grammar school, the rest to one of many secondary modern schools dotted around the town. Given the impact on a child's life, they were resented throughout the better council estates. Subsequent research has confirmed that the approach incorrectly classified about 20% of students. These late developers were penalized because there was no return once you had embarked on the secondary modern curriculum. Given my inability to grasp written instructions, I failed the Eleven-Plus. No-one was surprised. My mother and father reassured me that it was for the best. I believed them because they were my parents and meant well.

There were no more than 30 Blues at Fairfield Secondary Modern School for Boys, a tiny drop in the ocean of 500 Red Devils. Also, there were glory-hunting followers of Tottenham and Wolverhampton yet refreshingly – yes, I know that it's hard to believe – very few Kopites. It's likely that there were nocturnal Reds hiding in the nooks and crannies of the newly-built overspill areas which bordered the town but, with the exception of the ginger-haired sadist and friends, I rarely if ever encountered them. After his arrest, I've always thought that giant signs should have been erected at the town's boundary: 'Warning – Kopite-free Zone'. More recently, I've suggested that those same words should be posted at every point of entry to the USA or at the very least on the Washington State Ferry landing near my home on San Juan Island. Once again, I'm getting ahead of myself.

Parents play a key part in how their children deal with the temptations of life. Mine were very strict – Methodist strict – at home yet struggled to set rigid boundaries regarding Everton Football Club. Both Chemical Harry and Ma Carsley encouraged me to enjoy my travel adventures but voiced niggling concerns that I followed the beat of a different drummer than my school-mates. They were unaware that many of my more independent pals would talk about running away from home. Actually, one or two packed their bags, disappeared into the loneliness of the night and got as far as the town hall before tip-toeing home. Another made it to North Wales but had forgotten why he was fleeing by the time he got there. I know what you are thinking – only a truly troubled soul would run away to Rhyl. Despite my sense of abandonment - both real and imaginary - I had no reason to abscond. After all, I had Everton to lean on and could shelter in the arms of Mama Blue every fortnight.

It was too easy to become addicted to the royal blue opiate. Typically, young fans experiment before taking it regularly. Not me. The highs and lows at Goodison hooked me. Everton ruled my thoughts and controlled my waking hours. I lived for Saturdays.

Our new home was located near Farnworth Station and I was allowed to make the pilgrimage to Walton on condition that I showed my mother the matchday programme as proof that I had been to the game. Mama Blue seduced me with her lustful promises of good times so, to ensure that I had sufficient funds for the publication, I would walk from Central Station to Walton and frequent the Boys' Pen. More often than not, I was as excited as an able-bodied Hajji on his way to Mecca.

Old fans romanticize about the Boys' Pen as the best place to discover what it means to be a Blue but I was no advocate of confined spaces or young Blues screaming like they had been imprisoned against their will. Even as an 11-year old, it seemed to me that the purpose of the Pen hadn't changed since the day it opened in 1925 - the incarcerated boys were cheerleaders expected to re-ignite the rest of the Goodison crowd when it had gone too quiet. Even then, I concluded that the adult fans only joined in to drown out the ear-splitting screeching.

My aversion had nothing to do with claustrophobia associated with being trapped in a small cage possessing the mood of an asylum that you checked into voluntarily. I could never come to terms with the fact that some Blues liked to fight other Blues. I witnessed regular clashes between the juvenile delinquents from Scotland Road and those from Dingle's Holy Lands, or other districts where they boarded up the windows on Advent calendars. Oddly, the fighting started when Everton were leading by a couple of goals. Whereas, if the home side was losing the fists were unclenched and the inmates would unite in song.

At sixpence, it was by far the most economical place to watch matches. I survived by avoiding eye contact and never giving the slightest impression that I had my bus fare or a programme in my pockets. In truth, the experience stood you in good stead if later in life you found yourself locked up abroad. After a dozen or so games, I preferred to exit the Pen on the hour mark and loiter in Goodison Road before slipping into the Ground when the gates opened to let out the early-leavers. As for the missing 10 minutes of action, in my mind I had experienced it through a crescendo of oohs and aahs. My heart would rise and fall on the waves of sound.

Eventually, I graduated to the Ground where Woolybacks were viewed with less suspicion by those living closer to the Liver Building. My newspaper-round paid for this luxury. The only inconvenience was that I had to get back to Widnes to deliver them. With gates typically in excess of 50,000, I avoided the massive post-match queues for buses on Spellow Lane by dodging the traffic to hop on a non-football special speeding down the middle of County Road. Often, I was one of the first supporters to reach the city centre. As I scampered towards my train, my blue and white scarf converted me into the messenger of good tidings. From the doorways of Blackler's Department Store, known for its lavish Christmas grotto, men would plead: 'How did we get on?' I would proclaim: 'Three - nil.' There was no need to clarify that Everton had won, we always triumphed at home. I would repeat the news a half-dozen times, with increasing details of the scorers, as I approached the entrance to Liverpool Central Station.

It felt like everyone in the city shared my love of Everton Football Club and I was bringing real happiness into their lives.

16. Blue exodus

When my pockets were empty, I would jog back along Scotland Road replaying every goal in my head in order to educate my United-loving pals. I loved the famously insular city and can't talk objectively about its merits because, in my mind, Liverpool is the yardstick by which other cities succeed or fail. I grew up thinking that it was a place of superlatives steeped in history.

In the Nineteenth Century, some 40% of the world's trade including 80% of Britain's slave activity passed through its docks. In addition, its innovative citizens had pioneered some of life's important things – ferries, trains, trams, transatlantic liners and, of course, goal-nets. Also the Second City of the British Empire was known for the beauty of its architecture and thousands of listed buildings. The famous cathedrals of Christendom, which were under construction in the early Sixties, glared at each other from the opposite ends of Hope Street. The famous cathedrals of football, which eyed each other across Stanley Park, were less confrontational. I was dazzled by the streets in and around the city centre. One of my top spots was the manicured garden behind St George's Hall where a magnificent bronze statue commemorates Monsignor James Nugent. I was impressed by its inscription: 'The apostle of temperance, the protector of the orphan child, the consoler of the prisoner, the reformer of the criminal, the saviour of fallen womanhood, the friend of all in poverty and affliction.' Best of all, one of my uncles - I can't remember which one - claimed that he was an Evertonian.

Most of all, I've always liked the people. They are the type of folk who give you the time of day and are adept at a decent conversation. Even though the population has shrunk to 400,000, one thing hasn't changed. That is the conviction held by Liverpudlians that they have been put on this earth to make other people laugh. Merseyside is full of people armed with the natural ability to exploit any opportunity that comes their way to demonstrate their wit. Another thing that hasn't changed over the years, they show little affinity for the Southern elite who don't disguise their contempt for the city. Probably, Liverpool has more in common with New York and Hamburg than with London. I know that I do.

My travels to Walton coincided with those of John Moores who was about to change British football forever. The head of the UK's largest privately-owned company had accumulated Everton shares, usually two and three at a time, and even gave up the chairmanship of his Littlewoods Pools business to become an Everton director in 1960. With a billionaire on board you could say that the club was – brace for it – minted.

I first heard about him from a neighbour who collected coupons and cash for Littlewoods Pools. Because no-one had ever hit the jackpot, he was convinced that Moores had a license to print money. At Goodison, the First Blue Billionaire was much more than an Abramovich or a Mansour. He adopted a hands-on approach as his club lurched with near wanton abandon to capture a galaxy of stars. Within no-time at all, his cheque-book had snagged 10 much sought-after players for a total outlay of around £250,000. Believe me, this was a king's ransom a half-century ago. Many purists labelled his investment as obscene and his approach as a shameless way to grab the title. Few Blues complained.

The first arrivals were Alex Parker, the best right-back north and south of the border, and Eddie O'Hara from Falkirk. They were followed by Wee Bobby Collins from Celtic, who became the heartbeat of the club, Tommy Ring from Clyde, Welshman Roy Vernon from Blackburn and Englishman Mickey Lill from Wolverhampton. Later that season Jimmy Gabriel, then the hottest teenage prospect in the land, was added from Dundee. Billy Bingham, the Northern Ireland veteran, arrived from Luton before the doors were thrown open to welcome Alex Young and George Thomson from Heart of Midlothian.

Shamelessly besotted, I couldn't get enough of Everton and made every effort to travel to away games. After the Old Trafford experience, I was allowed to do so without an adult escort as long as I kept out of trouble. I trust that you detect the irony.

I've been told that following the club made me shrewd and streetwise. These aren't necessarily the most attractive qualities in a youngster. By comparison, my new friends in Sycamore Avenue possessed refreshing innocence. I was the latchkey kid their mothers warned them not to associate with. No doubt they worried about their off-springs picking up bad habits or, even worse, joining the exodus of 10,000, sometimes 25,000, Evertonians on excursions to Bolton, Blackburn, Blackpool and Burnley. The vast majority of my fellow travellers were males; clean shaven and smartly attired in coats and ties. Some wore homemade rosettes. A few sported lapel badges. Others twirled wooden rattles. One or two rang brass bells. I recall a bugler who loved to taunt our opponents by playing 'The Last Post' throughout the dying minutes of one-sided victories.

The walks to and from away grounds were filled with pride and a more than a hint of religious fundamentalism. Surrounded by Blues, I remember feeling so lucky to be one of them. While many things have changed in football during the past half-century - one thing hasn't. I'm still amazed by how many passionate supporters travel to away grounds irrespective of the club's fortunes.

Chemical Harry had advised me that there was more to life than breathing and I like to think that my membership of the Everton family taught me many things including how to deal with disappointments. I learnt to handle the numbness of defeat and progress via acceptance to hope. In my eyes, it made me more responsible. In those of my parents, I was mature enough to visit football grounds across the North West yet too small and too young for long trousers. Therefore, I had to wait until my thirteenth birthday and puberty to cover my knees in public.

I loved the grown-up feeling of wearing my first pair of grey flannels to school, church and football. These long trousers marked my transition into adolescence. Sadly, my new status evaporated after a few weeks. The incident is burnt into my memory. I had gone to Burnley, who were top of the table and headed towards the League title. They played us off the park. More than anything I remember the return trip to Liverpool Exchange Station. As the steam locomotive and its rolling stock completed the final 50 yards of its journey, the men in front of me opened the door and jumped onto the platform from the moving carriage. Like battle-hardened paratroopers, their landings were executed perfectly. To them it was a rudimentary manoeuver. So much so that most leapt with cigarettes between their lips. Clearly, the same was expected of me. Through inexperience coupled with a lack of athleticism, I hit the platform in a heap. Thankfully, the only damage was to my dignity. Or so I thought.

Closer examination showed that my left knee was badly cut and so was the fabric covering it. To my horror, I had ripped my long trousers. Though deeply upset. In Sycamore Avenue I received sympathy from my father and my sister, who understood the significance of my accident, but none from my mother. She darned the tear with wool. It was far from an invisible repair. Actually, I looked like I was wearing a knee pad borrowed from a roller-skater. I had to revert to my short pants for school and church but insisted on wearing my darned long trousers as a badge of pride to the match.

After all, I now had an image to maintain among the special forces of the Everton family.

17. Reading and writing

By my early teens I yearned to lead a normal life in a working-class society which equated illiteracy with idiocy. Secondary school should have been a fresh start. Despairingly, my new class-mates cottoned on to my difficulties and my days continued to be disadvantaged by not possessing the basic skills of reading and writing. By then, I was hardened to the students who mocked me but never accepted the teachers who punished me with their bamboo canes for being unable to read fluently. In front of my class-mates, one of them reminded me that I was a miserable reader, a hopeless speller but a very competent milk monitor.

Reading difficulties can be devastating to a teenager's self-esteem. People assume that children above a certain age and adults of all ages can understand the words printed in the books, magazines and football programmes which paper our lives. They find the concept of going through life with only rudimentary language skills inconceivable. Apart from missing out on a basic education, there are everyday activities like curling up with a page-turning novel, scanning a newspaper, conquering a crossword puzzle, following written instructions, heeding notices, filling out forms, etc. Reading opens up a world of opportunities — a world that had not been available to me.

I was bereft of all confidence at secondary school when one of my royal blue uncles gave me a copy of 'Soccer with the Stars' by Billy Bingham. The autobiography was a present for my fourteenth birthday - not an extremely cruel joke. With the possible exception of milk chocolate dentures, I couldn't think of anything more impractical. As I flicked through the illustrations, I realized that sooner rather than later I had better become proficient at reading the text and decided to tackle the Ulsterman's words.

Initially, I agonized over his silver-tongued eloquence. Then after four or so chapters, his nouns, verbs and adjectives fell into place. It was an epiphany and to this day I remain indebted to Bingham. He was a good right-winger for Everton, a great manager for Northern Ireland and a truly inspirational author. I remember the immense satisfaction of reading my next book which I had borrowed from the modest school library at Fairfield. It took me a few weeks to master 'Ten Little N-words' but was well worth the effort. With Billy Bingham and Agatha Christie under my belt, I moved on to the shelves of Widnes Public Library and the iniquities of Merseyside society portrayed in Silas Hocking's 'Her Benny'. Digesting this gripping tale was a huge step forward in many ways.

Next, I detoured to copies of 'Charles Buchan's Football Monthly' — the very first magazine of its kind. It had been introduced by the Sunderland and Arsenal star around 1951 and continued to be published for a couple of decades. As a schoolboy, there was one obstacle. Copies cost a massive 1/6 - several times that of matchday programmes. Therefore, I rarely bought a copy and simply devoured the contents at the newsagents before my paper-round. I would read them until their covers started to separate from their staples.

Charles Buchan's publications were followed by the daunting challenge of actually purchasing my first book. And what a book! It took me five or six months to read 'The Ragged Trousered Philanthropists' and much longer - possibly years - to fully digest its message. Written in plain English and easy to comprehend, Robert Tressell's words released the dopamine in my brain. Thanks to the author, who I discovered had toiled over his manuscript at his lodgings in Queen's Road in Everton, I was hooked on books in the same way that today's teenagers are tethered to electronics. I still have my copy of the working-class masterpiece. Today, it's cover is a little foxed and wrapped in yellowing Cellophane but the contents remain as fresh and resolute as ever. Despite musty odours emanating from the pages, the old paperback remains one of my most sacred possessions.

Shortly afterwards, I left Fairfield Secondary Modern School with a growing vocabulary and a healthy appetite for knowledge. It was more than hunger – it was voracity, possibly gluttony, which aided my transition from the monochromatic Fifties to a new and much brighter Technicolor decade.

Being a young teenager is difficult, as most of us remember. Being one in a house tormented by chaos has lasting unwanted effects. The atmosphere at Sycamore Avenue had progressed from turbulent to sour. In hindsight, it had been that way since we had moved from Gerrard Street. I recall that my father was never at home and my mother wasn't always aware of his whereabouts. Some men are unfaithful for thrills, others seek fulfillment or simply love. Years later, Chemical Harry confessed to me that he had simply grown tired of his family. Like a late-night poker player, I became sensitive to even the slightest changes in his facial expressions and his willingness to bicker over the smallest things. Emotionally numb, I thought that the cycles of rows and apologies were normal. I could handle the quarrelling, shouting matches and tongue-lashings but not the knock-down-drag-out fits of anger. They were frightening. There were no broken bones that I know of but we all suffered bruising of one kind or another. As the bonds within the France family strained towards breaking point, I didn't know what to expect at Sycamore Avenue and kept my home life a secret. Inviting class-mates over was impossible.

Needless to say, I grew up much faster than my closest friends and preferred my life to revolve around my Everton family. Mama Blue offered me a place to recoil from a world of confrontation. More often than I cared to admit, it was my refuge.

You don't find many centre-forwards of Dave's calibre nowadays

18. Season-ticket holder

Without question, Everton had progressed on the pitch during the Moores-Carey revolution. Even to my young eyes, it appeared that the manager didn't seem too worried if his side won or lost, so long as it entertained. I recall that his star-studded team surrendered too many leads – some quite beautifully.

While there weren't many complaints from the terraces, results weren't acceptable to John Moores. The ambitious chairman wanted trophies - immediately rather than later. So in April 1961, he dismissed his manager during an infamous cab ride from the annual meeting of the Football League in London. Consequently, 'Taxi for ....!' has become a staple jibe to anyone facing the sack. Moores sought a more authoritarian leadership figure and recruited Harry Catterick, an Everton former-player. The ruthless decision wasn't well received by the fans at Goodison and the chairman was booed throughout the next fixture against Arsenal.

As a proud season-ticket holder, I couldn't wait for the start of the new campaign. But with Bobby Collins absent through injury, Catterick's team appeared clueless. We gained only four points from the opening seven fixtures and were rooted at the foot of the table. My father and his older brother remained optimistic. His younger brother claimed to have heard the plaintive scream of sirens warning of impending danger. All three concurred that the new man had much work to do. Without question, Catterick was up to the challenge. With the signing of experienced Dennis Stevens, to replace Collins, plus the addition of a very young Gordon West for a world-record fee, Everton excelled. The stars of typical eye-catching team performances were Alex Young and Roy Vernon. They were electrifying. I'm sure they had poor games. But I can't remember any of them. In fact, they made the art of goal-scoring look easy and Everton finished in fourth spot, just five points behind champions Ipswich. It had been the first season that I thought winning something was important and, like most Evertonians, I rued the slow start in which the home defeats by Wednesday and City cost us the title. That said, we had evolved from entertainers to legitimate challengers.

With our continued dominance at Fortress Goodison, the following campaign was a revelation. Again, the football was fast and even more fluid. So much so that I went to home fixtures expecting victory and ventured to away grounds assured of one point irrespective of the opposition. The 1962/63 campaign is noted for the Arctic conditions which devastated the football calendar. I recall receiving a ticket for our FA Cup tie at Barnsley as a Christmas present. After the original fixture had been postponed due to snow, I was amazed to be granted permission to leave school early in order to cross the Pennines and attend the rearranged night game. The brutal weather didn't stop Catterick's team. Everton didn't put a foot wrong at Oakwell. However, it did make my return journey treacherous.

After our Home James coach slid to Speke, no amount of coaxing could convince the distressed driver to continue on to Widnes. With no taxis available, four of us set off on an eight-mile hike. We crunched along the middle of deserted snow-covered roads through Hale and Halebank. At the town centre, we were greeted by the headlights of a Panda car. The police officer was so alarmed by my fragile condition that he insisted on escorting me home. Ma Carsley couldn't mask her relief or silent anger. More than anything I suspected that she was fearful that the neighbours had spotted the police outside her front door at 4.00 am. My lasting memory of that trip is sharing steaming Quaker Oats with an impressionable member of the Lancashire Constabulary while I recounted my adventures under my mother's cryogenic stare.

Although the winter freeze postponed many fixtures, Catterick's new team – or rather Carey's old team – persevered to challenge for our first title since the days of Lawton and Mercer. As a rule of thumb, the world goes to war to celebrate Everton assembling a top quality side.

It did so in 1914 and in 1939 and threatened to do so in late 1962. Shortly after Catterick's team had topped the table, the USA discovered Soviet missiles in Cuba. The tension was immense for a fortnight as mankind teetered on the brink of nuclear war. Despite my father forecasting a bright clash in the sky and a painful death, the confrontation ended peacefully when Nikita Khrushchev blinked and withdrew his missiles. Days later, however, we were knocked out of Europe at East End Park. Yes, by Dunfermline Athletic. At the time I thought that it was an apocalyptic event - if not the end of the world. Performances suffered on the muddy pitches created during the Deep Freeze and, to guard against further slip-ups, the starting line-up was strengthened by the additions of the two most sought-after footballers in the land, namely Tony Kay to replace Brian Harris and Alex Scott to oust the aging Billy Bingham.

Blues, young and old, know that The Golden Vision's header against Tottenham took us to the top of the table and that we went into the last game of the season knowing that victory would clinch the championship. Of course, all fans remember the thrill of their first title. The memory never dims. For me, it was a magical day in which Roy Vernon was unstoppable. The Welshman netted twice and Scott scored another within the opening half-hour against Fulham before completing his hat-trick. Though there was no presentation of the famous old trophy, the scenes at full-time were spine-tingling. Surrounded by my Everton family, I enjoyed the sort of exhilaration that only football can provide.

Just a few hours later, however, it all seemed so trivial. I arrived home, still soaked in sweat with my body drained of everything except happiness, to a hullabaloo of noise. The tone of the screaming and the yelling indicated that my parents were not celebrating our triumph. I went straight to my bedroom without even attempting to share my joy. The house fell silent. After a couple of hours, I ventured downstairs to discover my mother with her head in the gas oven. Dressed in an under-slip, her head rested on a cushion placed on the oven door. Our society reserves its greatest disgrace and shame for those who have failed in their attempt to commit suicide. We avoid talking about such incidents and the subject becomes taboo. I don't know why people, by their own hand, choose death over life. Possibly my mother's trigger had been predictable — her helplessness associated with my father's extramarital affairs. Probably she had not intended to kill herself and it was a cry for help. Most likely she wanted her inner pain to stop and in the heat of the moment turned to the execution chamber in everyone's kitchen.

Nonetheless, she knew what she was doing and that the town gas supply was extremely toxic. Carbon monoxide binds to hemoglobin and progressively deoxygenates the blood and offers a painless exit. After I had dragged her into the garden, I discovered a brief note in the kitchen placed next to the bread bin. It was full of apologies and despair. It begged my father to look after my sister and my sister to look after me. The note closed: 'I'm sorry, I simply want peace.' I rolled it up into a ball and kept it that way for decades. Distressed and too embarrassed to go to hospital, she asked me about the match. I remember sitting on the back step telling her about my afternoon amid 60,000 deliriously happy fans as she gazed, distantly and implacably, at some imaginary point in the garden. Not for the first time, my mother asked me to move to the North East. I declined. It wasn't that I didn't desire a more stable home environment. It wasn't that I didn't want to change schools. Selfishly, I didn't want to leave Merseyside. Even at that tender age, I was aware that Mama Blue provided an escape from pain. Deep down, I recognized that the Everton family was the only thing that I could rely on.

I listened to my mother crying herself to sleep that night and vowed never to go to the match with my father again. Though the boycott lasted for four months — until the start of the new season, I remain scarred by her strangled sobs in the darkness. As for my parents, their marriage recovered and continued to co-habit, albeit imperfectly, before separating 25 years later.

19. Proof that God is a Blue

Supporters of my vintage are sentimental souls. We tend to dismiss the wonderful things that exist in the present and claim that everything was better in the past. So, permit me to tell you about my football hero. Here are a few clues. For 10 points: He worked in the coal-mines and served in the British Army. For eight points: He won every honour in the Scottish and English games. For six points: He suffered from a hearing loss and super-sized blisters. For four points: He was the most stylish British footballer of all time. And for two points: He is known as 'The Golden Vision'. Yes, my idol is Alex Young.

I'm sure that I speak for the vast majority of Blues on the bald side of 60 - when I say that once you've adopted Alex as your hero, life is too short to embrace another. Charles Buchan had informed me about his role alongside Dave Mackay and John Cumming in breaking the Old Firm's grip on Scottish silverware and I was thrilled to hear that we had signed him. Even so, I was ill-prepared for the sheer beauty of his play. For most Blues, it was love at first sight. He graced the game with an artistry that we had seldom seen before and hardly ever since. Alex made the game look so easy. His sublime technique allowed him to do things on the pitch that others wouldn't even attempt in training. Even my father was impressed. He claimed that Alex was the 'New Tom Finney' and indisputable proof that God was a Blue and wanted us to be happy.

Little footage exists for purists to marvel at his natural abilities. Therefore those who didn't see him play will never entirely understand why those of us who did remain convinced that Alex was more skillful than anyone else who graced Goodison in the Sixties. Without doubt, he is the most gifted footballer I've seen during my first six decades following Everton. It's worth repeating — he didn't run, he glided across the turf ... he didn't turn, he pirouetted ... he didn't jump, he floated ... he didn't kick the ball, he caressed it. I could tell you that his touch was like a mother's tender kiss. Such words don't do justice to him. Alex rarely failed to tame the ball no matter how hard, high or fast it came to him.

Never ostentatious, his feet stroked the football with the uncommon motion reserved for the foreheads of newborn infants. He shifted his weight from one foot to the other with balletic grace and glided past the opponents with an astonishing economy of effort. More than anything, I was enchanted by the way he employed his sublime ball control, delicate feints and elegant body swerves to make defenders fall over. Am I laying it on thick? If so, I'm guilty of simple amplification not aggrandizement. Believe me, my hero was that good.

The intensity of our adoration was reflected in the first football docu-drama of its kind. The 1968 play revolved around the relationships within a group of obsessive Blues and how their love for the club permeated their lives. It's packed with insightful interviews, tremendous acting and Merseyside-sized laughs. You would swear that you have known the characters all your life. More than anything, I was enthralled by the way that Alex punctuated 'The Golden Vision' with dignified and articulate analysis of his fluctuating form, self-confidence and respect for the people who paid his wages.

Despite the efforts of playwright Neville Smith, film director Ken Loach whose next project was 'Kes', and actors Bill Dean and Ken Jones, my idol has remained a Merseyside secret for decades. Descriptions of his skills had been passed by word-of-mouth from generation to generation before I sought to record them for posterity in a biography entitled somewhat predictably 'Alex Young — The Golden Vision'. To ensure that his brilliance remained undiminished by the passage of time, I solicited inputs from football fans across the football world. Hundreds of them recalled, mostly in reverential tones, their special memories of Alex. Others shared narratives about personal interactions which included invading the pitch to kiss his blistered feet and falling to their knees outside the players' entrance to smooch them.

It's hard to describe the way in which he excited the crowd. Remember when James McFadden flicked the ball over Madjid Bougherra of Charlton to score in 2007 and when Marouane Fellaini stole the ball from City's Craig Bellamy in 2010? Alex did something equally as astonishing most weekends. Was he really that good? Of course not. He was much better. If you don't believe me, then perhaps you'll embrace the opinions of Alan Ball: 'No-one plays football like 'Alex the Great'. Few have ever had the God-given flair or the arrogance-free class to do so.' Ball provided the biography's foreword. His respect for his old team-mate was obvious. In his draft, he underlined the words 'unique', 'elegant' and 'natural'. And he circled 'grace and guile', 'magic and majesty' and 'incandescent brilliance'.

Like George Best, he could beat defenders without appearing to change gear. But unlike the Ulsterman, Alex never received the recognition his skills warranted. Why? Although my hero didn't lack inner-belief to do extraordinary things but, perhaps, was short of the intense confidence that elevates great footballers to world-class stars. You need a giant ego to create a global legend.

In my eyes, The Golden Vision could do no wrong on or off the pitch. There has never been a shred of pretentiousness about him. At the height of his playing career, he lived in a semi, drove an old mini, talked to his neighbours and never sought a champagne lifestyle. Maybe he should have hired a publicist or, perhaps, caught the nation's attention by drinking himself into oblivion, kicking women, punching policemen, abusing the precious gift of a liver transplant, filing for bankruptcy or spending Christmas in prison. Harsh words? Well, I did warn you that I prefer art to porn.

Someone called Alex Young claimed infinity decades ago.
How about pi? Or perhaps sigma?

20. Alex the Great

The people who say that you should never meet your heroes because they often turn out to be miserable egotistical dimwits, have never met mine. In Alex's company, an everyday activity like walking into a pub turns into bedlam involving instantaneous applause and enthusiastic chanting by young fans. When it comes to the men who actually saw him in action, I can confirm that more than one wept uncontrollably at a book signing held at Radio Merseyside.

The adoration isn't limited to those of the Blue persuasion. I remember accompanying my hero to Goodison. The taxi ride was consumed by talk of the match. The driver said nothing until he pulled up outside the Winslow pub, I handed him a fiver. He smiled at me: 'No charge, I'm a Red but it's an honour to see that gentleman's halo in my mirror. Football gods ride for free in my taxi.' It was a special afternoon and his first visit to the lounge which had boasted his name for a decade. I recall that Alex was relaxing near the bar when an orderly queue formed to meet him. There was no need for stewards, everyone waited patiently for a post-game audience. What followed was the laying of hands on the sick and infirmed, the blessing of the young and the rejuvenation of the old. I remember Brian Labone whispering into my ear: 'Your mate may have bitten off more than he can chew - a steward has just confirmed that there's a colony of lepers making its way along Walton Lane.'

Alex's name is synonymous with excellence. His disinterest in self-promotion is as fascinating as his natural abilities and has diluted his legacy on both sides of the border. To remedy the situation and provide a sequel to 'The Golden Vision' drama, I worked with the film-makers at Tabacula on a documentary entitled 'Alex the Great'. Despite the exquisite coupling of dramatic music with equally stirring narrative, I fear that we were unable to capture his genius or his divinity. In an age when every Premier League throw-in and corner kick has been captured for posterity, I regret that there is little video evidence from 50 years ago to reinforce the consensus of the team-mates and opponents interviewed for the documentary who rated Alex's ball skills alongside those of Dennis Bergkamp, Lionel Messi and Cristiano Ronaldo.

Very few men have ever played like him. More humble comparisons are often made with acclaimed ball-juggling wizards such as Duncan McKenzie and Pat Nevin. Both of these gifted and natural entertainers concurred that Alex was more graceful and more ghostly, especially during a period when brutal tackles were part and parcel of the game. Perhaps the most commendable tributes were provided by his football foes. In particular, Ron Yeats, the fearsome captain and colossus of Liverpool Football Club, professed: 'Alex was fantastic in the air and simply sublime with the ball at his feet. Bill Shankly warned me that if you give him space, he'll take you to the cleaners. The wee man was the finest centre-forward I've ever seen and way ahead of his time.'

Yeats isn't someone you would disagree with. But if you remain unconvinced, then hopefully the endorsement of Sir Tom Finney may get your attention. Footballer of the Year in both 1953/54 and 1956/57 and widely respected as one of the finest players, if not the finest player, to have represented England. At a Hall of Fame dinner he told me: 'I've just been introduced as 'England's Alex Young'. It's a genuine compliment. He possessed such grace and balance; qualities no longer valued in the hurly-burly of the modern game.' Also Dave Mackay, Footballer of the Year in 1968/69 and hailed by many as the most influential midfielder that Scotland has ever produced, claimed that there were three kinds centre-forwards in the Fifties ... Alex Young ... Scottish footballers influenced by Alex's silky skills ... and those who should have been.

Then there is the man tasked with replacing Alex. Fred Pickering volunteered: 'Harry Catterick signed me to score goals. I repaid him with 50 of the best in my first 60 games, yet failed to win over the Goodison crowd. They expected more than goals from their No 9. It was an unenviable challenge – like following The Beatles onto the stage.'

It's possible that we'll see another Fred Pickering, Bob Latchford and Duncan Ferguson in royal blue. I've come to terms with the fact that we will never see another Dixie Dean or Golden Vision. They were so special that their relationships with supporters confirmed that true love is both unconditional and eternal. Of course, they were very different types of centre-forwards. Dixie's contributions can be measured by the number of times he hit the back of the net. In contrast, my hero's offerings can be characterized by the number of times he took my breath away. I like those words. After all, life isn't about the number of breaths we take but the moments in life that take our breath away.

Nostalgia plays strange tricks with the mind. Often we reminisce rather than remember. After watching re-runs of old games, more often than not I say to myself: 'This isn't how I remember it; I had thought so and so was awesome.' We remain fiercely protective of our heroes, however stardom rarely lingers and idolization seldom outlasts success. For as long as Everton Football Club survives, I pray that men will talk in awe of Alex the Great and his breathless skills.

Go south my son and pave the way for The Holy Trinity

21. Roll over Beethoven

It must have been frustrating for Blues to have come of age in the Fifties, Seventies, Nineties or Noughties. These decades are overshadowed by the ten years that stole the Twentieth Century and have hogged the cultural limelight ever since. The Sixties were a time of change. There was long hair, flower power, dolly-birds, mini-skirts, birth control, Bob Dylan, Alex Young and The Beatles - often referred to locally as 'The Fab Three plus Ringo'. We didn't know it at the time that the bluesy introduction to 'Love Me Do', courtesy of John Lennon's Hohner harmonica, would provide the soundtrack to my teenage years.

Merseyside was unlike any other place in the country. Make that the world. The city was on the cutting edge of both fashion and music. It had been for years thanks to the merchant seamen, known affectionately as Cunard Yanks, who brought records, leather coats, electric guitars and other treasures from the New World. The air was awash with the rock & roll sounds of Gene Vincent, Chuck Berry and Little Richard and the electric blues of Bo Diddley, Muddy Waters and John Lee Hooker which stirred an irreverent spirit of rebellion. One of my parents claimed that such music was a passing fad and a menace to established society. I'll let you decide which one.

In the days before the BBC embraced pop music, my sister and I relied on a Bush transistor radio to keep up with the local groups on Radio Luxemburg at 208 metres medium wave. There was no shortage of talent. In fact, the Beatles were just one component of the Mersey Beat. As a youngster, I had the good fortune to catch them at the Queen's Hall in Widnes. It was in February 1963. The converted church hall was set out for a dance with three rows of seats in front of the stage. The door staff let me in because my sister's best friend was dating Aaron Williams, the bass guitarist with the Merseybeats who were the opening act. At first, I stomped with my sister to rock & roll classics but, after she and her prettier side-kicks disappeared backstage, was left in the company of the ones who were pimpled, freckled and extremely understanding. On the dance floor I gave a good impression of a boy going through puberty; slightly uncomfortable in his own body and with oversized bits all over.

The set featured Little Richard's 'Long Tall Sally', Chuck Berry's 'Roll Over Beethoven' and other crowd-pleasers which lasted for two minutes or less. I'm still fond of the poetic lyrics about telling Tchaikovsky the news whereas I've never felt the same way about their slower numbers like 'Red Sails in the Sunset' made famous by Nat King Cole. I assumed that they were included to provide a break for Ringo, who had been banging away on his old kit like Grandad France on his anvil. His bass drum bore the words 'Premier' and 'Ringo Starr'. Most of the patrons at the Queen's Hall believed that it should have read 'Lucky'.

Everyone at school had a favourite Beatle. I don't recall any of my classmates claiming Ringo. The concensus of opinion was that he was an adequate time-keeper but not a virtuoso percussionist. One or two were convinced that he was no better than some of the older members of the town's BB bugle and drum corps. They were aware of the rumours that 'Love Me Do' had been recorded on three separate occasions with three different drummers, namely Pete Best, Ringo Starr and Andy White. The released single had White on drums with Starr relegated to the tambourine which was considered slightly more challenging than the maracas or the triangle.

The Beatles sang a few Lennon-McCartney originals. I remember 'Love Me Do' and 'Please Please Me'. Their other self-penned offerings weren't received with the same enthusiasm. When Paul or John announced: 'Here's one of our own songs. I hope you like it', the dance floor would clear. The perspiring stompers disappeared to the bar or elsewhere. As for yours truly? I'm guilty of visiting the toilets during a live performance by The Beatles.

The Fab Three plus Ringo were no strangers to my hometown. Their first single had bee launched officially on a wet October afternoon at Dawson's Music Shop and that evening at The Music Shop. Both establishments were modest even by the standards of Widnes's main street. It's fair to say that no-one who secured their autographs at theses launches dreamt that university dons would analyze their writings, museums would treasure their memorabilia or that their music would be the universal language heard around the world.

I saw John, Paul, George and Ringo again at the Liverpool Empire. In March 1963, they were advertized as the opening act for two Americans, namely Tommy Roe - who had enjoyed great success with a bubble-gum song entitled 'Sheila' and Chris Montez - who was more of a one-hit wonder with 'Let's Dance'. But because 'Please Please Me' had made its way up the UK charts, The Beatles were promoted to top the bill in their hometown. Shortly afterwards, they defected to London. I was honoured to watch them progress from obscurity to cultural icons, whereas many of my friends felt betrayed - especially those who had invested in collarless Beatle jackets and envied Ringo's luck.

I moved on to The Searchers, another Merseyside group who had worldwide hits with 'Needles and Pins' and 'Sugar and Spice'. It was an easy decision because Mike Pender could often be spotted on the terraces at Everton away games. Also my sister was dating Tony Jackson, the group's other singer, much to the disapproval of Chemical Harry. With so much rock & roll in the air, she was instructed to keep a watchful eye on me during the week. In exchange for his acceptance - make that tolerance - of my modest Beatle mop-top I was expected to reciprocate.

Royston, quitting is dead easy ... I've done it many times

22. Toilet rolls and darts

Everyone knew of my whereabouts on Saturdays. I had many different travelling companions to Goodison and would simply tag along with whoever was at Farnworth Station, now known as Widnes North, at 1:00 pm. Also since age 12, I had been allowed to venture as far as Yorkshire. These away-days must have been hell on my mother's nerves. Given the absence of a watch on my wrist, my most common misdemeanor was not complying with the conditions of her curfew. My punishment was two-fold – a clip around the ear and being grounded from sunrise to sundown on the next Saturday. Corporal punishment is considered abusive in some cultures but was accepted in our house. After all, caning was a common form of discipline at my junior and secondary schools. Opinions are divided on whether it is helpful or harmful to a child's behaviour. Personally, I can confirm that such punishment was nowhere near as painful as knowing that Everton had kicked off without me.

Hooliganism was a national problem throughout the Sixties. For a high-profile minority, going to away matches involved mindless vandalism and drink-fueled looting. The football specials were the prime targets for their anti-social rebellion. Between the steam locomotives and the guard's van, British Rail employed what seemed like 200-yards of its most bruised and battered carriages. Despite the presence of stewards in the corridors, the compartments were wrecked on their way to the match. That's right, on the outward journey. It was common for tables to be thrown out of the windows and emergency cords to be pulled before Crewe Station. Nowadays, there are various theories of crowd dynamics and the impact of policing upon public order. In the early Sixties, there was an unwritten etiquette on how fans should behave. If younger fans misbehaved on the terraces, the older ones would discipline them.

Blues received their share of bad press for the missiles launched from Gwladys Street. These transgressions led to the creation of the arcs in the perimeter walls behind both goals to separate the hooligans from their targets. Popular terrace-to-pitch missiles were rolls of toilet paper and darts. I understand that only certifiable nutters take darts to a football match but who wastes rolls of unused quilted, two-ply paper? For a boy raised in Gerrard Street, it was heresy. Other projectiles included old pennies with their edges sharpened. They were phased out after the conversion to decimal coinage in 1971 and replaced by Sayers' pies. Allegedly, the steak & kidney ones contained 15% meat. To this day, the contents of the meat & potato ammo remain classified. It's always amused me that someone calculated how far an intoxicated Blue could propel a half-eaten pie to determine the radius of the arcs.

Crowds foster anonymity and, on occasions, bring out the worst in people. Monkey sounds were no strangers to Goodison. I was raised to detest discrimination. Although a big fan of 'The Black & White Minstrel Show', Chemical Harry decreed that references to nig-nogs and honkies on the popular sitcom 'Love Thy Neighbour' shouldn't be a part of any decent person's vocabulary. Gwladys Street was far less enlightened. Racial taunts were aimed at Albert Johanneson and Paul Reaney of Leeds in the Sixties as well as West Ham's Clyde Best and our own Cliff Marshall in the Seventies. Then in 1987 some knuckle-head lobbed a banana at John Barnes and all Blues were branded as bigots. I regret that a racist undercurrent persisted into the Nineties and has yet to be fully eradicated. I can't imagine what goes through the narrow-minds of people who taunt their own players. Kevin Campbell was the target of vile abuse, even though his arrival saved the club from relegation. I propose that those found guilty of using racial slurs should be dispatched to the football's equivalent of the outer darkness, never to be seen or heard from again.

Racism, hooliganism and wanton violence weren't the worst thing to happen at away grounds in the early-Sixties. I witnessed shocking incidents at Bolton, Blackburn and Blackpool in which mobs of youths, with more testosterone than decency, would surround small groups of female supporters of the home side and interfere with them. I'm not talking about teenagers copping a sly feel of breasts during goal celebrations but the ripping and removal of clothing as trophies. Because the terraces were packed to capacity, no stewards or police came to their rescue and it was left to older Evertonians with the courage of Chemical Harry to put a stop to the shenanigans. Any reference to these disgusting incidents was taboo. When I mentioned them to my mother, she reminded me that a football ground on a Saturday afternoon, like a public house without a snug on a Saturday night, was no place for unaccompanied girls.

With little segregation and rival supporters intermingled on the terraces, you were never far from hand-to-hand skirmishes to enliven your matchday experience. I recall my adventure to Burnden in 1962. For the record, we won 2-0. After the game, there were outbreaks of trouble near Trinity Street Station. I got caught up in an ambush by some very sore losers and lost my dentures in the mayhem. Permit me to elaborate. I had forfeited my natural front teeth during a game of tick-and-pass at secondary school, in which there was some confusion with Mal Aspey, who was tough enough to play 570-odd times for Widnes, about what constitutes a legitimate tick. In the absence of dental bridges and implants, I've had to wrestle with partial dentures throughout the past half-century.

As a rule, I would pocket them for safekeeping at the first hint of pugilism. Unfortunately, they disappeared during the fighting at Bolton. I searched the battleground to no avail before hitch-hiking home. For reasons known only to a toothless 14-year-old, I elected to take the direct route home rather than appeal to the Liverpool-bound traffic along the East Lancs Road. It was an exhausting six hour journey in which I wasn't offered a single lift. I remember marching past the coal mines in Atherton, walking past the spinning mills in Leigh and trudging past the mental asylum in Winwick. A couple of cars stopped but, given my vampire-like appearance, the drivers avoided eye contact and sped away.

As a direct consequence of the Battle of Trinity Street Station, I've maintained numerous spare flippers – the technical term used by my American dentist. I keep them in neatly labelled boxes. 'The Corporate Smile' are ill-fitting pearly whites reserved for weddings and funerals. 'The Chompers' don't quite match the colour of my natural teeth but are well worn in and extremely comfortable. 'The Zahnersatz' were engineered in Karlsruhe, possibly for someone else. They are my false teeth of last resort. Then there are 'The Lucky Ones'. Yes, I own lucky teeth. They come in a special formation in which three big teeth dominate the space usually taken by four. They are 'The Holy Trinity' of dentures.

Over the years, I've grown fond of Bolton and people from that neck of the woods. Like the lass from Lancashire that I married, I remain in awe of King Cotton's role in the Industrial Revolution, the architecture of the civic buildings and town hall around Le Mans Crescent and, of course, the football heritage of Burnden Park. It was one of my favourite grounds. From its vast terraces, I had witnessed victories in two semi-finals. While I never set foot on the famous turf, I must reveal that my wife did so as a young girl. Apparently, she took part in a sports-day at the old ground and finished a very credible fourth in the sack race.

23. Battle of Goodison

In the Sixties, Goodison crowds were bigger and far more passionate than today. The packed terraces swayed with thunderous intensity and fostered a sense of belonging by reproducing the music of Lennon & McCartney and chanting rare Merseyside wisdom to get under the skin of opposition players and supporters. The matches themselves were far more physical. Two-footed challenges softened up opponents in the opening minutes. Cynical tackles from behind were termed professional. In fact, the game's hard men were more likely to be dismissed for dissent than violent conduct.

Looking back at my six decades of watching football at Goodison, my most memorable home game wasn't a stomach-churning relegation escape or a spine-tingling cup tie. To this day, my cerebral cortex is scarred by our 1964 battle with Leeds which has gone down in the annals of English football as one of its most notorious confrontations. The Battle of Goodison between Everton and Leeds burst into flames after only four minutes when Johnny Giles, notorious among opponents for going over the top of the ball, somehow left his stud marks on the chest of Sandy Brown. The defender retaliated by pole-axing his opponent. I was standing near the corner flag directly behind Brown and recall that his shirt was ripped and covered in blood. Also I can confirm that Sandy's monster left-hook was a thing of remarkable power and precision worthy of Smokin' Joe Frazier. It was a prototype for the one which knocked down Mohammed Ali in the final round of their first fight at Madison Square Garden.

Shortly after Brown had been dismissed, Mama Blue grew angry. Like witnesses to gladiatorial combat, the 44,000 frenzied Blues demanded blood. As Leeds seemed to get away with foul after foul, the crowd became even more incensed. Any Leeds player brave enough to stray within throwing distance ran the risk of being struck by the missiles fired from all corners of the ground. Nowadays frustrated fans dispatch pay-as-you-throw mobile phones and inflatable body parts. Back then, the skies rained cushions from the Bullens Road Stand and coins from the Gwladys Street terraces. Put it down to enthusiastic excess, a disgruntled Blue standing near me threw his bunch of house keys at goalkeeper Gary Sprake and had to plead with a photographer to retrieve them.

The men in blue stood toe-to-toe with those in white as the violence turned brutal. Like many in the Park End, I cursed the absence of Tony Kay, a respected hard-case out of the Vince Karalius mould, who would have banged more than a few heads together. In his absence, Everton's Roy Vernon, the thinnest man on the pitch, and Leeds's Bobby Collins, the shortest man on the pitch, relished the warfare. Along with the likes of Norman 'Bite Your Legs' Hunter, Jack Charlton, Billy Bremner, Jimmy Gabriel, Johnny Morrissey and Dennis Stevens, they were lucky not to join Brown in the showers.

Things came to a head after about 35 minutes when full-back Willie Bell launched a two-footed tackle at Derek Temple. It was at about neck height and one of the worst I've seen outside a wrestling ring. The crowd exploded into a seething mass of rage. As the Everton forward was being stretchered off by the St John Ambulance attendants, Mr Ken Stokes, the referee, ordered the other 20 players to the dressing rooms to give them, and also the crowd, time to calm down. Actually, I remember the weak referee marching across the pitch to the tunnel in a huff with the unruly players following like naughty schoolboys who had just realized that they had gone too far. We didn't know if the game had been abandoned and were surprised when the teams returned to the pitch.

The 10-minute ceasefire did little to soothe the fury of the players or the hostility of the fans. I remember that the rest of the match involved a long procession of fouls; the count was Everton 19 to Leeds 12. Inexplicably, only Hunter was booked. Amid the carnage, Leeds squeezed out a 1-0 victory. But there were no winners that Saturday afternoon. Both clubs were condemned for damaging the image of English football. Predictably, the media demanded the closure of the stadium. One or two journalists postulated that, given the game's growing preoccupation with money, the clubs and more important the guilty players should be penalized where it would hurt most - in their pockets.

Be that as it may, only the hosts were punished by the football authorities. Smokin' Sandy Brown was suspended for two weeks. Years later, he told me that his knockout punch was worth four weeks. Everton Football Club was fined £250. To this day, I remain convinced that coins worth more than that amount were retrieved by stewards from the Goodison touchlines.

Don Revie's men came out of the ordeal vilified as a brutally successful side. In and around Widnes, there was some unfounded speculation that they would convert to playing Rugby League or even ice hockey for the following 1965/66 season. Bremner, Giles, Hunter and friends weren't fazed by the criticism. In fact three months later, they returned to Goodison and knocked us out of the FA Cup in front of 66,000 blood-thirsty fans.

Even though Don Revie encouraged provocation and his side was widely regarded as a bunch of thugs, John Moores must have been impressed by his win-at-all-costs gamesmanship or perhaps the brotherly togetherness of his team. Often, it's forgotten that his Leeds side could really play and, sometimes, actually did. Prior to Catterick's retirement, Everton offered the Leeds boss a record-breaking annual salary plus a massive signing-on bonus to lure him to Merseyside. Surprisingly for someone known for his greed, especially tax-free cash, he preferred to take the England job for less money.

I'm sure that Revie's tenure would have been more productive than those of Billy Bingham and Gordon Lee. His arrival, however, would have delayed or even negated the need for Howard Kendall - the man who in my opinion remains head and shoulders above all other Everton managers, past and present.

Kay, get out of my sight ... I detest people who gamble on football

24. Veteran of the thumb

During my years at secondary school, my Everton money was earned through an assortment of part-time jobs. If I had possessed a curriculum vitae, it would have listed my stints as a sleepy-eyed paper boy, a diligent postman at Christmas, a begrudging potato peeler at a local chippy and an entrepreneurial recycler, specializing in coloured glass bottles. My most rewarding summer jobs involved labeling chemicals for laboratories and preparing wage packets for railway workers. It was during my stay at British Rail's maintenance sheds near Allerton that I first displayed my knack for numbers to the wider world. After word of my mathematical dexterity had spread, the staff placed bets on my speed against a state-of-the-art calculator made by Texas Instruments. The contestants had to add columns of numbers. The duel started with lists of three digits – no problem. It progressed to four digits – again no problem. The race became much harder with five digits. After a little auditing and much cheering, I was declared the victor and received 3/- for my troubles – the equivalent of one admission to the Paddock.

As a bonus, my grateful backers provided me with invaluable advice on how to navigate the national railway system in a cost-effective manner. I discovered that as long as I got to my destination, the British Rail ticket collectors wouldn't deny me safe rides home on the football specials. Therefore, I would thumb my way to the more distant destinations and catch the train home. It wasn't difficult. Widnes bustled with vehicles transporting products from the chemical plants to different parts of the country. My routine involved taking the bus to a popular cafe on the outskirts of town. Rather than stand by the side of the road with my thumb out, I would ask trustworthy-looking patrons if they were going my way. It's much safer to choose your driver. Other rules of the thumb involve common sense. Be patient, look friendly, never stand in a group of more than two and wear your colours with pride. Like many things in life, successful hitch-hiking is about prime location. The more cars that pass you, the more likely you are to get a ride. Therefore it's best to stand where the driver can pull over safely and legally.

The thumb is a magical phalange. It can make the rest of the body travel at 70 mph. Naturally, there were times when I worried that no-one would stop only for an articulated savior, often manufactured by Foden and driven by a Blue or a Red, to put my world into order. In truth, I preferred lorries. They had heaters. Such devices were optional extras on many popular cars in the Sixties. While these commercial vehicles were often tainted with a pungency unique to chemical works, their drivers were the true kings of the road. Many would make a detour to drop me at the ground or at a good spot where the traffic was headed in that direction.

Drivers stop because they are bored and want to hear the sound of their own voices. The contract between the hitchhiker and the driver is simple – a free ride in exchange for a friendly ear. I recall one driver chatting away about his domestic problems. After a half-hour he paused: 'That's enough about my life. What about you? What do you think about my life?' I learnt to listen with a look of astonishment as the drivers told me how great they were at this and that. It was a skill that I would use with no little success in later life. Also, it never ceased to amaze me that people willingly pour out intimate details. It must be something to do with the fact that the two strangers will never see each other again. I detected that car drivers enjoy a sense of adventure from picking up roadside wanderers. When they asked about me, I was keen to tell them about Everton and what it meant to be a travelling Blue. Few were interested.

Both of my parents had left home as teenagers and encouraged me to experience and enjoy life. It's probably worth clearing my conscience at this point by confessing that I rarely revealed the true risks of hitch-hiking to them. In contrast, most drivers wanted to hear about my road adventures, especially encounters with creepy misfits. Where to start? How about with an act of car-jaculating. A friend and I accepted a lift from a man in a Triumph Herald who looked like a harmless school teacher. Our risk assessment had much to do with his calfskin driving gloves.

After a few miles, he took off one glove, unbuttoned his fly and started to masturbate. We giggled at 'The M6 Wanker'. Mimicking Dick Emery, my friend demanded: 'Ooh, put that thing away … you're frightening the lorries!' The driver didn't laugh. His hand and car came to abrupt halts and we were dumped at the side of the motorway like a litter of unwanted puppies.

Then there were the two old biddies - possibly crossdressers -who described themselves as taking a trip to Naughtyland. At first, I thought that they were amusing but detected changes in their mood as the Ford Anglia chugged along. So much so that I feared for my welfare and suspected that the shining plastic covers had been installed to protect the car seats from incessant sexual innuendos or blood spatter. Concerned that the Sunday papers would report the discovery of a 14-year-old hog-tied with a blue and white scarf in a remote part of Cheshire, I threatened to vomit on the floor but gave an unconvincing performance. Consequently, I sought divine intervention. Celsius - the God of Steaming Radiators, responded to my prayers and, like a reporter from the News of the World, I made my excuses and bolted. And how can I forget 'The Prophet'? He articulated at tongue-twisting speed from Knutsford to West Brom. His sole topic? Humans are headed along the path of dinosaurs and will be wiped out by 2065. According to him, God has given up on the human race. We will be destroyed by disease spread via vermin. The non-stop doom-monger wished that the human race had died out earlier and given the rest of the species inhabiting this planet a chance. Yes I know what you're thinking, I should have asked him: 'Will Everton win the League Cup before 2065?'

Less hair-raising were the Old Pals who shared stories about serving in Lord Kitchener's Army throughout the ride to Bedford. In response to my callow questions, they described the stench of the death and the size of the fearless brown rats that fed on the corpses in the narrow trenches of Normandy. Both men brimmed with anger at the past and overflowed with optimism for the future. I recall that one claimed to dream of a better tomorrow where chickens can use zebra crossings without having their motives questioned. Born-again Baptists, they reassured me time and again that 'Jesus loves you', 'Man's way leads to a hopeless end - God's way leads to endless hope'. Before I left them they reminded me: 'Sex is the most disgusting thing on earth. You should save it for someone you love.'

As hitch-hiking became routine, I forgot about the risks associated with distracted drivers of unknown sobriety who were actively seeking a meeting with God while driving vehicles of questionable safety. The greatest threat, however, is the driver who looks normal but has evil at his core. Luckily, I had only one bruising experience during 100 or so rides. It occurred when another friend and I accepted a lift in a Ford Zephyr containing three inebriates in Army uniforms. It would be a stretch to call them soldiers. Immediately, they poked fun at John Moores buying the title. It started as light hearted give-and-take then turned ugly. Punches were exchanged before the car slid to an untidy stop and we were dumped at the side of the A57 where it traverses the Peak District. We licked our wounds in one of the most inhospitable spots on the Snake Pass, then questioned our sanity. Intense cold will do that to you. Should we give up and go home? My friend and I decided to flag down the first vehicle no matter what direction it was going. He stood on the road to Manchester. I stood on the one to Sheffield. Then, not for the first or last time, God intervened and a Hillsborough-bound car picked us up.

They say that hitch-hiking is something everyone should do in their youth. As a retired veteran of the thumb, I can confirm that it enhanced my self-reliance and taught me to handle the rejection of legions of passing motorists. Also the act of getting into an unfamiliar car honed my judgment. A hitch-hiker must make an immediate assessment of strangers whose wide smiles may not touch their eyes. Therefore, my advice is obvious. Be alert and cautious. If you've bad feelings about someone, even if it's raining cats and dogs, don't get into the vehicle.

25. Bone-shaking Blues

Most of my road trips were well-planned, others were spontaneous. In September 1964, one week after we had hammered the Reds by 4-0 at Anfield, I was busy fulfilling my paper-round. In truth, I was dreading the ride to deliver my last paper which was more than an uphill mile from the penultimate one and cursing the customer, who ordered the Daily Telegraph in the morning and the Manchester Evening News at night, when I bumped into two school friends. Their bikes were loaded with camping gear and pointed towards our next opponents in Birmingham. They invited me to join them on condition that I brought something to eat and bought a round at some country pub. Flattered by their proposition, I returned home with the orphan newspaper. I raided my mother's pantry for a tin of corned beef that had one of those pesky keys attached and scribbled a note: 'Gone to the match. Back Saturday night or Sunday morning.'

We cycled down the A51 and stopped at a pub near Nantwich. There was nothing special about the place, just six regulars sitting in their favourite nooks and crannies on a quiet Friday evening. Much as my father forbid me to drink, I was aware that mild was the cheapest beer and my preferred tipple. My friends were more evolved and selected Double Diamond which was gassed with carbon dioxide in order to work wonders. Anyway, we were sipping our beverages when the landlord invited me to buy a packet of Smith's crisps for the pub's mongrel which he claimed performed goalkeeping impersonations. With no little enthusiasm, we were informed that the canine called 'Dog' could mimic the contenders vying for the job between the sticks at Goodison. Both Gordon West and Andy Rankin could be brilliant one week and inconsistent the next.

Unlike the Alsatians that protected Widnes pubs, Dog didn't have anger steaming out of his nostrils. As the most expensive keeper in the world, he painstakingly scratched out an arrow on the grubby carpet with his paw and positioned himself between the open double-doors to the lounge. Following the landlord's instructions, I lobbed the packet towards the top right corner of the door-frame. Immediately, West leapt three feet off the floor to grab it with his teeth before swallowing the crisps, the bag, even the sachet of salt with one shake of his head before re-positioning himself between the door-jambs as Rankin. Dutifully, one of my friends bought another packet of crisps and threw it into the same corner. This time the canine didn't budge as the missile floated past him. After a few seconds, he barked at those in front of him before sauntering into the lounge to retrieve the packet. Again, he swallowed it in one movement. After our consumption of three rounds of refreshments, one of the regulars nodded towards me and mouthed: 'Give that schoolboy a lollipop. Give him two, he's a sucker!' As a result, 'Sucker' became my unwanted nickname for the rest of that school year.

I recall that we cycled for another three hours in darkness before erecting our tent somewhere near Walsall. My BB background proved invaluable until we were interrupted by the local constabulary. Concerned for our welfare, no doubt because we were consuming bread covered with Nestle's condensed milk, corned beef and pilchards, they moved us to a nearby bus shelter. There, we slept until disturbed by a gathering of Brummies headed to St Andrews. As for the match, Rankin played a blinder in a 5-3 win.

The 90 odd-mile trip seemed much longer pedalling northwards. I was handicapped by the fact that my old bone-shaker had a fixed-wheel which meant that its pedals were always in motion. We had got as far as Stafford when a Blue from Bootle driving a scrap-metal lorry spotted my blue and white scarf bobbing up and down and offered us a lift. You'll have guessed that I didn't receive a hero's welcome at Sycamore Avenue that night. Nor did I receive one at Chamberlain's Newsagents the next morning. The proprietor waited until I had completed my deliveries of the Sunday papers and the delinquent copy of the Manchester Evening News before giving me the boot. It was the first but not the last time that I was informed that my services were no longer required.

I didn't hitch-hike to Birmingham because I had lost faith in my seductive left digit which had failed to get me to the first-leg of the Unofficial British Championship in Glasgow. I threw the towel in around Charnock Richard but learnt an important lesson during that adventure. It was illegal for drivers to pick up hitchhikers on the M6 but it wasn't against the law for them to slow down and give them false hope. In my absence, we defeated Rangers by 3-1at Ibrox. As for the second-leg? I had never seen so many inebriated fans or empty whisky bottles. The latter covered the running track in front of the Paddock. I recall that Rangers were a decent side and retained the Scottish title, Scottish Cup and League Cup that season but were inferior to Everton. Therefore it remains a mystery to me why, despite out-classing the pride of Scotland, we've struggled against kilted opposition in the Inter-Cities Cup and the Texaco Cup – or, for that matter, never realized our potential in Europe.

In the first European Cup game played on Merseyside, the Champions of England hosted their counterparts from Italy in the preliminary round. Talk about the luck of the draw. Two things about the first-leg at Goodison come to mind. We played in all white and admission to the ground was increased to 5/-. If my memory serves me correctly, we enjoyed lots of possession and won a dozen or so corners, but failed to make the vital breakthrough. After Roy Vernon had a goal disallowed, Jimmy Gabriel was pushed up front in the Sixties' version of hoofball but the game finished scoreless. After we lost the second-leg by 1-0, Inter Milan progressed to beat Real Madrid in the final and we concentrated on retaining the League title. The set-back was no big deal at the time, after all the European Cup was for foreigners.

People who know far more about football than me insist that a manager should never change a winning-side. Harry Catterick didn't listen to them and signed Fred Pickering. The centre-forward was an instant success and scored nine goals in his first nine games. His introduction, however, upset the chemistry of the side and we gained only three points from the final five games. We finished in third position. The situation wasn't helped by revelations published by the 'Sunday People' in April 1964 that Tony Kay had bet against his own team at Sheffield Wednesday. Immediately, he was suspended by Everton and, sadly, never played football again. Kay was the most uncompromising competitor to have worn royal blue. If you don't believe me then ask the fans of Stanley Matthews. I remember the 50-year-old playing for Stoke when Brian Labone, Mick Meagan and their fellow defenders treated 'The Wizard of Dribble' with the respect deserving of a national treasure. Not so Kay. Ever the pro, he subjected Matthews to some ferocious tackles.

When I think about Stoke, my first visit to the old Victoria Ground in 1965 comes to mind. It was both memorable and uncomfortable. The game is remembered by many as the first in which the club used a substitute, namely John Hurst who had a goal disallowed in the final minute. I'm mindful of that fact because I lost my right shoe during the aborted celebrations of the 10,000 Blues gathered behind the goal. Somehow my winkle-picker came off in the crush and disappeared. After the crowd had exited, I rummaged through the littered terraces before checking with the club's Lost Property Office. It was stocked with the detritus of Saturday football. If I had been searching for a lonely-looking glove or a tartan umbrella, I wouldn't have been disappointed but no shoes had been turned in that afternoon. After my travelling companions had abandoned me to catch their train, I pleaded with the keeper of the lost property for any item of footwear to get me home.

He offered two alternatives. I could wait for the groundsman to bring a pair of wellies from his cubby-hole or make do with an orphaned Chukka boot. I must have cut a forlorn figure hitching at the entrance to the M6 motorway equipped with one black leather winkle-picker and one brown suede boot courtesy of Stoke City Football Club. Although they were of different sizes, my footwear had something in common – both were intended for the left foot.

26. World of the BTU

Do you remember your careers adviser? After a short interrogation, mine recommended that I leave school on my fifteenth birthday. His words were sobering. I hadn't thought about the future and had no idea what to do with my life except follow Everton. Process work at ICI, preferably in a not-too-toxic environment, would've topped my list if I had possessed one. My more ambitious class-mates wanted to learn a trade but, after they discovered there were no situations vacant, we all opted to stay on at school for another year. Amazingly I earned three 'O' level GCEs – mathematics, geography and woodwork. Nothing too academic. My mother wept at hearing the news. They were tears of delight. Her celebrations were not unlike those displayed by Andy Johnson in the 2006 derby.

Giddy with success coupled with my new zest for reading, I was more determined than ever to secure an apprenticeship. I wasn't picky - any trade would do. I made scores of applications only to be rejected by everyone from major corporations like Ford and ICI, where my father had worked for decades, to local plumbers, joiners and electricians. Finally, I was invited for an interview by the North Western Gas Board. The personnel manager was impressed, not by my academic qualifications but by the fact that I was from Widnes. Apparently, he had been let down by his preferred candidate from my neck of the woods and was desperate to fill the vacancy.

The job interview was an act of God; reward for my faithful attendance at Sunday school for so many years. I simply nodded and smiled a lot during the half-hour or so taken by the personnel manager to detail the terms of the indentured servitude and integration of on-the-job training with studies for a City & Guilds Certificate in gas-fitting, a derivative of plumbing, and possibly an Ordinary National Certificate in mechanical engineering. That was until he asked me about my hobbies. I abandoned my rehearsed fibs related to the works of Shakespeare, fly-fishing and overhauling twin carburetors and volunteered enthusiastically that I was a football fanatic who hitch-hiked to Everton away games. My candour must have scored points because I was offered the job there and then.

The gas industry was the least enlightened of the nationalized monopolies. It was set in its ways with local manufacturing plants, usually near coal mines, and appliance showrooms, always in town centres. Perceived as both dirty and dangerous, it struggled to compete with electricity. The world of the BTU, however, was about to change. Vast quantities of natural gas had been discovered in the North Sea by a group of American companies which included Texas Eastern, a name you will hear more about later. My initial training progressed from stints of shoveling coal into the retorts at the old gas works and digging up roads across South Lancashire to cycling around the new smokeless zones with coils of lead pipe around my neck.

Unfashionable or not, I really enjoyed the camaraderie. The older gas-fitters took great pride in their work. The only downside was that they possessed every tool imaginable and the novice apprentice had to take care of them as well as haul them from job to job on the front of my bicycle. By comparison, some of the younger tradesmen took pride in operating with the bare minimum of tools – screw-driver, hammer, chisel, adjustable spanner, propane lamp, knife, solder, pressure gauge, tub of tallow and packet of condoms.

At job-sites, the only liberties taken by the older tradesmen were to warn the lady of the house that her gas supply was about to be turned off and that she may want to boil the kettle to make some tea. Some of the younger ones sought other forms of stimulation. On more occasions than I care to remember, I was instructed to go home early because the tradesman wanted to finish the job on his own. I suppose high-speed sex was one of the hidden perks of high-speed gas. Without exception, I would return to the Gas Board's workshop and help the meter readers sift through their shilling coins. They spent hours separating those from 1900 to 1914 which contained significant amounts of silver and were worth much more than their face value. No-one asked why I wasn't gas-fitting. I assumed that they knew.

Quite literally, the low point of my apprenticeship involved an incident in Coroners Lane - one of the few leafy avenues in Widnes. I knew that it would be a short work-day by the way in which the middle-aged lady teased open the door amid a mist of perfume. My job was to run lead pipe under the suspended wooden floor to the fireplace. After lifting the fitted carpet, I disappeared through the trap-door. My progress along the 20-inch high crawl space was slowed by the need to knock bricks out of the foundation wall which allowed me to slither on my belly from one section to another. I had been out of sight for a short time when I received the anticipated instructions from my gas-fitter: 'Finish what you're doing and go home.' Thirty minutes later, I called it a day.

Unfortunately, the wooden floor joist had sagged where the bricks had been removed and, to my horror, I was trapped. I banged on the floor and shouted for help. No-one came to my rescue. Rather than panic, I thought about the important things in life such as my recent visits to London for the finals of the FA Cup and World Cup. Then, I set about predicting Everton's results for the new season. What if? The simple question has inspired scenarios. As a pessimist, I reckoned that we would go unbeaten at home. Actually, we would earn at least 18 wins from the 21 games. On the road? In alphabetical order I pencilled in a draw at Highbury, win at Villa, comfortable win at Bloomfield Road, win at Turf Moor, draw at Stamford Bridge, win at Craven Cottage, etc. to gain a total of 60 points in the era of two points for a win. I analyzed the fixtures again and again. As an optimist, I convinced myself that, with the recently recruited Alan Ball in our ranks, we would suffer narrow losses at Elland Road, Highbury, Old Trafford and, possibly, White Hart Lane and amass a title-winning total of 66 points.

A half-hour had passed before I began to fret about my internment. Some people suffer from claustrophobia; others have a deeper-rooted fear of being buried alive. I had neither. I simply turned off my torch to save the battery and in the darkness resorted to calculating the value of pi, the ratio of a circle's circumference to its diameter. Eventually, I re-inspected my surroundings and deduced that I would have to shrink my body size like a cockroach to squeeze through the crevice. Then all of a sudden, I sensed that I wasn't alone. I could hear the patter of hundreds of tiny feet. When I turned on my torch, I could see eyes — lots of eyes. I prayed that the 1,000 yard stares belonged to mice and not a legion of angry roaches intent on taking me hostage in reprisal for the atrocities suffered by their loved ones in Gerrard Street. In honour of the fallen, I hummed a verse of 'La Cucaracha', the Mexican folk song. In return, they respected my space.

The primary function of the cockroach is to mate. In fact, one female is capable of indirectly producing a million offspring in one year but it is possible that they could have learnt a thing or two from the activities on the top floor of the house. It must have been another half-hour before the gas-fitter finished what he was doing and noticed my bike in the driveway. Subsequently, the Gas Board's emergency crew used a series of hydraulic jacks to release me. I'm told that I resembled an earthquake victim embarrassed by the fuss. Only the emergency engineers and the man of the house, who had returned home from work, celebrated my return. The other witnesses shifted their weight from foot to foot as they stared at the concave floor. Their faces were something to behold, although not necessarily to admire.

For the record, United were crowned champions with 60 points. My subterranean forecasts were undermined by unexpected home defeats to Blackpool, Forest, Southampton and Stoke. We managed only 48 points and sixth place.

27. Made-to-measure Mod

With something of a cultural revolution underway, there was no shortage of distractions for a pubescent teenager with a couple of bob burning a hole in his pocket. My employment had coincided with my conversion to the Mod lifestyle in which it was important to stand out from the crowd, yet be part of an army that wore the same uniform. Everything had to be just right – the hairstyle with peyos borrowed from Orthodox Jews, the tailor-made suit and the Lambretta 150cc scooter. I'm not talking about an ordinary piece of Italian engineering. It was the type of head-turning transportation immortalized in 'Quadrophenia' and my calling card for a couple of years. The side panels had been hand-painted with RAF roundels and beautified with chrome mirrors of all shapes and sizes on the end of long poles. Also, there was a front rack covered in spotlights, a world-class collection of AA badges plus a somewhat faded pennant which as you may recall proclaimed 'Play Up Everton'.

The scooter resembled a wounded Christmas tree and its owner looked like a daft lad. That's how Chemical Harry referred to me. I'm not kidding. For a few months, my father called me 'Daft Lad' at home and in public. He claimed that my scooter had limited horsepower so as not to ruffle my back-combed hairdo and the mirrors were positioned so that I could see my reflection in every one of them. As a 17-year old Mod, I thought myself brave enough to challenge him for the first time. Though it wasn't a pleasant experience, I learnt an important life lesson. If you're going to rebel as a teenager then the last person to cross is Chemical Harry. Despite his name-calling, every weekend I would swap my green overalls for my charcoal grey suit - with thin lapels and narrow trousers - and tranformed into a dedicated follower of cheap fashion. While the Mods featured on Ready Steady Go! ordered their made-to-measure suits from trendy boutiques in Carnaby Street, Daft Lad bought his at Burtons.

As leaders of a generational revolt against the old order, the Mods' meticulous attention to detail was the complete opposite to our arch rivals - the Rockers who loved Triumph Bonnevilles, studded leather jackets and the rebellious look of the previous decade. Ironically, one of my match-going pals was an extra greasy biker who rode 'The Widowmaker' - an old 650cc Norton Dominator. His hair was styled like Presley – that is if King Elvis had graced Gilly Potter's chair. We were an odd couple who put Everton Football Club before our lifestyle decisions – at least on matchdays. Inseparable on the terraces, we rarely acknowledged each other in the street.

Compared to my troubled relationship with my father, I enjoyed a somewhat idealized one with my mother. It had something to do with the fact that I maintained a child's view of her and a more adult view of him. That said, I feared breaching her trust or upsetting him. Thanks to my away-day adventures following Everton I had developed the wherewithal to travel the length of the country and back without getting into too much mischief and was deemed responsible to visit the Twisted Wheel Club. With a small army of other local Mods, I attended amphetamine-fueled all-nighters in Manchester. I must clarify that purple hearts, surprisingly triangular in shape, were legal and not banned until the mid-Sixties. Experts will theorize that both of my parents wanted their son to embark upon voyages of self-discovery. Remember there is more to life than simply breathing? Indeed, I was heartened by their support until I discovered that Ma Carsley had opted for a trust-but-verify approach in which a young co-worker was her eyes and ears at the Whitworth Street nightclub.

There was one condition - I couldn't wear the dream-coat tailored by a young seamstress, whose nimble fingers toiled at the Golden Wonder crisp factory during the day, from discarded curtains and a suede handbag. I don't need to look at old snapshots to know that I was a sight for sore eyes. It wouldn't be the last time that I would hear those words, as other catastrophes would follow. Embarrassingly, a decade later, my wedding photos confirm that my wife married a cross between Cat Stevens and Bob Latchford. Oh wait, I'm running ahead of myself again.

My Mod garb was better received by my peers at Riversdale Technical College in Liverpool. The goal of the two-year sandwich course was an ONC. At the outset, we were informed that anyone who earned distinctions in all five of the mechanical engineering subjects would be considered for enrollment at the Royal College of Advanced Technology - soon to be renamed the University of Salford. No-one needed to tell me that this was my life-changing opportunity. Nevertheless, my mother warned me that it takes ten times the effort to get anywhere from a council house - especially one in Widnes.

She was the first person to recognize changes in my routine in that Everton had been placed temporarily to one side as I spent my weekends coming to grips with Saturated Steam Tables, a task somewhat similar to decoding the human genome. My sink-or-swim mentality was shared with a class-mate who was determined to escape from Lowton, an accumulation of dwellings near Leigh, where he had graduated from school clown to village joker. Some colleagues treated tech college as a relaxing interlude from the day-to-day monotony of installing gas cookers and water heaters. Whereas, we studied extra hard - as if our futures depended on it. Cognizant that our best chance of qualifying for university was as a team – granted, a very odd two-man team, we pushed one another to new heights. Grasping new concepts came easy to him, so much so that he took the time to tutor me. In return, I like to think that I offered him direction and structure and, as a bonus, educated him about Merseyside football and the world beyond Rivington Pike.

Two years later, we enrolled at Salford as part-time students and below-average gas-fitters. That's something he may dispute.

Mr Amokachi ... you've got the worst case of cup fever we've ever seen

28. Hijacked glory

Are you ready for another detour? If so, please allow me to put my odyssey into reverse and park in the summer of 1966. For me it was a time for realizing that there were too many demands on an apprentice's wages. Something had to be forfeited because at the top of my shopping list was the once in a life-time opportunity to watch World Cup football. The sacrifice turned out to be my Lambretta scooter, gleaming chrome accessories and weathered US Army fishtail parka. I used a big chunk of the proceeds to buy a booklet of 10 World Cup tickets for the Group C fixtures involving Brazil - the reigning world champions and red-hot favourites, Bulgaria, Hungary and Portugal at Goodison and Old Trafford plus a guaranteed standing spec at the Wembley final.

The games were played in a carnival atmosphere and elevated Mama Blue to the forefront of the world's stage. In my humble opinion, the best game was Brazil versus Hungary. It boasted breath-taking artistry and arguably the finest goal of the tournament. Centre-forward Florian Albert and right-winger Ferenc Bene had been thorns in the Brazilian side throughout the first-half. On the hour mark, Albert whipped the ball out to Bene. As he stormed down the flank, Janos Farkas rushed towards the box to meet a beautifully weighted cross. Farkas didn't break his stride to control the ball. He simply lashed his volley past Gilmar and put a grin on the face of Gwladys Street.

Without question, Florian Albert was the man of the match and received a standing ovation at the full-time whistle. No Brazilian sparkled quite like him at Goodison. Not Garrincha, not even Pele. His portfolio of silky skills encouraged many attendees to fantasize about the future European Footballer of the Year playing alongside Alex Young. Nicknamed 'The Emperor', Albert stayed loyal to Ferencvaros and life behind the Iron Curtain.

With all of their games played at Wembley, I didn't see much of the England side prior to the final. The nation seems to have forgotten that Northern fans were robbed of watching the host country in semi-final action. While my relationship with the Three-Lions isn't complicated - I opt for club over country - I think that my association with St George would have been far more intimate had it not been for the last-minute transfers of England's semi-final clash with Portugal to London and West Germany's battle with the USSR to Merseyside. It was a truly appalling decision by FIFA - then headed by Sir Stanley Rouse - and the Football Association.

Like many of my friends, I've never found it easy to support the England national team without a Blue in the line-up. No more so than in recent years when it included the louts who harassed stranded American tourists at Heathrow's Post House Hotel in the immediate aftermath of the September 11 attacks. These apparently untouchable players, tainted by allegations of binge drinking, nightclub violence, serial adultery and debauchery, don't represent me or the country of my birth. But back in the summer of 1966, it wasn't difficult to be patriotic with Blue Ray Wilson and soon-to-be Blue Alan Ball in the England side.

A school pal and I had hitchhiked to North London for the third-place play-off game between Portugal and the USSR and the final showdown between England and West Germany. You may remember that the host nation included five truly world-class stars in its 22-man World Cup squad, namely goalkeeper Gordon Banks, full-back Ray Wilson, captain and central defender Bobby Moore, mid-fielder Bobby Charlton and striker Jimmy Greaves.

Alf Ramsey had tinkered with various selections throughout the tournament. On the right-wing, he had started with United's John Connelly, tried other out-and-out wide-men Southampton's Terry Paine and Liverpool's Ian Callaghan before settling on the more versatile Alan Ball. Even at the eleventh hour there was some speculation about him reintroducing Greaves, London's favourite son who had missed a couple of key games through injury, at the expense of Geoff Hurst. The history books show that Ramsey stayed loyal to the players that had served him so well in overcoming Argentina in the quarter final and Portugal in the semi-final side.

As for the final against West Germany, in my eyes West Ham's Hurst, Peters and Moore - all fine players - hi-jacked the glory of England's success. Even worse, I think that the efforts of our own representatives have been overlooked by the nation and also by Everton Football Club. I've never understood the criteria for naming lounges but those honouring Ray Wilson and Alan Ball are long overdue.

Later in life, I was fortunate to befriend both men. I discovered that the classy defender is a gentleman - one of the nicest people you are ever likely to meet. There again it's easy to like someone who chooses his words carefully. When Wilson speaks, people listen. At first, I found Ball to be far more guarded. I wasn't too surprised. After all, he had won the world's top prize as a mere 21-year-old and his inclusion in the England team had coincided with noticeable shifts in football's tectonic plates. As the prototype of the modern midfield dynamo, Ball displayed unrivalled tenacity plus a touch of volatility. Often remembered for his displays of unflagging stamina, I believe that his real contributions were derived from his exquisite touch, control and vision as well as devastating use of the football.

Geoff Hurst scored a hat-trick in the 1966 World Cup final and Alan Ball - in the opinion of most observers - was the man of that memorable match but I feel that English football is indebted to all members of that World Cup squad.

Of course, I've seen it before ... we used loads of the stuff at my old job

29. Empire Stadium

I love the drama of knock-out competitions. They've been responsible for more royal blue tears, both of joy and sorrow, than other silverware. That said, I've just been informed that we've been eliminated from the League Cup. It's a bitter disappointment because I thought that our name was on the trophy this year. Mind you, I've felt that way for the past 50-odd seasons. Yes, we've never won the League Cup, even after the other big clubs stopped caring about it.

Everton, as we know, is a club with rich traditions. We have won more FA Cup ties than any rival yet for some reason have lifted that trophy on only five of the 114 or so occasions in which we have entered the competition. So why are Everton prone to coming up short in crucial games? The harsh truth, I regret to say, is that we are bottlers. Our inability to convert 27 semi-final appearances into a cabinet bulging with silverware means that for many Blues the road to the final has been more rewarding than the big event itself.

The unseeded format of knock-out competitions adds to the excitement with trips to play unfashionable opponents at unusual venues. For Everton, there have been some extremely embarrassing banana skins. While our worst-ever loss was to Glossop North End in 1914, the recent humblings by Tranmere in 2001 and Shrewsbury in 2003 still cause sleepless nights for me and the other eye-witnesses. Other defeats have caused even more anguish. The two losses to Liverpool at Wembley in the Eighties were tough to accept but perhaps no more painful than the cruel semi-final set-backs at the hands of our arch rivals. Of course, there have been many glorious cup memories, far too many to list. My favorites are Brian Labone's description of the royal blue veins in Princess Margaret's delicate hands as she presented the trophy to him, Jimmy Gabriel's crazed facial expression during the time consumed shielding the ball waiting for the full-time whistle and Eddie Cavanagh's famous pitch invasion.

Do you remember when Wembley was known as the Empire Stadium? My first visit to the nation's capital was to attend the 1964 Rugby League Challenge Cup final. Shortly after Vince Karalius had returned home to captain the Chemics, he recruited a few veterans to augment the local youngsters on the club's books. Their plucky performances in the annual knock-out competition, which included five replays, inspired the town. Its streets became a sea of black and white in preparation for the semi-final replay against Castleford. At Fairfield, the headmaster, who hailed from the Home Counties, threatened to punish anyone who left early. He had much to learn about cup fever. I've often pictured him searching the empty rooms for pupils to teach.

By early afternoon, some 15,000 fans, both young and old, had set off for Wakefield. I was among the travelling menagerie crowded onto the platform at Widnes North Station waiting for the special trains. You may be aware that Paul Simon composed 'Homeward Bound' in that station's waiting room prior to boarding a train to Manchester. There is no record of how Art Garfunkel spent his time. In contrast, my class-mates and I strolled up and down the platform day-dreaming about a weekend in London. Though the semi-final victory remains something of a blur, I do remember that the winning try was scored by Billy Thompson who ran a fish & chip shop in Lowerhouse Lane opposite Naughton Park. As for the Wembley final, it was an anti-climax.

Despite the tag of underdogs, the Chemics dominated the proceedings against Hull Kingston Rovers. It's claimed that 30,000 noisy Widnesians, half of the town's population, were at Wembley. Even more, including our headmaster, turned out to celebrate Karalius bringing home the magnificent Challenge Cup for the first time in 37 years. It was merely a rehearsal for the 10-year period in the Seventies and Eighties when Widnes teams brimming with homegrown talent appeared in front of the twin towers on seven occasions. I had been pals with a couple at Milton BB and played tick tick-and-pass with several others at school but I'm sure that everyone in the town was a neighbour or related to one or more members of those great teams.

Tickets for the Rugby League Challenge Cup final hadn't been a problem. I simply bought one at face value outside the ground. Brimming with teenage optimism, I expected to repeat the exercise before Everton's clash with Sheffield Wednesday in 1966. After an hour of pleading in and around Wembley Underground Station, I acknowledged my folly. So, with the community singing underway, I elected to work the Bakerloo Line. I caught the Tube to Finchley Park where I squeezed onto a northbound train and pestered the passengers for a 'spare' until the carriages emptied. I repeated the round-trip before a less than charitable tout sold me a ticket for the equivalent of an apprentice's weekly wage.

The run-up to the final had involved a big decision. By 1966, I was a big fan of Bob Dylan and had queued for hours to buy a ticket for his Liverpool concert. Cruelly, the timing of his gig coincided with that of the FA Cup final. Bob Dylan live at the Odeon, Liverpool versus Everton Football Club live at the Empire Stadium, Wembley was no contest, even though I had a ticket for the former and not for the latter. Shortly after the semi-final, I returned my concert ticket and bought one for his appearance at Manchester's Free Trade Hall. That was the infamous gig during which he was heckled. The mere sight of Dylan without his acoustic guitar and Hohner harmonica sent the political protest song-loving audience into apoplectic shock. But when an electrified Robbie Robertson and friends joined him, the crowd turned hostile. One Northern voice yelled: 'Judas!' In response, the Fender guitars crashed into 'Like a Rolling Stone' with the now ex-folk singer commanding them to 'Play it fucking loud!' Something he has done ever since.

Returning to football; whenever I've been privileged to watch video footage of the 1966 clash with Wednesday, I'm in awe of the precision of Mike Trebilcock's shooting. Also, I never fail to hold my breath and pray that Derek Temple will hit the target for the winning goal. He never disappoints. Not long ago, I had the pleasure of watching highlights of the final alongside him. You will recall that Gerry Young had lost control of the ball near the half-way line and the Everton forward sprinted 35 yards with the ball at his feet. I asked him: 'Could you hear the defenders behind you as you approached the box? What went through your mind as Ron Springett grew bigger and bigger? When did you decide to pull the trigger?' He confessed: 'If I had been Alex Young I would have dribbled up to the keeper before waltzing around him, nut-megging him and back-heeling the ball into the net. My practical alternatives were to chip the keeper or to blast the ball past him. I noticed that Springett had advanced from his line and decided to try my luck from the edge of the box. I knew exactly where I was going to hit the ball. Fortunately, the ball behaved itself.'

The FA Cup final was the highlight of my sporting calendar in 1966. No sights compared with Brian Labone wiping his hands on his white shorts before lifting the trophy. I was fortunate to hear him recall the presentation on many occasions and never ever grew tired of his detailed description of his fleeting interaction with the Queen's sister: 'Princess Margaret had delicate hands, porcelain skin and a very naughty twinkle in her eyes just for me. Or so I thought at the time. It turned out that she had somewhat strange tastes. Years later, I was told that she had a crush on Jimmy Gabriel who - like you - has no front teeth.'

The images of the massive crowds of both Blues and Reds gathered outside St George's Hall to welcome home the captain and his team-mates come close. The atmosphere was ecstatic, effervescent, exuberant and so much more. Though that particular trophy had graced the streets of the city on only two other occasions, I was convinced that we would lift the FA Cup on a regular basis and never thought we would have to wait until 1984 and then again until 1995. As for my most cherished recollection of the latter triumph at Wembley? That's easy. It was United's defence opening up before Anders Limpar and Matt Jackson like a working girl's thighs behind Lime Street Station.

30. Contagious cup fever

Please fast forward 40-odd years. Despite travelling so many miles following Everton, I can't claim perfect attendance at key cup games. Work prevented me from jetting over for the mid-week clashes with Bayern Munich in 1985. Poor health stopped me from attending the 2009 FA Cup semi-final against United. Declared unfit to fly by my doctor, I watched the semi-final on television alongside Elizabeth and Walter. The latter is an English Cocker Spaniel of the blue roan variety. He doesn't actually support Everton but can detect if we've won or lost. The gathering of the extended Everton family in North London in 2009 confirmed that few things in English football are as contagious as cup fever. It has been that way throughout the ages, from rosettes and rattles in the Sixties to modern-day counterparts of blue noses and banners proclaiming 'Wonder Woman wears Tim Cahill pyjamas to the Aldi'.

The pre-game show started at 6:00 am in Victoria BC. On seeing United's line-up, I thought that Sir Alex Ferguson had chosen a team for a FA Youth Cup semi-final. There was no Wayne Rooney, no Christiano Ronaldo and no Edwin Van der Sar. Thankfully, David Moyes treated the competition with more respect. So did the Everton supporters. As United's fans sauntered into the stadium just minutes before the kick-off, they must have been a tad intimidated by the raucous Everton end awash with royal blue.

I don't remember much about the match itself except for swearing at the screen on a couple of occasions. In contrast, my wife watched in suicidal silence and the dog curled up in the corner. She feared that United were more likely to score and continue their pursuit of a historic haul of five trophies in one season. To their immense credit, central-defenders Phil Jagielka and Joleon Lescott stymied United's initiatives and the game finished 0-0. Extra-time has never been a friend to Everton and Evertonians.This time we survived and progressed to the lottery of penalties. These shoot-outs have rarely been our friend either. If asked, I would have favoured a bout of eeny-meeny-miney-mo to pick the winner.

By now, the atmosphere in British Columbia was tense. Make that nerve-racking. The three of us abandoned our seats to stand in front of the big screen. Everton lost the toss and the kicks were taken at the United end. Our fans now had to blow rather than suck the ball into the net. My wife grasped my hand as Tim Cahill stepped up first to face Ben Foster: 'Is he any good?' I was about to reply when his penalty soared over the bar. I'm told that it's expected to dock with the International Space Station sometime soon. As the United fans screamed in delight, Cahill fell to his knees and looked up to heaven. His prayers were soon answered by a certain Dimitar Berbatov, complete with natty Alice band. He casually rolled a lazy back-pass towards keeper Tim Howard. The commentator claimed that it was the worst penalty attempt of all time and was destined for a long life on YouTube. The United fans seemed to agree.

Leighton Baines was next up. Again my wife asked: 'Is he any good?' The left-back confirmed my appraisal by sending Foster the wrong way and thumping the ball into the net. 'Yes!' I screamed at the screen. Next Rio Ferdinand strolled forward, exuding the confidence of someone planning to miss a drugs test. His effort was embarrassingly weak and Howard again saved. 'U-S-A, U-S-A' we screamed and hugged each other. Actually we jumped up and down like middle-aged pogo dancers. It was not a pretty sight. The count was 1-0. Had United cracked?

Now it was Phil Neville's turn. I blurted out 'No!' before my wife could ask her predictable question. Given his illustrious career with United, he was under more pressure than most. With immense calm, the Everton captain rammed his spot-kick past the United keeper. 'Yes! Yes!' we yelled. I had expected Carlos Tevez or Paul Scholes to enter the fray. They didn't and was encouraged to see Nemanja Vidic place the ball on the spot. His stuttered approach confused Howard and he scored with ease to make it 2-1.

The atmosphere in our media room grew tenser. We were shaking with excitement as James Vaughan prepared to take his turn. The youngster netted via his own stuttered run up. 'Is that legal?' asked my wife. 'Yes! Yes! Yes!' I replied. He was followed promptly by Anderson Luis de Abreu Oliveira. By the time the commentator had introduced him, the Brazilian had netted with a smirk. The count was 3-2. Elizabeth asked: 'Who'll take the vital kick?' The commentator answered: 'Phil Jagielka.' This was a surprise given the fact that he had missed a penalty against Fiorentina during the previous season. With little fuss, Jagielka placed the ball on the spot and sent the blue half of the stadium into ecstasy. The France household was already there. We joined the dog in howling at the giant screen.

It was one of those Spring mornings that you would love to bottle and keep for the rest of your life. We hugged for about a minute, which was the amount of time it took the United fans to evacuate the stadium. Then my wife went upstairs to answer the door bell. Walter and I remained glued to the television set. Apparently, our German-born neighbour had been concerned about the early morning racket. Elizabeth invited him downstairs. As he entered the basement he could see me - with tears trickling down my cheeks - transfixed by the giant television which by the way would not be out of place at a drive-in movie theatre. It was showing an advert for the Long John Silver's Restaurant chain. He declared: 'You English and your love affair with fish and chips!'

All Blues are aware that United got their revenge at Wembley. Seven years later, Everton wasted numerous goal-scoring chances and to snag an FA Cup semi-final against surprisingly poor opponents from Old Trafford. A missed penalty was one of five decent chances spurned by Romelu Lukaku alone. I was sat with Joe Royle and David Unsworth and encouraged our League winning centre-forward and FA Cup winning manager to either put on his old black leather shooting boots and replace Lukaku - the less said about the first touch of the human pin-ball machine the better - or put on his overcoat and replace Roberto Martinez in the Everton dug-out. Both smiled at me. But in hindsight, I've few doubts that these shrewd substitutions would have won the game.

After being booed off at the interval, Everton recovered to dominate a thrilling second-half. So much so that with Gerard Deulofeu — a late substitute - wreaking havoc down the right flank, I was convinced that we would triumph. My confidence grew after we equalized and steamed forward in search of the winner. Then it happened. Anthony Martial escaped his marker and netted in the dying seconds. Even though conceding such a last-minute goal was a trademark of the Martinez era, I was rendered speechless and held my face in my hands at the injustice of it all. I don't remember the final whistle or the journey back to my hotel. My mind was consumed with the fear that at age 68 this had been my last chance to celebrate my beloved club winning a piece of meaningful silverware.

That night, during the silence of my sleepless sleep, I concluded that capturing the FA Cup on five occasions - that is 1906, '33, '66, '84 and '95 - simply isn't good enough for a club of our standing. At the start of every season it should be one of the principal objectives of Everton Football Club to dominate all domestic knock-out competitions and for Evertonians both young and old to declare squatters' rights in North London.

Hand on heart; I really thought that we would lift the FA Cup in both 2009 and 2016. Now for readers aged 21 and younger, I must elaborate that I'm referring to a big shiny thing which you parade around the streets of the city in an open-top bus.

31. Great scientists and great gas-fitters

Now where was I? That's right, on the road to university. Besides matchstick men hunched against its drab industrial backgrounds, I knew only three other things about Salford. It was 32 miles away from a real city; its football club bore the name of another city; and there was something not quite right about its weather. My search for affordable digs concluded with a bedsit off Eccles Old Road. It was a quiet spot with a surprising amount of traffic, most of which was curb-crawling near a notorious brothel. Though there were no red lights, everyone knew that the street was twinned with Oudezijds Voorburgwal in Amsterdam. The prostitutes were nothing like I had imagined. The circus-ugly ones would stand at their front doors and accost passers-by: 'Hello love, want me to squeeze your blackheads?' Later I discovered that it was street talk for something far less intimate. Anyway, I took the banter in my stride. After all, I had read the gas meters at Todd's Drums where the female workers could have taught Salford's working girls a thing or two about harassment. I recall that after capturing a visiting apprentice, their initiation ritual involved attempting to smear his private parts with tepid bitumen.

I didn't know anyone who had been to a university never mind graduated from one and soon discovered that juggling part-time education with work wasn't easy. My aspirations weren't popular with everyone at the Gas Board. The older tradesmen wished me luck. One of them reminded me that it takes courage to fail. The younger ones preached that working-class boys should never rise above their station and predicted imminent humiliation. They must have known something about the academic environment because my friend and I were Eleven-Plus failures bobbing in a sea of bright grammar-school and public-school boys equipped with A-levels.

Our latent confidence evaporated after one member of the faculty predicted that 40% of our intake would drop-out by the end of the first year. He was staring at me at the time. One glance at the syllabus reinforced our fears that we were out of our depths. Our lack of preparation was highlighted under a cloud named Organic Chemistry - the study of the structure, properties and reactions of hydrocarbons. Personally, I was intimidated by the depiction of molecules via combinations of drawings and symbols. It was like being illiterate all over again. Thankfully, the chemistry professor recognized our distress and gave up his free time to tutor us. In return we got stuck into Organic Chemistry with the tenacity of Tony Kay. In no time, we concluded that we weren't thick and adopted the mantra: 'Ignorant – Not stupid'.

Most classmates were transitioning from sixth form to university. They seemed far less committed to their academic studies and didn't grasp the penalties for drinking at night and staying in bed all morning. We were more mature, no doubt that's something others may contest. After a few months at Salford, we returned to the reality of lead pipes and the organic chemicals that flowed through them. By then we understood that society needs both great scientists and great gas-fitters. While the University of Salford was our key to a different kind of life, it was clear that we weren't the smartest students in our university class. In truth, we weren't the smartest in our gas-fitting class either. Notwithstanding, we weren't at Salford to gain an education. We were there to do what we did best – pass exams.

My approach was three-fold. I scrutinized the lecturers' areas of interest, analyzed past exam papers using primitive data-mining and text-clustering algorithms and selected three topics within each subject where I could excel. It was so productive that we raised our sights by the start of the final year. Our new goal was a first-class honours degree. Even though none had been awarded in Chemical Engineering for six years, my friend and I were convinced that if we pushed each other harder possibly one of us would reach those extremely dizzy heights. Nothing, not even the comings and goings at Goodison, was allowed to break my concentration. During the final term, I abandoned the painted ladies of Manchester and travelled daily from Widnes. I swotted assiduously throughout the night and on the early morning train.

My mother didn't know how to help. Still, she insisted on staying up just in case I needed something. She need not have worried. Her son and his friend from Lowton may not have been well-rounded graduates but became Bachelors of Science with first-class honours. Both of my parents attended the commencement ceremony at which the presentations were made by the Duke of Edinburgh. To my surprise, his Highness spoke to me: 'Congratulations. What have you been reading during your time here?' I responded: 'Mostly big words.' He looked at me as if I was a three-dimensional chess board before declaring: 'I understand that you are the only graduate with a bookcase wider than his television?'

With the arrival of North Sea gas, my friend and I looked forward to exciting careers with the Gas Board. Inexplicably, our employer didn't know what to do with us. After treading water for a few months, he bolted to Hong Kong and I elected to further my education, perhaps to convince myself that my BSc was no fluke. I was fortunate to gain sponsorship from Radiation-New World which, coupled with lab work, enabled me to pursue an MSc by examination and dissertation. It was an anti-climax. I can remember four things about these studies. First, it's near impossible to walk around with massive decks of computer punch cards and fan-fold print-outs without dropping them. Second, it's not easy to defy friends and pursue your dream. Also to empower yourself through knowledge is one of the best ways of building self-confidence. Finally, the United Kingdom had turned its back on engineering - a discipline that had made it prosperous.

While engineering may be unfashionable, the recent glut of meaningless degrees is shameful. Allowing so many teenagers to pursue degrees in media studies at university demeans everyone involved. For many, it results in four years of alcohol-fuelled debt accumulation.

David France from Widnes ... reading gas meters

32. Famous hat

The combination of study and work didn't leave much time for mid-week distractions other than football. The city of Salford was home to Old Trafford and United's training ground. The Cliff, acquired from a defunct Rugby League club called Broughton Rangers, was just up the River Irwell from my university class-rooms. Therefore, I would watch George Best, Denis Law and the precociously talented Bobby Charlton go through their paces in training and practice games on most Wednesdays. The security was so relaxed that I would saunter inside to enjoy the action. I must have appeared harmless because no-one ever stopped me. If they had done so, I planned to reveal that I was a distant cousin of David Sadler, an unsung hero at United. To me, it sounded like something you wouldn't make up.

The practice games had everything – demonstrations of exquisite skills, raw pace and no little grit. In fact, I reached the pinnacle of my football career at the Cliff - thanks to the limitations of gritty John Fitzpatrick. The long-haired midfielder, who enjoyed a good tackle more than a good pass, sliced the ball into the assembled spectators. Instinctively, I trapped it and prepared to chip it into the grasp of Willie Morgan. But with my hands rooted deep into the pockets of my duffle coat, I tumbled into the mud. Worse, I got entangled in some discarded netting and struggled to return to my feet. After this embarrassment, I didn't need the Sadler connection. People readily identified me as the uncoordinated idiot with the mean air-shot.

Like everyone on the touchline and on the pitch, I was in awe of Charlton. I've seen few men kick the ball like him. He would dispatch missiles with either foot then pause to comb the fingers of his right-hand through what remained of his hair and dragged the strands kicking and screaming to where they weren't meant to go. With Law mostly absent through injury, I was unable to confirm Ted MacDougall's assessment of his heading prowess. As for Best, he rarely appeared or demonstrated his natural wizardry at training. I've no doubts, however, that they were three outstanding footballers and are rightly celebrated as the United Trinity. Even so, I don't think I'm alone in believing that as a triumvirate they paled in comparison to their biblical counterparts.

Obviously, I attended as many Everton games as practical. You won't be surprised to learn that my thumb provided my means of visiting Mama Blue. It was painless. When hitchhiking along the Rugby League corridor from Manchester to Merseyside the secret was to split the journey into segments. I would take a bus to the start of the East Lancs Road at Irlam o' th' Height. Then I would hitch to the Haydock Roundabout. After that, so long as I was wearing something blue and white, it was easy to get a lift from the Blues exiting the M6 motorway.

I knew people who have been picked up by Alan Ball in his Jaguar. Though never that lucky, I did hitch a ride in a similar top-of-the-range vehicle in late 1968. Draped in my blue and white scarf, I was sheltering from the rain at the traffic lights near Walkden when one of the occupants of a brand new XJ6 invited me to hop in. I had never opened such a solid car-door before, nor, for that matter, had I sunk into such plush upholstery. The smell of the new leather overpowered that of the ambient cigar smoke. Keeping me company on the rear-seat was a hat. It was no ordinary headgear. It was a fedora - with wide brim and indented crown - crafted from the finest cashmere complete with matching silk band. More specifically, it was Malcolm Allison's fedora. For the next 25 miles both Allison, who was Joe Mercer's assistant manager at Maine Road, and the driver, who resembled a Chicago henchman, quizzed me about our recent form. It was more like an inquisition. In particular, they wanted to know about the recent performances of Jimmy Husband, Tommy Jackson and Gordon West. Hand on heart, I swear that I told them nothing. Absolutely nothing. But to this day, two of his questions remain a concern. Big Mal asked me: 'How do you stop Alan Ball? Does he have an off-switch?' Honestly, I volunteered nothing in return. Absolutely nothing. Nevertheless, I could feel my body sweating and my old duffle coat sticking to the Jaguar's hide.

My friends on the Gwladys Street terraces weren't impressed by the fact that I had accepted a lift from Malcolm Allison. In their eyes, he was a flamboyant Cockney with an unhealthy zest for expensive champagne and voluptuous Playboy bunnies. After a half-hour in his company, I was convinced that he was a charming man with a genuine love of football. Many years later, my old pal Alan Whittle, who played for Allison at Crystal Palace, confirmed that he had been all of these things as well as a used-car salesman, a professional gambler, a nightclub owner as well as an innovative coach brimming with new ideas who revolutionized training methods.

For the record, Alan Ball was perpetual motion that afternoon and netted a superb hat-trick in a 4-0 victory over West Brom. The following weekend, Ball contributed another of his all-action performances and also opened the scoring in a convincing 2-0 win over City - who, by the way, were the reigning League champions. I don't recall Allison sipping bubbly or puffing on a Double Corona cigar on the way to Goodison and had no reason to do so during the return journey, but he had the last word when City lifted the FA Cup later that season after eliminating Everton in the very final minute of the semi-final at Villa Park. It was a tight game in which West, Jackson and Husband all featured and David Connor, a tough defensive-midfielder, was drafted into the City side to shackle Alan Ball and the fluency of The Holy Trinity. The tactic proved to be effective. I remember Ball becoming distracted and a little frustrated by Connor's constant - make that niggling - presence.

The history books show that City - without Connor - defeated Leicester in the FA Cup final. During a 5-year period, the Mercer-Allison partnership guided them to the Second Division title, First Division crown, FA Cup, League Cup and European Cup-Winners' Cup before it imploded.

33. Sent from Heaven

Allow me to indulge in another of my most cherished subjects — that's right, The Holy Trinity of Kendall, Harvey & Ball. Did you hear my sigh as their names rolled off my tongue? In the late Sixties, I joined other impressionable teenagers in believing that Goodison had been blessed by the gods of football when the twilight of Alex Young's reign merged seamlessly with the dawn of something equally aesthetic. Howard Kendall, Colin Harvey and Alan Ball may sound like fantasy footballers — those of us who witnessed them in action will confirm that they dovetailed perfectly to become the most stylish midfield trio ever assembled by an English club. Their rare blend of vision, technique, guile, courage, honesty and industry elevated them to the summit of the British game.

Respected as outstanding footballers in their own rights, Colin Harvey was the most naturally talented of the biblical trio. He was my personal favourite. I grew up watching him progress through the club's junior ranks. When the first-team was playing far away from home, I would marvel at him in Central League action. Even as a youngster, he looked like a seasoned pro. It had something to do with his technique. The left-sided midfielder was so sharp on the ball that no opponent could get near it. I loved the way in which he shimmied past them and pierced visiting defences with perfectly weighted passes. It was clear that Harvey would develop into a quality midfielder. How good was he? I would say that, until the arrival of Wayne Rooney, 'The White Pele' was the finest footballer produced by the Everton nursery system.

Then there was 'The Great Alan Ball', as he is known in the France household. The Sunday papers had speculated that the 21-year-old World Cup hero was destined to team up with Billy Bremner and Johnny Giles at Elland Road until Harry Catterick intervened and lured him to Goodison. Ball was an established superstar brimming with self-confidence. His boundless energy and inspirational leadership were the answers to the vast void in the manager's plans created by Tony Kay's life-time ban from football. Not necessarily approachable or instantly likeable, both Kay and Ball demanded improvements in the efforts of their Everton team-mates. Like Kay, Ball's fiery temperament got him into trouble with referees. He possessed such a refined first-touch that he rarely got into trouble with the football. There was something else about Kay and Ball. They were the worst losers that you are likely to come across on a football pitch. Perhaps it had something to do with their red hair and freckles?

Even with the acquisition of such a tenacious 21-year-old, Catterick believed that something was missing from his formula. Six months later, he remedied the situation by persuading another much sought-after youngster to join Everton, this time in preference to our red rivals. Mature beyond his years, Howard Kendall had captained the England Youth team to victory in the 1964 Little World Cup and was lauded for his passing and ability to read the game. Also there is the small matter of him converting tackling into an art form. Always fair, the midfielder had developed the uncanny knack of sliding into tackles and coming away with the ball.

A product of good planning or simply good luck, the Holy Trinity coupled ethereal beauty with supreme authority. So much so that Catterick's men kicked off every game with the genuine belief that they were better equipped for battle than any of their opponents. Bar none. I could wax lyrical about their sublime ball skills, sharp passing and movement, strong tackling, adroit positioning, superior stamina and never-say-die enthusiasm. Instead, I prefer to postulate that it's only once in a generation that the gods of football provide the ideal blend for the beautiful game. To this day, I remain convinced that Mama Blue had been duly blessed in the late-Sixties and that Colin Harvey and Howard Kendall plus their red-headed cohort had been sent from Heaven to teach three-part harmony to Crosby, Stills & Nash. While injuries and suspensions limited this mid-field triumvirate to only 140 outings together, I feel privileged to have seen the vast majority of them.

Fast forward to 2000 when Becky Tallentire, a Blue who knows about really big words, and I characterized the life and times of the iconic trio through interviews with hundreds of individuals who knew them best — their team-mates, opponents and fans - in a modest book entitled "Gwladys Street's Holy Trinity — Kendall, Harvey & Ball'.

Brian Labone told us: 'They were a sensational midfield unit. And in my official capacity as their skipper, I anointed them 'Los Tros Magnifico' or something like that. They were the only three-man team to win the League title.' Gordon West added: 'They were the heavenly darlings of Goodison. And just like the fans, I used to stand back and marvel at them. Seriously with them dominating the middle of the park - I had nowt else to do.'

Becky and I were wary that the title of our book seemed pretentious and guilty of religiosity. Neither of us can take credit for the Holy Trinity name. It was the fallout from my interactions with the fertile minds of Brian and Derek Hatton. At the time I was a tad perplexed that the member of the Trotskyist Militant Tendency and the undisputed champion of the People's Republic of Merseyside was unwilling to clarify which individuals were the Father, the Son and the Holy Spirit. The book's sub-title proved to be more of a challenge. We wrestled with different permutations of surnames. We tried alphabetical order, length of Everton service, tally of England caps and sequence of shirt numbers before settling on physical height in descending order. Hence Kendall, Harvey & Ball.

I'd prefer you to do this sort of thing somewhere else

34. What's our name?

I don't know about you but, during the past decade, I can count the number of games that I've enjoyed on two hands. More often than not, excursions to Goodison have been abstruse experiences in which my central-nervous system became befuddled. Reluctantly, I concluded that watching Everton was no longer about savouring the entertainment unfolding before my eyes. It involved peeking at the action through the gaps between my fingers. More often than not, I felt helpless, at the mercy of eleven men plus subs – few of whom share my connection with Everton and even fewer to have ever paid to stand or sit in Gwladys Street.

It wasn't always that way. Are you ready for the recollections of an old man? The 1969/70 campaign was a great time to be a Blue and one of the special seasons when our football reflected our Latin motto. Performances were simply divine. In the eyes of many journalists we were a one-man team with Alan Ball as our heart and soul. Of course, nothing could be farther from the truth. The champions were the most exquisitely balanced side I've ever seen. Rich praise indeed.

Have you noticed that successful seasons fly by from one important match to the next? Our 1970 fixture schedule was so congested that it was hard for Blues to catch our collective breath. After a lean spell in January and February, we seemed to celebrate a victory every other day. In fact, Everton notched seven victories in 25 days during the sprint to the finish line. At times, we were invincible.

To appease my mother, Chemical Harry and I placed our differences to one side and attended the much-hyped title-decider against Chelsea. It was an unforgettable afternoon. I recall that Howard Kendall netted before a visitor had even touched the ball. In fact, the darlings of the London media didn't show up for the first hour during which we went 5-0 up. At the final whistle, the Blues seated around us tempted fate by celebrating a title triumph. In contrast, my father feared Dirty Leeds situated on the naughty step in second place and insisted that there was work to be done. He suggested that we travel to Stoke a couple of days later to watch our heroes finish the job. Hand on heart, I was thrilled by his invitation. It had been years since we had done anything meaningful together. Like no other super glue, football has a way of repairing and strengthening the bonds between family members.

That Easter Monday, we weren't alone at the Victoria Ground. The terraces were packed with 20,000 noisy Evertonians. As for the match? It was a tense affair until Alan Whittle netted the only goal. I think that the blonde bombshell scored in all seven of the wins during the run-in.While I can close my eyes and picture the post-match hullabaloo, most of all I remember the return drive to Merseyside. We hadn't travelled far before my father stopped to help some fans who, in his sarcastic eyes, were too young to be hitch-hiking. Four youngsters squeezed into the back of the Ford Cortina. Another two crammed next to me on the front bench-seat. Before he proceeded, Chemical Harry schooled them in proper hitch-hiker etiquette: 'Fags out! Feet off the seats! No swearing!' We hadn't travelled another hundred yards before the driver complained that he was unable to access the gear nob. Sacrifice was required. Rather than ditch one or two Blues by the roadside, the smallest youth volunteered to join the spare tyre in the boot. With his spine curved, head bowed and limbs drawn up to his torso, the young Blue resembled a confused East German contortionist heading towards Checkpoint Charlie. Inexplicably, no-one objected.

My father was no fan of motorways, particularly the M6, and took the A49 through Cheshire. A self-proclaimed conscientious driver, he had never been involved in a traffic accident. I had suspected that given his zeal to tap the brake pedal at the slightest hint of danger, he may have caused a few fender-benders and immeasurable road rage.

No-one recalled the young Blue complaining. In truth, it would have been impossible to hear him above the merrymaking. The sight of the Cortina decorated with scarves prompted other vehicles to sound their horns. The honking was drowned by voices of my father and his adopted family. A powerful tenor who loved to warble along to the BBC's Songs of Praise, Chemical Harry spent most of the journey belting out: 'Bless them all, bless them all, the long and the short and the tall. Bless wee Bally and Big Joe too, bless all the boys who are wearing royal blue.' The verses were repeated until he had covered every member of the first-team squad including Frank Darcy. I had never seen him sing so passionately or laugh so uncontrollably before. It was obvious that our travelling companions liked him. It wasn't hard to do so that unforgettable evening.

Chemical Harry had missed our pre-war triumph because he had hooked up a squadron of Brylcreem Boys. Two decades later, he snubbed our title celebrations for a squadron of fancy ladies. That night, he sought to make up for 1939 and 1963 by ensuring that everyone enjoyed themselves during possibly the best road trip of their lives. As we approached Merseyside, this cacophony was augmented by fist-pumping pedestrians. Together, we screamed our undying love for Everton. At first, we sang: 'And now you've gotta believe us ... we're gonna win the League'. Through the streets of Wavertree, the youngsters on the rear-seat mimicked the taunts of Muhammad Ali to Ernie Turrel, the opponent who insisted on calling him Cassius Clay in 1967. The Ford Cortina reverberated with cries of 'What's-our-name ... Ev-er-ton'.

Our driver insisted on dropping off the youngsters near to their homes. It took him ages to navigate around the side streets of Kirkdale. Given his pride at squeezing eight males into a car, at one point I feared that he was searching for one of the cast iron icons designed by Giles Gilbert Scott to determine how many happy Blues he could shoehorn into a phone-box. As for the contortionist; I remember his release from solitary confinement outside St Anthony's Church on Scotland Road. The youngster, still in a fetal position, appeared slightly disoriented by his experience. Showing no signs of oxygen starvation, he mumbled the name of our rivals: 'Liv-er-pool'. Slowly, he opened one eye then screamed: 'Liv-er-pool ... Under-the-arm.' And ee-aye-adio, we secured the League title two days later. My mother insisted on converting the West Brom finale into a France family affair. Like me, she was excited at joining the other 60,000 Blues gathered at a building site where the partially-built Top Balcony, a massive physical structure and an even bigger sign of the club's ambitions, dwarfed the remnants of the old Archibald Leitch stand along Goodison Road. I think she knew that April Fools' Day 1970 would be the last time I would accompany them both to Mama Blue.

I doubt that anyone there will ever forget the radiance of our finest team being crowned champions. I often think about the warmth of that day. As expected, there was no stopping Catterick's youngsters. Immediately after Alan Whittle netted his mandatory goal, Chemical Harry wrapped me in the type of hug that a Kodiak bear would be proud of. After Colin Harvey scored an absolute cracker, Ma Carsley jumped up and down like the winner on an American game show. At the final whistle, she did something I've always wanted to do but have never found the courage to attempt – my mother started her own chant. The crowd around us was screaming 'Ev-er-ton, Ev-er-ton. Ev-er-ton.' That was before they heard a heavy contralto voice add: 'Champ-i-ons, Champ-i-ons, Champ-i-ons'. As her voice grew louder, the fans joined in. Within no time, the Upper Bullens Road Stand was screaming: 'Champ-i-ons, Ev-er-ton, Champ-i-ons'.

With Ma Carsley in seventh heaven, I glanced at my father. He was ecstatic. His face contorted with joy. As for his son, I was simply bewildered by the enormity of the accomplishment and the knowledge that Catterick's side was on the verge of a football dynasty. There was too much joy for me to take in. I felt blessed to be a Blue. More important, the Everton family had brought the increasingly dysfunctional France family closer together, at least for a few hours.

35. Curse of Nana Mouskouri

Like most Blues, I was convinced that the title-winning team would compete for the top honours for six seasons. I was wrong. Dead wrong. To this day, I've difficulty coming to terms with the regression. The 1970/71 season started with a victory over Chelsea in the Charity Shield match. Played at Stamford Bridge because the construction of the new Main Stand at Goodison had fallen behind schedule, the game was a stroll in the park.

The new campaign was a much different matter. After blunders accompanied gaffs and slip-ups partnered hiccups, the champions earned just three points from the first six games and slumped to the foot of the table. Chemical Harry blamed World Cup fatigue - Brian Labone, Alan Ball, Tommy Wright and Keith Newton having represented England in Mexico. Others claimed that our high-tempo tactics accelerated the wear and tear to key men. Ball struggled with a pelvic problem which prevented him from getting up and down the pitch as often as he would've liked, Harvey was troubled by a hip complaint and Labone suffered from Achilles tendinitis. The captain was the most significant absentee. I know this for a fact because he told me so.

More excuses for our poor form? There was the problem of inconsistency between the posts. Gordon West suffered another loss of confidence and was replaced by Andy Rankin who, after a short-time, suffered similar troubles. How Harry Catterick must have regretted the leak to the national press that had nixed the acquisition of Gordon Banks? Then there were the short comings in defence where Keith Newton had rarely shown his pedigree. His performances were so unpredictable that he was forced to compete against Sandy Brown and another Newton for his first-team slot. The new season was only two months old when the club signed midfielder Henry Newton for a record fee of £115,000 and converted him into an expensive left-back.

Others thought the decline had to do with not sharpening the champions' firepower. For reasons best known to him and his chairman, the manager resisted the urge to sign an experienced goal-scorer and alternated Jimmy Husband, Alan Whittle and David Johnson to dovetail with Joe Royle. To his credit, the centre-forward continued to net with some regularity as his young partners struggled. The Sunday newspapers, a popular source of gossip, cited the manager's interest in recruiting Bolton's Francis Lee. Looking back, our fortunes in the early Seventies may have been much different with Lee Won Pen in the line-up. It was an apt nickname. Lee could tumble unaided from outside the area into the six-yard box.

Decades later, Gordon Watson - a veteran of the coaching staff - hinted that the slide from champs to chumps had to do with the manager's strict code of conduct being more effective with malleable youngsters than reigning champions. That said, he thought that his boss was even-handed by treating everyone like juvenile delinquents and punishing anyone who arrived late for training. Irrespective of seniority, all players had to sign in at Bellefield. At 10:00 am precisely, Gordon or another coach with rhinoceros hide had the unenviable task of drawing a red line under which the latecomers had to sign. Worse still, Gordon was conscripted to patrol the streets near the more exclusive nightclubs looking for cars with familiar license plates. The old-timer joked that one or two of the first-team squad were as daft as a brush and used their own cars to break curfew. Embarrassed by his covert mission, he noted the transgressions but swore to me that he never reported them to his disciplinarian manager I believed him because he was Gordon Watson – the most decent man you could come across.

Gordon divulged that one player in particular had caused disharmony and grown too big for his white boots. Having played with giants like Dean and Lawton, he despised Alan Ball's swagger into the world of self-admiration. Gordon recalled one incident at Bellefield when Ball stopped a practice game to complain to Wilf Dixon, the first-team coach. Without a hint of humour, he yelled: 'Wilf, how do you expect me to play with these?'

I can remember the moment when I realized that all wasn't well. It was shortly after Gordon West had conceded a sloppy own-goal in the European Cup clash with Keflavik. For the first time in my life, I witnessed Mama Blue turn on her heroes. Aware that Gwladys Street was a refuge where normal behaviour was suspended and otherwise emotionally untroubled people berate poor referees and ugly opponents, I couldn't believe my eyes or my ears. My father raised me to believe that the Goodison faithful was entitled to criticize but never boo an Everton side. One of the subtleties of his blue etiquette was that venting frustrations at individuals was a different matter. When a player's performance fell below minimum standards, he should expect to be drowned in dark banter. The diehard Blues around me jeered the reigning champions. Even Alan Ball felt their ire. Before he took matters in hand and netted a hat-trick, the midfield maestro looked distraught. I sensed that no man was safe from the bile that pours from the terraces and his special relationship with Mama Blue would never be the same.

While I was confident that our ambitious billionaire would sort things out, there was no quick fix and the remainder of Catterick's tenure was undermined by scores of unforced errors, own goals and embarrassing incidents. Spoilt for choice, the one that comes readily to my mind is our inability to halt Ernie Hunt's volley from Willie Carr's donkey kick at Coventry in 1970. Evertonians of my vintage will recall the exquisite strike was shown every Saturday evening for years during the introduction to BBC's Match of the Day. They will prefer to forget that Keith Newton ducked to avoid the ball ruffling his hair while the rest of the Everton wall stood open-mouthed.

With the League crown conceded by September, the club targetted other silverware and, in the absence of Real Madrid, Barcelona, Juventus, AC Milan, Inter-Milan and Benfica, were tipped to recover their form and taste Continental glory. Had the European Cup been the club's prime goal? It looked that away after we defeated the favourites from West Germany via a penalty-shootout to qualify for a quarter-final clash with the minnows from Greece. Panathinaikos should have been a cakewalk. Indeed, we mauled them throughout the first-leg but failed to turn our dominance into goals. Then, sloppy defending allowed Antonis Antoniadis to net. Though David Johnson equalized in the last minute, my friends and I were shocked by the outcome.

I remained convinced that we would progress to the semi-final. But thanks to some extremely questionable decisions, we failed to score in Athens and were eliminated by the away-goals rule. The controversy surrounding the game hasn't dimmed with time. Was it the Revenge of the Elgin Marbles? Perhaps the Curse of Nana Mouskouri? Or something less subtle? Recently, it was alleged that Greece's military junta had intimidated the UEFA officials. Consequently, the no-score draw has been described as both the greatest triumph in the history of Greek club football and the most flagrant display of match-fixing paid in drachmas. Conspiracy or not, it's not too much of a stretch to speculate that our history would have been so different if we hadn't squandered the opportunity to bring the famous trophy to Merseyside for the first time.

When disaster struck again 72 hours later, I found it hard to imagine that any right-wing army officers were involved. At Old Trafford, Everton forfeited a 1-0 lead over Liverpool in an FA Cup semi-final. This time we were coasting to Wembley, courtesy of an Alan Ball goal, when an injury to Brian Labone changed the game. The influential skipper hadn't been 100% fit and blamed himself for the loss. He shouldn't have done. His boss was far more culpable by selecting Sandy Brown as a versatile substitute instead of Roger Kenyon who had been Labone's reliable deputy for most of the season. In the absence of a recognized centre-half, John Toshack's aerial supremacy allowed Alun Evans and Brian Hall to score for the Reds. In the wake of the unfathomable, I was stunned into silence for a day or two. No, make that a week or two. The defeat was much more than another example of self-inflicted disappointment. It signified the power-shift in Merseyside football.

36. Sale of Ball

Wednesday, 22 December, 1971 remains one of the saddest days in my years of following Everton Football Club. That was the day when we sold Alan Ball, still only 26, to Arsenal for a British record fee of £220,000. His departure came completely out of the blue and the speed of the transaction only served to fuel the ugly rumour mill. For me, the news didn't sink in for some time. When it did, I was incapacitated by sadness. Not anger, not betrayal. Just an overwhelming sense of sorrow. I was confident that the club knew what it was doing. Even so, I wondered how Harry Catterick planned to replace - never mind improve on - the world-class, white-booted maestro.

Even today, the details of the transfer remain shrouded in mystery. What we do know is that the buyers bought a superior asset, the vendors earned a 100% profit on their initial investment, the player received 5% of the transfer fee under the Football League guidelines and the Kop smiled every time our royal blue hero wore the red and white of Arsenal. Everyone appeared to get what they wanted. That is everyone except the Goodison fans. Years later Brian Labone told me that when the manager bragged about doubling his money, he had cautioned: 'Aren't you aware that the only way to do so is to fold your notes before you put them into your pocket?'

Alan Ball loved Everton. I know because he told me. At our final meeting, a week before his sudden death in 2007, he volunteered some heartfelt words about being a Blue: 'Three special words have had a special place in my soul as well as my heart for the past 40 years – Everton Football Club. I enjoyed my football throughout my career. People remind me that I played my best games in the famous blue and white. I adore Everton Football Club. I love being known first and foremost as an Evertonian. I never wanted to leave and had hoped to see out my days at Goodison. Like all of the club's ex-players, I recognized that once Everton Football Club gets into your blood your life can never be the same again.' In response, I confessed to him that he would be the first name I would put on a team-sheet. Ball appeared flattered. He smiled inquisitively: 'Me in front of Dixie? Before Big Nev?' He paused: 'Ahead of your mate Alex?' Without hesitation, I responded: 'Definitely. James Alan Ball Junior would be my first pick!' It was during the ensuing silence that I noticed The Golden Vision had crept up to my side. His facial expression mirrored that of someone who had been knifed in the back and my fingerprints were on the handle.

Everton struggled to recover from the sale of Ball. As the teams of Bill Shankly and Bob Paisley went from strength to strength throughout the Seventies - they were worthy champions in 1972/73, '75/76, '76/77, '78/79 and '79/80 - our downturn deepened with the untimely illnesses and subsequent retirements of Harry Catterick and, later, John Moores. There was no shortage of exciting young candidates for the Goodison hot-seat – for example Bobby Robson and Brian Clough – and I had thought that the club would move seamlessly to appoint new leaders. Surely there was a well thought-out succession plan filed away in some drawer at Littlewoods?

Catterick, a Goodison old boy, had upheld the club's tradition of cultured football and proved to be a tough act to follow. Whereas his record is comparable to those of Bill Shankly, Matt Busby, Bill Nicholson and Don Revie, his paranoid thinking, persecutory fears and the small matter of him treating outsiders with the suspicion usually reserved for smack-heads gathered outside a 24-hour petrol station, resulted in him not receiving equal acknowledgement. I have developed mixed feelings about The Catt.

My friend Brian Labone admired him. Make that worshipped him. Whereas my friend Alex Young loathed him. Catterick's supporters cite his astute deal-making; witness the signings of Alan Ball, Howard Kendall, Tony Kay, Fred Pickering, Alex Scott and Ray Wilson. Whereas his detractors counter that, within 12 months of losing its tenacious flame-haired terrier, his side had been diluted by the additions of David Lawson, Joe Harper, Mick Bernard, Rod Belfitt, Bernie Wright and Tiger McLaughlin - none of whom would have featured in that title-winning side even in their own wildest dreams.

Arguably Everton manager's greatest skill was his commitment towards developing promising youngsters. Unlike some of his successors, he understood that a club that fails to harness the potential of home-grown talent has no future. The manager blooded Tommy Wright and David Johnson at age 19, Colin Harvey, John Hurst and Roger Kenyon at 18, Jimmy Husband and Alan Whittle at 17, plus Joe Royle still in his nappies. All progressed to command first-team places and much more. Fresh faces bring hope and change. I hope that I'm not alone in detecting some modest similarities between Harry Catterick and Roberto Martinez. Of course, football has changed. By and large, teenagers in the Sixties had old heads on their shoulders and displayed no exaggerated sense of entitlement.

As for the retirement of the club's chairman? Chemical Harry thought the financial clout and ambition of John Moores were irreplaceable: 'Where do you find another billionaire prepared to spend his time running a football club rather than making more money?' My father had followed Everton throughout the barren Forties and Fifties and reminded me that there were cycles of success and underachievement in football. He claimed that I had been extremely fortunate to have enjoyed two League titles and a sensational FA Cup triumph by age 21 and predicted a period of mid-table adjustment. Deep down, Chemical Harry thought I was greedy and would remind me that success is not the be-all and end-all. In his eyes, disappointment – no matter how cruel – would reveal the positive character traits inside me.

Of course, we remember where we were when we heard the news
of your move to Highbury

37. Toffee lady

Adult life requires equilibrium. Unfortunately, I struggled to balance the demands of part-time employment, part-time education, football and other people. My priorities changed for a short time after I met Elizabeth Ireland, a nurse at Hope Hospital.

Born in Farnworth, the industrial oasis near Bolton and the birthplace of Fred Dibnah, Peter Kay, Tommy Lawton and a certain Alan Ball and isn't to be confused with the village of the same name in Widnes, I knew that she was different when during our second date she had a key cut in Bolton Market. Elizabeth paid for the item with a £1 note and the confused stall-holder gave her change for a £5 note. I'm embarrassed to admit that I would have scarpered to celebrate my good fortune. In contrast, she waited patiently for the key cutter to serve another customer before returning the excess change. It was equivalent to a week's wages for her. I was dumbfounded and obviously impressed. The fact that I ended up married to such a decent soul — someone who holds the comfort of other people above her own — remains a source of amazement to me.

To this day we share many shortcomings, including rhotacism - the imperfect pronunciation of the r sound. Speech pathologists grimace at our efforts in the same way that we react to another of our foibles — we despise the sight of onions. Don't tell me about the health benefits of its contents such as phytochemicals which improve immunity, chromium which regulate blood sugar and quercetin which may prevent cancer. You may disagree; my wife and I concur that the onion is an evil veggie planted on Earth to makes some people cry and others wince.

Our schedules kept us apart for a couple of years. Finally, we got together shortly after the sale of Alan Ball. She claims that I was inconsolable and needed her shoulder. By then, Elizabeth had been brainwashed. She knew about the important people in my life, namely Alexander Young, James Alan Ball and Leonard Norman Cohen. She was more than a little confused about Cohen's role and thought that he had replaced Morrissey — that's Johnny Morrissey not the former front-man of The Smiths — on the left-wing. A week later, in the words of the flame-haired Blue himself, 'the other good thing to come from Farnworth' and I went to the nation's capital for the weekend. Sounds romantic? Experts say that the first weekend spent together reveals much about a couple. Well, we watched Everton in an FA Cup tie — or rather an FA Cup brawl — at Selhurst Park.

I'm not sure what she had expected at Crystal Palace but it wasn't a picnic. The ground was empty except for the Arthur Wait Stand which was already overflowing with Blues. The fans seated nearby were friendly, funny and infected with cup fever. When they learnt that it was Elizabeth's baptism, we were invited to partake in their pre-match feast. First, they distributed blue paper cups and blue paper napkins. These were filled with triangular sandwiches without crusts, dainty pork pies and thick slices of Battenberg cake. Apparently, they had been destined for a la-di-da wedding reception somewhere near Crosby. Finally, they unpacked the liquid refreshments which consisted of a bottle of Gordon's best gin complete with Schweppes tonic water and a couple of neatly sliced lemons. Only the ice-cubes were missing. These passionate Blues confirmed everything that I had told Elizabeth about the Everton family.

Subsequently - I'm embarrassed to admit - my idea of a good night out was for us to wait in the freezing cold of Moss Side for the Maine Road gates to open so that we could catch the final 20 minutes. She knew that we didn't have two pennies to rub together and never ever complained - well, not to me. Indeed, Elizabeth has been by my side for 40-odd years and, despite being an Everton widow for most of them, has rarely grumbled. Like most young couples, we talked of travelling the world. Predictably, we started at the football grounds in the North West and the Midlands. Because Elizabeth distrusted unknown motorists, especially those driving erratically and actively seeking a meeting with God, we never hitch-hiked to matches.

Nonetheless, we were annual visitors to the Baseball Ground, Victoria Ground, Bramall Lane, Leeds Road, Filbert Street, Highfield Road and other stadiums that have been demolished. To her credit, she has never set foot in Anfield. Where as football fans on Merseyside are more or less identical to the lazy eye, she claims to be able to differentiate between a local Red and a local Blue on sight. Yes, our neighbours are more balanced and swagger pompously with a chip on each shoulder. For decades, she has harboured suspicions that there was something not quite right about Reds.

Her misgivings were confirmed in San Francisco before the game against Juventus in the 2013 Guinness International Champions Cup. We drove to California to join the remarkable turn out of Blues from the United Kingdom and equally amiable Italians from California. Before the match, we all gathered at Pedro's Cantina adjacent to the stadium. Everything was hunky-dory until the giant pub fell silent. Two Kopites had entered wearing their brand spanking new kits. Clearly unaware of their club's history, they seemed intent on harassing real football fans. Everyone ignored them – except my much better half. Elizabeth confronted them: 'Have you two no shame? If these Blues don't eat you alive, those Ultras will.' The colour drained from their faces as they noticed several hundred Italians between them and the safety of the pub's bouncers.

I know what you're thinking: 'What happened to these morons?' Well to the best of my knowledge, they vanished into thin air. Quite possibly, they were abducted or the victims of some other crime. My wife - who claims no responsibility for the disappearances - suspects that a giant hand inside a biodegradable dog poop bag descended from the royal blue heaven to dispose of them in an eco-friendly manner.

We can forget about Wembley this season ...

38. Man in black

The early Seventies evolved into a period of hope. For me, Goodison was the ideal place to get away from my academic studies and vent my pent up feelings. The chants had something of religious fundamentalism about them and the songs fostered a strong sense of belonging. Mama Blue was expensive in terms of time and other resources. On the other hand, she provided valuable stability during a time of self-discovery.

Elizabeth and I continued to attend home games. To finance these treats, I used my Saturday mornings to do foreigners for cash. That's sounds naughty. I had better explain that I specialized in installing second-hand fires and cookers. Thanks to Ma Carsley, I established a reputation in her neck of the woods for being cheap and tidy. I like to think that my customers were impressed by my skills with a blow-lamp, the traditional tool in which the methylated spirits flame is blown by mouth towards the solder, brass fitting and lead pipe. Many would stop what they were doing to watch me in action. The gentle blue flame allowed the solder to melt with great precision and avoid the tears caused by propane-fueled torches on the copper fittings of today. Some enquired: 'Did they teach you that at university?' My soldering bore the signature of an artist. Embarrassingly, the same couldn't be said about my plastering. On more than one occasion customers questioned if I had trained to the melodic chimes of Mister Whippy.

In the absence of a steady income and the demands of courting, I resorted to looking for away results in the Echo and enjoying a quiet moment of delight at discovering a victory. Then one day I decided to become a better spectator by enrolling as a referee with the Liverpool County Football Association. I know what you are thinking, why would anyone in their right mind volunteer to be a referee? In my defence, I thought it would provide a sense of self-assurance to help me grow as a person. In truth, I liked the black uniform. That said, my willingness to inflict such pain on myself still troubles me. Encouraged by one of my match-going pals, we waltzed through the written exams. The on-the-job training was more challenging. Unlike me, he appeared unaffected by criticism, committed few errors and, most important, kept games running smoothly. Within a few years, he progressed to officiate in the Football league.

My performances were so-so. In fact, I mastered the knack of never quite being in the right place at the right time. More often than I like to admit, I arrived at the scene after the action had moved on. Nonetheless, like most local referees in the Widnes & District Alliance I was treated with respect. It had something to do with the influence of Rugby League in which no-one dared to badger the man in the middle. The players accepted my bad decisions along with my even worse ones without exhibiting the anger of football terrorists like Gary Neville and Rio Ferdinand.

Hand on heart, I like to think that I was impartial until confronted by my past at Halebank. That's where the class weasel from secondary school taunted me after I had ruled him off-side: 'France, you illiterate wanker ... France, you illiterate dunce.' His voice grew louder and more confident until he was punished — not by me. The weasel was nearly dissected by a two-footed tackle executed with surgical malice. The culprit was the hosts' enforcer who rolled down his socks like Dave Thomas and wore his shorts so high that they looked like a thong. He invited idiots to kick him so that he could kick them. I was about to caution him for both his wrongdoing and his fashion sense when he whispered: 'I heard what he said to you. I was born out of wedlock too.' Five minutes later he clattered into the weasel again. I screamed: 'Play on!'

I never had problems with rough or dirty players. I respected their decisions to misbehave in the open and almost enjoy receiving their marching orders. In contrast, I detested cynical players such as the class weasel from secondary school who performed their deceitful tricks away from prying eyes. When caught, more often than not , they would encourage a swarm of pleading, whining and eventually sulking team-mates to surround me .

The second-half was even more eventful. The pitch was surrounded on three sides by council houses. It was a fortress for the hosts, figuratively and literally, complete with snipers. If my memory serves me correctly, the visiting keeper was about to take a goal-kick when he was shot. The home captain speculated that it was a lone marksman taking pot-shots with his air rifle from a bedroom window in Baguley Avenue. To this day, conspiracy theories have proliferated.

Two weeks later my whistle-blowing days came to an abrupt halt at Kirkby Town. The home team was 2-0 up and claimed a third when the ball entered the goal through a gaping hole in the side-netting. In the absence of a neutral linesman never mind goal-line technology, I elected to award a goal-kick. My decision was greeted with the type of exaggerated hysteria that should be reserved for an arrogant little man from Treorchy. The crowd, a sprinkling of 60 friends and family of the home team, sounded like 60,000 baying for blood - my blood. While I understood that verbal abuse is an essential part of the learning curve for every match official, I was disappointed that the grassroots of our national game had become spattered with the vilification of amateur referees. People don't seem to appreciate that without them you can't have an organized game of football. So after several dozen games stretching from the quagmires of Speke to wastelands of Sankey, I decided to relinquish my dream of refereeing at Anfield. You know the one in which I awarded a hat-trick of controversial penalties in the final minutes of Liverpool's relegation decider.

Actually, my decision wasn't influenced by the goings-on in Kirkby, I quit refereeing because I could hear Mama Blue calling my name. Also I had realized that it was one of the many things I wasn't very good at it.

We may be famous for our pioneering initiatives
... but cubeball won't be one of them

39. Mind your car

Life is easier when you're organized with a plan, even if it's not necessarily your own plan. With unemployment at the one million mark, which was considered a national disgrace in the Seventies, Elizabeth expressed fears that she would fall down the pecking order behind Everton and my career, if and when I found full-time work. My future better-half talked about a code involving hard work and honesty as well as buying quality and never borrowing against future earnings.

I took some consulting assignments. My initial gig involved designing an industrial furnace to melt scrap aluminum. For the first of many times in my life I became a consultant — the curse of the modern business world. It was much later that I was warned that the scientists at Porton Down planned to use consultants instead of laboratory mice in their chemical warfare research. Why? There are more consultants than mice. You don't get less attached to the consultants. Finally, there are some things that even mice won't do.

I was amazed that people listened to my advice and were prepared to pay for my modest know-how. One assignment led to another and within no time I had enough to break the code about buying quality. For some reason, perhaps genetic in origin, I mirrored my father's love affair with his Jowett Javelin by purchasing one of the 9,000 Lotus Europas ever produced. A light-weight fiberglass vehicle powered by a tiny 1,500cc engine, its aerodynamic design ensured race-car acceleration and unrivaled handling. Horrified by my conspicuous consumption, Elizabeth claimed that instant gratification was a trait of people with low self-esteem. It's too easy to stereotype why someone drives a certain vehicle. All sports cars carry a whiff of overindulgence. So what did the Lotus say about me? You're right, I was a shameless show-off.

The car had few miles on the clock. That wasn't by luck. The low mileage was related to its chronic unreliability. I knew that only the truly misinformed buy a Lotus for its Swiss watch durability but had anticipated a certain degree of mechanical fallibility. Nevertheless, my father was delighted. While encouraged that the France acorn hadn't fallen far from the tree, he cautioned me that the learning curve associated with a flash car would more than likely take a turn through my Trustee Savings Bank account.

One Saturday, I invited him to drive it along the winding country roads through Cronton and Tarbock to Goodison. To me, it was a modest gesture intended to strengthen father-son bonds. To him, it was a dream come true. I understand that the overture signalled to him that I could be his biological son after all. That said, it was a truly terrifying experience. After the first bend I had abandoned gripping my seat to concentrate on biting my blue and white scarf in order to stifle any noise from my mouth. Gone was his affinity to hog the gutter as he craved the adrenaline surge that comes from attacking tight corners at speed.

He yelled above the engine noise: 'Isn't this fun? Driving extra fast is about smoothness. Sharp movements unsettle the car. Always change gear before a corner. Treat the pedals with respect. Squeeze them - never stab them.' With my mouth full of wool, I simply nodded in his direction of the Merseyside version of Emerson Fittipaldi - the Brazilian who had captured the Formula One World Championship in an infinitely more reliable Lotus rocket ship. I concluded that Chemical Harry was a very good driver because he didn't touch the brake pedal throughout the 10-minute journey. Thankfully, I couldn't read the instruments to ascertain his exact speed but remember my legs trembling as we walked along City Road.

Though our visit to Goodison would confirm that there are only two good days when you own a Lotus Europa — the day you buy it and the day you sell it, the afternoon started with a stroke of good fortune. A polite youngster welcomed us into his street near to the ground by proclaiming: 'Mind yer car, mister? Please mister, mind yer car?'

For a shilling, he promised to protect it from vandals - especially himself. We agreed to his terms and parked between the kitchen chairs outside his terraced home. When we returned two hours later, I never expected to be involved in hostage negotiations. The Lotus was surrounded by the children of Bodmin Street. Their innocent faces and open palms mirrored those from my Methodist Sundays. As for the polite car minder, he was sat behind the wooden steering wheel making noises usually associated with a turbo-charged internal combustion engine.

The car minder-kidnapper pleaded with Chemical Harry: 'Go on mister, gizza ride in yer fancy car.' Displaying the diplomacy of Kurt Waldheim - the UN Secretary-General, my father agreed to a short spin around Stanley Park. I recall that he and the youngster sped away in style but returned on foot Apparently, a galaxy of red and orange warning lights had illuminated the dashboard. Nervously, my father apologized to me and said that he had left the Lotus on Walton Lane. Back in Bodmin Street, we waited for an automotive expert from the AA. His diagnosis was succinct: 'Beyond me. Need to tow you.' We retired to enjoy baked beans on toast and watch Saturday night television with the family of the kidnapper. Eventually, a big yellow truck showed up. Its driver reported: 'Fibre-glass. Need a trailer.' Around 10.00 pm, another mighty vehicle arrived to transport the car to the dealership on Aigburth Road. En route, Chemical Harry looked embarrassed: 'Son, has this had happened before?' I confessed: 'Every month.' He continued: 'This car reminds me of Jimmy Husband – it runs like the clappers until it breaks down. My father, who loved nicknames, considered 'Chapman's Bitter Lemon' before christening it 'Skippy'.

I know what you're thinking about the folks in Bodmin Street – the typical kindness of Blues? No, our new friends were Reds.

Three-nil down at half-time ... how did it finish in Istanbul?

40. In the shadows

The 1972/73 campaign started with a flourish. After the first eight games, which produced five wins and three draws, we topped the table. Lamentably, these heady days didn't last long. Performances deteriorated alarmingly to those usually associated with relegation. One sequence of 23 League games involved just four wins and five draws. As a result, Billy Bingham was recruited to replace Harry Catterick. I thought that the Ulsterman was a terrific author but lacked meaningful management experience. My father concurred and predicted that the appointment of Bingham, who had been in charge of the part-timers at Linfield only 12 months earlier, would challenge our royal blue faith.

Regardless, I lived in hope that silverware was just around the corner. My optimism heightened when I heard a newspaper seller in Deansgate, Manchester announce Bill Shankly's departure from Anfield. Buoyed by the unexpected news, I thought the premature exit of the man who had transformed a Second Division club into - let's be honest - a football giant would erode Liverpool's dominance. Clearly, I was wrong.

After Bingham splashed the cash on Bob Latchford and Martin Dobson, I believed that it was a simple matter of patience before we regained our crown. After all, his team boasted some of my favourite local players of all-time. My mother called them 'The Pals', as if they were an Army battalion in which friends had enlisted together during a neighbourhood recruitment drive. Certainly, there was something special about Mick Buckley, Terry Darracott, Gary Jones, Mike Lyons and Steve Seargeant. They were young and honest footballers of my own age. Best of all, they were diehard Blues.

Indeed, Bingham's team dominated the 1974/75 title race until the campaign imploded. The fuse was lit at Brunton Park in March. This defeat mirrored an earlier one to Carlisle at Goodison. After this second set-back to a club experiencing its only season in the top flight, I was convinced that my presence would salvage the season. To do so, I hitch-hiked to all away matches during the run-in. It rekindled fond memories of my mis-spent youth. Also I discovered something special about an articulated truck. The engine noise provided the ideal rhythm for both celebrations - which were rare - and commiserations.

The journey home from Luton masked the reality that the power of my thumb was eroding. Or maybe it had something to do with my long and somewhat tatty hair. I remember being stranded at the Newport Pagnell Services on a miserable Wednesday night after we had been beaten at Kenilworth Road. Though crestfallen, I accepted that such disappointments are like cold waters to red-hot steels — they strengthen Blues. Nonetheless, I questioned if a raised digit is an indecent gesture in that part of the world. The parking area was frequented by what are now known as lot lizards and most of the lorry drivers looked at me in disgust. During the next four hours I managed to progress only 20 miles to Watford Gap, the UK's oldest services which are the home of the invisible boundary of humility dividing the North from the South. I must have appeared desperate because my lift was provided by the motorway constabulary. They suspected that I was loitering and just wanted to move me on.

While nobody had promised that supporting Everton would be easy, I had become disillusioned. It was during an extended sulk at Watford Gap that the penny dropped finally. Bingham was destined to be the worst kind of boss — an unlucky one. Part of luck is random — a force of nature, coming and going as inevitably as the tide. Another part relates to state of mind. Some men have an inexplicable abundance of good fortune. Others, like Bingham, stumble repeatedly.

My fears were confirmed when, despite my presence, his team picked up only eight points from the final 10 games - which included losses at Carlisle and Luton plus a draw at Chelsea.

Everton choked against these three relegated clubs to finish three points behind champions Derby. To make matters worse, our neighbours - now managed by Bob Paisley - overtook us to pinch second place.

After too many seasons of famine, most Blues had come to terms that we were second best on and off the pitch to the Reds. Initially, I found it hard to accept that we had slipped into their shadows. Liverpool bigger than Everton? Absolutely not. Less than 20 years earlier, our lovable neighbours had never won a domestic cup and had never played European football. Liverpool bigger than mighty Everton? Never. We had a bigger ground and, thanks to John Moores, more money at our disposal and could buy any British player we fancied. Then I realized that no matter how much we spent on top-class footballers such as John Gidman, Asa Hartford, Mike Pejic, Bruce Rioch, the majestic Dave Thomas, the supernatural Duncan McKenzie, and the sublime Colin Todd, the Seventies were destined to be a barren decade for Blues. In search of an answer, I concluded that Everton Football Club was still under the curse of that bespectacled Nana Mouskouri woman.

In 1977, the First Blue Billionaire replaced Billy Bingham with Gordon Lee and stepped down from the board. I can't imagine his disappointment but, given his ruthless nature, he must have been tempted to sack the entire board, the administration, the coaches, the players and the tea lady. Even though he continued to attend home matches during the Eighties, the club failed to replace his vision and ambition. I was a great admirer of self-made men like Moores. I still am. In contrast, Chemical Harry wasn't. He believed that clubs were first and foremost rallying points for local pride. As such, he favoured the democratic ownership of all football clubs.

I was bullish that Gordon Lee's organized approach coupled with his predilection for caution would grind out a path to silverware. Though he had inherited two promising cup runs, some 10 weeks later we had forfeited our dreams of League Cup glory at Old Trafford after draws in finals at Wembley and Hillsborough and FA Cup success after a controversial draw in the first semi-final at Maine Road. The semi-final loss to Liverpool in the replay was hard to take. Not just the high-handedness of referee Clive Thomas but the deep significance of the missed opportunity to pick up a very elusive trophy.

The League Cup final against Villa was even worse. It caused my wife to question my judgment. We had travelled down to North London without tickets confident of buying a couple from Cockney touts before the kick-off. I ventured alone to find two spares. I did so because I didn't want her to know how much I was prepared to spend for them. I managed to unearth one but sadly not two. So I returned empty handed and settled for listening to the crowd noises. She claimed that only a religious zealot would travel ticketless to such a major event. I took the term as an attempt at flattery. Until recently, Elizabeth didn't know that I had put spending my time with her ahead of watching Everton at Wembley. Experts would say that it was a clear sign of her growing importance in my life.

We both struggled to come to terms with the loss to Villa in the second-replay at the home of Manchester United. A goal up thanks to Bob Latchford with 10 minutes to go, we had hold of one of the three handles of the trophy when Chris Nicholls avoided a challenge from Jim Pearson and struck a hopeful 40-yard effort. To our horror and the amazement of the Villa fans around us, the central defender scored. It was a fluke. I don't know how else to characterize his effort. A polite word has not been invented to describe David Lawson's attempt to stop it.

The game went to extra time, where in the dying seconds we forfeited our best-ever chance to capture the elusive silverware by 3-2.

41. Hooked on America

I sought a meaningful career and, given the strength of my academic qualifications, was invited to interviews in the nation's capital. All bar one were unproductive. It was my own fault. I despised snobs. I still do. I've been fortunate to live in four different countries. The United Kingdom is the only one where potential employers enquire about my father's occupation. Picture their response to my revelation: 'He's a manual labourer. And from all accounts, he's a pretty good one.'

The only permanent work on offer was with British Gas in London. So reluctantly, I retreated to a dingy yet roach-free flat in Fulham. I'm told that such insects drew a line at living in that part of the capital. It was in SW6, however, that I first observed that promotions to the best jobs were reserved for people who glide effortlessly - like cockroaches - into positions of influence regardless of performance. To their credit, my employers recognized my ambitions and the fact that I didn't fit in. I'm not sure in which order. They encouraged me to embark on a doctorate. On hearing the news, Chemical Harry referred to me as a professional student who should get a proper job. Nothing was further from the truth. All of my studies had been self-financed. My education had been built on my ability to secure part-time jobs, scholarships and other forms of sponsorship. But in his eyes, I remained a good-for-nothing university student.

I won't bore you with the details of my research except that I was one of the first scientists to employ lasers to measure the combustion characteristics of fuel gases. All I did was point them at different types of flames, in the same way that today's police determine traffic speed. I've always been amazed that no-one else had thought of doing so. My thesis, a monumental piece of work, perhaps in quantity rather than quality, spawned 20 scientific papers which were published in academic journals worldwide and almost as many invitations to speak at symposia in Europe, North America and South America. I never deluded myself that my research would have a lasting impact. A scientist must be content with the personal satisfaction of having changed the way that one or two people think.

It took time for the scientific community to digest my efforts. When the recognition arrived in the form of gold medals named after Bone-Wheeler and Townend, it was far more than my work merited. Peter Walker, the UK government minister presented me with the latter at a banquet organized by the Institute of Fuel. After learning that I had attended the University of Salford, he joked: 'Tell me, is disadvantage a blessing?' Seeing that I was lost for words, he concluded: 'Since you've mastered fire, you should focus on earth, wind or something visionary.' In response, I shared my thoughts on the hydrogen-based economy proposed recently by scientists in Michigan. To cut a very long story short, some years later I was awarded the prestigious Joule Medal - which had been struck to commemorate his discovery of the mechanical equivalent of heat - for my work with the lightest and most flammable of all elements. I must add that I've never been an H-fan and refuse to embrace its utilization as an emissions-free automotive fuel. Why? The colourless, odourless and tasteless gas is too dangerous. Despite my reservations, the international publications summarizing my findings caught the attention of people in North America where hydrogen's reputation had recovered from the explosion of the Hindenburg airship in 1937. Contrary to my fears, the everyday use of hydrogen appeared to excite them.

No award was more satisfying than the ICI Brunner-Mond Fellowship. Perhaps the UK's top company decided to repay some of its debt to the local community as part of its centenary celebrations. Whatever the reason, ICI's generosity allowed me to visit North America. I never thought of treating my travels as holidays - they were listening missions. Allow me to elaborate. I had developed a methodology for predicting the suitability of substitute natural gases and sought American feedback to refine it into propriety tool. To achieve my goal, I gave seminars at universities, research institutions, industry associations as well as the utility companies worried about the quality of their future supplies of fuel gases.

Most people are content to wait to become the person that their pet dog thinks they are. I've never been one of them. Far from it, I made a list of potentially interested parties, bought a map and scheduled 40 seminars. I mirrored an over-the-hill pop star or an ambitious sales rep. It was a different day - a different city but the same old song. I'm still tickled by the irony that ICI was responsible for changing the direction of my life by opening my eyes to the New World but had elected not to interview me for a craft apprenticeship only eight years earlier. Perhaps the giant of the chemical industry and bellwether of the British economy had been looking after my best interests all along.

At that time, foreign exchange restrictions were enforced to narrow the balance of payments deficit. Consequently, travellers could pack £50 only. It was an obstruction to one of the dearest freedoms — the ability to move among other peoples and in other countries. Not surprisingly, buses were my preferred form of transport. I became well-acquainted with Greyhound Bus Lines. Given that this icon of the US freeways could take you to almost anywhere in North America, I organized my itinerary to travel during the night and spend my days at different hubs. In total, I made three one month-long sorties across the continent yet spent no more than a dozen nights in hotels. I travelled from New York to San Diego and onto New Orleans to the nation's capital and was encouraged by audience reactions. My next foray followed Route 66 from Chicago to Los Angeles. By the time that I had ventured from San Francisco through Houston to Miami, my seminars were word-perfect and I was hooked on America. All in all, I crossed all of the 48 contiguous states with little sleep and even less soap before concluding that the size of the USA isn't measurable by the places you are able to visit but by all of the ones you don't.

My travelling companions were a mix of Americans who didn't have cars, namely aerophobics, misers, hippies who claimed to have been at Woodstock, runaways, crying babies and practicing musicians. Most were friendly. A few were scary, the types of unsavory characters who travel by bus because they couldn't pass through airport security. Only one was confrontational. This burly serviceman interrupted my sleep one evening to enquire: 'What part of Europe are you from? The part whose butt we saved or the part whose butt we kicked?' I answered: 'Both.' The basic rule of the Big Dog is the nearer to the back you sit, the more likely you will collect material for a bestseller. Other advice includes never stray outside the urban bus stations, read a book or feign sleep to avoid unwanted chatter and board late so that you decide who you sit or sleep with. Today, Greyhound is often associated with horror stories about unruly passengers and surly drivers. In the Seventies, their buses were reliable and friendly. The latter may be attributed to the smell of marijuana wafting over the passengers.

It wasn't hard to make new friends as the Big Dog scampered down the US freeways, especially during the community singing. The passengers took turns to perform songs which reflected their roots. There were Negro spirituals, Delta blues, folk songs, Grand Ole Opry classics and Led Zeppelin unplugged. In the eyes of Americans, the planets had aligned and placed Merseyside at the hub of the universe. Those expecting the sounds of the British Invasion were disappointed. I rejected the popular choices of 'Ticket to Ride' and 'All You Need is Love'. Accompanied by a newly released convict on a four-string guitar and a toothless pensioner on a duelling banjo, I sang 'The Leaving of Liverpool'. My version of the chorus went something like: 'So fare thee well my royal blue love … when I return united we will be … it's not the leaving of Liverpool that grieves me … but EFC when I think of thee.' I may be wrong. I recall that my freeway vocals, influenced by Bob Dylan's nasal twang, were received with spirited applause.

What about Everton? Now and then I came across exiled Blues. I remember meeting a handful in San Diego. One of them, a merchant sailor from Bootle, boasted a tattoo of his idol. It read: 'Duncan McKenzie is magic.' He laughed that he was the only man with three tits on his chest.

42. Behind the Iron Curtain

My wanderlust came in handy after an unexpected award from the Deutscher Akademischer Austausch Dienst allowed me to accelerate my research at the Universitat Karlsruhe. Bordering the Black Forest and the Alsace, the institution was haunted by the aroma of the good science. Three old boys come readily to mind. Karl Braun developed the cathode ray tube, Heinrich Hertz discovered electromagnetic waves and Edward Teller is hailed as the father of the hydrogen bomb. Then there was my favourite. Karl Benz gave us quality motor cars with the advertising slogan 'the best or nothing'. Sound familiar? I suspect that he was a Teutonic Blue.

In the mid-Seventies, we liked to compare ourselves to West Germans usually with a sense of superiority associated with victories in two World Wars and one World Cup. We were deluded. Unlike Liverpool, Karlsruhe boasted magnificently restored architecture and spotlessly-clean streets. Most of the British people that I knew would rather wade through litter than pick it up; it was evident that German society embraced rules that enhanced communal life at the expense of individual freedom. Teutonic pride overflowed to the football pitch where they were the reigning World Champions. My university colleagues believed that football produced a narrative that took them to places where even the Brothers Grimm couldn't dream of going. In my company, their preferred topics of conversation were England's third goal in the 1966 World Cup final and the opinion of Tofik Bakhramov, the Soviet linesman, that the ball had crossed the line.

After Geoff Hurst had added a fourth goal, Kenneth Wolstenholme proclaimed famously: 'Some people are on the pitch, they think it's all over … it is now.' To this day, they are some of the most contentious words in the history of the German game. One colleague was infuriated by the BBC commentator. It had something to do with the fact that Wolstenholme had been awarded the Distinguished Flying Cross for flying hundreds of bombing missions over his home town of Essen. Within no time, most of them were aware that Everton was interwoven into the tapestry of my life and of our dramatic triumph over Borussia Monchengladbach in the European Cup in 1971. To educate the rest, I excelled at providing a shot-by-shot account, complete with hand gestures and crowd noises, of Andy Rankin's heroics. Even though my ability to communicate in German was limited, we agreed that the penalty shoot-out had transformed a team sport into an individual one.

I survived by smiling and nodding during the appropriate pauses. I adopted this approach on the morning that a colleague informed me that a famous English club was to play at the local stadium. For one reason or another, I failed to follow up on his lead and missed the pre-season visitors - Everton Football Club. After all the bravado about my unswerving devotion, I didn't have the guts to admit not going to the game. Yes, sometimes I've been guilty of screwing up my priorities and failing to maintain the correct balance between career and football.

Karlsruhe loved scientists and engineers. They were hailed as the bedrock of a vibrant economy and enjoyed a different status to their UK counterparts. Not surprisingly, the university possessed some of the most advanced laboratories in the world and enjoyed long-term relationships with other prestigious institutions across Europe. As a result, I was invited to review my research plans and findings at some of them. Somehow my modest scientific credentials had qualified me to follow the path of the royal blue pioneers in 1905 and enter the restricted lands of Hungary and Czechoslovakia. To do so, I had to tackle the Iron Curtain which separated countries belonging to the Warsaw Pact from those in NATO. My mode of transport was an old Mini. Teal blue in colour with an unforgettable harvest gold interior, it was a veteran of round-trips between London and Merseyside. The car's maintenance history, however, would have been an embarrassment to Sir Alec Issigonis. With that in mind, it displayed two badges of honour. One was issued by the Automobile Association; the other was acquired from the Toffee Shop on Goodison Road. The latter read 'Everton Are Magic'.

Winter had arrived by the time that my paperwork and visas had been approved for me to lecture in Budapest, Prague and East Berlin. I was in good company and, for that matter, in good voice as my old car rattled towards the ideological divide. I must add that I wasn't alone. My travelling companions were Leonard Cohen, Janis Ian, James Taylor, Neil Young and Eric Clapton. Also, even though I hadn't smoked since age 10, I carried a generous stash of tobacco. The contraband was the product of savvy advice from a German student at Salford. He encouraged me to take plenty of shilling coins which were the exact size and a fraction of the value of Deutschmarks. They could be used to buy US cigarettes from the autobahn vending machines and traded for goods and services on the other side of the Iron Curtain.

My route cut a path through Yugoslavia, actually the bits now labeled Slovenia and Croatia, and along the River Danube to Budapest. The tension at the check-points was straight out of a B-movie. There were lots of barbed wire and barking dogs in the heavily-fortified no-man's lands as well as lots of guns and barking soldiers at the border-crossings. In contrast, the other Magyars were friendly. Now and then, I would bump into football fans who were aware that Ujpesti Dozsa had dumped us out of the Inter-Cities Fairs Cup a few years earlier. I used non-filtered Camel cigarettes and music cassettes, the preferred currency of Eastern Europe, to ease my passage. Of my four tapes, 'Layla' had got tangled up before I reached Ljubljana and 'Between the Lines', 'Sweet Baby James' and 'Harvest' were confiscated by members of the Hungarian Army with good taste.

After my debut at Technical University of Budapest, it was on to Czechoslovakia with only Leonard Cohen for company. Make that very good company.

Don't worry Bob ... all strikers go through a loss of confidence

43. Behold bearded Bob

In Prague, I had arranged to stay at a youth hostel which doubled as a shelter for the local transients. Now, I had been warned about bed bugs, the small parasites that feed exclusively on the blood of warm-blooded footballers; I'm sorry I'm confusing them with WAGs. Anyway these accommodations were full of cockroaches on a day-trip from Leipzig. Small by Gerrard Street standards, the German roaches goose-stepped in formation up and down the bare wooden floors rounding up the bed bugs. Worse still, the air was filled with an unpleasant odour during these nocturnal hours. Apparently, insects fart when they are excited or frightened. Yet again, they have much in common with WAGs.

The following night, I elected to avoid further interactions with bedbugs and kip on the rear-seat of my Mini. To do so safely, I ventured 30 miles north of Prague city centre where I found a quiet parking spot near a transport cafe. At sunrise, I attempted to make an early start only to discover that my car was covered with a foot of frozen snow. Worse still, it had died from hyperthermia. Those with experience of British Leyland Minis will know that it had something to do with the Lucas electrical components. Alone in the deserted car park with no knowledge of the local language, I waited for a Good Samaritan. From the comfort of my sleeping bag, I began to worry about my predicament. After all, I didn't know anything about my location except that it was near a transport cafe with very few vowels in its name on the road to Poland.

Eventually someone tapped my decals on the rear window. Dr Zima's first words were reassuring: 'Behold Bob Latchford!' Initially, I thought that it was a supernatural communication. Then, he repeated the name of the bearded centre-forward: 'Behold Big Bob!' Slowly, I clambered from my cocoon to discover a thin man with a white coat and stethoscope and, wait for it, a passion for football and motor mechanics. I couldn't believe my fortune and feared that other men in white coats would drag me away. Even though my Good Samaritan had never seen a Mini or a transversely mounted engine before, he swiftly remedied the problem – namely, the points were frozen. It turned out that he was a doctor at the local A&E hospital who had popped out for a breather after spending the night tending to the victims of a traffic accident. There is more to this wintry tale and it's a beauty – he had Blue tendencies. Dr Z was a supporter of Dukla Prague who had developed a fondness for Everton after the Czechoslovakian Army side hammered us in New York in the early Sixties.

While thawing out in the transport cafe, he confirmed that football is a unifying force with an amazing ability to bring people together. The good doctor had learnt the English language via Voice of America and acquired his knowledge of English football via the BBC World Service. Therefore, with no little charm, he spoke enthusiastically about the exploits of Big Bob and Little Dunc in a New York accent. With the zeal of a missionary, I told him about my royal blue faith and welcomed him to join the Everton family. I reassured him that the club embraced all types of new supporters including a Soviet trained ex-Czechoslovakian Army doctor with lust for American cigarettes. After we had raised glasses of homemade elderberry wine to toast both Everton and Dukla, he echoed the words of Chemical Harry: 'You can like several clubs. You can support only one.' Little did we know that two years later his club would eliminate us from the UEFA Cup via the away-goals rule.

He invited me to join his friends for dinner at his home that evening. The host introduced me to them by claiming that I wasn't normal. I feared that it was a professional diagnosis until he elaborated that his concept of freedom of movement would never ever be the same after meeting a long-haired, Everton supporter from England brave enough to venture behind the Iron Curtain in a clapped-out Mini. As for the dinner conversation, it covered a wide range of subjects from the unreliability of Skoda cars via the ability of Bearded Bob Latchford to walk on water to the unreliability of Dai Davies.

One taboo subject was the efforts of the proletarian revolution to overthrow bourgeois society and abolish all private property, in the belief that this would lead to a classless and stateless world. Their words, not mine. Mostly, we talked about football. Dr Z proposed that young fans should experience formal rites of passage into the Promised Land. The new status should be characterized by outward symbols such as - wait for it - branding. No-one laughed. Under the influence of the elderberry wine I suggested that, because I had spent so much time with Blues during my lifetime, there should be an Everton family cemetery where the remains of deceased Blues are buried or otherwise interred. No tombs. No mausoleums. No fancy monuments. Just a simple place with standard plaques and modest headstones for us to remember our loved ones. Again, no-one laughed.

I learnt many things that frosty evening. One fact in particular has stayed with me. Dr Zima had to work a 10-hour day repairing mangled bodies to earn a carton of 200 Soviet cigarettes. When I think of the austerity of the communist world, another example haunts me. We were served a feast of potato soup followed by cauliflower and cheese. Both courses were hearty and filling. As the guest of honour, my meal included a fried egg, sunny-side up. To my unease, my plate was the only one topped with protein. I recall an older guest staring at it. Worn down by years of totalitarian rule, she confronted me: 'Are you going to eat all of that egg?'

Much has changed since the mid-Seventies. The Iron Curtain no longer exists nor, for that matter, does Czechoslovakia. I'll never forget the good doctor's instantaneous kindness or his final nugget of advice: 'Smile at every stranger you see in Eastern Europe. It could be the only sunshine he sees all day.'

You're both wrong ... a Brazilian is a really big number

44. Brazilian Blue

Upon returning home, I continued to spread the royal blue message. After all, it was God's work. By far my finest recruit was a post-graduate student from Brazil who had yet to master the English climate or language. He was hard to miss. Tall and slim, he wore a bowler hat and wire-framed glasses. This dead ringer for Carlos Santana was football crazy and the first person to tell me about the other Everton, our siblings across the Andes in Chile.

I was fascinated but more intrigued that he knew about Alan Ball, Brian Labone, Keith Newton and Tommy Wright. Of course, all Brazilians of his vintage remember the 1970 World Cup clash with England in the baking heat of Guadalajara. They don't need to be reminded that Pele, Rivelino and team-mates, arguably the greatest Brazilian side of all time, went on to lift the Jules Rimet trophy. My friend could describe the save by Gordon Banks, the miss by Jeff Astle and the tremendous play of Tommy Wright. Surprisingly, I had to remind him of Bobby Moore's perfectly-timed tackles on Tostao and Jairzinho. Apparently, they were nothing special in Brazil. He thought that the Everton right-back had been the top defender on the pitch that day. After watching a re-run of the game recently, I'm inclined to agree.

At the first opportunity I took him to the School of Science. It was a night clash with City. My Brazilian friend was more impressed by the escalator which took him to the Top Balcony than our crude interpretation of the beautiful game. I remember him referring to the action unfolding before his eyes as grotesque. In particular, he was critical of the unwillingness or the inability of the teams which occupied the top and third positions in the table to control, never mind master, the ball. My friend claimed that the trickery of Ronny Goodlass, the only footballer on show with any flair that evening, scared his own team-mates more than his opponents. I invited the Santana wannabee to embrace Mama Blue on other occasions. Now and then, he would tag along. More often than not, he found one excuse or another to decline.

Years later I visited him in Rio de Janeiro where he had convinced his pals that John Barnes played for the Pride of Merseyside - that's right, Everton Football Club. And because they talked enthusiastically about his dribbling skills and wonder goal against Brazil in 1984, I didn't correct them. As for English football? They weren't impressed and believed that the 1966 World Cup was badly-organized and biased against South American sides. Even worse, England had traded its reputation of fair play for one of skullduggery to steal the Jules Rimet Trophy. Shortly afterwards, we went to the Maracana Stadium to watch the Classico Vovo - the Rio derby between Fluminense and Botafogo. The match was played with Samba rhythm. But it was the banners, chants, drums and general mayhem that made the afternoon so memorable. Plus, of course, the riot police who were on hand to contain the missiles which included potatoes containing razor blades - the Brazilian equivalent of meat & potato pies. I concluded that the crowd was made up of inmates who had been released too early into the community and without their medication for some time. After the game, I agreed with my friend's observation that Evertonians play football in rhyme and Brazilians play football in poetry. I had no reason to revise my opinion for a couple of decades. Then I witnessed Jo - who believe it or not was awarded 20 international caps - turn out for Everton at Goodison. Vividly, I remember a neighbouring Blue ask: 'Anyone checked his passport?'

I know what you are thinking: What happened to Nurse Ireland? Well to confirm that we were compatible, Lancashire Lass — which makes her sound like a retired, yet to be adopted, greyhound — and I decided to conquer the Pennine Way. The 270-mile hike along England's backbone from the Peak District, via Bronte Country, the Lake District, the Yorkshire Dales and Hadrian's Wall, to the Cheviots Hills in Scotland is regarded as the most taxing in Britain. There were conditions. The major one was that there could be no mention of the past, present or future of Everton Football Club.

There was nothing technically difficult about the hike. For most people, the test is a psychological one against the terrain, climate and awesome sense of loneliness. Whereas for me, not talking about my Everton for two weeks was an even bigger challenge.

I could tell you that such shared experiences ignite feelings of togetherness and deep love. But I won't. As a matter of fact, it was several days before I grasped that our adventure up and down rugged mountains and across endless seas of bog was a dummy run for a long-lasting marriage. That's right, after a short time the novelty had worn off. In our case it was near Malham's limestone pavements at around 80 miles. I didn't have the guts to confess this realization until we had reached the half-way point. As we rested at the Tan Hill Inn, which at 1,700 feet above sea level is England's highest and remotest ale house, I mentioned to Elizabeth that it was as far back as it was forward so we had to grin and bear it. Eyebrows raised, my wife-to-be claimed that I had taken the words right out of her mouth. As a result, we marched on in unison to Kirk Yetholm chatting about Gordon Lee's adoration of Bob Latchford and apparent abhorrence of Duncan McKenzie and got married four months later.

As you know, Elizabeth's initial failure to realize that she had tied a knot with Everton Football Club led to the Malta Protocol. Remember 14 years as a slow learner, 14 years as a fast learner, 14 years at work, 14 years doing something more useful and 14 years doing nothing but watch Everton? Well after 41 years of wedlock, I can confirm that walking the Pennine Way replicates marriage. There are parts that are difficult, that bore you even, but the more you put into it, the more you get out of it. Especially if you possess a code, a plan and a mutual love of all things blue.

You three are same after every international break

45. Life without Everton

Aspirational Britain remains a myth. It's hard to disagree with the Granada TV documentaries, 'The Up Series', which hypothesized that class structure was so strong in 1964 that a child's life path was determined by age 7. People remain unwilling to tackle the entrenchment of privilege. Advancement isn't the matter of gaining academic qualifications; you need social networks and to follow their unwritten and unspoken rules of how to dress, walk and talk.

My doctorate thrilled Ma Carsley. She relished bragging to strangers: 'My son is a doctor but not the kind that helps people.' Others were less impressed. At job interviews, I encountered more discrimination than is good for the soul. On one occasion, I introduced myself to the panel. In the haughty tone used to divert an apprentice gas-fitter to the tradesman's entrance, the chairman replied: 'Sorry old boy, can you repeat that?' I reintroduced myself: 'My name is David France'. He corrected me: 'Rather Northern old boy, don't you mean Fraaaance?' Later he enquired: 'I note your degrees and work experience but don't seem to have the name of your prep school.' I would like to think that he heard the response from the corner of my mouth: 'Aaaarse hole.' To this day, my wife claims there is nothing more threatening to the social elites, with their toxic air of self-satisfied superiority, than an educated working-class boy who supports Everton.

My prospects were so bleak that I signed on. Chemical Harry was appalled. In his eyes, accepting state benefits was something for deadbeats. He claimed that I had enough letters behind my name to spell 'LOSER' and that I should have taken his advice and left school at 15. There was no Full Monty-style line dancing at the Labour Exchange in Chorley, just the voicing of anxieties by middle-aged men tagged surplus to requirements after spending their lifetimes at local munitions and truck manufacturing plants. Among them was a sage who challenged me: 'What do you want out of life? What are your plans for getting it? Lancashire is a good place to come from. Not a good one to end up at. Thought about emigrating?' He joked: 'Ever thought that if you move to the USA, you'll raise the average IQ of both sides of the Atlantic.'

I embraced the meritocracy advertised in arguably the most diverse country in the world. Even more important, I concluded that science had simply been my means to an education and, though deemed over-qualified by many, sought to complement my CV with an MBA - a course of study only available in North America. And by a stroke of good luck, I was offered a Fulbright Fellowship in which my tuition fees and living expenses would be paid by International Telephone & Telegraph, a conglomerate that had acquired 300 or so companies in an alarmingly short period of time. Apparently, ITT desired to enhance its image worldwide and with yours truly as the face of the United Kingdom. I was accepted by all of the six universities on my short-list and selected the one-year intensive programme at Purdue University over the two-year offerings at MIT and Harvard University. To this day, my decision confuses most Americans. I picked the Indiana home of the Apollo astronauts because - wait for it - I had been impressed by their endeavours. Neil Armstrong and Gene Cernan, both graduates of Purdue, were the first and last men on the moon. When I think of it, I'm sure these brave men would have advised me to enroll at Harvard.

Before we emigrated, Elizabeth and I bid farewell to Everton at the Baseball Ground. It was three days after we had conceded the League Cup final second replay to Villa and we thought that the fixture would provide an opportunity to display our steadfast loyalty before starting our new lives. As a rare treat, I purchased tickets for the stands. Elizabeth was thrilled that we would cheer our heroes in comfort. Or so she thought. As always, there was a massive turn out of Blues. None, however, were in Derby's grandstand. The locals around us appeared irritated by our presence. Given their belligerent mood, we stifled our enthusiasm as the Rams dominated the early proceedings on the pitch. Then it happened - Big Bob scored. In a flash I leapt out of my seat screaming my head off. A split-second later, Elizabeth mirrored my behaviour.

This incident sticks in my mind because the goal was disallowed and I had returned to the anonymity of my seat as she jumped up and down amid a torrent of intimidation. Like a naive soul, it took her another second to comprehend that the abuse was aimed at her. Some advised: 'Sit down! Shut up old duck!' Embarrassed, she was about to retake her seat when someone yelled: 'That Latchford is a lazy lummox!' I believe that there are times in life when you must defend the honour of your loved-ones. This was hers. She addressed the menacing individual sat behind her: 'Excuse me, Bob is deceptively mobile. Surely, you're aware of his magnificent muscular legs!' As her words reverberated around the grandstand, the fans around us moved to safer seats.

Following Everton in the Seventies was an adventure of elation and disappointment, often in the space of 90 minutes. Trailing 2-0 at half-time, we refocused and led 3-2 thanks to goals from three of our favourites - Big Bob, Mike Pejic and Little Dunc - before our hero was injured. Elizabeth displayed a monastic level of silence as he was carried off but celebrated at the final whistle with the wild enthusiasm of someone who would never visit the city of Derby again.

I'm back ...

46. Belfast Candies

The nameless people with whom I shared an intake of breath during the opening bars of Z Cars had become my family. We all have them. Mine included an old chap who claimed to have been at Sheffield when the club was relegated in 1951. There was a spy with his collar turned up who shared the latest gossip extracted from a cook at the Bellefield canteen. Also, the prematurely bald fellow who bragged about having turned out for the Everton C team in his younger and slimmer days. And how could I forget the fan who, once upon a time, had won the Golden Goal competition? Irrespective of what happened on the pitch, their collective fidelity invigorated my life. I was sorry to leave them.

Some people are content to go wherever the road may lead. Others prefer to go where there is no path and leave a trail. The Frances were simply economic refugees with $100 in cash, a dark blue Globetrotter suit-case, a plan for life's journey and appetites for hard work. The latter came in handy because I soon discovered that the Krannert Business School at Purdue, like the USA in general, was no place for slackers. Ranked third in my marketing major in the All-American league tables, it was no place for dummies either. Krannert helped me to break my bounds of conventional thinking and see questions not as a place to linger but as barriers to overcome as swiftly and cheaply as possible. More than anything, business school taught me to identify problems before others did. Later in life, when training for marathons, I became so fit that my feet didn't touch the ground. Seriously, I floated on air. It's a fantastic feeling. My year in Indiana tuned my mind in the very same way. I had never been so mentally sharp.

Like Harvard, Krannert promoted a case-method approach in which collective knowledge was shared. Accordingly, MBA students were required to perform intensive analyses of real business scenarios. Some were invited to write cases for extra credit. One student from Boston outlined the development of new cranberry products for Ocean Spray, another from Chicago tackled the introduction of electric powered vehicles by Sears Roebuck and a New Yorker examined the expansion of Macy's department stores across the USA. It should come as no surprise that my efforts addressed a small private company - The Everton Football Club Company Limited. Based on actual financial statements extracted from a half-dozen annual reports, I thought that my case would interest my professors and fellow students. Especially since John Moores, who had just stood down from the board, had been an autocrat and left behind a gaggle of yes-men whose most popular phrase was 'Oh, Mr John won't like that.'

Though rejected, my case generated innovative feedback. The consensus of my classmates was that the club must expand its markets. A student from Taiwan, possibly a Kopite, suggested the relocation to a geographic location with less competition, namely Dublin: 'Rebrand the franchise as the pride of all-Ireland, change the uniforms to emerald green and the nickname to The Mighty Shamrocks. All people with Irish blood will pledge allegiance to the franchise.' Another student was equally creative: 'Move the Everton Tootsie Rolls to Belfast. The UK government should build a stadium in that war-torn city, so that the club can alternate fixtures between there and Merseyside. Boosters of the same club are unlikely to kill one another.'

I still have the class-notes of an intellectual who pioneered research into the use of automated checkout systems - known as the ubiquitous barcode. Our most esteemed professor didn't rush into an opinion without the expenditure of much agonizing thought. He recommended that my beloved club promote initiatives to expand its customer base and enhance its non-traditional revenue sources. He promoted strengthening brand loyalty by enriching what we now call the matchday experience of fans both young and old, developing succession plans for all key business executives and establish a worldwide scouting system to trawl for the best talent in North and South America. Clearly he was an oracle. At the time, however, I was more impressed by his role as a strategic adviser to Hugh Hefner's Playboy Enterprises.

The downside to Indiana? I missed Mama Blue and some things about the old country. While my British friends at Purdue pined for real bacon and proper custard, I yearned for the sounds of home - people laughing and saying sorry. I think apologizing makes up half of our conversations. We're sorry for things that aren't our fault. When it comes to politeness, we can't help ourselves.

Also I missed the whirring noise made by the letter-by-letter typing of the BBC Grandstand's teleprinter and the heightened anticipation during the wait for the full-time scores. In the absence of telephones and televisions, I subscribed to 'The Football Pink' which arrived by airmail on Thursdays. In addition, my mother corresponded regularly. She wrote the same one-page letter every week, always on Basildon Bond airmail paper. While her handwriting changed over time, her correspondence followed the same format throughout the 1977/78 season - the only one in which I didn't cross the Goodison threshold - and the next decade or so. In this day and age it would be termed Una's Blog. Her insights started with the weather and the health of the roses in her garden. They progressed seamlessly into the comings and goings around Sycamore Avenue and recorded all births, deaths and illnesses. She identified the latest local factory to file for bankruptcy, the latest shop to be closed on the main street and the latest mountain of gallygu to be converted into golf fairways. Ma Carsley was frustrated. Merseyside was being converted into the set of a post-apocalyptic science-fiction film. She had never seen anything go to pieces so quickly. It was her way of encouraging me to stay in the USA.

Her letters concluded with Una's Blue Update. It read something like: 'We won again on Saturday. Chelsea 0 Everton 1. We were lucky. Latchford scored as usual. Pearson missed a sitter as usual. Woods and Lyons played blinders. Sunday People reports we're about to sign another spotty youth from somewhere or other.' It was an eventful campaign. Besides Latchford amassing 30 League goals, we spent most of season in second-place chasing Forest before fading. How badly? Before the final game - a 6-0 win over Chelsea - we collected only three points in five games. Worse, shortly afterwards Liverpool retained the European Cup after beating Brugge.

My mother adored Mike Lyons. He could do no wrong. It had much to do with the colour of the blood pumping through the massive heart displayed on his sleeve. Years later I had the privilege of sitting next to him at Goodison. It was a bruising encounter. He kicked my shins and elbowed my ribs as he contested every ball. While most ex-players analyze the proceedings in silence, Lyons roared motivation towards the boys in blue as well as the referee. His instructions were last employed at Rorke's Drift in the Anglo-Zulu War. That evening, the Main Stand was empty except for the extended families of the participants in the FA Youth Cup tie. I'm sure that they all felt the resonance of his passion and understood why my mother loved him.

What did I learn from my MBA studies? How about if you can't handle each piece of paper only once, then you must minimize the number of times you touch it. I discovered also that wise folk speak because they have something to say. Fools speak because they have to say something. Most stuff is gained from trading time. So before you exchange a piece of your life to acquire something, make sure you need it. And perhaps just as important, you must buy an expensive pen because, unlike a Biro, you'll always know where you put it. Unfortunately, I didn't embrace the best bit of advice until much later. During our final semester, my class-mates and I focused on securing decent jobs. Most targeted the industrial behemoths of the Mid-West or the faceless titans of Wall Street. One friend argued: 'You're all making a big mistake. Relocate to your perfect spot then find something to do when you get there. I'm off to Portland, Oregon.' It took a decade of hot and humid summers in Houston for me to embrace his wisdom. Since then I've tried to compensate by residing in Victoria, BC, San Juan Island, WA and Sedona, AZ. The latter is surely the most beautiful spot in North America. Set among a geological wonderland of red rocks jutting from the desert floor, it's a place of spiritual renewal for an old Blue.

47. Wilberforce Trophy

Upon graduating from Purdue, I was thrilled to accept an offer from Science Applications Inc, a consulting firm, to participate in their nuclear and synfuel projects in Oak Ridge, Tennessee and their propulsion and aerospace projects in Los Angeles, California. Sounds high-tech?

While not much to look at in the flesh, I must have appeared better on paper because I received my Green Card thanks to the support of Senator Ted Kennedy. I've no idea why JFK's youngest brother sponsored me. I hadn't met him and didn't know that much about him except that he sought to change the lives of every man and woman in the USA and farther afield. I knew that he had authored hundreds of legislative bills to aid the less fortunate. Like most people, I was more mindful of his flaws. He had been expelled from Harvard for cheating and had starred in the Chappaquiddick incident which drowned Mary Jo Kopechne. I understand that, courtesy of rigorous background checks conducted by several government agencies, he was aware of my shortcomings. Thankfully, the folks at the FBI ignored my lack of judgment involving cigarettes along Bundesautobahn 8 and bubble-gum cards at Bungy Parr's Tuck Shop and allowed the Senator from Massachusetts to tease open the door to a world of equal opportunity.

Oak Ridge was a giant step from the dole queue. Just about everyone was a world-class expert in something or other. Known as the town that did not appear on maps, the US government had selected this area near the Smoky Mountains as the site for the Manhattan Project. Its mission was to produce enriched uranium for the first nuclear weapons. By 1945, Oak Ridge had shipped 100 pounds of the stuff to Los Alamos, New Mexico where the Hiroshima bomb was assembled. Codenamed 'Little Boy', the bomb vaporized everything within an area of 200 acres, including 66,000 civilians.

Thirty years on, after the removal of the perimeter fencing and guard towers, the town had evolved into a cultural oasis populated by highly qualified people from across the globe. Their numbers included three other Blues. One came from County Antrim. Another hailed from County Meath near the site of the Battle of the Boyne. The third was from Birmingham, Alabama. We became good friends and formed our own unofficial supporters' club - the Smoky Mountain Blues. We even wore sweat-shirts personalized with those words.

The third Smoky Mountain Blue preferred to be known as X rather than his slave-master's name. His connection with the club was inspired by the first name of his Jamaican grandfather. I know you couldn't make it up; it was Everton. Grandad X had fallen in love with the club during our North American tour in 1956. A part-time student for eight years at the Knoxville School of Law, X financed his quest for a degree by working several jobs including the graveyard shift at Science Applications. To handle the monotony of operating a yoke of photocopiers for hour after hour, he smoked ganja. X would inhale through a glass bong and exhale through his own filtration contraption . There was something even stranger about him. After midnight, he liked to place his body parts on the glass of the Xerox machine and press the green button.

More politically aware than politically correct, X suffered from unwarranted giggling and excessive references to race discrimination in the Deep South. When stoned, he reminisced about taking part in the March on Washington and the Soul Train television show. Also he bragged about flying a small plane along the Mason-Dixon Line. Few people believed him. His credibility was undermined by his constant teasing and preening of the biggest afro in Tennessee. It came with a wide-toothed comb on the side.

Something of a football prophet, X predicted that the USA would win the World Cup before England. He was convinced that blacks with their longer legs and bigger feet would dominate world soccer in the way that they had gridiron football, athletics, basketball and boxing.

Shortly after Viv Anderson had been capped by England, X claimed that within a half-century the Everton first-team would be made up of 10 players from Africa plus a local goalkeeper. X was bold enough to envision Everton Africans contesting Liverpool Africans for the William Wilberforce Trophy in 2020.

The other Smoky Mountain Blues thought he was a bit of a blowhard. I concurred until X borrowed a Beechcraft plane from the University of Tennessee Flying Club and invited my wife and I to join him for some sightseeing over Clingman's Dome in the Great Smoky Mountains National Park. It was only after we were airborne that she realized her life was in the hands of someone who liked to photocopy his Jamaican black snake. The colour had drained from her face by the time that a somewhat confused X pointed to a remote strip of tarmac and the single-engine plane started to lose altitude. After we touched down, a man in denim overalls rushed towards us. He stopped abruptly when he saw the gravity defying afro hanging out of the window. Tentatively, he asked: 'Engine trouble?' Our pilot responded: 'No, just lost.' The mechanic couldn't resist telling us about the Fukawi tribe of small people who would get lost during their hunt for food and chant 'We're the Fukawi, we're the Fukawi' until they found their way out of the rain-forest.

Shortly afterwards, I caught a much bigger plane to the old country. After being greeted at Manchester's Ringway Airport like a biblical prodigal son, I accompanied Chemical Harry to Ayresome Park. The triumph over Middlesbrough elevated us into second-place behind our loveable neighbours. With 13 League games to play, I returned to the USA convinced that the 1978/79 season would be the one in which we popped the top off the Silvo. Sadly, it wasn't. Inexplicably, we won only two of these games to finish fourth.

Under no circumstances mention his own goal at Anfield in 1979

48. X and Zen

Initially, the Smoky Mountain Blues were reluctant to share our love of Everton with others. Wrongly, we thought no-one who isn't a Blue could love a sports team in the way that we loved ours. Then in an ambitious attempt to spread the royal blue gospel with parables about The Golden Vision and The Holy Trinity, we infiltrated a local football club.

Luckily for me, Tennessee football was primitive and some what slow. Teams were composed of enthusiastic novices and adopted a common core. The most rotund individual accepted the goalkeeper's jersey without serious argument. The gangly hot-head with extraordinarily skinny legs assumed the role of the defensive kingpin. Up front, the hick with the most outrageous mullet and matching swagger was the spearhead and captain.

Blount County FC was different. We played in all green, apparently to repel mosquitos and boasted a secret weapon - a goalkeeper known affectionately as 'Zen the Buddhist Monk'. Immaculately turned out in orange - shirt, shorts, socks, head-band and wrist-bands - even his fingers were stained by nicotine or possibly Doritos, the former-US marine could punt the ball higher and occasionally more wayward than any other human. That claim may be a bit of a stretch but he could kick it 60 yards with a hang-time of 4.6 seconds.

My friend from County Antrim — the same neck of the woods as the family of David Moyes — took advantage of Zen's talent and developed rudimentary tactics in which the job of three Smoky Mountain Blues was to win the ball and pass it back to the keeper. Nothing more was asked of us. Subsequently, Zen would punt the ball into the clouds where it would hang from sky hooks until X and his fellow forwards reached the penalty box. Then and only then would the ball fall to earth. At 6 feet 2 inches excluding his afro, X was our star striker. A master at keepy-uppy, his confidence was so fragile that his ability to control the ball fragmented as soon as he stepped onto the pitch. Though pacey, X could have been much faster if he hadn't run like an abandoned giraffe calf.

Our primitive tactics - nicknamed skyball - confused opponents and increased the demand for the services of osteopaths, chiropractors and physical therapists to treat defenders with neck aches. That said, we enjoyed no little success and were headed for regional glory until Almighty God intervened. One Wednesday night at training - I'm serious, we practiced our hoof-and-pray tactics - Zen informed us that he planned to become a Jehovah's Witness. His religious calling wasn't a problem. We had a spine of Southern Baptists and our right-back was a follower of the Unification Church founded by Reverend Sun Myung Moon. That's right, we boasted an overlapping Moonie. More than anything, we were confused by his demands to wear mosquito-resistant green like the rest of us. Lamentably, Zen struggled in his new role on the left wing. So much so that one abiding memory is of his painful attempts to cross the ball. Time and time again it soared over the goal-mouth and directly into touch on the opposite side of the pitch. I concluded that although Zen had no difficulty hoofing the ball 60 yards, he lacked the finesse to kick it less than 40 yards. He was like a golfer using a Callaway Great Big Bertha to putt.

Not long afterwards, my wife and I moved west where, in addition to constant sunshine, pristine beaches and bikini-clad babes, Los Angeles boasted a professional soccer team. Despite the recruitment of Johan Cruyff to replace George Best, who had defected to the Fort Lauderdale Strikers, watching the LA Aztecs was a joyless experience. Their home performances were awful. But to their credit, they provided opposition for visiting franchises crammed with old names from the old country. Nostalgia plays strange tricks with the senses and I met several Blues chasing a royal blue high at the Rose Bowl. Like me, they had come to support the likes of Dave Clements, Jimmy Gabriel and Jimmy Husband as well as some of the Pals such as Terry Darracott, Roger Kenyon and Steve Seargeant who had been lured by the mighty dollar to the North American Soccer League.

Many of my tastes changed in the USA; however, my football palate remained unblemished and defined by Everton Football Club. Hand on heart, I never suffered from homesickness - few people from Widnes do. That said, I did experience separation anxiety. Seeing our ex-players in action made me pine for Mama Blue and, as a result, I would jet home to watch the current boys in blue.

I loved returning to Merseyside. Goodison reminded me of the homes of some of my mother's elderly neighbours. The unchanged surroundings were a time capsule - a reminder of my youth. Sadly, the club was still troubled by The Curse of Nana Mouskouri. No matter how much we spent on new signings such as John Gidman, Asa Hartford, Micky Walsh and Colin Todd, arguably the finest defender in the land, our local rivals captured the title. I was a tad peeved yet never ever resentful. Liverpool were an outstanding side and worthy champions. Towards the end of the Seventies, the penny finally dropped that we needed a new leader. Preferably, someone with the Durham grit of Bob Paisley.

Everton Football Club was in much better shape than its environs. My mother's descriptions were accurate. The city was in turmoil. The docks were closed. The factories were idle. The shops were boarded up. The architecture was crumbling. The society had become unequal and divided. The indigenous working folk had been discarded by Margaret Thatcher's London-centric policy and anti-Merseyside bias, then neutered by cheap beer, cheap drugs and non-stop television.

By systematically destroying mature industries and frittering away the revenues from North Sea oils and gas supplies, Mrs Thatcher caused significant human damage. Her Britain was a cruel place for too many people.

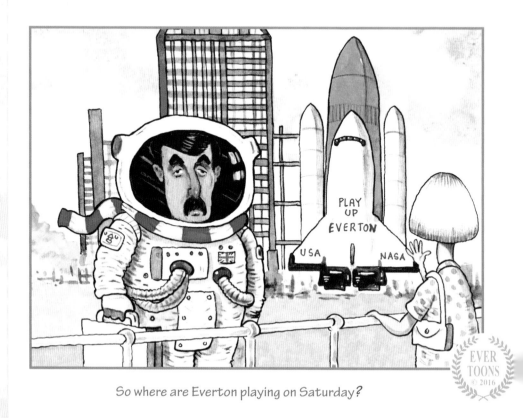

So where are Everton playing on Saturday?

49. Don't mess with Texas

In addition to the advent of the new pecking order mandated by the Malta Protocol of 1975, that is 1 Work - 2 Everton - 3 Lancashire Lass, my life changed when I was head-hunted by a polymath who could speak languages, play musical instruments and write poetry. A man of moral conviction rare in any walk of life, his rounded education provided him a unique perspective of the oil & gas industry.

During my first interview, the Renaissance Man and I explored the need for independent thinking and real-time communications in increasingly competitive markets. Because he was concerned about my youthful appearance, I know the precise moment that I grabbed his attention. Straight out of a business school manual, he asked: 'How old would you be if you didn't know how old you are?' In a flash, I responded: 'Old enough to discuss what business Texas Eastern Corporation should be in?' I think that he mumbled 'smart-ass' under his breath in either Mandarin or Farsi.

At my second interview, he focused on my weaknesses and seemed taken aback by my aversion to the colour red. So much so that he engaged a behavioural psychologist to follow me around for five mornings and five evenings to determine how I reacted to different situations and no doubt to the 40 or so shades, hues and tints from auburn to vermilion. I did my best to appear normal. After a day or two, however, I reverted to my usual self.

Fascinated by the shrink's observations, I reviewed his dossier with Elizabeth. I read aloud: 'David doesn't suffer fools ... That's wrong. I'm as tolerant as the Dalai Lama.' She snarled: 'Tell me, who else uses the noun 'Fahrenheit' to describe jerks with the IQ of room temperature?' I continued: 'David is highly assertive in relationships ... That's completely wrong, I'm a consensus builder.' She sniggered: 'In your dreams.' I read on: 'He is far more mature than his chronological age ... Now, that's more like it.' After my better half had stopped sniggering, she concluded that Texas Eastern hierarchy could have saved the shrink's fee by chatting one-on-one with her for five minutes. Thankfully they didn't and, at age 32, I became the baby of its corporate executive headquartered in Houston.

The second bumper sticker I saw during my inaugural commute to work read: 'Don't Mess with Texas - the Home of the Free Because of the Brave.' It captured the spirit of my new stomping ground. As the fourth largest city in the land, with a metropolitan population in excess of six million, behind New York, Los Angeles and Chicago, Houston's dramatic growth coincided with the introduction of air-conditioning in the Fifties to conquer the oppressive combination of heat and humidity. By my arrival in 1980, it was experiencing the type of expansion that Merseyside had enjoyed a century earlier. Houston was a place where concrete grew faster than grass.

Downtown skyscrapers seemed to pop up over-night; many of them belonged to Texas Eastern. Nonetheless, the company wasn't a household name. It had only 10,000 employees. Most of its assets were hidden below ground. As the largest pipeline company in the world, it supplied natural gas and petroleum products to both coasts. It was also the largest US supplier of propane. And to add icing to the tasty corporate cake, it owned massive reserves in the North Sea and Gulf of Mexico. Through these enterprises, my employer had more cash than it knew what to do with and had dabbled in real estate and all sorts of businesses. By the way, the first bumper sticker read: 'Honk If You're Horny for Success!'

Three years after stagnating on the dole, I had secured a dream job. Initially, it wasn't easy for me to accept my giant slice of good fortune. Deep down, I feared that I was the subject of a cunning social experiment - possibly designed by the Houston shrink - in which fresh meat in the shape of yours truly had been dropped into a corporate jungle.

The reactions to my arrival were predictable. Rather than acceptance, my presence caused skepticism, puzzlement and intrigue in no particular order. Also, it brought out the naked aggression of the alpha-types that had applied for my job. In response, I adopted the Karlsruhe approach - smile, watch, listen and nod. I could tell you that I was analyzing the corporate culture. In truth, I was trying to cull the arrogant braggarts, narcissistic complainers and manipulative bullies and confirm that the work-place was free of Kopites and others with persecution complexes.

Nonetheless, I worried that someone would spread the rumour that there had been a mistake and I had only dropped by to read the gas meter. That was until I received a leather-bound binder containing updated organizational charts of the corporation and its many subsidiaries. Tucked away on the third row on the very first page was my name. Surely the social experiment had gravitated into a bad joke. The abundance of charts indicated a highly structured corporation with little, if any, room for raw entrepreneurial spirit and that only hard work coupled with the ability to satisfy the hopes and expectations of the corporate hierarchy would keep me on the first page. I embraced the challenge. After all, I was used to turning up my sleeves while others turned up their noses or didn't turn up at all.

Within no time, I was elevated to the almost heavenly forty-fifth floor of the forty-six story building. To be honest, I didn't understand the significance of my corner office. No-one in the dole queue had mentioned it was the most coveted place in a skyscraper and a sign that I had been blessed by the corporate gods. Innocently, I was chuffed that it allowed me to view the world from two directions. My office was sterile and not the place for displaying Everton or other football knick-knacks. In contrast, my private conference room boasted a giant lithograph by Roberto Matta, the Chilean abstract surrealist, which incorporated 32 penises. I know because I've watched numerous visitors count them. Surrounded by a parliament of Willies, I earned a reputation for tackling the problems that more career-sensitive executives avoided.

The scene at the weekly executive meeting would have made my mother proud. It starred six battle-hardened veterans perched around a Texas-size boardroom table encircled by the naked ambitions of me and a half-dozen other advisers. With security guards in position and a helicopter pad on the roof, the Chief Executive would navigate the sophisticated control panel to slam and secure the massive mahogany doors, lower the microwave-proof window blinds and extinguish any hint of laughter.

All attendees were dressed for success. We wore Hart Schaffner Marx suits, Brooks Brothers cotton shirts, black socks and black Church's shoes. No snakeskin cowboy boots or rhinestone belt buckles were evident. In fact, there was nothing flashy about our uniforms — except the silk ties and the mandatory diamond encrusted watches. My plastic Casio, courtesy of H Samuel in Bootle, made a bold statement. There was another tell-tale sign that yours truly was a tad different from the other executives. Today, only aging porn stars and even older women - who have given up on life - cultivate facial hair above their upper lips. Back then, I was convinced that a manicured moustache would disguise my youth.

Mine was no ordinary tache. It looked like something borrowed from a death-row inmate or, even worse, Graeme Souness.

50. Republic of Evertonia

I'm indebted to the four men who moulded my career. They displayed such diverse strengths. My first boss – the Renaissance Man - had headed up ARCO as well as Ethyl Chemicals in his previous life and outpaced his contemporaries in his grasp of complex issues. Rarely loquacious and a patient listener, even to my tales about visits to Mama Blue, my polymath stressed that leadership wasn't about doing what was easy. It was about doing what was right.

For some reason or another, he assumed that I knew what was right and tasked me with the weight of both corporate-wide and operating responsibilities. The former included international development, new business ventures and research & development and enabled me to poke my big nose into everyone else's business from different angles. My operating subsidiaries were involved in specialty chemicals, catalysts and engineering services. They had been conceived by scientific geniuses who had registered thousands of patents and designed more than 300 chemical plants worldwide. Their founder has a building named after him on the MIT campus and their previous leader had served on the boards of ICI, BP, PowerGen and Eurotunnel. For a moment, I conveniently forgot about the minerals business which involved uranium and copper resources. I must add that some of these companies were like shaggy dogs with fleas. Their names, such as American Hydrocarbons Incorporated and US Copper Company, were more impressive than their health.

I prospered by surrounding myself with lots of people smarter than me. Believe me, that's not difficult. Recruiting highly qualified people was one thing - converting them and their egos into team-players was a bigger challenge. I imagine it takes similar skills to manage professional athletes. As you may know, many bright and successful people are over-confident. A lifetime of praise has led to an unflappable faith in their own abilities and it's hard for them to graciously accept that every now and then they may be wrong.

Given that their struggles to accept constructive feedback often leads to toxic professional relationships, I was amazed that most of them followed my directions. It helped that I'm keen to embrace the intellectual curiosities and unusual hobbies of bright colleagues. I strove to connect with many of them through their fascination with Harley-Davidson hogs, minerals and rocks, Native American tribes and the New York Yankees. And to this day, I take no little pride in being able to differentiate between Sitting Bull on an Electra Glide and Babe Ruth on an iconic Low Rider. Many demonstrated as much passion for their hobbies as someone besotted by a football club located some 5,000 miles away. In contrast, I rarely shared my love of English soccer with them. To me, Everton Football Club was more than a hobby. It provided an identity, an escape from everyday life and a sense of belonging. There were a couple of ex-pats - neither from Manchester - who supported United. They were aware that I was a royal blue fanatic and respected the fact that my club meant much more to me than their club did to them.

In the Eighties, US corporations focused on short-term financial performance and beheadings were common-place. Enter my second boss who had been responsible for his fair share of blood splatter as he climbed Texas Eastern's spiral staircase. Surprisingly for the president of a large oil & gas conglomerate, interactive decision-making wasn't one of his strengths. He managed by blending Haitian voodoo with the knack of knowing which backs to slap in order to get things done. Also, he knew which butts to kick in order to get them done faster. His uncommon methods made the long workdays fun. More often than not, we would wind down our late-night meetings talking about professional sports. The Voodoo Master was fascinated by the chemistry of winning teams, the tools employed to motivate people who possessed more money than sense and the vast divide between the in-crowd - that is the players, agents, executives and franchise owners - who earn a living from the game and those who pay for that living. He often referred to fans as stadium decorations for the benefit of US television audiences.

A keen psychologist, he was enthralled by football's impact on my makeup and claimed that Everton had been my most reliable companion during the first 35 years of my life. This boss loved social history too and was fascinated by my plans to secure football artefacts from the nineteenth century. Intrigued that Everton was the first football club to wear numbered shirts and install goal-nets, he couldn't believe that Merseysiders were playing professional sports when Texans were playing cowboys and Indians. Beneath his Kevlar veneer, I discovered that he was a compassionate humanitarian who like to remind me that what we do for ourselves dies with us, only what we do for others is remembered.

Throughout his corporate life, the Voodoo Master had encountered sycophancy from the people around him and suffered from delusions of wisdom. Fearlessly, I told him the truth - especially the inconvenient truth - about problems and their likely solutions. In the boardroom, he loved to brag about my ability to make problems vanish. He didn't know that I was simply someone who had made three correct guesses in a row. His boasts were challenged when, as a diversion and addition to my day-to-day grind, I was asked by my former-boss to put on a rodeo to entertain the delegates and their entourages attending the Twelfth World Petroleum Congress. This get-together was the Oil & Gas Olympiad. Held every four years, it involved industry leaders and political big-wigs from 100 or so countries across the globe. My rodeo qualifications weren't immediately obvious to me. I had been to one at the Texas State Penitentiary and must admit that I wasn't too keen on attending another. In very few words, I was informed by my boss that the experience would come in handy someday. Therefore, I treated the challenge as a novel examination of my executive potential.

At the prison rodeo, the male inmates volunteered to take part in calf roping, steer wrestling, bull riding and bareback-bronc riding as the highlight of their incarceration. I was mesmerized by the cowboys who climbed on to the backs of angry 2,000-pound bulls and used one hand to stay aboard for an eight-second ride. The other hand grasped a rope which was wrapped around the bull's chest and woven through his fingers to secure his grip. I was impressed equally by the female inmates who had their own event which involved something equally as dangerous with greased pigs. Within weeks I had recruited the necessary quota of professional cowboys, buxom cowgirls, courageous clowns and animals with suitably mean dispositions.

While the World Petroleum Congress was riddled with intrigue and friction, no country boycotted the rodeo. There were no political demonstrations. No cowboys were hospitalized. No animals were injured. That said, some South Americans weren't too happy. I recall that the extravaganza started with a parade in which the cowgirls rode into the arena with the flags of the participating nations held high. Because I hadn't received one from the Argentinian embassy for the dress rehearsal, I substituted my blue and white triband from Rotterdam. Though scuffed and worn, it didn't look out of place during the rehearsal or the actual parade. Yes, I forgot to exchange my Everton flag for the Argentinian ensign.

Despite my negligence, the round-up was deemed a triumph. The head of the World Petroleum Congress was delighted that delegates seemed to get along with one another. I was simply chuffed to witness visitors from China, Norway, Russia, Venezuela and even Saudi Arabia, chugging from long-necked bottles of Lone Star - the national beer of Texas - and raising their brand-new Stetson hats to the battle flag of the Republic of Evertonia.

I've been reassured the event was an unmitigated success but must add that, for one reason or another, 1987 was the only time in more than 80 years that the Oil & Gas Olympiad has been awarded to the USA.

51. Flaming fireworks

Immediately after the bull-shit had been cleaned up, I was charged with another extracurricular assignment which provided me with fleeting fame across Space City USA and the rest of the Lone Star State. Again it had nothing to do with oil or natural gas. It was another examination of my leadership prowess by the Voodoo Master. This time I was saddled with organizing the grand opening of his pet project - the George Brown Convention Center, which is a massive complex with 1.8 million square feet of air-conditioned floor space named after the founder of Texas Eastern. Again he advised: 'You'll draw on this experience some day.'

The City of Houston had planned a Texas-size bash to celebrate its new Texas-size building. Without informing his fellow directors and for reasons known only to his voodoo doll, my boss had engaged an obscure Italian company that specialized in Baroque fireworks. Clearly, he was unaware of the logistics involved in importing unlicensed handmade explosives. After I had arranged for their trans-Atlantic transportation in a specialized munitions ship, military-type vehicles escorted the convoy of trucks carrying them from the docks in Montreal to a storage facility in Houston, which was protected by an electrified fence and patrolled by armed guards and extremely nasty-looking dogs. It was a lot of planning and worrying for an extravaganza that lasted precisely 23 minutes and 25 seconds.

Synchronized with Tchaikovsky's 'Capriccio Italien' performed by the strings, wind, brass, and percussion of a 75-strong symphony orchestra, the colours and sounds of the fireworks dazzled the one million spectators more than any Fourth of July celebrations. My wife suspected that it was my special way of applauding Everton's second title in three seasons - which had been secured earlier that year. She was right. Never before has a club's ascendancy been lauded so spectacularly. The artillery shells were propelled from 12-inch diameter pipes sunk deep into the earth. More than a few of them had 'Southall', 'Sharp' and 'Reid' as well as 'In bocca al lupo Sig Kendall' chalked on their sides by friendly Italian hands. They soared 1,000 feet before crackling into mystical shapes. Royal purples changed to titanium yellows and sapphire blues; metallic fuchsias sparkled into radical magentas and cosmic silvers. The final explosion was unforgettable. Liquid fire filled the heavens as if commanded by some celestial hand.

To ensure public safety, I arranged for the suspension of flights from both Houston airports and the closure of the freeways circling downtown. Nevertheless, the event wasn't without incident. There was a couple of shootings - which is common when Texans and strong alcohol get together - and an international fall-out between the Italian pyro-maestro and American music-maestro. Though skilled at massaging prima donnas and aware that many egos fail to understand why other egos don't think the way they do, I couldn't get them to talk directly to each other. The biggest unexpected problem was the cloud of smoke which followed the display. It wasn't an issue for the audience. However, the Neville Brothers - not Phil and Gary but Aaron and his siblings in the New Orleans rock band - suffered some distress. Also chunks of space debris showered Chinatown where the Voodoo Master claimed that fiery objects descending from the skies were considered lucky.

The extravaganza wasn't as expensive as the opening of the London Olympics but, at a cost equivalent to 100,000 barrels of crude oil, was a ridiculously wasteful undertaking. Worse still, the expenditure was poorly timed. It coincided with a glut of OPEC production which triggered petroleum prices and Texas Eastern's stock price to tumble. With no little irony, shortly afterwards I was tasked with slashing operating costs via a worldwide profit improvement initiative. The concept of austerity was alien to my boss. As you know by now, I'm a master of understatement. The tone of the kick-off meeting highlighted the challenge ahead of me. In any other US company, the carcass of the business would be dragged into the boardroom and the assembled executives would use scalpels to scrape every morsel of fat from its bones.

By comparison when Texas Eastern's plump Thanksgiving bird was wheeled onto the forty-sixth floor, our top men reacted by slapping one another on the back. I thought I heard one reciting verse: 'May our stuffing be tasty; may our turkey plump. May our gravy never lump. May our spuds be tasty and our pumpkin pies take the prize. And may our feast stay off our thighs.' It took a month or so to get their attention and much longer to generate $200 million in annual savings. No-one remembers this accomplishment but everyone reminisces about the flaming fireworks.

My next boss was a young man who wore his genius with little if any humility. He was destined for something special. What that was nobody quite knew. Given my experience in buying and selling assets and discovering skeletons in closets, he tasked me with developing a blueprint for the corporation's future. I needed no encouragement to focus my strategic plan on expanding our traditional core businesses at the expense of oil exploration and production, oil refining, oil field services, minerals and real estate interests. At the same time, he was fine-tuning his own master plans for navigating the white heat of international world business. Indeed, he progressed to serve on the board of directors of BP, BHP Billiton, BAE Systems and Qantas Airlines. I learnt something important from our brief collaboration - not every American likes association football. Without fear of contradiction, I can say that he had the psyche of the most ardent soccer atheist. Therefore I never ever talked to him about my love of Everton and the beautiful game. It would have been a waste of my breath.

My promotion was announced shortly after Enron Corporation had been formed by Inter-North's acquisition of Houston Natural Gas in the mid-Eighties. It was an extremely timely merger. The US natural gas industry was about to be deregulated. Significant change lay ahead and our counterparts at Enron addressed the new opportunities with unwavering innovation and revolutionized the way in which all pipeline companies conducted their business. Within no time at all, US energy markets became far more competitive and Enron was lauded as the world's dominant trader. Predictably, its share price soared above that of Texas Eastern on Wall Street. Our chairman - a neighbour of Ken Lay the infamous leader of our new adversary - would ask: 'How on earth can Enron afford to do this in Louisiana? How in hell can Enron make so much money from their activities in India?' Though he expected a detailed analysis, my riposte was always the same: 'Beats me. There must be something in the water at 1400 Smith Street.'

A decade later, he and the rest of the world discovered that our rival's water was non-potable and its management had committed the crime of the century. You may recall that many of their reported profits were either inflated or nonexistent. From all accounts, Enron's demise was a result of bad habits, flawed values and - let's be blunt - criminal fraud and other illegal acts that spiralled out of control. And let's no forget the weak and sloppy auditing by Arthur Andersen. It wasn't a victimless scenario. The more ambitious members of my staff - who were lured to Smith Street by a smorgasbord of higher salaries, mouth-watering perks and opulent offices - lost their pensions when Enron's shares dropped to junk status.

52. Good time to be a Blue

My business career coincided with the most successful spell in our illustrious history. Was it happenstance or some strange synchronicity? No, the credit belongs to one man and one man only - Howard Kendall.

I was at LAX airport, scouring the newspapers for the result of our encounter at Molineux, when I read that Gordon Lee had been a casualty of our neighbours getting better and better while his expensively-assembled side was sinking in the other direction. I had a soft spot for Lee and had been convinced that his tactics of hard running and hustling would capture the title. I recall that we finished third in 1978. Also we enjoyed an 18-game unbeaten run at the start of the following season and topped the table in February 1979 before faltering and finishing fourth. As I digested the news of his dismissal, I discovered that God had intervened and blessed Goodison with one of his own. I loved Howard. Given his self-effacing charm, it was easy to do so. Not for one minute can I overlook that he left us on three occasions and was responsible for one unwanted flirtation with relegation. Nor can I ignore his Mickey Mantle-like fondness for red wine which, allegedly, on one occasion required Gary Speed to give the half-time talk because the manager was incapable of speech. The man that I admired was a top-class footballer who matured into a master alchemist equipped with the knack for blending young legs with old heads into trophy-winning sides.

Much like his predecessors Bingham and Lee, I expected Howard to be given three or so seasons to return the club to the top. His early days in the hot-seat were not promising. In particular, his scattergun approach to recruitment had yielded one hit and too many duds. To their credit, the club's directors remained patient while the new gaffer fine-tuned his formula. It was such a fitful process that Howard decided to put his playing boots on again. I wasn't privileged to see him as a player-manager. If his performances were anything like the ones he produced after the exits of Alan Ball and Colin Harvey then they must have been phenomenal. People forget that he single-handedly kept us in the top flight in 1973.

All Blues are conscious of his darkest afternoon in 1982 when he oversaw a 5-0 thrashing in the Goodison derby. Yes, it was the game in which Ian Rush scored four and Mark Lawrenson netted the other. The sickening spectacle still gives me sleepless nights. Local lore blames Glenn Keeley for the humiliation even though he had left the scene of the crime after 25 minutes. I'm convinced that dark times make us more committed to the cause. After that debacle, Blues dug deep into that special place where our passion lives and nothing is impossible. The remainder found other things to do and home gates dropped to below 20,000 for the next 12 months.

From the other side of the Atlantic Ocean I could hear Mama Blue: 'You don't have to visit but I'm here if you need me.' In response, I embraced Goodison as my corner of paradise. Possibly, I was hankering for somewhere that didn't or couldn't exist and found comfort in the unchanged surroundings as a time capsule - a taste of yesteryear. It provided a cathartic escape from the stresses of the oil & gas jungle. My wife referred to it as stress-busting therapy – a special kind of royal blue yoga. I remember attending the League Cup tie against Chesterfield when we scraped a 2-2 draw in front of 8,000 at Goodison. You could hear the players shouting encouragement to one other. As a teenager, I had been to Central League games with noisier crowds. It was around that time that I accepted reluctantly what the football world had known for the past 10 years - Everton had slipped behind Liverpool.

I can recall a Southampton fan questioning my heartfelt opinion that the Merseyside giants shared equal standing. His ridicule forced me to examine the records of the clubs. It wasn't pretty reading. The Reds had won the League title in 1973, '76, '77, '79, '80 and '82 plus the FA Cup in 1974 and the League Cup in 1981 and '82.

Then there was the not-so-small matter of them conquering the Continent with triumphs in the UEFA Cup in 1973 and '76 followed by those in the European Cup in 1977, '78 and '81. The only thing that Everton picked up during this period was bitterness related to the antics of Clive Thomas. As for silverware, we captured sweet nothing.

Media claims that the turnaround occurred during the course of a League Cup tie at Oxford in early 1983 are inaccurate. It happened at a near-empty St Andrews a few weeks earlier. I saw it with my own eyes. After a grim and goalless Christmas period, in which we lost 3-0 at Wolverhampton - who were bottom of the League, and drew 0-0 at home to both Sunderland and Coventry, we looked like a very good side in Birmingham. I didn't question what I saw that day. I simply appreciated it. Howard had found the right blend or perhaps some magic dust.

History books show that we progressed to the 1984 Milk Cup final against Liverpool but not that we were robbed. Nevertheless, I was confident that we were primed for something special. And a couple of months later we defeated Watford to lift the FA Cup, our first trophy after a hiatus of 14 years. It was a terrific time to be a Blue. Howard's next season was more productive. Driven on by Andy Gray and Peter Reid, two veterans from football's top drawer, Everton went from strength to strength. We dominated opponents and captured the League title in comfort. Aside from the individual brilliance of the world's finest goalkeeper, there were no super-stars - we were simply a balanced team of great footballers with enormous hearts, indefatigable work-rates and a rare willingness to fight for one another.

It's worth repeating — the mid-Eighties were a tremendous time to be a Blue.

Doctor, there's a Kopite who saw Sharp's goal with the same symptoms

53. Good times zipped by

One highlight of the campaign was Graeme Sharp's winner at Anfield. After witnessing that wonder goal, I remember thinking: 'What I've just seen can't be unseen. It will stay with me forever.'

The goal is in good company. Many spectacular ones come to mind. Of those that I witnessed live, Alex Young's header over Tottenham's Bill Brown makes my top dozen. In 1962, I thought it would never ever be equalled. Recently, I saw a video recording in which it didn't appear quite as magnificent as I had remembered. Mike Trebilcock's superb leveller at Wembley remains undimmed by time. It was responsible for the most famous one-man pitch in the history of the FA Cup final. Then there was the sensational swing of his left peg by Diniyar Bilyaletdinov against Portsmouth. It was the final and arguably the most sensational kick of the 2009/10 season. That goal wasn't quite as eye-catching as the famed 20-yard scorcher from Andy King against Liverpool. The goal was as unforgettable as the roar that greeted it. Some 20 years later in the relegation battle against Coventry, Gareth Farrelly struck the ball from the same spot into the same top-right corner of the Park End net. Of course, it was greeted by a collective sigh of relief.

And how about Kevin Sheedy's free-kick at Anfield, one of many sublime strikes from his magical left foot? The goal in 1987 is remembered more for his celebration than the free-kick itself. And how can you forget the glorious technique exhibited by 16 year-old Wayne Rooney to end Arsenal's 30-game unbeaten run? Another cracker was Leon Osman's goal against Larissa. It involved an exceptional move in which Cahill passed to Baines, who crossed to Pienaar, who set up the goal-scorer with a back-heel. Osman's shot was exceptional. And what about James McFadden's exquisite skill and execution against Charlton? Absolutely breath-taking.

My three favourites? Graeme Sharp's 30-yard strike past Bruce Grobbelaar, which secured our first win at Anfield for 14 years. Simply spine-tingling. How can you beat that derby-winning thunderbolt? Incredibly, Andy Gray and pals did it twice against Sunderland later that season. Gray's headed efforts, just four minutes apart, were mind-blowing and confirmed that, at that moment in time, Goodison was at the vortex of the football world. As for the very best of the best? I was standing in the Paddock adjacent to where Paul Bracewell clipped the ball to Peter Reid in the action leading to the first goal. The fluency of the move was remarkable. The cross by Reid and finish by Gray were things of rare beauty - the finest goal I've seen at Goodison.

I feel fortunate to have seen Sharp's goal with my own eyes. Thoughts of it silencing the Kop kept me warm the next morning as I flew to Northern Norway. For those of you lucky enough never to have been there, Tromso is a town located 200 miles inside the Arctic Circle. In the winter, when the sun rises at 10:00 am and sets at 2:00 pm, it is miserable. Upon my arrival I noticed that the Viking Reds were more frigid than usual. Possibly, it had something to do with the inflated prices of smoked reindeer and aquavit. Probably, it had more to do with our derby triumph. Tromso is a great spot to view the curtains of iridescent green shimmering across the sky caused by the solar winds entering the earth's atmosphere at the magnetic North Pole. I wasn't there to marvel at the Northern Lights. As part of an industrial cooperation initiative with the Norwegian government, I had structured a joint venture to exchange our seabed geochemical technology for brownie points towards oil exploration licenses. I had planned to spend seven days there but after witnessing so much squabbling among the other partners, I set off immediately for Egypt where we were having problems collecting monies after the commissioning of a major chemical plant.

Based near Alexandria, the complex produced ammonium nitrate. I'd expected to wait for hours before being granted an audience with the company hierarchy. To my surprise the president was punctual. Also he was a connoisseur of English football and proclaimed: 'Sharp kicks like a Bedouin's camel.'

Aware that the locals believed the dromedary had been blessed by Allah, I took his description as a complement. So instead of a bout of international arm-wrestling over money, I offered him an eye-witness account and retreated with a receipt from a multi-million dollar wire transfer and a grossly-inflated opinion of my negotiating skills.

In good times and in bad times I placed business ahead of football during the workday. Only once did I plan to realign my priorities. I must confess that I had hoped to return from Cairo circuitously via Bratislava, where we were due to play in the Cup-Winners' Cup, meet up with my Good Samaritan - remember Dr Zima? - and then travel to the United Kingdom, where we were scheduled to host United at the weekend. I telephoned Houston from the Egypt Air check-in desk and received the following instructions from my boss: 'Drop by Kuala Lumpur while you're in that neck of the woods!' Possibly the size of Texas had distorted his concept of distance.

Texas Eastern had been invited to construct a natural gas pipeline through the rainforest jungle to Singapore and I was required to lead the preliminary negotiations. Mercifully, my stay in Malaysia was brief and buoyed by the news that we had beaten Internacional Bratislava. It was developing into a good week until I discovered that all of the local prayer mats were pointed towards Old Trafford. Even 25 years ago, Malaysia was teeming with young Red Devils. The United badge plus images of Bryan Robson and Mark Hughes were everywhere. Never before had I seen toilet seats painted in a club's colours. My wife may disagree; I like to think that it was the first time that I didn't lift the seat before urinating. Definitely, it was the only time I've heard a taxi driver declare: 'Supporting Everton will lead to a slow and painful death.'

Because the construction project was both ambitious and expensive, the parties scheduled a brain-storming session with the money men in San Francisco to determine the required financial guarantees. It was Friday lunchtime before I left California for the old country where I arrived just in time to witness Everton maul United 5-0. Surely, life couldn't get any better for a Blue? The next day, I completed my circumnavigation of the globe by returning to Norway. As I listened to the Viking Reds bickering about how best to pillage the North Sea, I was tingling not from jet lag but from the realization that we had beaten the red shirts of Liverpool and Manchester in the same week. For the record, I was still in Norway a few days later when we unceremoniously dumped United from the League Cup.

The good times zip by. Thank goodness their memories linger. Our football was telepathic. Its quality approached that of Kendall, Harvey & Ball. Our team was so good that visiting teams arrived at Goodison in fear of a good hiding. Hand on heart, I was convinced that we were destined to grab the unparalleled treble of League title, FA Cup and European Cup-Winner's Cup.

Indeed months later, with the title captured, one of my American colleagues accompanied me to the Netherlands for our first Euro-final even though I refused to buy him a ticket. My rationale was that I didn't want him to deny any Blue the opportunity to witness history. My colleague bought one from a German tout and, from the other end of the stadium, claimed to have been intimidated by the passion of the Blues as we triumphed. With two trophies in the bag and the treble within our grasp, we were expected to wrap up the season with an FA Cup final victory. Our prospects looked even more promising when United were reduced to 10 men after 75 minutes. Sadly, we didn't take advantage of the extra man and lost to Norman Whiteside's goal in extra-time when winning seemed inevitable. His curling shot around Pat van den Hauwe and Kevin Ratcliffe and beyond the reach of Neville Southall into the far corner was a spectacular effort. So much so that few Blues complained at the time. As for my American colleague, he thought that it was unfair for a team to take part in two major sporting events within 72 hours.

54. Two titles in three seasons

The 1985/86 season ended in tears when Kenny Dalglish's Reds rather than Howard Kendall's Blues became only the fifth club to win the double. It's likely that the outcomes in the League and FA Cup would have been different if Neville Southall hadn't damaged his ankle ligaments while on international duty. Before the keeper's injury, the reigning champions were 11 points ahead with only 11 League games to play. Our slide started at Luton in March when our usually water-tight defence shipped two late and sloppy goals. The following month, we forfeited our crown by drawing at Nottingham and losing to another late goal at Oxford. I've heard that Gary Lineker's favourite boots literally went missing at the Manor Ground. Some claim that Nana Mouskouri borrowed them. Fact or fantasy, he had to wear new ones and missed a couple of decent scoring chances that could have retained the League title.

As for the heart-breaking reality of the FA Cup final at Wembley, Everton suffered stage fright. Leading at half-time thanks to a Lineker goal, we weren't only rampant - we had our opponents fighting amongst themselves. Then we choked and allowed Jan Molby and Ian Rush to shred our dreams. By the final whistle, some of the Blues around me were traumatized. It was the first time that I had observed grown men blubbering about the pendulum swinging towards Anfield. I'm aware that a man's tears are fine in a hospital delivery room or at a funeral but is weeping at Wembley acceptable?

It had been a long and exhausting season in which we played 60 or more first-class games but to compound our disappointments Everton sold Lineker to Barcelona during the summer. To this day, it seems absurd that an ambitious club would sell its top striker, especially after a highly productive first season during which he netted 38 times in 52 games. Despite the club investing the funds in signing Dave Watson and Ian Snodin, I approached the new campaign with more than a little apprehension. I feared that injuries to key men, namely Bracewell, Reid, Sheedy, Stevens, Southall and van den Hauwe would undermine the rediscovery of our trophy-winning ways. Indeed, we appeared to dawdle through most of the season before striking a rich vein of form with a dozen fixtures remaining. Except for an off-day at Anfield, we trounced all opponents and were crowned champions with a handsome nine-point cushion over our local foes.

With two League titles in three seasons, our future looked bright - make that incandescently bright - until we suffered the truly catastrophic blow of Howard Kendall moving to Bilbao. He was a giant Blue, a genuine gentleman and our greatest-ever manager. Nonetheless, I still feel let down by him and by the directors who failed to stop him from leaving. Years later, after we became friends, I told Howard that he had ripped at my heart using a blunt knife with a grudge and should have stayed to build a dynasty. His departure heralded a decline in our fortunes. Managers come and go; some all too quickly and some not quickly enough. A good manager like Harry Catterick takes his team to the river and makes it drink. A great one like Howard Kendall makes his team thirsty. He was a hard act to follow. Like all Blues, I considered Colin Harvey to be Howard Kendall's natural successor. Unfortunately, our expectations were so inflated that he was replaced after taking us to two Wembley finals - we lost both in extra-time - and finishing 4th, 6th and 8th in the League. Colin was sacked in 1990 after our worst-ever start to a league season. I was saddened but not surprised. I remember the game at Maine Road. City, under the management of Howard Kendall, fielded five former-Blues and won 1-0. The goal, scored by Adrian Heath, placed us firmly at the bottom of the table.

It's an old adage that football managers should never go back. Nonetheless, I was excited when Howard Kendall Mark 2, as Blues like to call him, returned to the Goodison hot-seat, especially with Colin at his side. Wary that perfection gained once is rarely repeated, I expected that we would be fighting for the title sooner rather than later. Sadly, I was wrong. Their magic had deserted them.

My frequent references to Liverpool Football Club and its followers may hint that I'm jealous of their success. I'm not. In truth, I'm in awe of their achievements. I hope not to appear obsessed with them. Again, I'm not. I just like to push the buttons of people who are homo-erotically excited by old photographs of Stevie G in his Liverpool kit.

Our period of ascendancy under the guidance of Howard Kendall Mark 1 and Colin Harvey was tremendous but fleeting compared to the continued success of our neighbours. Brace yourself mentally for more unpleasant stats. The Reds won the title in 1983, '84, '86, '88 and '90, the FA Cup in 1986, '89 and '92, and the League Cup in 1983 and '84. They added another European Cup in 1984. I found the stats sobering before it dawned on me that there is much more to supporting a football club than the quest for trophies. It was a rather novel outlook because in the eyes of the football world, we - like every other English club - lived in the shadows of Liverpool Football Club.

Now where was I? Back in 1991, I had a premonition that all wasn't well under Howard Kendall Mark 2. It occurred at Luton. First of all, my plane arrived late at Gatwick. Next, my Hertz car wouldn't start. Then panic took over amid the congestion on sections of the M25 motorway. It peaked when I discovered that all tickets were reserved for registered members of the Luton Hatters' Club. To my surprise, away fans had been banned or discouraged from visiting Kenilworth Road. The capacity of the dilapidated stadium was about 14,000 at the time and I thought its owners would welcome every single penny. I walked around the outside of the ground to discover clusters of Blues that had been denied entry. Obviously I needed to be resourceful. I appealed to different turnstile operators to squeeze me in and even resorted to bribery without success. Like a hoodie outside an off-license, I begged around the main reception area and skulked near the players' entrance before a spotty youth in a muddy Luton tracksuit put his head around the door. He handed me an envelope: 'Mr Simpson? These are for you.' He disappeared before I could identify myself. Now my wife would have made every effort to track down the real Mr Simpson. Not me. Immediately, I set about finding three other Blues to share my windfall.

The Main stand was so full that we had to occupy Mr Simpson's premium seats near the half-way line. I must admit that I had a nagging sense of foreboding. Something wasn't right. When I gazed at the pitch, I noticed that our players were wearing Luton's orange kit with brown tape masking the Vauxhall logo. Apparently, someone didn't know that our change kit was similar to our hosts' home colours. Guilt is such a heavy burden that I kept looking over my shoulder expecting an angry Mr Simpson to claim his seats at any minute. He didn't and everything went smoothly until about 20 minutes from the end. That was when winger Robert Warzycha dispatched one of the most clinically executed strikes I've ever seen. It was a beauty. Our quartet reacted simultaneously. We shot out of our seats straight into the arms of the stewards. As we were escorted from the ground, I cursed Luton Football Club.

I regret to inform you that my jinx worked because the Hatters were relegated at the end of that season. It was the start of a slippery slope for them because the last time I cared to look they were playing in the Blue Square Premier League or somewhere similar.

55. Paisley RIP

Back to our loveable neighbours. The Houston area has always been a popular oasis for oil industry nomads. People arrive from places across the globe and stay awhile before leaving for other places across the globe. Most of them, irrespective of geographic origin, support Liverpool or Man U - that's how they refer to Manchester United.

One wayfarer, an acquaintance of my wife, planned to accompany her husband, a Red from Newcastle - I know, you couldn't make it up - on a short-term assignment in Columbia and begged Elizabeth to mind their family cat. Even though the red tabby possessed a gentle temperament, I wasn't keen. It had green eyes - one of which was shifty, the other lazy. After an incident-free get-together with Wellington, our American cocker spaniel, we agreed to take care of Paisley.

I'm not a cat lover. Neither was our dog. When the fluffy feline threw herself onto the carpet and rolled around like Arjen Robben, my wife claimed she was expressing her love for us. When she purred like a badly-tuned diesel engine, my better half said she was trying to seduce us. While I can't speak for man's best friend, I wasn't impressed by her antics. Elizabeth was more understanding when the cat abandoned her faux diamond collar and cavorted around naked. It was only when she started to shred the curtains like One Minute Harrison with a pair of sharp scissors that Paisley lost her sponsor and was given a verbal warning that she was scratching the hand that fed her.

Neither Wellington nor I was surprised when our guest skedaddled within 48 hours. Convinced that Paisley was hiding nearby, my wife spent hours calling her name. Still confident of the return of the collarless cat, she placed fresh tuna at the back-door and taped posters to telephone poles. After searching high and low, her hopes turned into fears that the domestic feline wouldn't survive in the woods inhabited by armadillos, skunks and snakes. My pessimism was reflected by a simple wooden cross. On its horizontal member I had scribbled 'Paisley RIP'.

To heighten our discomfort, Geordie Red's wife airmailed treats at regular intervals. These included clockwork mice that scurried across the carpet, catnip-scented balls and the type of ribbons that cats love to bat around with their claws. My better half didn't have the heart to confess that Paisley was missing - presumed dead. A couple of months later, Geordie Red and his wife returned from South America holding a new pet carrier in one hand and an Inca scratching post in the other. With sadness in her eyes, Elizabeth showed them the glittering collar and wooden cross which had been placed in a flower bed. She explained that Paisley had passed away peacefully in her sleep. The words sat awkwardly on her tongue. I'm aware of the intense bond that most people share with their pets and the sadness when a beloved one dies. Everyone grieves differently. Therefore I added: 'Do you have any more little Kopites for us to look after?'

I've never been one to seek the company of ex-pats. Actually, I've squirmed at their failure to grasp that when you move from one country to another some things are better and other things are worse. I embraced many of the interests of my adopted land and showed more than a passing interest in country music, BBQ and baseball. As you know, I had no input into selecting my football team. On contrast, I had my pick of all 30 MLB teams. Yet again, I resorted to eeny-meeny-miney-mo. Certainly, no-one can call me a glory hunter because I rejected the glamour of the Dodgers and Yankees in favour of the Astros. Why? Well, Houston's finest were everything that the Toffees weren't. They played in an air-conditioned dome lauded as the Eighth Wonder of the World and wore truly garish uniforms highlighted by a rainbow of hoops. The young franchise were habitual under-performers. To this day, Houston's record is one of the most fruitless in baseball. They have won one National League pennant in 56 seasons. Nothing else.

I watched them about 10 times a year but preferred to listen to play-by-play commentaries during my evening commute. Veteran Gene Elston - the Voice of the Astros, and Milo Hamilton knew when not to talk and allow radio listeners to hear the sounds of the ball-park such as the crack of the Louisville Slugger as it made contact with the baseball and the eruption of the crowd after the ball cleared the fence. Within no time, I became familiar with the game's nuances and thought that I knew something about baseball, perhaps in the same way that so-called Man U fans know something about football.

Oklahoma Crude was an Astros fanatic with premium season-tickets behind home-plate. Every Monday before our corporate management meeting, I was required to update him on the state of the company. Always, we concluded with talk of the weekend's sinkers, sliders and knuckleballs. By the way, the latter pitch creates vortices over the stitched seams of the ball during its trajectory, which causes it to change direction in mid-flight. I imagine Leighton Baines does something very similar at set-pieces. Now and then he would make reference to soccer as a game for butch women who can't comprehend the subtleties of baseball. He had made up his mind that it was synonymous with Mexican skulduggery, Italian bellyaching and English violence.

He was horrified that 55 people had perished in the Bradford fire and disgusted by the events at Heysel two weeks later. On several occasions, he asked me to explain the so-called English disease. It was impossible. From my experience, whenever large groups of males get together under the influence of alcohol there is the potential for disorder, regardless of whether a football match or a child's birthday party is taking place. I believe that football grounds have always been safer than the average town centre on a Saturday night. He remained unconvinced. In his mind, English soccer fans were hooligans with a capital H. Actually, he wasn't too impressed by Englishmen in general and often referred to them as a nation of functioning alcoholics who liked to cross-dress in private. Predictably, he despised Scotsmen who he thought were antisocial drunks who liked to wear women's clothing in public.

By and large, the US media exaggerated the hooliganism problem. This was evident when I dragged an American colleague to Fratton Park. He had never been to a soccer match and was apprehensive. We stood in the Milton Road End which was open to the elements and light years away from the sanitized Astrodome. Besides Graeme Sharp netting the winner, he was not impressed - especially after the Portsmouth stewards detained all visitors for 15 minutes after the final whistle. My colleague postulated that the local constabulary's assumption that all visiting fans are inherently dangerous could become a self-fulfilling prophecy. I'm sure that the Hampshire Police thought it was for his own good. They may have felt the same way about the broken glass and barbed wire fixed to the top of the stadium walls.

To my relief, there was no violence, no pitch invasions and no pools of blood on our way to the car. Deep down, I think my colleague was disappointed. Throughout our journey to Central London he complained about his loss of liberty and the violation of his human rights. At one point, he threatened to send a letter of complaint to Amnesty International.

56. Heavy breathing

Remember Oklahoma Crude — indisputably the most pragmatic executive in the oil & gas industry? At one meeting, I made the mistake of mentioning that I had planned to watch baseball at the Astrodome that weekend before getting tied up in the congestion associated with the Houston Marathon. Even worse, I hypothesized that long- distance running was all in the mind. My exact words were: 'Anyone with our mental toughness can run 26.2 miles. Even I could do it.'

I had forgotten about my bravado until an entry form for the next Houston Marathon appeared in my internal mail. Deep inside I had admired people who could reach down and come up with the strength to complete such a daunting challenge. As a 40-year-old with dubious athletic abilities, I thought of the marathon as something best reserved for masochists who gain pleasure from pushing themselves to the point of physical exhaustion. I scrutinized the entry form and toyed with two alternatives. Either I could cite my childhood accident in which my right ankle was mangled in the bicycle wheel or I could take up jogging. With four months to the race day, I decided on the latter. So out of shape that my inner thighs chafed together as if covered in Velcro, I enrolled in an aerobics class at the gym. I twisted, gyrated and perspired for a half-hour. By the time that I squeezed into my kit, the class was almost over.

Houston is hot and humid even in September. It was 90-odd degrees when I set off on my first training session. My goal was one circuit of the roads through my neighbourhood. About two miles. Even though that sounds like a piece of cake, my brand spanking new Adidas footwear stopped three times during the first mile and walked the final one. I concluded that jogging provides a warm glow and a feeling of being at one with the Texas sun. More important, I resorted to eating more pasta and, possibly, my words. The next week I turned to what I knew best. That's right, you guessed it - I read a book. 'Jeff Galloway's Book on Running' offered a training timetable for the novice and practical advice on diet, fluid intake and the psychological aspects of endurance activities. Stimulated by his words of encouragement, I soon mastered two miles then four miles and finally six miles without stopping.

Ill-prepared for 26.2 miles, I re-read the book's checklist: buy quality shoes - tick; lubricate body parts - tick; drink plenty of water - tick; do lots of jogging - cross. Apparently, a marathon is 500 miles long. The race is just the final 26.2 of them. Much more training was required. Indeed, Galloway claimed that to run a marathon you must have completed one long run of 20 miles to store glycogen in your muscles. The next day I tested my hypothesis that long-distance running is all in the mind. By chance, I lived 25 miles from my downtown office and set off at 3:30 am on a genuine long run to work. Amazingly there was traffic at that dark hour, mostly pick-up trucks heading home from honky-tonks. No doubt they had contributed to the road-kill, better known as the carcasses of skunks and armadillos, which dotted my path. To relieve the boredom, I picked up every coin I discovered at the roadside. For the record, this amounted to two dimes and 14 cents by the time I ran out of steam in one of Houston's more notorious areas.

My Dixie Dean t-shirt was a revelation in the Yale ghetto, a part of North Houston renowned for the citizens killing one another as though it was an Olympic sport. That's right, it was the type of high-crime neighborhood where the houses have wheels and the cars don't. Even before sunrise, it boasted hookers on the corners of Jensen Drive and drug dealers slinging outside the convenience store. The working girls, who were so ugly that they had to sneak up on a glass of water to get a drink, yelled racial abuse. The other locals enquired: 'Yo! Who da fuck is Dixie?' Definitely, it was the wrong place for me to explain that my grandfather had lauded him as the greatest-ever centre-forward or that his name was derived from the Mason-Dixon Line which had separated the free and slave states. Not surprisingly, I developed a Messerschmitt twitch as I shuffled over to the public pay phone and appealed to my secretary to come and get me.

That January, I completed the Houston Marathon. It wasn't a pretty sight. After crawling into work the next day, I made no reference to my ordeal or that I had been overtaken in the home stretch by a man wearing only a Ronald Reagan mask and tie-dye underpants. Before we set off for the executive meeting, my boss smiled: 'What else did you do yesterday?' He had been monitoring my progress for four months and concurred that the mental toughness honed at Texas Eastern made long-distance running easy and by staying relaxed and positive you can handle anything. In total, I managed to haul myself around 97 marathon courses during a 10-year period. I flitted between the middle and the back of the pack. I've no reason to brag about my times except that I ran in Boston having met the 3 hours 15 minutes prerequisite. Besides fleeting senses of accomplishment, my reward was a mountain of donations to various charities and a pile of colourful cotton t-shirts. They were converted into four quilts, big enough for California king-size beds, and donated to a homeless shelter in Vancouver, BC. It was repayment for the patchwork one supplied by the Canadian Red Cross during my childhood.

In the remote chance that you are inspired to attempt a marathon, here is something for you to pin on your kitchen wall and read before opening the fridge door. Everything you ever wanted to know about yourself, you can learn during the race. Without question, the person who starts isn't the same as the one who finishes it. There are three phases. The first involves scheduled training sessions and abundant Vaseline. If you can run eight miles without walking then you should be able to complete the marathon course, regrettably in some agony. To run in comfort you must average four miles per day and have completed the long run prescribed by Galloway. Phase 2 involves running to the 20-mile marker in a good state of mind and body. To do this you must learn to maintain a rhythm and overcome boredom. Many chat with fellow runners. Some visualize pleasant thoughts. Others count their strides per mile. I even know someone who hallucinates about the value of pi.

At some point you will hit the dreaded wall, this is when your glycogen levels are at their lowest and you struggle to take the next step. Fear not, if you've slept soundly and carbo-loaded the night before, drunk plenty of water and maintained your usual pace then the ordeal will be fleeting. In Phase 3, the challenge is overcome the Wall - which evades definition but, like other things, you know it when you hit it - and endure 6.2 miles of excruciating pain and debilitating tiredness. The less masochistic of runners must learn to forget about exhaustion, muscle aches, blisters and nipple chafing and accept that the pain is simply weakness leaving their bodies. Drained of physical and emotional strength, you will hear the words of unknown cheerleaders: 'Looking good. You can do it!' Then there are the signs such as 'Pain is temporary, pride is forever' and 'Black toenails are sexy'. I recommend that you ignore them. The final 10,000 metres are all about disciplined breathing and good posture.

Regarding strategy, unless you're an elite runner from Kenya's Rift Valley, start towards the back and run at your own pace - not someone else's. The target for most first-timers is to complete the course. The more ambitious hope to better the time taken by Oprah Winfrey at 4 hours 29 minutes. I remember passing her - or rather her posse of bodyguards - during the Marine Corps Marathon in Washington, DC. The only other celebrity that I've encountered with a similar entourage was Jimmy Savile. The yet-to-be-disgraced disc jockey was chatty with runners and spectators during the Leeds Marathon. He wore a gold tracksuit and gold bangles to augment his peroxide dyed locks. He looked like an old Kopite. As I overtook Mr Fixit, he emitted the type of strange yodel that only a Liverpool fan from Yorkshire could make. I assumed he made it with his mouth. If you want to brag about your time, you must improve your respiratory capacity, cadence and stamina. I discovered that I ran faster with a Body Mass Index below 20 - somewhere around welterweight. To get there, my diet involved eating only apples - preferably the Granny Smith and Golden Delicious varieties. It was a poorly-disguised approach to starvation.

As for kit, I never considered myself worthy to wear the club's official colours. When competing, I preferred a white tee-shirt. Acquired at Widnes Market, it had been customized masterfully by Ma Carsley. Both sleeves had been removed for aerodynamic purposes. 'Ev-er-ton' had been printed on the front and 'Slow but raised as an Evertonian by an Evertonian' added to the back. I'm told that all true wisdom is found on such cotton garments. For example, 'Kopites are Gobshites' - been there, done that, got the Vaseline-soaked shirt. I trust you understand that this off-colour message is just a bit of good-humoured razzing and ribbing. Honest.

Running marathons is much like supporting Everton in the Premier League era. At the start you know that you're not going to win, finish second or even third. Still, you expect exuberant support as you battle on. For this reason alone, my best-loved run is the New York Marathon. The crowds throughout Staten Island, Brooklyn and Queens create a carnival atmosphere. And nothing beats the cacophony which greets the runners as they turn into First Avenue and head through Manhattan towards Harlem and the Bronx. The noise reverberates between the skyscrapers and I've never failed to hear pockets of spectators shouting 'Ev-er-ton … Ev-er-ton … Ev-er-ton'. If one or two start the chant, it's amazing that others join in. Possibly they had read my t-shirt or more likely had enjoyed 'Blood Brothers' the night before.

So much for my advice; two weeks after completing my ninety-sixth marathon I experienced profuse sweating, excruciating chest pain which extended to my abdomen and a shortness of breath. Yes, it was a real heart attack. Myocardial infarction was an uninvited running companion. I was fortunate because I had ignored the same symptoms one week earlier. Confined to a hospital bed with my body hooked up to an assortment of medical tubes, I feared that I would never see my nearest and dearest again. I'll let you decide who I'm referring to. Fortunately, I didn't require angioplasty or bypass surgery. To regain my confidence I entered and completed the Majorca Marathon. It was such an unpleasant experience that I elected to hang up my New Balance shoes without completing my ton. People have asked my better-half why I've ran so many marathons: 'Does it provide him with time to process his thoughts in peace or does it allow him to escape from his thoughts altogether?' Elizabeth never tires of responding: 'No, he likes the sound of heavy breathing.'

While I was working, running and following Everton around the world, my better-half kept busy educating her flock of under-privileged school children. To broaden the ambitions of her pupils, she had invited a procession of carpenters, postmen and insurance adjusters to visit her school and explain what their jobs entailed. Elizabeth assured me that her pupils would be fascinated to learn how oil is produced and processed before it reaches the petrol pump. I was unconvinced yet agreed to take part. After listening to me practicing and inspecting my homemade props, she proposed a contingency plan involving either long-distance running or football. Because trying to describe the agony of a marathon to someone who's never run one is like explaining the concept of shame to a Kopite. I agreed that the round ball would be my safety net.

Though I had never addressed a classroom of children before, I was brimming with confidence. That was until I heard that another teacher had arranged for her husband to attend the same 'Bring Your Spouse to Work Day'. As luck would have it, he worked at the US Drug Enforcement Administration and brought along a Sikorsky Black Hawk. Yes, a helicopter. The children swarmed over the machine parked in the schoolyard. My party piece followed immediately after his jaw-dropping presentation. Within less than a minute I detected that the pupils weren't interested in the oil & gas business and I reverted to Plan B by producing a soccer ball with their first names handwritten on the white hexagons. Rather than providing a tutorial explaining unusual geometrical shapes, I asked my young audience - which boasted predominantly Hispanic roots - to name some famous soccer stars.

Immediately, a chubby girl called out: 'Diego Maradona'. A boy yelled out: 'El Pibe - you know, Carlos Valderrama with the blond curly hair.' After another called out: ' Hugo Sanchez.' I invited all three to step forward. Next I sought worthy opponents to play against the very best of Argentina, Columbia and Mexico in a three-on-three contest to demonstrate the concept of teamwork. Given that all American children, irrespective of sex, size and athletic ability have played soccer, I pointed to a bespectacled boy with his hand raised: 'Whose your soccer hero son? Is it Pele? Or Zico?' Nervously he said: 'No sir, it's Magic McKenzie.' The small-boned girl next to him, who was obviously the teacher's pet, added: 'Please pick me sir. Pick me. Mine is Hot Legs Latchford'. Clearly, my wife had done a good job educating her flock in the more important things in life. Also she was a good sport as Dai Davies - the third member of an unlikely Everton trinity.

The match took place within the confines of the basketball court at Aldine School with traffic cones for goal-posts - because, as you can imagine, no-one wears wooly sweaters in Houston. In front of two dozen cheering class-mates, I refereed the proceedings in which the pride of South America took turns elbowing the ribs and kicking the shins of their favourite teacher and her favourites.

Afterwards, Elizabeth reassured me that her charges had really enjoyed chasing the soccer ball. Sympathetically, she proclaimed: 'Who needs a helicopter with its fancy bells and whistles when you've got the likes of Maradona, Valderrama and Big Bob on the same schoolyard?' There was an extremely awkward silence of 30 seconds or more before I uttered my considered response: 'Why a Black Hawk helicopter? Was the Space Shuttle busy?'

All together now ...

57. Blood brothers

You may have noticed that I possess an abiding loyalty to my ancestral homeland and have served as Merseyside's unofficial envoy to the USA for decades. Trust me; it has been an honour to do so. Word of my origin, however, paints concentric circles on my forehead. I'm sure you've heard the old gags: 'What do you call a young man from Merseyside in a brand new suit? The accused. Or a young lady from Merseyside in a white tracksuit? The bride.' Of course, I've been conditioned to laugh at myself, especially in the company of people who are ill-equipped to reciprocate. Indeed, I've gained comfort that our spontaneous sense of humour has sustained us as a people for 800 years.

Let's not kid ourselves, Merseyside has its fair share of benefit cheats and gun-toting drug dealers. But they represent a tiny minority of the population; in the same way that only a few people from North Wales think their sheep are extremely good looking. Unfortunately, the lazy stereotyping of Merseysiders emanated from the South of England in the early-Seventies. A decade later, the jokes based mostly on poverty, crime and unemployment - all designed to offend - had crossed the Atlantic Ocean. I must recall an interaction with a trade representative of the British Consulate-General in Houston. While waiting to see me, he quizzed my secretary about my roots. Upon discovering that I was from Merseyside, the man with the old school tie and matching accent cautioned her: 'I hope you keep your handbag hidden from the Scousers.' My secretary hailed from Louisiana and had a lovely way with words. She replied: 'Sir, I thank you kindly for your concern. With your permission, I'll store it in a safe place. Would you like me to put your silver spoon with it?'

So what do Americans know about the Second City of the Empire? Three things come to my mind – African slaves, Liverpool Football Club and the words to 'Yellow Submarine'. New Yorkers, in particular, are in love with The Beatles. I've met several who have taken a day-trip from London to follow in the footsteps of John Lennon, their adopted son, from Menlove Avenue through the Philharmonic Dining Rooms, which as we all know boast the finest urinals in the world to the replica of the Cavern Club. The more enlightened ones have seen Jimmy McGovern's 'Liam', Alan Bleasdale's 'No Surrender' and Willy Russell's 'Blood Brothers'.

The musical is everything that great theatre should be. It doesn't rely on intricate scenery, complex choreography or a big name to give you an earworm that will make your brain itch and linger there for hours: 'Tell me it's not true ... say you didn't mean it ... say it's just pretend ... say it's just the end ... from an old movie of long ago ... from an old movie of Marilyn Monroe.' I must caution you not to reread those lyrics or you'll be humming the tune over and over to the annoyance of those around you. I've seen 'Blood Brothers' dozens of times. Mrs Johnstone, the principal character, reminds me of the young mothers and other heroines of my childhood in Gerrard Street. All looked old before their time. My list of Mrs Johnstones is comprehensive and includes Barbara Dickson, Stephanie Lawrence, Kiki Dee, Rebecca Storm - arguably the best - and Carole King. Some were more authentic than others but all were terrific.

Now for a bit of serious name-dropping; I remember meeting the American singer-songwriter, whose album entitled 'Tapestry' - which included 'You've Got a Friend' - topped the charts for six years, in a small coffee shop located a couple of blocks from the Music Box Theater on Broadway. She revealed to me that Bill Kenwright had introduced new scenery highlighting 'Everton for the FA Cup' in graffiti and a special start to Act 2. After the intermission, the entire cast burst onto the stage chanting 'Ev-er-ton ...Ev-er-ton ... Ev-er-ton'. I detected that she didn't fully grasp the relevance of the name except that it was the love of the theatre impresario's life. In fact, she seemed a little confused when I suggested a spiritual twist to the nature-versus-nurture plot. I proposed that after the Johnstone twins are separated at birth, one should be raised as a Red, the other as a Blue.

As I chatted with Carole King, I thought about Blue Bill. I don't know what he did in a previous life. But it must have been something pretty good for him to have been reincarnated as such a massive Evertonian.

I've bumped into other celebrities in New York City. Most were so nice that I suspected they were hiding some deep dark secret. Others were far less chatty. One example of the latter involved sitting next to the Reverend Jesse Jackson on the Trump Shuttle from La Guardia to Washington, DC. If I remember correctly, I had been to the US Baseball Hall of Fame in Cooperstown to discuss their rules and selection criteria which ensured inductees covered a cross-section of eras and avoided the usual slant towards the more recent past and was documenting my preliminary ideas for something very similar at Goodison. Throughout the flight, I sensed him glancing over my shoulder at my note-pad.

We made eye contact but I was far too star-struck to engage him in conversation. Reverend Jackson didn't talk to me until we prepared to touch down at Washington's National Airport. He cleared his throat before he spoke. I anticipated that the two-time candidate for the Democratic Party's presidential nomination, renowned for his eloquence, was about to offer me some wisdom from his days as a civil rights activist working alongside Reverend Dr Martin Luther King, Jr. and Ralph Abernathy. Indeed, I recalled that he was on the balcony of the Lorraine Motel when Dr King was killed in 1968. Therefore, I was prepared for something like: 'Everton Football Club is not a blanket woven from one thread, one wool or one color. Michael Trebilcock must be inducted into your Gwladys Street's Hall of Fame.' Instead, he looked at me with his huge doleful eyes and mumbled: 'Nuts. You want your peanuts?'

58. Switch-hitter

If you are impressed by blatant name dropping, then let me tell you about my dinner with Mickey Mantle. During my frequent stays at the Waldorf-Astoria, I often walked around the block to dine at Christo's Steak House. One winter evening I had arranged to meet my New York attorney there. It was raining cats and dogs as I waited to cross Lexington Avenue and offered to share my umbrella with an immaculately suited man who was headed also to the restaurant. We dried out in the bar and chatted about the weather and sports memorabilia. After the maitre d' informed me that my attorney had cancelled, my new friend and I decided to share a booth. Even though he mentioned spending his time at fantasy baseball camps in Florida and baseball card shows across the nation, I had no idea that he had played 18 years with the Yankees and was on a marble pedestal at Cooperstown alongside Joe DiMaggio, just below Babe Ruth.

I suspected that he was a celebrity when diners nodded with child-like wonder in his direction. My new friend was explaining that the T-bone steaks had been hand-cut thick for succulence and carefully aged for tenderness when a patron asked for his autograph. That signature encouraged others to flock to our booth. It was the first time that I had been in the company of a sports legend and witnessed the infringement of their privacy. Mantle seemed to revel in the attention and declared: 'I like you Dave because you don't know who I am!' Of course, I had heard about 'The Mick'. The boyhood hero of Oklahoma Crude, Mantle had been a switch-hitter who when batting right-handed had struck one ball 550 feet over the stands and out of Griffith Stadium in Washington, DC and as a left-hander had exceeded that mark when he slugged one out of Detroit's Tiger Stadium. The distressed ball was discovered 650 feet from home plate.

Mantle's entertaining tales of pranks involving team-mates Whitey Ford and Billy Martin were presented with impeccable timing. My favourite? One night at the Book-Cadillac Hotel in Detroit, Ford, Martin and Mantle, all worse for wear, climbed onto the window ledge to spy into the rooms of their team-mates. They tired of their adventure when they discovered nobody's lights were on. Unfortunately, the ledge was so narrow that they couldn't turn around and had to crawl around the building to return to their rooms. They were staying on the twenty-second floor.

By now, our conversation was purely baseball. The Mick told me that he autographed baseballs for a living. While he commanded huge appearance fees at organized signing sessions, he took pride in never turning down requests from fans in the street and signing one autograph after another until all of his fans were happy. The Yankee icon cautioned: 'When collecting autographs, there's only one way to be sure about their authenticity. You must witness the signing with your own eyes.' Next he waxed lyrical about the Yankees archives compiled by Barry Halper. It contained documents, photographs, ticket-stubs and uniforms in addition to bats, balls and gloves signed by that game's icons. It also included Ty Cobb's dentures. These were no ordinary false teeth. Their previous owner had received the most votes in the inaugural Baseball Hall of Fame ballot in 1936; seven more than Babe Ruth. Apparently, Halper's approach to collecting was simple: if a Yankee or other baseball star had thrown it, hit it, caught it, wore it, signed it or posed for it, then he collected it. Halper amassed one million baseball cards, 1,000 uniforms and 3,000 autographed baseballs before selling his collection for $38 million. Six years after his death, some of his more spectacular items were determined to be far from authentic.

After I told Mantle that I was compiling something similar about Merseyside football - without the forgeries, he professed awareness of Dixie Dean and his achievements. At first, he confused the great man with Dizzy Dean, a pitcher with St Louis Cardinals during the Depression. Then to my horror, he claimed that the Goodison icon had played for Liverpool Football Club. 'The Mick' was a man of opinions which weren't weakly held. So for that evening, William Ralph Dean was as red as my companion's hearty steak.

I mentioned to Mantle that some of our stars from the Eighties had become less approachable as their signatures became more hurried. I didn't reveal their identities but noted they were just as miserable as ex-players. Mantle smiled and suggested that these Everton legends dole out pre-signed cards to their fans: 'This card certifies that you've met me and I refused to provide you with my autograph because I'm both dour and dumb.'

Besides his passion for America's favorite pastime, what I noticed most about Mantle was that his personality changed with his blood-alcohol level. After a few vodkas on the rocks, he bragged about his tolerance to the savage waters of Tzar Nicholas II - his description, not mine - and became somewhat boisterous. So much so that he confessed to having played with hangovers and bouts of gastrointestinal distress: 'God-given talent trumps a healthy lifestyle any day of the week.' After a few vodka martinis, he was a tad cranky towards his fans. Next he sank glasses of Chardonnay and Cabernet Sauvignon. White wine and red wine? It didn't matter as long as there were demons in the bottles. By then, he was downright rude to everyone in the restaurant and it struck me that there can be nothing worse than discovering your hero is an inebriated jerk.

There was sadness about 'The Mick'. He was a prisoner of fame who had forfeited his privacy. As I made a polite exit, he was mumbling obscenities as he added his 'Mickey Mantle #7 moniker to the pile of cocktail napkins placed in front of him. I wondered how much these intoxicated signatures eroded his reputation as a baseball star or possibly enhanced his eminence as a national treasure. I shouldn't have worried. My next sighting of Mantle was 20 years later. His smiling face was featured on a 39¢ US postage stamp.

That's right ... we were banned for five years

59. Blues and Reds

I was living overseas and insulated from the period when Liverpool lifted so many shiny pieces of silver that many Blues suspected that Anfield had made a pact with the devil. Aware that envy is a poor companion in life, I don't think I was a chameleon who changed from blue to green when I read about them picking up their trophies. Honestly, I've never been jealous of Liverpool Football Club; I simply harbour pathological contempt towards anything to do with it. Cross my heart, I'm only teasing. It's just a bit of fun. I must confirm that I've retained an aversion to the colour red. I've never owned a red car and, on several occasions, have refused to accept one from Hertz.

My father didn't dislike Liverpool supporters. He claimed that the rivalry had been somewhat benign before the appointment of Bill Shankly because it was extremely difficult to duel with a club languishing in a lower league. My grandfather got the occasional urge to do so but never did. That said, he helped to propagate the urban myth that every Merseyside midwife is required to dangle a newborn child in front of a freshly polished mirror. If she cannot detect the baby's reflection, it's rejected to the red heap.

Thanks to Anfield Arrogance, fueled by the red bias of the UK television and print media, Kopites are despised throughout Europe. Personally, I've never had a problem with Merseyside-born Reds. I can joke with them and argue with them because, like me, their allegiance has been passed down as an heirloom. Nowadays, I feel sorry for them. After the turmoil associated with Luis Suarez's racial abuse of United's Patrice Evra, they discovered that you can't defend the indefensible and retain your credibility. As a consequence, they have been taunted as murderers, racists and, perhaps worst of all, Norwegians. Obviously, it's unfair to tar an entire fan-base with the same brush. But there can be no excuses for those who mock the Munich Air Disaster. Nor for those who accused Blues of poking fun at the Hillsborough Disaster. The only chant I've heard from Blues about that horrific day is 'Justice for the 96'.

Believe me, I try hard to like them. I suppose I've encountered too many Cockney Reds who have no connection to the city except for the collection of John Lennon's songs on their iPods. They simply want to add a pinch of glory into their lives to feel less miserable. I've discovered that few things are more amusing in football than watching these most self-righteous fans arrive at Lime Street lost in their own deluded world. The glory days are long gone. The deluge of silverware has given way to drought. Not surprisingly, they have much in common with American Reds who express their undying devotion to a club they adopted because it guaranteed glory. Often, I've thought about contacting the US Department of Homeland Security in Washington DC about the development of a national register of American Reds. Surely, no-one wants to live next door to a Kopite. Not even a Kopite wants to live next door to a Kopite.

Some Blues believe that the friction with Reds wasn't helped by the errors of judgment made by some dodgy officials. When it comes to referees who have favoured our local rivals, one man comes immediately to my mind. Though 34 seasons have passed since Mr Clive Thomas dashed our dreams of FA Cup glory by disallowing the winning goal in the semi-final clash, his ruling rankles as if made yesterday. As the prospect of a replay loomed Ronny Goodlass crossed, McKenzie flicked the ball to Bryan Hamilton who diverted it past Ray Clemence for a deserved winner. Or so it seemed. All Blues and Reds believed that the last-minute effort had taken Everton to the final. You could tell by the reaction of the Liverpool players that they knew it was a goal. Even the linesman was on his way to the half-way line. Then Thomas signalled for offside. Or handball. Perhaps force majeure. As a battle-scarred veteran of the Widnes & District Alliance, I'm not someone to belittle referees. We all make mistakes. Therefore, I propose that instead of maintaining umbrage for an error of judgment made decades ago, we forgive the conceited, pompous and shameless cheat.

Mr Thomas wasn't the last match official to be demonized. Another was Mr Alan Robinson, the referee who controlled the 1984 League Cup final - the first all-Merseyside affair. In the no-score draw at Wembley, defender Alan Hansen cleared Adrian Heath's goal-bound effort with his hand. Actually, he fondled the ball as if it was a pert female breast. Somehow, the referee turned a blind eye to the foreplay.

Next was Mr Graham Poll who disallowed Don Hutchison's goal in 2000. Only half of the two minutes of added time had elapsed when Liverpool keeper Sander Westerveld hoofed the ball against Hutchison's back. Inexplicably, Mr Poll blew his whistle bringing the game to a premature end as the ball trickled over the line. Then there were the actions of Mr Mark Clattenburg. Mama Blue rained so many grievances at him in 2007 that I don't know where to start. I can still picture the referee changing his mind about showing a yellow card to Tony Hibbert after a friendly word from Steven Gerrard. The Liverpool captain nodded his approval when the card was upgraded to red.

Hand on heart, I'm not bitter about these incidents. If football was fair it wouldn't be the same. Injustices are part of the game's attraction. While these key decisions frustrated us, Blues often forget the giant one that went our way when Bolton had a goal disallowed unfairly by Mr Steven Lodge during our scoreless draw at the brand new Reebok Stadium in 1997? Video replays show that Gerry Taggart's header had crossed the goal-line before it was cleared by Terry Phelan. At the end of the season, both clubs finished on 40 points and Bolton were relegated on goal difference. If goal-line technology had been in use, we would have no arguments about our demotion to the Nationwide Football League.

Listen you bitter and twisted Blues ... it's just a bit of banter

60. Andrea Casula

The Heysel tragedy is cited as another reason why the Merseyside derby has soured. It's a story of territorialism, intimidation, violence, shame and much more. I've heard that the trouble at the 1985 European Cup final started an hour before the scheduled kick-off and escalated when the Belgian police failed to prevent some Liverpool fans in Section Y from tearing down the wire fencing and charging across the no-man's land towards their rivals who had snapped up most of the tickets in the neutral section. The Italians in Section Z tried to flee by climbing over the perimeter wall which collapsed under them. The violence escalated to the point where the match and the score-line meant nothing.

Some 39 men, women and children died and 600 others were injured during the pandemonium. Though no formal inquest has ever been held to ascertain the causes of the disaster, a dozen or more Liverpool fans were extradited and jailed for involuntary manslaughter. Even though there was no malicious or prior intention to kill, the acts of violence were inexcusable. No doubt there were mitigating circumstances. But was the provocation sufficient for reasonable people to lose self-control? Would Blues have behaved differently? To be honest, given our appetite for hooliganism in days of yore, I doubt it.

Having won the title earlier that month, it was the turn of Howard Kendall's Everton, one of the finest teams to emerge from the shores of the United Kingdom, to follow in the footsteps of Villa, Liverpool and Forest and maintain England's stranglehold on European silverware. I was shocked when all English clubs were prohibited from taking part in competitions and even pre-season tours in Europe. Immediately, I feared that the five-year ban would rob us of the chance to build ourselves into a global brand to rival that of our esteemed neighbours. I've heard that Margaret Thatcher's government pressured the clubs to accept their penance. As a result, we were denied the opportunity to challenge for the European Cup and the European Super Cup in 1986. Of course, given our track-record and the curse of Nana Mouskouri, it's possible that we would have floundered again in Europe. We'll never know.

Liverpool spent six years in exile and an eternity in shame. Like the grief of those who survived, the stain on the reputation of Merseyside football will never fade. My rancour doesn't stem from our five-year ban. While Everton fans might not have behaved differently during the chaos, I'm confident that the Goodison board would have reacted with a more mature sense of right and wrong and shown genuine remorse. The reputation of Merseyside has been tainted by people who should know better than paying lip service to such a disaster. So let's peer into the shadows of my loathing. Kopites adopt sneering attitudes and voices of revisionism to blame others for the events at Heysel. In no particular order they point fingers at UEFA, Belgian police, maintenance staff at the stadium, mischief-makers of the National Front, bloodthirsty Ultras and, of course, Italian fans and children who fled in terror. But rarely themselves.

Yes, I'm a bitter Blue with much to be bitter about. Let me tell you about Andrea Casula. During one consulting gig, I was responsible for 30 offices scattered across Europe. My proposals for tightening operations weren't well received in Turin. The staff had been warned that I was a big shot from the USA but when they discovered my true roots, one of them became agitated. Before storming out of the meeting, he yelled: 'Casula! Casula!' I was embarrassed because I didn't know that he was the youngest of the Heysel victims or that his 11-year old body was discovered under that of his father. The remaining Italians explained that, even though it had been a decade since the slaughter, the wounds hadn't healed. They weren't ready to forgive because there had been few words of contrition just conspiracy theories. In their minds, no-one outside of Italy talks about the Heysel Disaster or Heysel Denial for that matter and complained that there had been no exhaustive re-examination of the event, just a manipulation of the historical record.

There had been a disturbing mental blindness associated with this tragic loss of so many innocent Italian lives in some parts of Merseyside until Juventus and Liverpool were drawn together in the 2005 Champions League. During that match, the Kop held up a massive banner proclaiming 'Amicizia'. In response, some visiting fans turned their backs on the tardy offer of friendship. Again, they weren't ready to forgive.

It doesn't help that many Reds have put Heysel to the back of their minds. Their reluctance to accept responsibility damaged their relationships with Blues. As for the impact on Everton, it's unlikely that we'll receive a formal apology from the hierarchy at Liverpool Football Club. Anfield has ignored the fact that an admission of culpability for the actions of its fans will cost them nothing but mean everything to the English clubs banned from Europe. As a direct consequence, even though the region possesses an uncommon sense of community, it's a myth to suggest that we're one big happy family or will return to the days of chanting 'Mer-sey-side' in unison. Thankfully, club loyalty doesn't preclude Blues and Reds from befriending one another.

Perhaps because we've won only 28 League and cup games - about 20% of the 133 derbies contested during my lifetime, Blues of my vintage have learnt to show humility and dignity in both defeat and victory. These qualities, however, seem to have eluded some Kopites, especially those from outside Merseyside. Whereas we have a healthy disregard for Liverpool, they hate Everton, United and everyone else. Gratefully, none of my red pals display a delusional sense of superiority in my company. Also they are well aware that when it comes to me calling them gobshites and them referring to me as bitter and twisted, it's good-natured banter between friends - some of whom, others would say, are outraged by everything and ashamed of nothing.

61. Heart-breaking tragedy

The Merseyside community is principled and strong. It is united by blood and divided by football. One of its strengths is the ability to unite in adversity. So, now it's time to reflect on the events of April 15, 1989, when 96 Liverpool fans were crushed to death and at least 750 were injured physically at an FA Cup semi-final in Sheffield. Why, you ask? Well, the heart-breaking tragedy affected every true football supporter on Merseyside and beyond.

Though the problem was fading, hooliganism influenced the behaviour of the police. Most of us who attended matches in the Eighties were treated like cattle - penned in for 90 minutes, locked in at the final whistle and then herded to the nearest train station. Even though occasional stampedes were part of the matchday experience, catastrophes had been rare. I recall being alarmed by the news of the1971 Ibrox disaster when the failure of crush-barriers caused 66 deaths and 200 injuries. This isn't to be confused with the 1902 Ibrox disaster during the Scotland-England match which involved the collapse of a newly-built wooden stand. It resulted in 25 deaths and 500 injuries.

The Hillsborough tragedy was much worse. That morning I had listened to the second-half of our clash with Norwich on the BBC World Service and knew that the other semi-final had been abandoned due to crowd problems. Later that day, the US television networks covered the unfolding disaster with sympathy. They highlighted clips of young fans being pulled to safety. It took some time for them to grasp the enormity of what had happened. Subsequent reports included the heart-breaking scenes of the pitch filling up with bodies. My wife and I watched in horror. I remember feeling a sense of disbelief mixed with shock and numbness. Elizabeth claimed that my face went white with purple snakes thrashing at my temples. I didn't need to be told the obvious - it could have been us. Had the cup draw handed Liverpool semi-final against Norwich, rather than Nottingham Forest, then it would have been Blues dying at Sheffield.

Within days, I had heard a first-hand account of the carnage. A friend from Huyton who had been at Hillsborough wept as he talked about fans turning blue through a lack of oxygen and their faces contorted in pain as they gasped for breath. He confided to having been traumatized by the sickly-sweet smell of death and blamed the errors of judgment made by the Football Association, South Yorkshire Police and Sheffield Wednesday Football Club as well as some of his fellow Reds. He was the first to claim that the police were more interested in the prevention of public disorder and failed to protect the Liverpool supporters.

With about 400 local murders per year, death is no stranger to Houston television. American interest in the Sheffield bloodshed was fleeting and cited as just another example of soccer hooliganism. Everyone blamed drunken Liverpool fans. No-one questioned the failure of the much-loved British Bobbies to control the crowds. During the days that the story was deemed newsworthy, the local media focussed their interest on the sea of flowers that covered the pitch at Anfield.

The pain touched all Merseysiders. Everton and Liverpool are closer than other clubs, so much so that their local fans are able to divorce football rivalry from human tragedy. I agreed to brief interviews with both Houston newspapers. I think they expected me to criticize the fans. I didn't. The journalists appeared unaware that English football fans were regarded as subhuman by the authorities. They were used to the sanitized facilities at the Astrodome and failed to grasp basic queueing theory or that entering the stadium through a small number of antiquated turnstiles could have added to the congestion outside. Rather than delay the kick off, Exit Gate C had been opened to alleviate the crush. The influx of fans caused chaos in the central pens. Obviously, the latecomers had no idea of the compressive asphyxia at the front. I recall telling them that if someone had opened the gates at a football match, I would have been one of the first to go in.

I tried to explain that - from my experience in big crowds - you can't see what is in front or to the side. Certainly, you can't stop or turn round. Hemmed in, there is nowhere to go. Clearly, the police and stewards should have directed the fans towards the side pens when the central one approached capacity. Finally, the journalists asked me about fans urinating on police officers and picking the pockets of the dead. I felt trapped and repeated - somewhat loudly - my firm belief that such claims were unimaginable: 'Some people think we are work-shy, dishonest and strike-happy but no-one from Merseyside would do such things!' Sadly, my comments weren't published in the Houston Chronicle or the Houston Post. Later, they reported that Chief Superintendent David Duckenfield, the police officer in charge, claimed that fans had broken into the stadium. He added that they had conspired to do so by arriving late, ticketless, drunk and determined to force entry. The media in Houston bought his hooliganism line. They weren't alone.

Truth was as much a casualty as those carried from the ground on makeshift stretchers. It wasn't until Lord Justice Taylor established that the cause of the disaster was poor crowd control that the world listened. He acknowledged that the consumption of alcohol and attempts to bunk in without tickets had aggravated the situation but were secondary factors. It beggars belief that Duckenfield was allowed to retire on a full police pension and that the prosecution was abandoned when doctors declared him unfit to stand trial due to post traumatic stress disorder. I've often wondered how he sleeps at night.

As for the 1989 FA Cup competition, some of my friends - Blues and Reds alike - proposed that the abandoned semi-final should not have been replayed. Furthermore, I thought that after Liverpool had eliminated Forest at Old Trafford, we should have withdrawn politely from the competition. Indeed, the FA Cup final should never have been played. After all, it would have been insensitive for Everton players and supporters to have celebrated a victory at Wembley never mind in an open-top bus through the streets of Merseyside. To me, winning or losing seemed of little importance. In truth, I would have voted for the club to use Littlewood's sponsorship money to erect a suitable memorial at Goodison.

Because no-one was held accountable, Hillsborough grief turned into Merseyside anger which caused most of the world to believe that self-indulgent victimhood pervades our culture. Many propagated that myth. These included Boris Johnson, then editor of 'The Spectator' magazine, who took the position that people in Liverpool cannot accept that they might have contributed to the misfortune at Sheffield and seek to blame others - deepening their sense of shared tribal grievance. Similar sentiments were voiced across North America. Steven Cohen, the self-proclaimed US voice of soccer on Sirius Satellite Radio, complained that Liverpool fans have failed to take their share of responsibility for the disaster. He reported: 'People hell bent on getting into somewhere where they shouldn't be going because they didn't have tickets are the root cause.' Later he added: 'Two events, four years, two different cities, two different countries, two different stadiums, 135 dead ... one common link.' Cohen was sacked but his mud stuck and I've had to correct many Americans making lurid allegations about the events that took many lives and ruined so many others.

While many sighed and asked the city to move on, such vilification served Merseyside's need to discover the truth about what happened on Saturday April 15, 1989. I had been in awe of the pursuit of truth and justice but must confess that I had become desensitized to the images of the lucky fans being hauled into the upper tier and the unlucky ones being carried away on the makeshift stretchers. A couple of years ago, I was reminded of the depth of the horrors at a memorial service at Anfield. There was emotional nakedness throughout the old ground. At 3:06 pm precisely, the crowd stood for two minutes of silence.

During the period of contemplation it became clear that the people of Merseyside weren't hooked on grief. They knew their loved-ones hadn't died in the way that the authorities claimed. The reading of the victims' names was a reminder that Bill Shankly and Vince Lombardi had got it wrong. Life is far more important than football.

Successive governments did nothing to challenge the inquest verdicts until Andy Burnham, former-Secretary for Culture, Media and Sport, sought full disclosure. Along with Steve Rotherham, the red MP for Walton, he was instrumental in setting up an independent panel. Hand on heart, I feared that the bereaved families would be dismayed again by its findings. My doubts were misplaced and, after a 27-year battle, the Liverpool fans were exonerated and the South Yorkshire Police and South Yorkshire Ambulance Service were exposed as parties to a blatant cover-up. The 450,000 pages of evidence exposed flaws in the policing at the ground. Without question, the most heartbreaking of the panel's findings was that 40% of the victims could have survived had the emergency response been coordinated properly.

The football world was appalled at the conduct of the police. In addition to errors at the scene, a hundred or so officers' statements had been doctored to remove criticisms of its leadership and the media had been briefed with false information to deflect the blame into the fans. To their eternal shame, senior officers had launched a concerted campaign to smear the innocent. Why did the police officers allow their words to be changed? Don't they know that telling the truth is a brave act during times of widespread deceit and evil prevails when good men stand by and do nothing? The conduct of the ambulance service was no better. Who ordered the testing of the asphyxiated corpses of children for alcohol?

Without doubt, the Football Association failed the fans. Even though it was the preferred neutral site for clashes between clubs from the North West and Midlands, Hillsborough was an antiquated ground. Its turnstiles at the Leppings Lane End were inadequate to process big crowds safely and prevent a build-up of people outside the ground. In fact, the Football Association had stopped using the venue after complaints of overcrowding in 1981 when about 40 Tottenham fans were injured in an incident, some with broken legs. Hillsborough was reinstated in 1987 yet, despite a series of modifications to the old ground, didn't have a valid safety certificate. Inexplicably, Sheffield Council failed in its statutory duty to ensure compliance with their legal requirement. Clearly, the stadium should never have been selected by the FA without proper documented safety checks. Liverpool, with a larger support, asked to be allocated the larger end of the ground. When that was rejected, the club asked for the game to be moved to Old Trafford.

The disaster was a catalogue of heinous acts of negligence and the collusion between the press and senior politicians was a catalogue of criminal acts. Clearly, the police judged that protecting their own reputation was more important than shedding light on inadequacies which resulted in the massacre of 96 members of the public. Their senior officers must accept the consequences of such shameful behaviour. Also questions have to be asked of the West Midlands Police who investigated the conduct of their South Yorkshire colleagues and found no evidence of wrong doing. The culprits should be dragged to court to face criminal charges.

Given that the campaign for truth continued for a quarter of a century, it's hard to believe that so many people doubted the families. Thankfully, the fans of many football clubs were supportive. None more so than those of Everton. In September 2012, we hosted Newcastle in the first game played after the publication of the findings. You'll recall that a girl in blue and a boy in red led the players onto the pitch. Her shirt displayed a number nine, his a number six. I'm sure that the image of them standing side-by-side is burnt into the cornea of every Merseyside eye.

As Allan Clark of The Hollies belted out: 'The road is long, with many of winding turns ... that lead us to where, who know where? ... but I'm strong ... strong enough to carry him ... he ain't heavy ... he's my brother', the faces of the victims were shown on the giant video screens sited in two corners of the stadium. The players and supporters of both Everton and Newcastle applauded as the montage lingered on the LED displays. It was a beautiful demonstration of solidarity with the bereaved families and captured that special something that makes people from the North of England so extraordinary. The tribute brought tears to my eyes and sent chills down my spine. The manner in which Mama Blue showed her empathy made me proud to come from a united Merseyside. It's been said before but is worth repeating, future generations of Blues must never forget the fans who went to watch a game of football and never came home.

A two-year inquiry determined that the victims were unlawfully killed and that the fans had done no wrong. I must add that while 96 died that tragic day, thousands lost their lives. The verdict is a triumph for the entire population but no one should have to fight for truth and justice decade after decade. I'll never know how those bereaved families have lived through 27 years of torment. In April 2016, my visit to St George's Hall was a pilgrimage. The mood was one of relief, respect and reflection. There was a sense of civic pride that the families of the victims and people of Liverpool fought a relentless battle against the Establishment. Reds and Blues stood shoulder to shoulder that evening. I held the hand of a stranger. I'll never forget his assertion: 'I'm a Red. You're a Blue. We are one.' Nevertheless, some things remained the same that night. While those around me sang the infamous Anfield ditty. I shed a tear but couldn't even lip-sync the words.

Bitter, twisted, proud ... it's full-blown Evertonitis

62. UnAmerican

Back in Houston, the mantra of maximizing shareholder value was more than a little inconvenient because, despite our portfolio of healthy businesses, our corporate stock price didn't fully reflect the value of our hydrocarbon and cash reserves. Drastic action was required to deter unwanted advances from industry admirers. Cue the introduction of my final boss, a hard-nosed, sharp-tongued executive who specialized in takeovers and corporate restructuring. This big-shot lawyer, who allegedly had sorted out Kerr McGee with a Louisville Slugger, was brought in to implement the strategic plan. Unlike his predecessor, he didn't need a bobble-head dog on his Texas-size executive desk to constantly agree with him.

People called him 'Oklahoma Crude' behind his back. Though we were unlikely bedfellows, I've been told - not by him - that he was impressed when I declined an offer to serve as dean of a business school to concentrate on solving real business problems. One of which involved the then largest settlement in the history of the US Environmental Protection Agency. The regulator mandated the cleanup of waste pits contaminated with polychlorinated biphenyls located at remote sites along the 10,000-mile transmission corridor. Decades earlier, these cancer-causing PCBs had been added as flame retardants to the lubricants in the turbines which powered the pipelines. It was no small irony that the company took pride in the immaculate condition of its gold-plated compressor stations which were cleaner than many NHS wards.

I must clarify that both the board and the corporate management team had made environmental awareness part of our business ethos and had operated to standards above those required by law. So much so that we were pioneers and one of the first US corporations to implement the environmental auditing of all operations. Our problem was that Federal and state standards had become more stringent. In addition to the mind-numbing burden of the subsequent remediation at around $1 billion , the corporation was prevented from implementing my strategic plan until a rigorous clean-up programme had been implemented. This involved excavating and transporting contaminated soils to the biggest hole in the ground I've ever seen. Located in Alabama, the landfill could have swallowed up Widnes, St Helens and possibly Anfield.

Eventually, the non-core operations were sold off. The shareholders received more for the sum of the components than Wall Street's valuation of the company. By then, I had deduced that instead of managing people I was spending my time managing what people thought of me. Possibly, I was tired of cleaning up other people's shit, both figuratively and literally. Probably, I was burnt out. Certainly, it was time to keep my promise to my wife and retire undefeated from the corporate jungle. And at age 42, I complied with the Malta Protocol and the pecking order of my life was revised to 1 Everton - 2 Lancashire Lass - 3 Work. It had been a grand innings. I had been fortunate. Make that extremely lucky. I spent my brief career at a company where the executives and directors inspired the values of sacrifice and concern for others, rewarded both endeavour and responsibility, and tolerated my devotion to Everton Football Club.

All four bosses thought I was insane not to fulfill my potential and maximize my personal wealth. The Renaissance Man claimed that I had been blessed because few people of my age had been invited back-stage to see how the oil & gas business hid the rabbits in its hat. Oklahoma Crude warned me that retirement at age 42 was simply unAmerican. The Voodoo Master encouraged me to attend sessions with his mental health professional before finalizing my decision. None of them, of course, had given their word to my much better-half. At our final meeting, both the Voodoo Master and Oklahoma Crude embraced me. With tears of admiration in their eyes, they proclaimed that the major regret of most oil & gas executives is that they spend so much time on the treadmill of work. One told me that the road to happiness involved tough choices. The other claimed it takes courage to enjoy a life true to yourself, not the one others expect of you.

I was convinced that the few bob I had put away coupled with a commitment to sharing my life with a loving wife is more fulfilling than being mega-rich and suspicious of other people's intentions. In the late-Eighties, Texans measured success by material excess. Yes, I know it sounds vulgar. The appetites of my peers for the showy accoutrements were seemingly infinite. My rewards had been significant. And, like my peers, owned too much stuff. The infamous Lotus Europa,however, had taught me a valuable lesson. There were no fast cars, exotic boats, demonic motor-cycles, diamond studded watches or other fancy bling.

When you've been poor, you never ever forget what it feels like to be poor. Therefore, my yardstick of material success was more personal and measured in - wait for it - toilet rolls. By 1989, I had 10 bathrooms at my disposal thanks to two homes in Houston and a 200-acre ranch in Colorado. The Texas lavatories even had names - Bog, John, Khazi, Latrine, Crapper, Thunder Box and the biggest toilet of all - Anfield. Such a list appears a tad indulgent even for someone raised with no indoor plumbing and fake Izal but for me there was nothing quite like holding a wad of ultra-soft tissue in front of Thunder Box to remind me of how far I had come.

That act raises important questions side-stepped during my childhood. Both have continued to plague mankind: Should toilet paper be hung over or under? Does your preferred direction characterize you? Advocates of both orientations argue about aesthetics, cleanliness and con-servation. By default, I'm an over practitioner. Elizabeth, who claims to have researched such matters, says it allows for an easier one-handed tear. I believe her because she is my wife and, having learned to pick my battles with caution, see no joy in a battle over quilted Andrex. Most important, I don't care about the orientation as long as it's within arm's reach.

Every morning I check the list of the richest men in the world ...
if my name is on it, I go to my office at Goodison ... if not, I come here

63. Leaving the rat race

Wiser men than me have written that ambition is the road to success. Whereas I discovered that when ambition ends, real happiness begins. Also, I found that two things happen after you reach age 42. The first is your memory goes. I'm sorry, I can't remember the other one. Upon retirement, some oil & gas executives move their watch to their other wrist to remind them that their day-to-day routine has changed. Not me. I did something far more radical. I suggested to my Elizabeth - my much better half - that we spend more time enjoying ordinary things together. I proposed that instead of popping out to local Mexican, Chinese and Italian restaurants, we enjoy home-cooked food at our own dining-room table. To do so, I encouraged her to conjure up four tasty and wholesome meals to fuel the rest of our lives.

My request for homemade nourishment sent a shockwave through the France household. Even though our kitchen was packed with the necessary appliances and gadgets to indulge culinary passions, I often joked that the only thing she made there was a telephone call to Pizza Hut. Since that day there have been no Mondays or Tuesdays in my life. No Wednesdays or Thursdays either. Only the days named after the four dishes. Their titles have changed over the past 25 years. Today Chicken Korma, Grilled Sockeye Salmon, Chopped Salad and Pasta Thingy are served up in strict rotation. Some meals are better than others. The early litmus test was Wellington. I would feed him a portion and monitor his reaction. A recipe was deemed successful if he didn't lick his anus to get the taste out of his mouth.

What else do you do after retreating from the daily grind? I took stock of my life and fine-tuned a checklist clipped years earlier from an airline magazine. It was entitled: 'The 40 things to do at least once before you reach 40'. Certainly, it's important for everyone to detail their goals to be achieved, dreams to be accomplished and simple pleasures to be enjoyed. In truth, I couldn't imagine how any 40- or even 42-year-old could find the free time to do so many things and travel to so many places described in the magazine without first winning the lottery.

Because mine didn't have the scent of a cemetery, it wasn't a bona fide bucket list. More like a simple to-do list. After realizing that I could tick off half of my items already, I perceived that things were pretty much on track and under control. My achievements to date? Climb a mountain. Get fired from a job. Live in a foreign country. Drive a fast sports-car. Ride something bigger than a horse. Visit the Grand Canyon, the Taj Mahal, the Vatican and a Nazi concentration camp. Fly around the world. Swim with stingrays. Skinny dip by moonlight with stingrays. Attend a ballet. Run a marathon. Watch a movie at a drive-in theatre. Hitch-hike. Howl at the moon. Sit on a jury. Answer the phones at a telethon. Serve at a soup kitchen. Then I cheated. Instead of attending the Super Bowl, I substituted celebrating a World Cup triumph at Wembley.

I understood that compiling such a list was an exercise in wishful self-improvement and living life to the full. Also, I was aware that these lists were tiresome. Nonetheless, with time on my hands, Elizabeth and I set about reducing the remaining things to be accomplished and never repeated. Again, it wasn't difficult: Take an African safari. Attend a bar mitzvah. Donate a gallon of blood. Visit Petra. Milk a goat. Float in the Dead Sea. Stroke a hairy spider. Kayak around orcas. Ride in a hot air balloon. Watch a solar eclipse. Prepare a mouth-watering salad. The remaining items proved far more troublesome. I failed to master another language or a musical instrument. And as for writing a good book – it's an ongoing challenge.

This left three biggies – win a raffle, meet your hero and change the life of a stranger. Since I don't gamble, I've never bought a lottery ticket, wagered on the Grand National or donated to the Moores family fortune. As for raffles, I've bought my share of tickets at sportsman's dinners. More often than not, I've left before the draw. Indeed, it was at the dinner to celebrate Dave Hickson's career that I enjoyed good fortune.

It was greeted with skepticism and derision from attendees who knew of my friendship with the guest of honour. My embarrassment was made worse by Billy Butler, the master of ceremonies, who demanded that I join him to make my choice of the prizes: 'Forget the microwave. You don't want the bizzies catching you with it under your arm at this time of night in Walton.' Embarrassed, I opted for the voucher for a two-week holiday at Pontins in Jersey which I gave to a young couple at the next table who were raising two blue boys and two blue girls.

After crossing off the places to visit, experiences to undergo, things to master, I focused on the task of meeting my heroes. Wary that such initiatives could destroy the fantasies I had constructed about my idols, I limited my list to just two names - The Golden Vision and The Golden Voice. That's right - Alex Young and Leonard Cohen. When I think of the beautiful game, instinctively I think of Alex. As you know, he could do things will the ball in a match that no other player would even attempt in training. My last sighting of my football hero had been as a member of the understrength side fielded at Upton Park one week before the 1968 FA Cup final. Even though Alex didn't have the best of games that day, my adoration was undimmed. The manager was less impressed. Despite being promised the No 12 role that he had served with distinction in the semi-final, Alex didn't play at Wembley and departed to Northern Ireland.

Except for friends in Belfast who saw him turn out for Glentoran and others who had witnessed him illuminate Edgeley Park, no-one had seen Alex for years – not even Brian Labone. Thanks to Neville Smith, the author of The Golden Vision screen-play, I tracked down my hero to a small village outside of Edinburgh. Even though Neville had cautioned that 'The Golden Vision' was an ordinary man who had achieved extraordinary things, I was intimidated by the thought of meeting him. In my eyes, Alex embodied the Soccer School of Science, he was a Goodison god, arguably the most gifted British footballer of his and all other eras, who had won everything there was to win in both English and Scottish football. And had done so with rare panache. Nancy, his wife, invited me to their home. My fears that her husband would not exude an aura of greatness evaporated immediately. Alex greeted me like a long lost Blue There was an instant bond. The type enjoyed by Evertonians. His modesty and humility took my breath away. In the 20-plus years since that first meeting, one thing has remained unchanged during our ongoing friendship - I remain overwhelmed by his kind and unassuming manner.

Some years later, he crafted the preface for the first edition of 'Gwladys Street's Hall of Fame' and confirmed his love for Everton and Evertonians. I'll never forget his words …'I signed on November 23, 1960 and since that day I've had blue blood pumping through my veins. I was just a wee lad and had no way of knowing that my life would never be the same again. Everton was more than a football club, even more than a football institution. It was a way of life on Merseyside. Playing alongside Bobby Collins, Jimmy Gabriel, Brian Labone, Alex Parker and Roy Vernon, and a wee bit later with Alan Ball, Tony Kay, Ray Wilson and Tommy Wright was a true pleasure. Together, we conjured up some glorious flowing football. My biggest privilege was being accepted as an Evertonian by fellow Evertonians. For me, it was a real thrill to experience the passion of belonging to something important. Nothing in my life has come close to the pride of being an Everton No 9 and the honour of following in the footsteps of giants. I know first-hand how much the club means to the players. Everton gets into your blood and stays there. I doubt if any other club generates such lifelong affection among its former-players. There has always been something regal about the blue shirts, the inspiration of the Latin motto, the legends of the School of Science, the atmosphere at Goodison and the loyalty of the fans who follow the club around the world irrespective of its playing fortunes.'

I've said it before … What a Blue. What a friend. What a football hero!

64. Pi

While there isn't one item in my new home in Sedona to reflect my unwavering support for Everton Football Club, the same can't be said about my music hero. There is a room dedicated to Leonard Cohen. With walls covered with his art work, it's a simple place for relaxation and meditation.

His poetry and songs have provided the sound-track to my adult life. Upon hearing his debut LP, I became a big fan of 'The Poet Laureate of Pessimism'. It was the honesty and authenticity of his songs that made them so appealing. You may be aware that the album was hailed as music to cut your wrists to. With no little irony, its arrival in UK record shops coincided with our loss to West Brom at Wembley. At the time, I found strange comfort listening to someone who made my heart bleed. Even though 'Songs of Leonard Cohen' spent 18 months in the UK album charts, to speak lovingly about his music back then resulted in questions about my emotional darkness.

Before I proceed further, I must reveal that Elizabeth and I have attended his concerts across the world throughout the past five decades. Always, he has exhibited his talents in an unguarded fashion with performances stripped of everything except an old guitar and an unmistakable voice. He has never disappointed. Unlike North America's other poet-troubadour, Lennie displays warmth coupled with a self-deprecating touch. So much so that every member of his audience feels that he was speaking to them directly. As a result, I've accompanied him on his journey through the complexities of love, social justice and psychological depression. In return, Lennie has comforted me as we buried so many seasons in unmarked graves. Sincerely, I believe that only someone who had witnessed the highs and lows of being a Blue could craft such lyrics.

In the Nineties I developed a cunning plan to bump into him at one of his favourite hang-outs. Attracted by its reputation as a place to rub shoulders with rich black sheep and other outlaws who may know him, I opted to stay at The Chelsea Hotel during my consulting assignments in Manhattan. This tired outpost of Bohemianism had been frequented by Dylan Thomas and Andy Warhol and immortalized by Sid Vicious in Room 100, Bob Dylan in Room 211 and Lennie with Janet Joplin in Room 424. The hotel was bewitching. You never knew which starving artist, tortured poet or avant-garde nutter you would meet on the stairs. I never bumped into my music hero but met his manager, Kelley Lynch. She confirmed the rumour that, after a lifetime of womanizing coupled with the pursuit of enlightenment through drugs and alcohol, 'The Patron Saint of Angst' was preparing to enter a Zen monastery in the San Gabriel Mountains.

With his head shaved and black robes flowing, Lennie became Jikan, an ordained Buddhist monk, in 1996. Immediately, I thought of Jikan in orange robes and the vacancy at Blount County. Close your eyes and image, Lennie as your goalkeeper. Perhaps not an unreasonable fantasy. Surely, his limitations at punting the ball into the opponent's area would be compensated by his peerless prayers of faith and petition to the gods of football. Of course, my fantasy assumes that he wouldn't rely on futile star-jumps to thwart advancing strikers.

All Cohen fans are indebted to Lynch. She embezzled $5 million from his retirement fund and forced the septuagenarian to pick up his old guitar again. As the poet's voice has deepened, his worldwide popularity has increased. Until recently, Lennie was better known in Europe. In fact, few Americans know who he is. And if it wasn't for 'Hallelujah', an anthem that has slowly percolated into the most covered song of the new millennium, the number would be even smaller. I'm delighted that his delicious melodies, lyrical imagination, subversive wit and ability to meditate in an Armani suit have enjoyed newfound popularity world-wide. There maybe more to the story because I found it somewhat out of character that Lennie filed a civil suit against his former manager. Subsequently in 2005, he was awarded over $9 million. The ugly episode didn't finish there. Some seven years later, Lynch was sentenced to 18 months in prison for her unrelenting barrage of harassing behaviour towards my music hero.

With his return to the road in 2008, my wife and I attended his three gigs at the Place des Arts in his hometown of Montreal. Backed by a handful of the finest musicians and singers, his tattered baritone delivery held the audience spellbound throughout each three-hour concert. Cohen's majesty rendered us breathless, sometimes weepy.

It was the afternoon before the second show that I sought my one-to-one with my music hero. To do so, we tail-gated Neil Larsen - the man who tickles the Hammond organ during Lennie love-ins, into the concert hall - past the venue security in their immaculate uniforms and along a maze of hallways to backstage. There we encountered a frail gentleman in an immaculate double-breasted suit. It was Canada's most dapper Jewish-Buddhist poet-balladeer. So what do stalkers say to their hero? I thought about telling Lennie that I'd heard every note he'd recorded and read every word he'd written. I didn't. Thankfully, I stifled proclaiming 'I'm your biggest fan' and 'You gave my life meaning.' Surely, the least inspired words to say to someone who hears them constantly. Knowing that his works-in-progress can simmer for decades, I considered enquiring how he knew when a song was finished. Again, I didn't. Given that Lennie is privy to the secrets of the universe, I was too tongue-tied to ask when Everton would capture the League Cup. I didn't even ask for his answer to the riddle 'What do you call a lifetime devoted to Everton?' I was too star-struck. I remember, however, our verbal exchanges as if they happened yesterday. I said 'Hi'. My hero mumbled 'Pi'.

Afterwards, my wife and I imagined that he returned to his quarters and, drawing upon his Zen coolness and Bohemian charm, composed a dark verse plumbing the depths of the human condition about meeting two tortured Blues.

And they call us brain-addled junkies ...

65. Change life of a stranger

The final biggie was to transform the life of a stranger. Coincidentally, that had been the goal of Joseph Williamson, someone else who retired at age 42. This tobacco merchant spent the rest of his days employing soldiers and sailors from the Napoleonic Wars to create a maze of winding tunnels under Edge Hill. Theories about their purpose include building a haven from an imminent Armageddon. It's most likely that Williamson simply wanted to provide paid work for idle hands.

Big-hearted deeds were in my corporate blood. Everyone at Texas Eastern was expected to tithe part of their salaries and assist local charities in tackling education, poverty and health care issues. Therefore, despite my deep-seated guilt about American materialism and the number of toilets at my immediate disposal, I was convinced that random acts of kindness and philanthropy should be a part of everybody's life. But how do you change the life of a perfect stranger? First, I volunteered to serve meals to the inner-city poor, drive underprivileged children to the zoo and walk dogs at animal shelters. All were worthwhile. When you volunteer, you vote every day for the world you want to live in. While the pursuit of such noble deeds restores your faith in human nature, I wanted to do more.

Next, I offered my services as a reading buddy - someone who tutors nine-year-olds to build their confidence in reading aloud. Illiteracy has plagued the USA for decades. Everyone is implicated, including those entrusted to educate them. I know because a reliable source told me. After graduating from the University of Manchester and University of Tennessee, my wife became a school-teacher. Her first-grade pupils were African-Americans from single-parent homes. She reinforced the importance of spelling, grammar, punctuality and manners but complained that her job was exacerbated by her co-workers. Many were under-educated.

Her evidence? When all of Houston's teachers were required to take competency tests in 1983, more than 60% failed the reading exam. Some 46% failed the mathematics test and 26% could not pass the writing exam. If that wasn't bad enough, more than 20% of them cheated. In Texas, dumbing down had become more of an ambition than an ailment. She cautioned that the way some of today's youngsters are brought up, by role models who laze around drinking beer, eating junk and watching television, is shameful. Elizabeth warned me that education was a bureaucratic minefield and suggested that I seek a more intimate challenge.

I toyed with converting a Red into a Blue. After all, Howard Kendall had prevailed with Peter Reid. I was dissuaded not by the challenge but rather the nagging concern that you're never sure if the exercise has been successful. Remember, Joe Royle failed miserably with Nick Barmby. Deep down, I wanted to rescue an abandoned soul in a physical sense rather than spiritual one. So instead of rescuing a Kopite from his self-imposed victimhood and delusions of grandeur, I focused on changing the life of a more laudable candidate – a heroin addict.

The first recipient of my good deeds was a homeless Vietnam veteran. That's what it said on his cardboard sign. He spent his days begging at one of the busiest intersections on FM 1960, an eight-lane road in North Houston. Like many of the motorists who stopped at the traffic lights near Willowbrook Shopping Mall, I would make a donation with maximum friendliness and minimum chatter. There was something intriguing about him. Raging Cajun was better dressed than the other dope-sick panhandlers. His hands and nails were scrubbed. Also, the lapels of his jacket boasted badges. One supported Ross Perot for US President. Another shaped like an electric guitar paid homage to Stevie Ray Vaughan. Always polite, he thanked me for my donation with the words: 'It's hell to be poor in America. One afternoon, my wife spotted him with a new sign: 'Vet needs tent.' Immediately, she hunted through our garage for the one used in Key West some 15 years earlier. Upon receiving her gift, Cajun skipped into the woods where

Through my travels I've learnt that everyone's got a story if you're prepared to listen, so now and then I would bump into the Vietnam vet and buy him a cup of decaf at McDonald's. His coffee had to be decaffeinated. He was equally as careful about what he ate and preferred chili con carne provided at the local food-bank to fast food. Cajun talked about hopelessness and homelessness. He insisted that an addiction to drugs is no excuse for slovenliness or bad behaviour,. Indeed, he was proud to be a tidy, polite and somewhat choosey beggar rather than a shoplifter. Shortly afterwards, he revealed that his career in the Louisiana petroleum services industry in addition to his wife, children and family dogs had vanished within a matter of weeks. Why? They had been replaced by heroin. Initially, he had injected the drug between his toes. After the majority of his veins had collapsed, he resorted to smoking the drug. To fund his daily fix, he sought to raise $50 from begging at different high yield, high turnover locations – his description, not mine - and $10 from scavenging for aluminum cans.

I had been cautioned by people who know about these things that junkies destroy everything they come into contact with through an endless cycle of lies, thefts, abuses and profuse apologies. No matter how hard you try, they will drag you down to a place that you no longer recognize. Regardless, I arranged for Cajun to spend an afternoon or two working at a storage unit complex. I paid his wages and innocently enabled his addiction. Even though the warm glow of heroin controlled what he saw and more important what he didn't see, his toil with a cotton string mop and bucket appeared to re-establish a sense of routine. More than anything, I was impressed that he turned up on time. Then one day he scarpered with a pair of aluminum step-ladders. After listening to his apologies and redeeming his swag from a local pawn shop, I made arrangements for him to work part-time at an office-cleaning company. There, he lasted two weeks or so before disappearing. This time he borrowed a commercial floor-polishing machine complete with scrubbing and buffing attachments. Such unacceptable behaviour is part of the challenge of helping an addict. I retrieved the machine from the same pawn shop and fixed him up with a lawn maintenance job. Whenever I dropped by his workplace, Cajun appeared happy and optimistic. So much so, that several months later I proposed to sponsor his treatment at a clinic where he would be sedated for 48 hours while his body withdrew from heroin.

I would like to report that my adopted smack-head got clean, found a full-time job, reunited with his family and became a life-long Blue. I can't. No doubt you have guessed what happened. Cajun bolted on the eve of his detox. I don't know if he got cold feet or found a dragon to chase. From the saddle of my high horse, I didn't feel used – simply useless. Hand on heart, I like to think that I did my best with Raging Cajun and his successors. Yes, I tried to rescue other junkies, alas with similar outcomes. After 12 months trying to change the life of a perfect stranger, I conceded that helping damaged people who don't want to be saved is frustrating and rescuing the disenfranchised was not an area for idealists like me. So having seen more discarded kitchen foil than Jamie Oliver, I can confirm that heroin doesn't discriminate according to age, sex, race or religion. It's something you would not wish on the most insufferable Kopite.

I've never been reluctant to explain to addicts what it means to be a Blue and to clarify the responsibilities associated with being a good one. One smack-head told me: 'Some days I love it more than life itself. Other days I hate it more than anything. It's the effing devil. Compared with the demands of supporting Everton, my six-year addiction to black tar sounds almost sensible.' There's no point in lying to myself, let alone anyone else - football is more than a recreational pick-me-up. Yes, Everton is my Class A drug of choice. It provides unrivalled euphoria and makes me feel alive. I realize that my happiness is out of my hands. I'm powerless to influence the very thing that exerts so much control over my emotions. There have been times when football wasn't so important. Thankfully, they weren't very often and never lasted for long. But what would life be like without the boys in blue?

66. Out of our league

After my miserable failure as a do-gooder, I kept myself busy by developing a management consulting practice to advise investment banks involved in mergers and acquisitions and to supervise the streamlining of service companies. Even though I cherry-picked my restructuring assignments, more often than not I was called in at the eleventh hour take the blame for the client's dirty work.

All organizations benefit from fresh eyes. As a rule, my immediate challenge was to generate cash – the faster, the better - by reducing overheads via compassionate liposuction, discarding poisoned apples and exiting loss-making operations. Conscious of the dehumanizing effects of downsizing, I never got used to the repercussions on innocent people's lives. Nor, for that matter, the hate mail which often referred to me as a blood-sucking scumbag. It could have been worse, they could have called me a blood-sucking Kopite. After the dust had settled, I would focus on improving income streams by refining the ways in which the client conducted its business. While cost cutting is easy, no little finesse is required to drive change and innovation. More often than not, the client tired of my involvement as it grew stronger. At the often premature conclusion of each job, I would buy a piece of modern art.

The Pablo Picasso gig involved turning around a group of engineering companies based in New Jersey. To do so, I commuted 5,000 miles every week for six months to deal with clients whose tongues could open bottles of wine and whose voices maintained a code of silence usually associated with the cast of 'The Sopranos'. Another, the Salvador Dali gig, involved stabilizing the European operations of a technical services firm that specialized in the disposal of spent nuclear fuel and excess weapons-grade materials. Its success was based on the ability to attract and retain top-notch talent. Before my arrival, the company's board had established a novel criterion when recruiting staff: 'Is he or she good enough for Liverpool Football Club?' Without hesitation, I proposed that they should set the bar higher because, as we well know, only the best was good enough.

During this period, I was offered significant opportunities to return to the mainstream. As the head of a new UK business school, I could have hand-picked my own team. As the US head of a French oil & gas giant, I could have named my own salary. My wife declined both opportunities on my behalf. Then not long afterwards, an associate at Goldman Sachs faxed to me an intriguing job advert from 'The Daily Telegraph'. It was for the position of Chief Executive of Everton Football Club. Even though he had sent it as a prank, the advert stirred contradictory emotions. Of course, I wanted to help the club yet suspected that Goodison had yet to enter anywhere near the modern business world.

Regardless, I wrote to David Marsh, the club's chairman, highlighting my successes in turning around organizations, improving profits, pursuing new business opportunities worldwide and developing strategic plans for wrestling with change. I still have his response: 'Thank you for your letter dated 28th May regarding our recent advertisement for a Chief Executive. Your application is first-rate but I am afraid that salary consideration will be far below what you are currently earning or are expecting upon a return to the UK. I do not believe that someone of your calibre is in our league.' Needless to say, I wrote back clarifying that I would do the job for nothing and elevate the club into my league.

Not for one minute am I suggesting that I would have succeeded in challenging the status quo and laying the foundations for a strong future. I doubt that I would have lasted as long as Trevor Birch did a decade later. Even though this highly-regarded business executive had previously developed a 10-year plan for Chelsea and secured massive investment from Roman Abramovich, he survived less than six weeks on Merseyside.

Compared to the complex operations of oil & gas companies, a Premier League club football is little more than a local supermarket which just happens to hog the back-pages of the UK national newspapers. Even United is insignificant in the grand scheme of things. I'm told that running a Tesco store is made much easier by implementing strong fiscal controls coupled with establishing a culture of mutual beliefs and shared goals among the people behind the scenes. All staff must be committed to Tesco. No-one must shop at Aldi or Waitrose. I've suggested to more than one Everton executive that he should apply a similar rigid standard to the non-Blue members of his staff: 'Is he or she good enough for Liverpool Football Club? Would they get the same jobs at Anfield?' To reiterate, I doubt that I would have lasted five - possibly six - weeks at Goodison.

A heart attack accelerated my exit from the part-time consulting scene and return to early retirement. For many, life without work would be shapeless. They have little idea what to do with their free time. Because everyone benefits from mental and social stimulation, my answer was Everton Football Club. With mortality on my mind, I did what any good Blue would do. That's right, I bought a season-ticket and made frequent crossings of the Atlantic to relive the best parts of my childhood without the need to hitchhike in pouring rain. The initiative caused an unforeseen identity disorder. In the New World, I was Dr David France - a respected and somewhat reserved executive with a passion for English soccer. In the old country, I was Widnes Dave – just another diehard Blue with mysterious Woolyback roots.

I would depart from Houston IAH at 6:00 pm on a Friday and, motorway-traffic permitting, would be sheltered, albeit a tad bleary-eyed, in seat R-25 of the Joe Mercer enclosure by kick-off. I was in good company. To my left was a Scottish Blue; a hybrid of Billy Connolly and a genuinely funny comedian. Next to him sat his boss who possessed the uncanny ability to sense an Everton goal. Always, he was the first to get to his feet and punch the air. To his left were two lawyers who despised all referees. The more outspoken one was the charming nephew of Lord Carrington. He rarely spoke about his uncle who had served in the cabinets of Churchill, Macmillan and Douglas-Home and was Thatcher's Foreign Secretary during the Falklands War. Perhaps confrontation runs in his family because my lawyer pal - a fellow shareholder - is infamous for his AGM wisdom. First, he cautioned Peter Johnson: 'The club is like a White Star liner on her maiden voyage. She's hit the iceberg but hasn't quite sunk yet.' Then years later, he advised Bill Kenwright: 'You've murdered the soul of this great club!'

Our group was completed by my future UK lawyer, his perceptive daughter who attended Imperial College and my dealer from Merseyside Football Programmes who protected my latest stash of memorabilia under his seat. He attended all first-team, reserve-team and youth-team fixtures and was a tremendous source of artefacts. Also a supplier of Bellefield gossip and Goodison intrigue, especially about the club's day-to-day cash flow struggles, he would greet me: 'We're doomed Dr France. We're effing doomed!' Then there was the Blue in front of me who jumped up and down like the over-optimistic father of the fat kid in a school football team. He had been the manager of a rock star - Van Morrison comes to mind - and claimed to suffer from attention deficit something-or-other.

With one or two exceptions, they assumed that I lived in Widnes and it was mid-season before I confessed to travelling 11,000 miles to enjoy their company. Both lawyers declared that I was Everton-mad. The others thought that I was Everton-sad.

67. Super-sonic Blue

Even though the airlines were remarkably punctual, I missed a handful of Everton matches due to mechanical problems. On one occasion my flight had to return to Houston after the pilot reported engine troubles shortly after take-off and had to jettison aviation fuel over the Gulf of Mexico. Another time the fuselage was struck by bolts of lightning. I can still hear the loud bangs and see the spectacular flashes as the aluminum oxidized.

One of my most frustrating experiences was on a British Caledonian DC 10 from Houston to Gatwick. The big old plane developed rear-engine problems and had to put down in Newark. The whirling sirens of the reception committee confirmed that my weekend plans had been left up in the air. British Airways came to our rescue and escorted me across Manhattan to JFK Airport to catch their flight to Heathrow. It arrived at 9:00 pm and I was tucked into my hotel bed just in time to watch Jimmy Hill introduce 'Match of the Day'. Early the following morning I returned to Houston. The journey of some 10,000-miles was another clear sign that the two lawyers were correct. Then there was the time I arrived at Manchester airport to find that my flight to New York had been cancelled. British Airways offered two alternatives to its frequent flyers. Either we could wait for them to redirect their Heathrow - New York plane to Manchester or we could take the shuttle to Heathrow and catch a JFK bound flight later that evening. The second alternative didn't make sense until I suspected that it would be on a very special plane.

Concorde cruised at 1,300 mph and an altitude of 60,000 feet. I sat across the narrow aisle from Sir John Harvey-Jones, the retired chairman of ICI, who by then was much better known for hosting a popular BBC television series called 'Troubleshooter' in which he advised struggling UK businesses such as Morgan Motors and Norton Motorcycles. Part-way through the flight, he boomed: 'Business or pleasure?' Rather than chat about the frustrations of management consulting, I volunteered that I had been to watch Everton and, in fact, attended most games at Goodison. Initially flabbergasted, he appeared genuinely intrigued by my obsession. So much so that when the cockpit crew greeted us at the plane's exit Harvey-Jones smiled, turned and roared to the 50 passengers: 'Captain, did you know that you had a lunatic onboard? Dr France here goes to the effing match on Concorde.'

You can no longer fly super-sonic across the Atlantic. Still, if you talk football, it can cut your travel time in half. There again, if you have the misfortune to sit next to a Kopite it doubles your travel time. My first contact with a Cockney Red was on a trans-Atlantic flight. I wasn't impressed. He had never been to Merseyside, let alone Anfield, because - wait for it - he didn't like Scousers. Since then, I've discovered that a quick quiz usually silences them: 'Who was your manager before the great Bill Shankly?' It never ceases to amaze me that they appreciate so little about their heritage. If they know that the answer is Phil Taylor, then I follow up by enquiring: 'Who was your captain when you first won the League title? Who was your captain when they first won the FA Cup?' The answers are Alex Raisbeck in 1901 and Ron Yeats in 1965.

No incident compared with the flight during which I was woken by an announcement that we had mechanical problems. Our plight was exacerbated by the fact that we were half-way across the Atlantic and several hours away from an emergency landing at Gander, Newfoundland, the nearest runway on the East Coast. The news was received with a collective gasp of fear. The paranoia increased with every unusual sound and movement of the aircraft. My own dilemma was made worse by the passengers seated around me. They had been transformed into nervous wrecks. People deal with such stressful situations in many different ways. Some reach for Absolut vodka, I prefer absolute silence. For almost three hours I kept my fears to myself as my immediate neighbours circulated photos of their loved ones. I failed to reciprocate because I had no snaps of either Alex Young or Leonard Cohen on me.

When one of them asked me to spell 'hydraulics', I noticed she was writing a message to her husband and children on an air-sickness bag. She grabbed my arm and asked me to pray with her. Behind me, I could hear others in prayer. Even the babies had stopped crying and were looking towards the man upstairs. Like someone who had died and come back to life, she described heaven as a place of splendour and majesty where angels strummed their harps while lying on soft fluffy clouds. A minute later, she grasped my hand and confronted me: 'What will you say to God if we don't make it to Gander?' I thought long and hard before uttering: 'How did Everton get on?' She didn't laugh. In absolute silence amid clear-air turbulence, I speculated that the Big Blue in heaven would smile: 'We won.'

As for the most unforgettable incident. That's simple. It started when a British Caledonian Airways flight attendant woke me during a trans-Atlantic flight to Gatwick. Loudly, she appealed: 'Dr France, please follow me to the rear of the cabin. Please hurry!' There we discovered a serious looking passenger wearing a bright purple turban standing in the aisle. He was staring open-mouthed at an elderly and motionless passenger slumped over his tray table. The flight attendant asked me: 'Is he dead?' I searched for a pulse, a skill acquired during my first-aid classes as an apprentice. I couldn't find one and asked the Sikh for a second opinion: 'What do you think?' He confessed: 'How should I know? I'm not that type of doctor. I'm a professor of economics at Texas A&M University.'

It was only when we were moving the deceased to an empty seat behind a privacy curtain that I revealed to them - in the words of my mother - that I wasn't the type of doctor that helped people - especially dead ones.

As for the good news ... you're getting Saturdays off

68. Toffee lady

Shortly after my father retired through ill-health, he elected to walk out on his 40-odd years of marriage. My mother was devastated by the timing of his disloyalty and, as a consequence, her health deteriorated. I visited her frequently and was shocked to learn that the authorities considered that the onset of Alzheimer's disease had made her a candidate for a nursing home. She was terrified at the thought of forfeiting her independence.

Determined to make up for my years overseas, I asked her to list a dozen things she would like us to do together while still mobile. To be honest, I had anticipated days out in Southport and Chester. Her plans were far more adventurous. Immediately, we set about fulfilling them in style. I can vividly see her in front of the Wailing Wall, the Parthenon and the Statue of Liberty as well as seated amid a mariachi band in a Tijuana bar. I can picture her discarding her ubiquitous white socks - poor circulation along with hardened arteries had turned her feet black - to paddle in the Pacific Ocean. Also, I can see her in a natty hotel dressing gown hobbling around a deluxe corner-suite at the Waldorf Astoria in New York as well as enjoying room service at the Savoy in London. My mother claimed that the Savoy mini-bar provided a look into the future - a world in which Mars bars cost £2. She ran the staff ragged at this remnant of the British Empire. Ma Carsley wasn't seeking their help; she simply wanted to tell them about her fan mail.

For those of you who think that football has always been soulless, one glance at my mother's treasured correspondence would change your minds. It was a direct result of me contacting six of her football heroes and encouraging them to forward a kind word or two to cheer her. I knew them by reputation only and never expected that every one of them would take the time to write to her. Mike Lyons, her favourite footballer, summarized his pride at being a fellow Blue. Alan Ball, then at Southampton, sent a beautifully personalized photo. Bob Latchford, Howard Kendall and Kenny Dalglish expressed their best wishes. The most remarkable correspondence came from Brian Clough who dispatched four handwritten pages describing the special bond between a son and a mother. Always outspoken, sometimes insensitive after his reputation became tainted by allegations of financial misdealing, there will never be another like him.

Why Clough - especially after his heartless contention that Liverpool fans were killed by Liverpool people at Hillsborough? Well for starters, he was a working-class hero from her neck of the woods. People tend to forget that he had been a top-class goal-scorer, netting 251 times in 274 games for Middlesbrough and Sunderland. His goals-per-game ratio was higher than that of Dixie Dean. I had seen Clough in action. My father and my step-uncle, a previously unknown kin in the North East, had taken me to Ayresome Park to watch Boro against Alf Ramsey's Ipswich in 1961. The Second Division fixture saw Clough overwhelm the table-topping visitors with a heroic display. That afternoon, he was unplayable and scared the life out of the Ipswich defenders.

When a knee injury cut short his playing career, he developed into a top-notch boss who took two provincial clubs, Derby and Forest, out of the depths of the Second Division and converted them into champions and more. In particular, I liked the fact that his teams were exciting and skilful. Unfortunately, there was to be no place in our history for Clough. He stands alongside Don Revie and Bobby Robson as the greatest managers we never had. It could have been so different. After the sacking of Billy Bingham in the summer of 1977, the media had elevated Clough to odds-on favourite for the hot-seat. The club's hierarchy, however, was too conservative to appoint such a controversial maverick. So instead of Brian Clough, we got Gordon Lee.

At the top of my mother's bucket list was her wish for one more afternoon in the Top Balcony. I took the liberty to enquire if there was anything that the club could do for an old Blue who had experienced some bad news.

We were in Texas when a member of the staff invited us to meet him outside the main entrance at noon on the next Saturday. In a flash, we packed our bags and headed across the ocean. Ma Carsley was thrilled at the idea of visiting Mama Blue again. Perhaps not as much as me. Neither of us knew what to expect, possibly a brief tour of the stadium and the then bulging trophy cabinet. No, this was the Everton of 30 years ago – a truly grand old club that went out of its way to please its faithful customers.

There are some things in life that money can't buy and being treated like a Toffee Lady is one of them. From the moment she crossed the Goodison threshold, the truly grand old club went out of its way to make her afternoon special. She was greeted with genuine kindness and displays of thoughtful gestures and actions - the type that make such a big difference in someone's life. After the stadium tour, we returned to the home dressing room for what can only be described as a love-fest.

Howard Kendall, a warm-hearted gentleman with impeccable manners and a lovely way with people, took charge of the proceedings. He re-assured me: 'I'll look after your mum'. I remember glancing at her wrapped up in a hand-knitted blue and white scarf holding his hand. For the first time in months her face beamed with happiness. They were like two old friends. The manager insisted on introducing every player to my mother. It was a demonstration of compassion way beyond the call of duty. I was more than a tad jealous of her perched on the bench between an injured Derek Mountfield and a ravenous Kevin Richardson, who was finishing off his bag of chips. She was so excited that it was hard to understand her Geordie words and Richardson acted as a flawless interpreter. The manager escorted the reigning champions towards her. One by one he introduced Kevin Ratcliffe, Gary Stevens, Graeme Sharp, Gary Lineker, Trevor Steven, Adrian Heath, Peter Reid, Paul Bracewell et al. Predictably, Neville Southall gave her a bear hug. So did Colin Harvey and Mick Heaton. Each and every one of them was a credit to the Everton family.

The atmosphere created by Howard Kendall was so relaxed that I found it hard to believe that his team was about to tangle with Arsenal. After 30 minutes of laughter and giggles, assistant manager Colin Harvey approached me: 'Please tell Una that the boys are a bit shy and want to take their clothes off.' We started to make our way towards her favourite spec and hadn't gone five yards before Howard Kendall and Kevin Sheedy approached her. Kendall prompted: "Go on, tell her.' In response, Sheedy smiled: 'I just want you to know that your name will be on the ball when I score today.'

I don't need to remind you that these fine footballers were at the top of their game. That afternoon my mother along with 30,000 other Blues witnessed Howard Kendall's team of gentlemen humble the Gunners by 6-1. Lineker netted a brace, so did Heath. Steven and Sharp added the others. Although Sheedy's magic wand failed to propel the leather into the onion bag, my mother spoke about Kevin Sheedy and Howard Kendall in biblical terms until the day she died.

69. Name on the ball

Subsequently, I returned to Widnes to look after Ma Carsley. It was a truly wonderful experience, possibly the best of my life. During those 12 months, I got to know my mother as a person and grasped the opportunity to express my appreciation for the sacrifices she made in the name of her children. Far quicker than I had anticipated, Alzheimer's disease stole her memories, independence and dignity by eroding her ability to manage even basic tasks. It was painful to watch her mind shutting down. She forgot things. She couldn't find words. Thankfully, even when she didn't know my name, my mother retained her kindness.

My return was made easier by a joint venture set up in London and Chester by some American acquaintances and Lord Rothschild. Let's call it the Andy Warhol gig. Even though I had enjoyed the support of Texan aristocracy, I entered the world of their British counterparts with caution. My fears proved to be unfounded. His lordship made me feel welcome and organized regular lunches at Spencer House, located next to my London office, to introduce me to his business buddies. To this day, I'm convinced that the guests were more impressed with the ostentatious surroundings than anything I had to say to them. I know that I was. The home of Princess Diana's ancestors is the capital's most magnificent private palace. His lordship had invested a small fortune over a 10-year period to painstakingly restore the neo-classical architecture to its full splendour and then adorned the interior with truly magnificent oil paintings, marble sculptures and antique furniture borrowed from the Royal Collection and the Tate Gallery.

Away from the nation's capital, I was shocked by the distressed condition of the rest of the United Kingdom. The country had frittered away the North Sea revenues which should have been used to upgrade or replace its clapped-out industries and infrastructure. I'm no expert but it appeared to me that the indigenous working class had been abandoned and were void of real hope. A London-based friend claimed that, in the absence of traditional moral norms, they were turning into a feral underclass.

It won't surprise you to learn that my London colleagues demonstrated immense confidence derived from gilded lives and were members of a clique you could only belong to if you've been to a prep school with manicured lawns. While the majority was supportive, one of them postulated: 'Listen old chap, no matter how hard you work and how many sacrifices you make in life - you'll never earn as much money as I stand to inherit from my dear Pa Pa.' He thought of himself as enlightened culturally yet every so often looked down his nose at me and my interest in professional football. Hopefully by now, no doubt from his executive boxes at the Emirates, the Bridge, the Lane and even the Queen Elizabeth Olympic Stadium, he has grasped that footie - as he like to call it - is the world's only transcendental art form.

At first, I ignored him and bit my tongue. After all, I was well aware that what we've been given is not what makes us who we are. Later, I reminded him that the best things in life weren't things. Finally, I showed him a snap-shot of Ma Carsley sat between Derek Mountfield and Kevin Richardson in the Goodison dressing-room. He wasn't impressed.

My most celebrated encounter with the type of British people who achieved glory while giving the impression of making no real effort was at the Annual Meeting of the Law Society held at Cambridge University. Prior to my speech which highlighted the hidden risks in US mergers and acquisitions, the organizers asked me to jot down a few things about my background. The chairman misread my scribbles to the audience of 500 lawyers, solicitors and barristers: 'Those of you expecting a member of Rothschild family will be bitterly disappointed.' He laughed and continued: 'I don't know too much about the last-minute replacement, except that he's British by birth and - for some unknown reason - American by choice.' 'I understand that although our next speaker hails from Merseyside - a place in the North Country where virulent strains of anti-establishment run rampant, he was raised as an Etonian by an Etonian.' I stifled my chuckles and decided not to correct his words.

I realized that my cover would be blown wide open as soon as I opened by big Widnes mouth. Anyway, for the next hour and more I wore the imaginary black and light blue neckwear of the school to attend if you want to get ahead in the United Kingdom or, alternatively, keep quiet about if you don't want to be seen as obscenely privileged. I was told by an American acquaintance at Fulbright & Jaworski that my words were delivered with guarded confidence and received with genuine interest but muted applause from the public school old boys sat near him.

Upon returning to Widnes, Ma Carsley wasn't amused by the recollection of my deception at Cambridge University. Always, she preached brutal honesty, generosity of spirit and good housekeeping. Even as a pensioner fighting a cruel and degenerative disease that no-one has ever survived, she spoke frankly, displayed compassion and continued to save her pennies. I encouraged her to spend them on little luxuries for herself. She wouldn't hear of it and insisted on saving them in order to leave something to her two children.

Because such things aren't worth arguing about, I told her that - with her permission - I planned to purchase shares of The Everton Football Club Company Limited with my inheritance and, with her permission, would like to distribute them to my friends. In response, she whispered: 'Play up, Everton.' They were her final words to me.

A fiver for the tape and another five hundred for
the Betamax machine to play it on

70. Blue for life

Now to another of life's really big decisions – what to do with your mother's ashes? Given the increasing speculation about a ground-move, I didn't want her remains spread at Goodison and decided to drop one handful into the River Mersey and another into the River Tees. Because Chemical Harry had returned to comfort my mother during her final days, I invited him to accompany me to the North East on a bitterly cold January afternoon. Even though the path to the High Force waterfall was treacherous, we hiked to a vantage point where the Steel River plunged perpendicularly into the basin below. The swirling mist above the turbulent waters was like that at Niagara's Horseshoe Falls.

Against my advice, my father climbed some icy rocks to throw the ashes into the heart of the falls. Predictably, they blew into his face and temporarily blinded him. He stumbled and, for once in my life, I exhibited the type of athletic reflexes with which he had impressed so many patrons in the Paddock decades earlier and bundled him to safety. While I don't believe in karma, I fear that I prevented my mother from having the last word.

Elizabeth and I departed to Texas with the rest of her ashes. The journey wasn't without incident. Looking back, I shouldn't have been surprised that we raised suspicions at Houston airport. After all, we were people with unusual accents holding US passports and fiercely protecting a package containing an unknown substance. My interactions with the immigration officials didn't go well. Flippantly, I described myself as 'British by birth, American by choice and a Blue for life.' Their counterpart with the US Customs Service took me into a room for further interrogation and - wait for it - a cavity search for contraband. I trust that you understand that I'm not talking about nostrils, ears or my big mouth. In response to his demand, I declared: 'May I remind you that I also hold a British passport and don't bend over for anyone.' He replied: 'Well your highness if that's the case, you had better curtsey onto this Latex glove.' I don't know how best to describe the subsequent experience. Later in life, I discovered that such invasive frisking was like a prostate exam without the finesse acquired at medical school.

When I was cleared to go, the tetchy customs official smiled: 'Welcome home. Have a nice day!' After living in the USA for 40 years, I'm immune to such Americanisms. After all, it's a young country where you can say what you think - without thinking. Though I've adopted more than a few American spellings, I cringe at inelegant phrases such as 'hike the price', 'do the math' and 'gotten'. Their frequent use on the 'NBC Nightly News' makes me shudder.

The people in the United Kingdom are different from those in the USA. Not better, not worse, just different. By and large, I've concluded that older Americans are Anglophiles who aren't reluctant to express what they think of their English-speaking cousins. That's not a bad thing because Brits appear even keener to voice their opinions about Yanks. Stereotypes bound. Let's see - morbidly obese, beer-swilling, gun-toting, war-mongering people preoccupied with buying stuff on the never-never. I'll let you decide which nation I'm characterizing.

Many Brits and Americans of my vintage fear retirement. Some express anxiety about not having enough savings. Others anguish about leaving the routine and sense of purpose provided by the workplace. A few agonize over how to spend their free time. Surely, excessive worry about such things can shorten life expectancy so much that you need not be concerned about them? As you know, I discovered that you must make sure that you retire from work, not from life. It took me years to accept and validate Dr France's First Law: Devotion to the royal blue cause expands to fill the time available.

In retirement, I've been very fortunate to bump into Blues in just about every corner of the North American continent, even in the tranquility of the Pacific Coast where I straddled the 49th parallel. The driving forces behind ToffeeWeb, the longest-running website for Blues, reside in my neck of the woods near Seattle and San Francisco. I must confess that I'm hooked on my daily doses of chatter and opinion on the independent websites. Most contributors are eloquent and passionate. So much so that their archives combined with those of the NSNO website will become important parts of the club's history in the Twenty-First Century and should be preserved.

Then there was my barber in Victoria BC, a less reliable source of football gossip, who welcomed new customers by proclaiming loudly: 'I must warn you, I'm a far better Evertonian than I am a hairdresser!' before launching a tide of royal blue propaganda towards whoever was trapped in his well-worn chair. Obviously, I loved the sound of his words as well as his Crosby accent. However, they could be troublesome for unsuspecting walk-ins. I remember one summer's afternoon when he was confronted by the owner of a vibrant Carlsberg shirt. The visitor queried: 'Of all the teams in the effing EPL, why on earth did you pick the effing Toffees?' Instantly the Johnson Street shop fell silent - make that near deadly silent. Through the expanse of floor to ceiling mirrors lining the walls I could see my friend holding his mother-of-pearl handled razor and glaring at the nape of the Kopite. But rather than take his scalp - in the manner perfected allegedly by the local Songhees tribe - and perhaps his tongue from his potty-mouth, he leaned over his hostage and growled sinisterly: 'Because Evertonians eat Scouse.' His response was very similar to the Moyesiah's insightful proclamation that the indigenous people on the streets of Merseyside prefer Everton.

In retrospect, I feel that it's possible to stand up for your strongly held beliefs and empowering thoughts about our beloved club without foisting them down someone else's throat when holding a very sharp blade.

Image how fast Donovan would run if he wasn't an American

71. American soccer

Stateside soccer has had a royal blue rash for several decades. Throughout the Seventies and Eighties, wrinkled Blues popped up on playing fields across North America. The club, however, continues to maintain something of a low profile. Woe betide any Blue wanting a replica shirt because they aren't sold alongside those of United, Liverpool and Chelsea. My wife jokes that they must be kept under the counter like porn at an old-fashioned newsagents shop. Despite its association with Joe-Max Moore, Brian McBride and Predrag Radosavljevic -better known as Preki, US legends who amassed 224 caps between them, Everton Football Club wasn't a household name until very recently. The change coincided with the signings of the two most recognizable faces of the North American game. The enthusiastic manner in which both Tim Howard and Landon Donovan have spoken about their times at Goodison has elevated us to among the 20 most popular European clubs on this side of the Atlantic.

Like the country itself, US professional soccer is a work in progress. Thirty years ago, it boasted Beckenbauer, Cruyff, Pele and a legion of aging imports. After the NASL folded in 1984, there was a vacuum until the MLS kicked off in 1996. Despite Americans' dislike of no-score draws and blatant diving, the game's popularity has increased season after season. So much so that the Seattle Sounders - my nearest club - sold 32,000 season tickets for the 2016 campaign. That figure placed them 50th on the list of the best supported football clubs in the world.

Market growth has been driven by the fact that most children in Houston and farther afield have been exposed to soccer at one time or another. Encouragingly, our club has taken some important steps by the introduction of Everton America in Texas, Maryland and Connecticut. This grass-roots approach for youngsters aged 6 -18 emphasizes our enviable development record. Unfortunately, it came too late for one Canadian. Let me explain. A friend who coached the Alberta Under-16 team telephoned me about a promising teenager who had been invited for trials in Europe. He asked if I could arrange something similar for his protege on Merseyside. I'm sure real talent slips through the net all the time. In fact, I bet you can name more than one youngster released by Everton only to return and earn international honours. None of them, however, have won two UEFA Champions Leagues, four Bundesliga titles, three German Cup finals and one Premier League title plus 42 England caps in a truncated career. I imagined that the club was inundated with similar requests and asked my friend for objective evidence about the abilities and merits of his young hopeful. In response, I received a dossier containing data on the boy's speed, endurance and strength. I still didn't know if he was a decent footballer. The technical data, however, confirmed that the youngster was as fit as a proverbial fiddle.

Since the Canadian teenager had been invited for kick-abouts at Sheffield United and Crystal Palace, I deduced that he must have something to offer and forwarded the dossier to the folks at Bellefield. I even volunteered to drive the boy from London to Merseyside if they would take a quick look at him. Many former-players have told me that a professional eye can tell if a youngster has potential simply by the way he addresses the ball. Sadly, the club couldn't find the time to do so. Apparently, it was overflowing with the YTS players and responded that there was no point in bringing him to the training ground. Owen Hargreaves took this set-back in his stride. Even though his subsequent playing career was blighted by persistent knee injuries, United were keen to pay £17 million to Bayern Munich for the mid-fielder's signature some 12 years later.

This reference to United leads me to David Beckham. I'm not sure what specific crime the USA committed to have been burdened with his public relations machine. No doubt his advisers thought that US soccer would orbit around him. Well, it didn't. Beckhamania focused more on his role as a publicity whore than soccer player and more Americans know the names of his children than the clubs he has played for.

In California, his contributions were ridiculed. In six seasons, he made 100 or so appearances for LA Galaxy - allegedly, each time with a different hairstyle. Because Landon Donovan and his team-mates seemed to play more free-flowing football without him, many Galaxy fans believed his absence wasn't such a bad thing. I must concur. Every time I watched him, Beckham conspicuously failed to influence the proceedings against modest MLS opposition.

In retirement, I discovered that the best thing about being a Blue is that you never have to take a day off. That said, I wish that I had pulled a sickie on November 28, 2010 - the day when US television reported that David Moyes had invited the 35-year-old clothes horse, who can't raise a gallop because of the weight of his gratuitous international caps, to telephone him about a loan spell at Goodison. Immediately, I grabbed the remote control and clicked to the Weather Channel to see if hell had frozen over. What was Moyes thinking? Surely he was aware that the man craves so much attention that we were more likely to see him alongside Ulrika Jonsson in the Celebrity Big Brother House than tracking back to help right-back Tony Hibbert.

72. Paid to lose - allegedly

Today, I barely recognize Merseyside as its skyline is dotted with the cranes of regeneration. The region, however, lost something during the transition to service-related enterprises in the Nineties. I believe that when a community manufactures things, it reinforces the connection between effort and reward. To make things, you need to understand concepts, materials and skills. To make money, you simply need the morals of a whore.

Returning to football; nobody promised me that supporting Everton would be easy but going to Goodison in the Nineties was like attending the bedside of a sick relative. It was a duty bordering on a moral obligation that drained me emotionally. My response was to put on the proverbial brave face to hide the sense of betrayal. Who was to blame? There were plenty of condemnations to go around. Even though I'm aware that it's a physical fact that by pointing a finger at someone results in three fingers pointing back at you, I aim my index finger at Mike Walker, and the people who recruited him in early 1994 as the major conspirators to my misery. Those directors included Dr David Marsh, Sir Desmond Pitcher, Sir Philip Carter, Keith Tamlin and Bill Kenwright. We all make mistakes; it's part of being human. But what were they thinking? The appointment of 'The Silver Fox' was epochal. Within no time, it induced a week-by-week erosion of our hopes and major readjustment of our expectations. Walker, his very name turns my stomach, lasted 10 months - the shortest tenure of any Everton manager. During that time, we won a half-dozen League games. That's right, six League games. To add insult to injury, the Premier League fined the club for inducing him to leave Norwich. What's that? We should have kept our receipt and demanded a refund.

Where to start? The manager's tactics were grim. Performances were atrocious. Results were shocking. His acquisitions were distressing but no worse than the man he failed to sign. What a farce! Luis Antonio Correa da Costa, a Brazilian mercenary better known as Muller, walked out of Goodison shortly before the press conference arranged to announce his signing. Perhaps he became aware that within seven seasons we had tumbled from champions to relegation candidates. The striker rejected Walker's Everton for Kashiwa Reysol in the Japanese J League.

After witnessing an abject 5-1 defeat at Hillsborough followed by a 3-0 home loss to Blackburn, I concurred with the other diehards in Row R that we resembled dead men walking to the gallows. After the last match of that UK trip, an encouraging 1-0 win at Upton Park, I reviewed our remaining fixtures and predicted that we would lose at Leeds, snatch an away point at Loftus Road and scratch out three home points against Coventry to edge our way to safety. I became pre-occupied with the horror of relegation. My fears heightened after we gained only one point from those three games. Even if we picked up all three points in our final game against Wimbledon, I was aware that we would need a little help from elsewhere. I visited Rothko Chapel in Houston to communicate with the football gods. I begged that Neville Southall, Dave Watson and Tony Cottee wouldn't let me down and even promised to forgive Mike Walker and his side-kick Dave Williams for pushing us towards the abyss. I was no stranger to the octagonal structure or Mark Rothko's massive artwork that covers its walls. It's impossible to describe the power that transcends the black and purple tones of the paintings. Now listed in the National Register of Historic Places, some people consider it gloomy. To this day, the chapel is my tranquil place for meditation and, if appropriate, for contemplation of life in a lower division.

Before the advent of the internet, when American television was no friend of soccer, I started every Saturday by decorating our living room with a homemade apparatus designed to receive the BBC World Service. I'm told that it looked like RAF Fylingdales in the Yorkshire Moors, with antennas stretched across the ceiling. My Sony short-wave radio, which had brought much joy to our Texas household, was primed to receive the signal. It was faint on the morning in question, no doubt because it was relayed via Canada, Antigua and heaven.

My heart sank when the radio crackled with the sound of the fat lady gargling. We were 2-1 down at half-time. Before commencing the live commentary, the reporter summarized the first-half. Nerves had got to the boys in blue. Anders Limpar had needlessly handled in his own area. Southall had got to Dean Holdsworth's spot kick but the ball slipped into the net. Worse still, we had panicked whenever the ball was in our half. Wimbledon had increased their lead when Dave Watson and David Unsworth collided and Gary Ablett sliced his clearance into his own net. I heard Wellington, our American Cocker Spaniel howl: 'Why? For the love of God, why?'

We had pulled one back when Limpar collapsed inside the Wimbledon penalty box despite the absence of a discernible challenge. I didn't approve of the acrobatic manoeuver in which his body rotated and twisted before reaching the pike position but did applaud Graham Stuart's successful penalty kick. Around that time, the radio commentator mentioned that the visitors' team bus had been destroyed in the early hours of that morning in Runcorn. Arson was suspected. More importantly, he noted that the half-time scores from the other important fixtures offered some encouragement to listening Blues. Alas, not to those in Houston.

My wife couldn't stand the tension and insisted that I hand over my shoelaces and belt before she took the dog for a long walk. Via the radio I could hear blue sleeves being rolled up high. I did the same as I scowled across the living room carpet blocking every Wimbledon attack and kicking every item of furniture in the process. When Wellington and Elizabeth returned to check on me, the dog sensed that things weren't going well. American Cocker Spaniels can detect anxiety. He sat at the front door and refused to cross the threshold. Consequently, they made an about-turn for another lap around our sub-division. In their absence, the referee ignored calls for a Wimbledon penalty after Graham Stuart and yours truly unlaced the ball on the line.

Not long afterwards, Barry Horne got the better of Vinnie Jones in midfield and ventured forward to send a rocket into the top corner. My screams must have alerted Wellington and his handler because they bounded into the house. It was 2-2 and the three of us howled at the radio as we strained for the vital winner. Our pleas were answered when Tony Cottee knocked the ball into the path of Graham Stuart whose shot evaded the lethargic dive of the Wimbledon keeper. The dog couldn't believe his luck. He did a couple of somersaults before thinking of Mike Walker and vomiting on the carpet. The final whistle brought scenes of wild jubilation as news of Sheffield United's loss at Chelsea confirmed our safety. Then, the house fell silent. We realized that we had survived by the skin of our teeth. It was our most serious flirtation with relegation for 43 years.

There were many Blues at Goodison that day including referee Robbie Hart, Hans Segers and the big fellow upstairs. Cynics allege that Walker's team nearly lost a game in which the opposition was paid to lose. Never? I'm aware, however, that football is a murky world of cheating players, bent managers, rogue officials and muscular betting syndicates that matches are fixed more often than we think. On occasions, old players have mentioned games against suspiciously inept foes such as the penultimate match of our 1962/63 title-winning campaign when we triumphed by 4-0 at the Hawthorns. West Brom lost a player through injury after eight minutes. The remaining 10 men conspired to donate a soft penalty and an own goal to our quest. Fixed or not, no-one complained about the outcome on the road to our first silverware for 24 years.

While May 7, 1994 isn't a date to be celebrated, it's one that no Blue should forget. Imagine if Segers had saved Graham Stuart's tame shot and we had been relegated. The ramifications? Drowning in debt, we would have been forced to sell our best players and slash operating costs. The academy at Netherton would have closed and a 9-year-old Wayne Rooney would have joined the Reds, albeit against his will. Heaven forbid, we could have been docked points and discarded to the third-tier because Peter Johnson owned two clubs in the same division.

73. Rideout suit

Everton Crazy? Quite definitely. Superstitious? No not me. I would gladly walk under ladders, step on cracks, spill salt and smash mirrors even on Friday the Thirteenth. That was until the first night I wore my lucky suit. Dark blue, single-breasted and nothing fancy, it was a gift or rather compensation from British Airways.

Let me explain. I had flown from Houston to Manchester. It was an uneventful journey except that my checked luggage - an old Globetrotter suitcase - didn't make the connection in Gatwick. For some unknown reason, it had decided to spend the weekend relaxing in London. BA' staff were understanding and advised me to purchase a modest suit from say Marks & Spencer at their expense to tide me over. The half-priced bargain enjoyed its first outing that Monday night at Goodison. It was a memorable debut. Rooted to the foot of the League table, Everton had won only one of its first 14 games prior to my UK visit but defeated the old enemy by 2-0. I must admit at that time it flashed through my mind that the new suit could be a good omen. These feelings were reinforced the following weekend when it witnessed Paul Rideout steal the points at Stamford Bridge. It was larceny. If my memory serves me well, we also defeated Leeds before I returned to Houston.

During my next UK visit, a month or so later, I wore the suit when we battered Norwich in the League and also the FA Cup. It had not gone unnoticed that Rideout had scored in all of these games. Could it be a lucky charm? Brian Labone thought so. He brought his suspicions to my attention and insisted that I wear 'The Rideout Suit' until the end of the season. He didn't demand that I follow any special ritual of putting it on right leg first or left arm last, as long as I wore it every time I watched Everton. Then things became a little odd, make that spooky. To attract the favor of the football gods, Brian would produce a pocket-size clothes brush before every Goodison fixture to ensure that my shoulders were shipshape.

We were still holding up the League table when I returned to the old country in April. As you would expect, I now travelled in my lucky suit to avoid any luggage problems. During that trip, we hammered Tottenham in the semi-final at Elland Road, defeated Newcastle and drew at Hillsborough. Rideout didn't score in those games but, thanks to the suit and possibly Joe Royle's Dogs of War, we edged towards safety and the FA Cup final. Stained with sweat and tears, it was present in May when we picked up three points at Ipswich to secure our place in the top flight, drew at Highfield Road and then beat United in the final. Rideout, of course, scored the most important goals of his career in the 1-0 victories at Portman Road and Wembley.

Superstitious? Who me? I'll say so. At the start of the following season, the blue suit looked tired around the elbows and shiny at the seat. Even so, it was at Anfield when Kanchelskis scored his double and Hillsborough when he netted a magnificent hat-trick. However, the cruel reality of life was that I had stopped long distance running and had put on some pounds. My wife decided that the garment had earned its retirement. Her exact words: 'You're not going to England in that thing!' Her tongue-lashing was nothing compared to the one from Brian Labone who admonished me in the crowded Joe Mercer Suite before the game with Wimbledon for wearing a blue pin-stripe replacement. His fears were realized when, even though the Ukrainian wide-boy scored, we lost by 4-2. Afterwards Brian looked disheartened and close to tears. So much so that I felt like I had betrayed him.

Now, fast forward to the end of the 1997/98 campaign. The appointment of Howard Kendall for a third term was as ill-conceived as the recruitment of Mike Walker. The rumours of heavy drinking were disturbing. While attitudes towards lifestyle had been liberal in the glory years, alcohol should not have been a part of team bonding in the late-Nineties. Our progress was plagued by the stench of mediocrity, internal strife and spilled red wine.

The suit had languished in a closet in Houston throughout the season which had involved one calamity after another. Like most Blues, I feared for our future after witnessing the deplorable capitulation to Wednesday which appeared to drive a giant nail into our coffin. I wasn't alone. Pat Hickson approached me after the match. She cautioned that the fear of relegation and his memories of his early days in the Second Division had got to the Cannonball Kid. She asked me to comfort her husband. Aware of the red mist swirling around him, I approached Dave in the manner of a bomb-disposal robot before placing my hand on his shoulder. My old friend turned to face me. With tears in his eyes, he sobbed: 'We're not good enough. We deserve to go down. Don't we?' He added: 'And it's your fault. Where's your lucky suit!'

The concept of relegation sickened me. Never before had I experienced such gnawing pains in my stomach. I seemed to spend my days and nights processing the remaining fixtures and the different permutations of outcomes in my mind. If we win this game here and they only pick up a point there and then they lose to them, etc. In a state of high anxiety, I telephoned Elizabeth in Texas and encouraged her to join me at the final League fixture, namely the famous showdown with Coventry, and to bring the lucky suit in her hand-luggage. Also I begged her to find a rabbit's foot, a four leaf clover, a horseshoe, scarab beetles and anything else she thought would emit positive spiritual energy. To my amazement and her eternal credit, she agreed.

Later I learnt that she had been genuinely concerned that I may have another heart-attack or a lethal episode of Evertonitis, an equally congenital condition. It's an odd phenomenon, difficult to explain. When it strikes, you know what it is. In the interim, my worst fears had been confirmed at Highbury where we surrendered in a miserable 4-0 defeat.

Regarding his inability to read the game ... there's nothing wrong with his eyes - he's got dyslexic feet

74. Women and children first

Neither my old garment, whose artificial silk lining had been turned inside-out for extra luck, nor my old lady, whose stomach had been turned upside down by a cocktail of panic and anxiety disorders, made it to Goodison. They stayed in the blue rental car parked near Walton Hall Park and hugged each other for two hours. Innocent passers-by must have thought that Elizabeth was taking part in a witches' Sabbath. I'm sure that any football fans that saw her understood that it was a prayer vigil.

Our fate was out of our hands. We would be relegated if Bolton won at Stamford Bridge. Before the kick-off, Mama Blue held her breath as the Everton women's team took a bow for capturing their League title and the Everton youth team were saluted for winning the FA Youth Cup. Once again the lawyer sat near me claimed: 'Everton Football Club was like RMS Titanic - women and children first.' He was wrong. The history books show that the previously maligned Gareth Farrelly and 40,000 new members of his fan club brought the city centre to a standstill that rain-soaked Sunday evening. My response to his all-important goal in the sixth minute was surreal. I remember the Irishman knocking the ball up to Duncan Ferguson and the big man nodding it into Farrelly's path before his right-foot shot flew into the net off the post. My brain didn't process what had happened for a split second. I was in shock. My initial silence was followed by a lot of shrieking and jumping up and down before anxiety returned to the pit of my stomach.

I looked around for reassuring faces to calm my nerves. In their absence, my uneasiness gave way to panic. My mind was tormented by fear. Yes, we had scored too early. I prayed, an act cunningly disguised by the nibbling of my finger nails, throughout the rest of the game. The news that Gianluca Vialli had scored for Chelsea didn't cheer me. I was convinced that Coventry would recover and send us down. The tension was incredible. Nick Barmby's feeble penalty kick and Dion Dublin's sublimely headed equalizer in the closing stages served to heighten my agony. I felt dizzy. I felt breathless. I know people who hid in the corridors and locked themselves in the toilets during the final minutes. When referee Paul Alcock brought the proceedings to an end, the Blues around me went delirious.

My own reaction? The 1-1 draw was more emotional than any cup final victory. Perhaps under the weight of good fortune, I sank to my knees seeking celestial succor. My heart was beating as fast as that of a racehorse. It was all that I could hear. I felt drained and remained in the Main Stand for 10 minutes mesmerized by sights of thousands of strangers embracing like long lost brothers and dancing across the hallowed turf and hundreds of others ripping it up with their bare hands for souvenirs. Among the bedlam I was enthralled by the sportsmanship of the visitors. The Coventry fans were applauding our Premier League survival.

As I made my way along Goodison Road, I asked one of my friends to climb a lamp-post not to thank the football gods but to retrieve one of the many Echo placards that screamed 'Come On You Blues!' I carried it aloft as I jogged to Walton Hall Park. In a state of unabashed ecstasy, I embraced everyone who crossed my path and changed my path to hug others whose relentless support had inspired the team. My wife greeted me with open arms. She was wearing the suit jacket. From the car, the trousers sighed with contentment.

From the driver's seat, Elizabeth noted that cruelty as a public spectacle is abhorrent to the civilized mind and claimed that the final scoreline had involved divine intervention. Possibly, there was a hint of a miracle about Gareth Farrelly's life-saving goal - with his weaker right foot - because the Irish midfielder played only another dozen minutes for our first-team during the next two seasons. If you don't want to look that high perhaps destiny played its part. Definitely, there was a perceptible interruption of the laws of nature about the outcome.

As we drove eastwards along the East Lancs Road, I wondered how a club with such steadfast support and such a distinguished past could have fallen so far as to rely on an out-of-form midfielder and a worn-out suit to cling to its place in the top flight on goal-difference. How had a football club that had boasted the first billionaire owner in British football plunged so deep into the game's abyss of hopelessness? Surely the previous last-day-of- the-season escape against Wimbledon in 1994 should have been a wake-up call.

The Echo placard is now a part of the Everton Collection. The lucky blue suit isn't. It was donated to the Salvation Army shop in Chester. Yes, I know that I acted in haste. In its absence, I've watched Everton performances move farther and farther away from entertaining football to the mind-numbing hoofball of Walter Smith and David Moyes and equally tedious tippy-tappy of Roberto Martinez. I've endured some truly atrocious performances as they guided their sides along unimaginative ruts and would love to proclaim that I've never ever been ashamed of the boys in blue. Sadly, that's not true.

I trust that everyone who visited the Dell for the final game of the 1998/99 season feels the same way. Effectively unopposed, Southampton won 2-0 and side-stepped the trap-door. The Blues in front of me were disgusted by our limp performance of Walter Smith's team. I remember Oliver Dacourt throwing his boots into the crowd and, in the manner of Islamic protesters, the Everton fans chucking them back. All Blues should be thankful that Chelsea demonstrated more integrity under very similar circumstances. The Londoners had nothing to lose except their honour yet refused to go through the motions against our relegation foes - Sheffield United in 1994 and Bolton in 1998.

Be fair ... if you pick the tea lady we're stuck with Claus again

75. Reds didn't force us to sign Angell

It's hard to swallow but there is no escape from the fact that my beloved club trails behind its traditional rivals — by some distance. During too many of my 60 seasons as a Blue, the red juggernauts garaged in Liverpool and Manchester swept all before them. While United were picking up 33 trophies and Liverpool even more, we captured just eight. Worse still, it's been two decades since our last triumph - the longest drought in our history.

Now and then, I'm guilty of peering through the mists of time to re-discover the vibrant club of my teenage years and identify the undermining causes for our regression. So let's start with the usual suspects. First, the vagaries of misfortune. Tell me, is it pure coincidence that we were the reigning champions when the hostilities associated with World War 1, World War 2 and Heysel interrupted our plans? Who knows how many trophies we would have won if it wasn't for the Kaiser in 1915, the Fuhrer in 1939 and, let's call her, the Iron Lady in 1985.

Tragic deaths in Belgium allow some Blues to feel morally superior, however, the inconvenient truth is that even though the actions of red hooligans and Margaret Thatcher barred the reigning League champions and favourites from competing in the 1986 European Cup, they can't be blamed for our subsequent decline. That said, I do believe that Liverpool should have paid financial compensation to Everton and Arsenal, the innocent League champions during that five-year period, or invited them to take their place in future European competitions when the ban was lifted. Sounds preposterous? Well, I've been told by lawyers with expertise in this area that Goodison season-ticket holders could have sued Liverpool Football Club for anticipated loss of enjoyment.

Previously, our European ambitions had been hindered by the fact that we resided in the same city as Bill Shankly and his annoying habit of finishing slightly higher up the table than Harry Catterick. Everton were penalized by the one city-one team rule of the Inter-Cities Fairs Cup, which morphed into the UEFA Cup, at a time when English clubs dominated the competition. I recall that the entrants for the 1968/69 season, after we had finished fifth in the table, included Liverpool in third place and the eventual winners Newcastle tenth. Our misfortune was exacerbated the following year when we had finished third and the entrants for the 1969/70 season were Liverpool who came second and the eventual winners Arsenal fourth. Our tough breaks weren't limited to European woes. Shortly after Catterick's star-studded side captured the 1962/63 title, Tony Kay was banned sine die for the foolish deeds he committed in a previous life. We were left to wonder what the most expensive footballer and arguably the most influential mid-fielder in the land might have achieved. I speculate that we were the victim of a jinx inflicted by some evil power. In all likelihood by that bespectacled Greek girl.

Enough talk of bad luck and curses. To the best of my knowledge, neither Bill Shankly nor red hooligans forced Mike Walker to sign Brett Angell, Joe Royle to sign Marc Hottiger or Walter Smith to sign Alex Nyarko. Let's be honest, it's more likely that self-harm contributed to our plight. I prefer not to fret about transfer failures but, in the spirit of fair play, must mention the comings and goings of big money men such as Niclas Alexandersson, James Beattie, Diniyar Bilyaletdinov, Mo Johnston, Per Kroldrup and Tobias Linderoth. And how can I ignore the likes of Vinnie Samways, Steve Simonsen, John Spencer, Richard Wright and a Croatian whose name I no longer speak? I ask you: 'How many, if any, were good enough for Anfield or Old Trafford?

Along with the duds we bought, our decline was hastened by the gems we sold and failed to replace. My father described the sales of Tommy Lawton and Joe Mercer by Theo Kelly in the Forties as impetuous. If so, then the disposals of Bobby Collins and Roy Vernon by Harry Catterick in the Sixties were reckless. I shook my head in despair after the same manager committed the unthinkable act of selling Alan Ball. Every Blue from that era remembers where they were on that cold day in December 1971. It was worse than the death of a US president. More like the murder of Santa Claus. Decades later the assassin struck again when we failed to hold on to Gary Lineker, Andrei Kanchelskis and Wayne Rooney. After the last of these defections I was surprised to find that the globe was still spinning, albeit on a slightly different axis.

Enough talk of bad luck, curses and self-harm. What about paralysis? Our history could have been more glorious if we hadn't lost our nerve at critical times. Choking or bottling has been an Everton trait since our early days. How else can we explain finishing runners up in the League in 1890, '95, 1902, '05, '09 and '12 and in the FA Cup in 1893, '97 and 1907? That's nine hard luck stories in 22 years. Surely, 'Everton jitters' … meaning cock-up on the line between success and failure … is worthy of a place in the Urban Dictionary. Given our near misses in 1985, '86, '89 and 2009, sometimes I wonder if Blues have been conditioned to accept second place.

Cast your mind back to 1975. You may recall that we headed the League table for most of the season before imploding during the run-in. That wasn't bad luck; it was an untimely case of complacency. At the time, I didn't dwell on what might have been. I simply yearned for silverware to lift the gloom - even the League Cup. Perhaps that's not a good example because 22 clubs have captured the trophy since its introduction a half-century ago. Alas, not Everton. There have been 11 US Presidents in the White House, 10 UK Prime Ministers in Downing Street and six Popes in the Vatican since we first entered the competition. Inexplicably, we have performed no better in the other Mickey Mouse competitions held at Wembley. You may prefer to forget that we reached the finals of the Simod Cup and the Zenith Data Systems Cup only to falter.

If I'm honest, few indicators of our decline have caused more anguish than our inability to enlist some gifted baby Blues. I'm sure that local talent slips through the fingers of all clubs but there must have been a systematic flaw in our recruitment process not to have hooked Robbie Fowler, Steve McManaman, Michael Owen or Ian Rush. Can you imagine the impact these young Blues would have had on our line-ups during the past three decades? Why were we unattractive to them? Was it our stench of mediocrity? Our lack of ambition? Worse, we didn't attract Jamie Carragher and he boasted an Everton season-ticket in his pocket and an Everton tattoo on his heart. I had the pleasure of sitting between him and Dave Hickson at Goodison. Both gentlemen may have played for Liverpool but boasted more than a touch of Mike Lyons about them.

This leads to our struggles to fill the hot-seat. They started with the deteriorating health of Harry Catterick. We delayed replacing him and reassigned the day-to-day preparations to coach Tommy Casey who from all accounts wasn't a graduate of the School of Science. After Catterick finally stepped aside, the directors courted Don Revie and Bobby Robson before opting for the untried Billy Bingham as his replacement. After the Ulsterman was terminated, they returned to woo Robson. This time, the Ipswich manager agreed to a 10-year deal only to change his mind and we made do with the inexperienced Gordon Lee. Almost two decades later, after two stints by Howard Kendall and one by Colin Harvey, we were knocked back by Robson yet again. I recognize that this was a major blow but it was no excuse for offering the job to Mike Walker. Then, after Peter Johnson had failed to lure the elusive Robson to replace the so-called Silver Fox, we settled for Howard Kendall and his disastrous third term.

Many claim that Howard's departure to Spain in 1987 caused the club to fall behind its rivals. While his exit was untimely, our decline had been triggered a decade earlier. The origins of so many of our woes can be traced to the Goodison boardroom in the Seventies. That's right, even though the Moores party finished nearly 40 years ago, the hangover lingers to this day. How could the first football club in England to boast a billionaire owner have experienced such a riches-to-rags plunge? Clearly, something went wrong.

76. Imagine LFC being sold to a Blue

As I've watched the Merseyside Millionaires of my childhood disappear before my eyes, I've concluded that it must be wonderful to be a member of the Moores family. Imagine winning the pools every week and not having a care in the world. Prior to his retirement, John Moores had decided that none of his children exhibited the drive and savvy to run Littlewoods or Everton profitably and that they should focus on looking after the great man's name rather than his business interests or beloved football club. I'm convinced that he was mindful of the need for seamless continuity but, in his absence, both organizations slipped into a Kafkaesque world of bad judgment and internal squabbling.

For reasons known only to him, Moores selected a fawning subordinate as his representative on earth. Throughout his 42-year association with the Goodison boardroom, Philip Carter displayed the characteristics of an unassuming gentleman who allowed both football and administrative staffs to get on with their jobs. Or so I've been told. Normally, delegation is an attractive trait in a leader. Unfortunately after half-dozen years of relaxed stewardship, the club had tumbled into debt - so deep that it had to switch banks to arrange for a £60,000 overdraft to sign Peter Reid from Bolton.

All Blues know that we captured five trophies during his time as a director. Four of them were lifted in a narrow window between 1984 and 1987, the other must be credited to Peter Johnson in 1995. During the rest of his time, the club spent season after season in the doldrums. Unlike Will Cuff, whom many historians cite as Everton's most successful chairman, responsible for four titles, one FA Cup and a world-class stadium, Carter has been criticized for his tendency to look down his nose at the club's rank-and-file supporters - something that my wife and I witnessed first-hand.

Having sat or stood in just about every vantage point - obstructed and unobstructed - and watched from every angle including the fetal position at Goodison, my wife accepted Blue Bill's invitation to join the other white heads on the front row of the directors' box. During the post-match chat in the boardroom, Carter brought up the subject of young Wayne Rooney. We listened to his spin about the greedy youngster wanting to leave and didn't respond that the timing of the sale would rescue the club from financial meltdown. We bit our tongues until he started to rant about his interactions with the Rooney family. He stated: 'They are not - I repeat not - the type of people I like in my boardroom.' I couldn't hide my contempt for his snobbery and responded somewhat firmly that they were no different from the France family and the tens of thousands of other devoted fans who pay hard-earned money to pass through the turnstiles week in, week out. My words weren't well received. And just before he turned his back on me, I cautioned him that someday he would be working for them. To tell the truth, I've always thought that the club should keep well in with the Rooneys. Their son is set to earn at least £250 million during his playing days and there is more chance of them buying the club than any other Merseyside family.

Whatever the Moores family was thinking when they sold Liverpool Football Club to Tom Hicks and George Gillett must also have been going through their minds when they transferred their Everton shares to Peter Johnson. Instead of buying out the Moores family, who owned some 44% of the club, Johnson agreed to inject £10 million via a rights issue into the club's coffers. There was a small snag. The Football Association ruled that no-one could own a controlling interest in more than one club. Saint, sinner or something in between, Johnson agreed to sell his Tranmere shares.

After years of depraved indifference, the club was teetering on the brink of insolvency when the self-proclaimed Red grabbed control. His coronation was a quiet affair on Merseyside.

To the best of my knowledge, there were no street parties and banks, schools and post offices remained open. It was rumoured, however, that there was an extra public holiday in the Norwegian cities of Oslo, Bergen and Trondheim to allow his fellow Kopites to celebrate.

Secretly, I was confident that the savvy Merseyside businessman would re-establish the secure foundations required to return Everton to the elite. He had worked miracles at Tranmere where, with the help of Johnny King - our former-player, he had guided them from the very foot of the old Fourth Division to the gates of the new Premier League. At Goodison, Johnson displayed more ambition than the previous regime. After his hounds chased Mike Walker out of his lair, he made meaningful progress by constructing the club's Megastore and refurbishing the bridewell featured so proudly on the club's badge.

Also there was the small matter of him arranging for the funds to smash the club's transfer fee record three times in consecutive years. You may recall that he underwrote transfer kitties of £40 million for Joe Royle to sign Daniel Amokachi, Duncan Ferguson, Andrei Kanchelskis, Gary Speed, Nick Barmby and Slaven Bilic and another £20 million for Walter Smith to attract Olivier Dacourt, Marco Materazzi, John Collins, Steve Simonsen and Ibrahima Bakayoko. His greatest successes? He captured the FA Cup and the FA Charity Shield as well as - wait for it - deciding not to sign an Italian mercenary named Fabrizio Ravanelli.

Many Blues remained unhappy. To them he was Agent Johnson - a Kopite who wanted to relocate the club to a new stadium. Their distress was understandable. In your wildest dreams, can you imagine Liverpool Football Club being owned by a Blue?

Dumped Z Cars, introduced red season tickets, sold Big Dunc
... and you won't believe what I plan to do with my shares

77. An unwanted giant-killing

Even though they guided Everton to FA Cup glory at Wembley, Peter Johnson and his faithful lieutenant Clifford Finch could do nothing right in the eyes of most Blues. They saw a reign littered with insensitivities. These included replacing 'Z-Cars' with 'Fanfare for the Common Man', evicting the supporters' club and supplying season-tickets with red covers - I know, you couldn't make it up - and planning to abandon Mama Blue. More important, the increasingly skeptical fans criticized his failure to attract a top manager to replace Joe Royle who had left after being prevented from signing Tore Andre Flo from Brann.

The recruitment fiasco included a drawn-out rejection from experienced and accomplished Bobby Robson and a sharp snub from inexperienced and raw Andy Gray. By then, Johnson's popularity was so low that his hardest job was to keep the fans who believed he should have his head covered in tar and goose feathers from influencing those that remained undecided about the type of feathers to be used.

I received a poignant reminder of his fall from grace in the most unlikely of locations - the Valley of the Kings. My wife and I were accosted in the Luxor souq by a young shopkeeper named Mr Happy who was wearing an Everton shirt. He offered the usual patter: 'Come inside. Asda prices!' I asked him which team he supported. He looked at me with polite puzzlement: 'Mr Happy loves One & One.' Next I enquired his source of such a fine article of clothing. After much reflection, he admitted to finding it in a rubbish bin. It seemed ironic. Since then I've wondered about the previous owner. I imagine that he was a young Blue from Merseyside who took his prized shirt on holiday and discarded it in disgust, possibly after discovering that the yellow, white and blue hoops were different to those worn by the players.

Throughout the 1997/98 season, Everton were an absolute laughing stock. Rather than blame Howard Kendall, the fans blamed the Kopite. At the end of the season, Everton hung on to their Premiership lifeline by goal difference. At that time, I was invited by Johnson to submit a proposal to reduce costs and enhance revenues as well as provide a strategic framework for longer-term operations at Goodison. My approach involved a team of four diehard Blues, experts in legal, management, accounting and public relations issues, who would volunteer their time. Yes, for free. No consulting fees. No expense claims. No percentage of savings. The chairman embraced the idea but claimed to have received little, if any, support from his fellow directors of longer standing. I understand that one gentleman in particular - I'll let you decide who - asserted that my team lacked football experience. More likely, they were uncomfortable with the likelihood of our experts identifying loose controls and questioning generous perks in an essentially cash business. I was frustrated not to have been involved in influencing our future especially when watching the club drift from one financial crisis to another.

When Norman Jones, our mutual lawyer, and I dined with the new Everton chairman in Chester, I detected no preference towards the dark side of Stanley Park. That was until he asked me about my favourite goal. 'Was it Alex Young's header that won the title? Or was it Derek Temple's shot that captured the FA Cup?' I told him: 'No, it's the next one we score against the Reds'. He didn't laugh. His muted reaction was surprising because he had been both charming and jovial all evening. Indeed, my lasting impression of Johnson is his ego confronting me about the caricature planned for inclusion in Gwladys Street's Blue Book. Vainly he asked: 'Did you have to make me look so bald and so fat?' He blushed when my wife responded: 'Of course not. But I do think that it makes you look virile.' The chairman countered: 'Don't worry, I'll have the last laugh.'

Despite the amount of hope invested in Johnson's reign, it ended in controversy with the banks pounding on his door shortly before he sold our prized asset. On November 23, 1998, Johnson transferred Duncan Ferguson to Newcastle without the full knowledge of Walter Smith. To this day, I've wondered about the deal - especially since Smith and Ferguson had the same agent.

I recall attending the match with Alex Young and Brian Labone greeting us in the Joe Mercer Suite: 'We've sold the big man to reduce the overdraft.' I assumed he was joking and waited for his punch-line. It never came. Alex was flabbergasted. No ambitious club sells its most popular player behind its manager's back. After four tumultuous years, during which his personal fortune shrunk allegedly from £150 million down to £50 million, the Everton chairman resigned in late-1998 and, after another 12 months of negotiations, sold his controlling stake for £20 million to True Blue Holdings. Johnson returned to Prenton Park where Tranmere embarked on a dazzling cup run - eliminating several Premier League clubs - to reach the 2000 League Cup final. Perhaps Johnson was more of a Blue than a Red after all because his side lost to Leicester and failed to capture that elusive trophy.

As for the last laugh? Johnson's Tranmere side - including our former-players Paul Rideout and Graham Allen - humiliated Kenwright's Everton in the fourth round of the FA Cup. It occurred on January 27 - now celebrated on the south bank of the River Mersey as St Yates Day. Surely, no Blues will disagree that Tranmere out-played their hosts and won deservedly thanks to two goals from Steve Yates and another from Jason Koumas. Vividly, I can recall the scenes after Tranmere went 3-0 up. Their supporters sang loudly and danced wildly as the home fans headed for the Goodison exits. One chant reverberated around Mama Blue. It was unforgettable: 'One Peter Johnson - there's only one Peter Johnson'. This unwanted giant-killing remains one of the most embarrassing afternoons I've ever experienced as an Evertonian.

Buck up Duncan ... all you've done this year is fight crime

78. A book inside of them

As you know, I disagree with the skeptics who say that you should never meet your hero but have concluded that if you get too close to your football club you'll be disappointed. That was the case in the mid-Nineties when Everton Football Club lacked identity, strategy and more. I sought to channel my love of all things blue into something productive while the club tackled the more pressing financial and operating problems. I met with Michael Dunford — then club secretary - and Philip Carter to review my list of ideas. They included the type of self-financing initiatives that a leading football club should be pursuing.

Some were better than others. Proposal 1: celebrate our identity and the forgotten men who had made the club what it is ... via an Everton Hall of Fame elected by the fans. Proposal 2: promote our history ... via exhibits of rare memorabilia, an Everton museum, top-class website and a heritage society. Proposal 3: Take care of our old players ... via an ex-players' charity. Proposal 4: propagate the Everton story ... through a series of books. Proposal 5: commemorate the players and fans who perished during warfare ... through formal memorials. There were some more creative ideas ... an Everton Day - for Blues to celebrate being Blues ... an Evertonians-only cemetery - for Blues who don't want to be buried next to a Kopite - and annual tours to developing international markets in the USA and China.

The club secretary claimed: 'Good ideas. I've already thought of them'. The ex-chairman simply smiled in disapproval. My response? I assembled a team of diehard Blues, rolled up our sleeves and tackled them. I was confident that if we were successful then sooner rather than later the club would seek to get involved. Where to start? It was an easy decision. The club's history speaks with such a velvet tongue that I set about writing a series of books to tell the Everton story from different perspectives. By now, assuming you've read the proceeding pages, you will have determined that my literary skills are not to be confused with those of the distinguished American wordsmith of the same name. His most popular book, entitled 'Our Fathers', examines sexual abuse within the Roman Catholic Church. It's a heartbreaking portrait of the victims as well as a searing indictment of those who concealed the crimes. Yes, serious stuff. Possibly, he will research the Kings Dock saga one day. I'm sorry, I'm getting ahead of myself.

Some Blues assert that my own modest offerings — all 16 of them — provide a bridge to our past and platform to our future. I wish I felt the same way. I've never been a big fan of the words I've picked nor the order that I've put them in. My better-half is even more scornful. She claims that I've produced the same publication with different covers. As always, she is correct - partly. The contents are different but my message is the same. I've sought to communicate to the football world that the first club of Merseyside and its followers are peerless. Supposedly, everyone has a book inside of them; my critics claim that's where mine should have stayed. Most people dream about writing one. Some take notes and make outlines only to give up at the first sign of writer's block. I've discovered that patience is crucial for finishing anything, especially something as daunting as a manuscript. You may think that producing books is a solitary activity. It isn't. An author requires loyal enthusiasts in his corner. I've been lucky. The Blues at the Liverpool Echo and Daily Post in Old Hall Street provided gracious reviews and the airways around Paradise Street, the home of BBC Radio Merseyside, offered generous endorsements. Equally as valuable, the independent websites rallied round with their bountiful blessings. In many ways, my efforts became Everton family initiatives.

Selling books is an even bigger challenge. As a literary virgin, I conducted some market research to verify the appetite for such printed propaganda. A visit to WH Smith in Church Street revealed that there hadn't been a decent release in years. They had relied on a couple of anodyne biographies as well as a couple of glossy histories crammed with the same old photographs.

My contact encouraged me to assemble a prototype and review it with the people who claim to know about these things at Goodison. Subsequently, the club's representative showed genuine interest in my work before - you're not going to believe this - demanding a backhander of £2,000 to stock it on the shelves of the Megastore. I thought he was joking. Clearly, he was confident of doing so with impunity. Given that I planned to donate the net proceeds to a local charity, namely Alder Hey Children's Hospital, I was disgusted. So much so that I suggested that he and his office should be dipped in Dettol. No, make that industrial strength hypo.

Dismayed by his skullduggery, I re-approached the national retailers who wielded great influence over book sales. Believe me, it wasn't easy to capture the interest of WH Smith and Dillons, now known as Waterstones, and near-impossible to have my books incorporated into their window displays or promotions near the front of their shops. I remember my first sales visit to WH Smith. Elizabeth guarded the car, which was crammed with 40 boxes containing 480 books, as I attempted a cold call. Within minutes, I returned triumphant. She asked: 'How many?' I replied: 'Three'. She said: 'Three boxes - not a bad start'. I clarified: 'No, three books!' Luckily, she stifled her laughter because by the end of that week WH Smith wanted the whole print run. Vividly, I recall the request from the store manager: 'We've no idea what you put in your books. Nonetheless, we'll take everyone you've got!'

When it came to the book releases, my approach was simple. I converted them into royal blue celebrations in Liverpool city centre. At one event or another, I enlisted Messrs Labone, West, Parker, Wilson, Young, Hickson, Ratcliffe, Stubbs and Unsworth to keep me company. The launches attracted long queues of book-buying Blues. Believe me, I wasn't deluded that they had turned up to meet the author. Far from it, they had come to snag the autographs of their royal blue hereos. Typically, my cohorts would sign 100 or so books per hour. It was such a demanding task that one or two proponents of neat cursive penmanship complained of cramp or scrivener's palsy. Miraculously, their symptoms vanished after a brief excursion to Yate's Wine Lodge.

At one signing session, the bookshop manager engaged a group of local musicians to entertain the crowd. Their specialty and possibly the only song they knew was 'Johnny Todd'. Over and over they sang: 'Johnny Todd he took a notion for to cross the ocean wide ... and left his true love behind him waiting on the Liverpool side ...' Brian Labone hypothesized about the power of the sea shanty that evolved into 'Z Cars' : 'Don't you love it. Muzak for the Everton soul. And best of all, it keeps the Reds away.' Few things compare to an interaction with one of your royal blue heroes, especially if he is Brian Labone. Everyone fortunate enough to have met the famed 'Last of the Corinthians' will be well aware of the extra time he took to engage his fellow Blues in conversation. He always made eye-contact and took extra care to dot the 'i' in his name.

Similarly, Alex Young made book signing sessions extra-special. He created a family atmosphere by greeting every fan with a warm handshake and an even warmer smile. More often than not, the teary-eyed, middle-aged Blue would confess: 'I've been waiting all of my life to meet you.' Alex would blush, exchange a more than few kind words before taking his gold pen into his left-hand to personalize a dedication. Finally, he would rise from his seat to present the signed book. The ceremony reminded me of the etiquette displayed during the exchange of business cards in Japan. Alex made a tiny bow before offering the signed book with both hands and another friendly smile. He treated his biography as an extension of himself. No request seemed too much trouble for him. Indeed, Brian Labone and Alex Young never refused a photo request and signed everything placed in front of them - from baby's bibs to their mother's skin. While some modern-day stars consider such intrusions to be a nuisance, most of the ex-players I've had the good fortune to meet admit to dreading the day when Everton fans no longer recognize them or remember their names never mind ask for their autographs.

As for the books themselves, I first dipped my nervous toes into the ocean of printed words with 'Toffee Pages – The Post-War Years'. It told the Everton story without the boring bits through extracts from post-war programmes. The novel concept was lauded nationally but wasn't to everyone's taste locally. This fact was reinforced when I discovered that someone had broken into my old Volvo parked outside the Adelphi Hotel. A few items were removed from the glove box and a six-pack of Diet Coke from the rear-seat. Thankfully, they didn't take my Leonard Cohen CDs nor, for that matter, any of the 20 boxes of books, even though they opened a couple of boxes to examine the contents. Clearly, the crime was perpetrated by a weight-conscious Kopite with extremely poor tastes in both music and literature.

Encouraged that the book sold out within two weeks, I adopted a similar approach for my second publication later that year. With permission from the major tobacco companies, I gleaned images and biographical information from old cigarette cards to record the early story of the club. It would be an understatement to claim that 'Toffee Cards – The Tobacco Years' was novel but not to everyone's fancy. The most positive review included the following words: 'The one good thing about the decline of the cigarette as a tool of social intercourse is that you don't run the risk of Duncan Ferguson's head popping out of the packet'.

I was chasing a royal blue high when I released 'Gwladys Street's Hall of Fame' in late-1998 to celebrate the inaugural inductions. Given the lack of photographs from the pioneering era, I commissioned artist Peter King to capture the character if not the exact likeness of all Hall of Fame members for posterity. Love them or loath them, his caricatures have become the enduring images of many men who had been long forgotten. Most players believe that his efforts flatter their team-mates but not themselves. Only one demanded cosmetic brushwork to enhance his hair-line. No, it wasn't Wayne Rooney. I prefer not to reveal the Irishman's identity. The book was so popular that it disappeared from the bookshop shelves within days and I had to produce a Second Edition for the first Hall of Fame dinner in February.

Through these offerings I became fascinated by the recollections of footballers and learnt that by asking open-ended questions, they will talk for hours about the highs and lows of their careers. Having discovered that the lifeblood of the Everton family is enriched by the shared experience of storytelling, I recorded the insights of Gordon Watson. He had seen it all. You may know that he was a left-half who had played alongside Dixie Dean in the first-team and reserves, won the title with Tommy Lawton and Joe Mercer, played war-time football alongside TG Jones and Ted Sagar, coached the first-team containing Roy Vernon and Alex Young, guided the careers of promising teenagers such as Colin Harvey - the most skillful player he coached - and Tommy Wright, and was the very first stadium tour-guide at Goodison. Not a bad curriculum vitae?

You may not know that this lovely man - the type of friend everyone should have - enjoyed every minute of his 64 years at Everton Football Club. For me, it was a privilege to spend afternoons at his home. Typically, Gordon started by reviewing an old team photograph. He had something good to say about every player. I wallowed in his candid insights and royal blue tales about life with Dixie Dean and friends. When it came to Harry Catterick, who had been his team-mate and then his boss, Gordon revealed that there was too much wheeling and dealing and not enough leadership at Bellefield. He claimed that the manager was most interested in money: 'Pound signs rolled in his eyes like the windows on a one-arm bandit.' As for his teams, the manager was adamant that his line-ups include someone with a fighting spirit - that is, a bit of the devil about them - such as Bobby Collins, Dennis Stevens and Tony Kay.

As for the Dixie Dean-Tommy Lawton debate. Gordon had played alongside both of them and revealed that no-one could hold a candle to Dean - a terrific player and inspirational captain.

'While everyone on Merseyside - irrespective of club allegiance - loved him, Bill could be quite a handful on and off the field. I remember him being interviewed with Ernest Edwards at the end of training. Alan Storey, the Goodison groundsman, demanded that the Everton star and Echo journalist get off the pitch so that he could cut the grass. Bill cooperated but returned to seek revenge. We watched as our captain marched to the centre-spot, dropped his trousers and left a steaming souvenir for the groundsman.'

Gordon enjoyed working with the club's apprentices. He recalled: 'The youngsters would look at me and chuckle: What can I learn from this old man? So every pre-season I had to prove myself. I did so by placing a dozen footballs in the centre-circle and lining up six or so doubting apprentices on both touch-lines. Then I would ping the ball 50 yards to the feet of each and every one of them and shout: If you think I'm good, you should have seen Cliff Britton in his prime!' In the role of father-figure, he thought that most of his charges were financially illiterate and would advise them not to live like a king for a few years but like a prince forever. Some listened, others bought E-type Jaguars.

His favourite tale involved John Moores: 'During the American Soccer Cup, Everton trained in Central Park and changed in a park shelter which was supervised by a local named Hank the Yank. He looked after the kit and ran errands. Because nothing was too much trouble for him, I tipped him $10 in appreciation of his services at the end of our stay. Mr Moores disapproved and instructed me to recover the gratuity. After I explained my dilemma to Hank, he approached the two directors - Mr Moores and Mr Holland Hughes - holding a container labelled 'Tips' and emptied the contents at their feet. Training came to a standstill as we watched the Littlewoods millionaire kneel down and count out $10 in nickels and quarters.' The resulting publication, entitled 'Gwladys Street's Blue Book', was co-authored with Dave Prentice - someone who makes good writing so easy. Deep down, I feared that if we hadn't done so his precious memories would have been lost forever. More than anything, Gordon taught us that the Everton story must be told with feelings as well as facts and, though my old pal passed away before it was printed, I know that he would have been humbled by the sight of hundreds of rain-drenched Blues queuing down Church Street and along Paradise Street just to read his recollections and opinions.

What next? Well, Dave and I set about detailing Everton's pioneering days and commemorating our status as the first English club to spend 100 seasons at the top. To date, no rival has matched our consistency or undiluted hunger for top flight football. Our publication entitled 'Virgin Blues' captures the story of our first season in the Football League. It was well-received nationally. It featured never-before-seen photographs, extracts from the club's minute books, match reports from the Daily Post and home programmes to provide a fascinating window into the day-to-day deeds of our Victorian forefathers. Appropriately, we published only 1878 copies and every one of them vanished within one week.

Deluded by this and other modest literary successes, I decided to take a significant change in direction and produce a children's book entitled 'Gwladys Street's Big Book for Kids of All Ages'. Illustrated beautifully by Peter King, the contents told the Everton story in small words and big images. I make no apologies for this less-than-subtle tool for indoctrinating youngsters or for the Everton pledge highlighted on the final page. Fondly, I remember Jeanette Rooney receiving a copy at a Hall of Fame dinner shortly after she had accepted 'Gwladys Street's Young Blue of the Year Award' on behalf of her 17-year-old son. She promised to get him to sign the pledge before she cooked his tea the next day. One of my haunting memories of that evening was Mrs Rooney's pride when autographing hundreds of copies of the book. She signed them: 'Love, Wayne's Mum'.

79. Books stroke an author's vanity

Let me be honest, freshly published books stroke an author's vanity. I was thrilled to see my early efforts rubbing jackets with the works of Stephen King and James Patterson but didn't watch them as much as Peter King. He would patrol the aisles daily and smile when customers picked up copies of the books crammed with his PAK caricatures. The store detectives considered him a nuisance. This description may trouble him. Not as much perhaps as the sight of any customer brave enough to return a book containing his artwork onto the shelf.

Now and again my own ego would tip-toe around Dillon's to stroke my latest book in the new releases section. That was until the shop manager warned me that half of her inventory was missing. She proceeded to describe the apprehension of two thieves in Bold Street. Upon searching them, the police discovered three copies of my latest book, three Jeffery Archer novels and four Jamie Oliver cookbooks. They claimed that the shoplifters had been stealing to service their drug habits. At first I was flattered. Then my ego took a bruising when I realized that I wasn't as popular as the Naked Chef among Merseyside smack-heads.

Around that time, the advent of central purchasing policies at the major chains restructured the book business and I noticed that there were more titles for Chelsea than Everton in many of the Merseyside outlets of WH Smith and Waterstones. Without the full cooperation of these major chains, it's difficult to sell even 1,000 units. This observation was confirmed by my next project, a double edition released in 2006. The top-side, in recognition of my old barber, was titled 'Evertonians Eat Scouse.' Notwithstanding the fact that all proceeds were to be donated to local charities, no major bookshop would touch it. Why? Apparently, some of their staff didn't like the cover which carried the bold warning: 'Mature subject matter. May offend hyper-sensitive Kopites'. Others cited my recipe for Walton Scouse: 'Ingredients to feed four: one pound of lamb, two pounds of potatoes, three carrots, one large onion, splash of Worcestershire sauce, one tablespoon of mixed herbs, salt and pepper. For vegetarians, replace the lamb with cod. For vegan guests, replace the cod with cauliflower. For Kopites, replace the salt with laxative.'

The flip-side was less controversial. 'Moyesiah' was based on a poem penned by Roger McGough for inclusion in the third edition of the Hall of Fame book. Unable to attend the dinner, he sent his apologies attached to the rhyme. It was a magnanimous gesture by a great performance poet and a terrific Blue. Now before you proceed, it's best to pinch the sides of your nostrils and read the following in a monotone voice. Here goes: 'The chairman dreams about our football team … who play in royal blue … we win the Cup … and win the League … then conquer Europe too … the manager claims that we're the club of the people … and prays to make our dreams come true … but because only the best is good enough … the Moyesiah has more work to do!' The book was published in 2006 and, I think that many but not all Blues will agree, remained relevant until the manager defected to Old Trafford in 2013.

Have I mentioned that selling football books is a challenge? More frustration followed when the Megastore fell into the hands of JJB. This company baulked at stocking my own personal favourite 'Alex Young – The Golden Vision'. Yes I know what you're thinking, you couldn't make it up. In truth, after interacting with JJB representatives in Wigan, I'm convinced that they didn't know or care who he was. Therefore, in the days before Amazon and eBay, I took a mail order route to satisfy the initial demand for the biography. This approach was augmented by well-attended signing sessions at Radio Merseyside and in the lounge named after him at Goodison. Both events were emotional. Without doubt, no-one who attended the radio station will ever forget the displays of passion during the signing session and the live broadcast of 'An Audience with Alex Young' hosted by Billy Butler. I've fond memories of the line of old Blues clutching copies of the biography as if they were their pension books. Many were in tears.

Elizabeth never moaned about the number of days and nights I devoted to writing these books or that she spent proof-reading them. She had assumed that I would retire undefeated after 13 books and wasn't too pleased when Philip Carter suggested a scholarly publication to profile my collection of memorabilia for posterity. It turned out to be a massive undertaking at a time when I was suffering from extremely poor health. My wife complained that I should make better use of my time and selected an insensitive working title, namely 'The Everton Folly'. Most Blues know that the completed book known as 'Everton Treasures – The David France Collection' is now a collector's item befitting its contents. Only 400 units were produced, all in handsome slip-cases. Most were incorporated into fund-raising sets for the Everton Collection Charitable Trust. Subsequently, I've been flabbergasted to discover used copies listed on eBay at £900.

In early 2007, in what must have been a very slow week, it was selected as The Independent newspaper's Book of the Week. In truth, I was shocked by the excessive praise. Its success led to the production of an expanded version of the limited edition. Appropriately titled 'Dr Everton's Magnificent Obsession', I encouraged the publishers to commit to a large print run and price the book so that it would find its way into lots of blue and white hooped stockings at Christmas. Thanks to my co-author Dave Prentice, it was hailed locally as the most important book on football history ever written. While I don't believe the hype, I do think that it's the nearest thing that exists to a football time-machine. Cards on the table, it merely scratches the surface of my collection which could spawn another half-dozen similar books.

My fondest memory of the book business was when my co-author and I visited Alder Hey to donate a few hundred copies of 'Dr Everton's Magnificent Obsession' to the young patients, both Blues and Reds. We thought that it was only fair that little Kopites learn something about the city's rich football heritage. I'm well aware that a stay in hospital can be stressful for a child at any age. Fear of needles, pain and the unknown is common. The parents and hospital staff were marvelous in comforting the children and sought to engage them with the outside world. My co-author and I met many sick children. We had invited a photographer from the Echo but, after a few pictures, asked him to stop. Why? Because I had seen an angel. Dressed in her white outfit with gossamer wings for the Christmas party, she was a tiny Blue – age 7 with no hair. She smiled at me: 'Dr Everton, can you cure me?' I responded: 'I'm sorry love, I'm not that kind of doctor but I can tell you a story about your favourite football club: Again, she enquired: 'Will it make me better.' I offered: 'I do hope so. I know it will make me feel better.' It was a truly humbling experience.

By the way Robert Philip, the prize-winning journalist, labelled me 'Dr Everton' when he described my pursuit of memorabilia in a 'Daily Telegraph' article in March 2008. I was a bit embarrassed and have tried to grow into the nickname. Many years earlier, Brian Labone had used the term of endearment to introduce me to some of his drinking cronies in The Exchange pub in Old Hall Street. Coming from someone who had played in excess of 500 games for the club that we both loved, it was the equivalent of a Papal blessing.

I don't think mankind will be damaged if I don't write another book. Every now and then I come across well-thumbed copies of my books in second-hand bookshops. I'm rarely impressed. Actually, I feel a little ambivalent towards them. They remind me that I have written for Toffees yet still can't write for toffee.

80. Forget the rest

Reds claim that football kicked off with Bill Shankly. Red Devils assume that it began with Alex Ferguson. Regrettably, some Blues are just as guilty in believing that the start coincided with the signing of a certain William Ralph Dean. This understandable tribute ignores the fact that Everton was already a national institution when the great man was kicking a tennis ball around the playground at Laird Street School in Birkenhead. Such has been Dean's celebrity that these many Blues have forgotten that the club had fielded 40 international stars before 1925, including some of the greatest forwards in the history of the British game. Six of them, namely Jack Southworth, Jimmy Settle, Sandy Young, Bert Freeman, Bobby Parker and Wilf Chadwick, had topped the League's goal-scoring charts. I know what you are thinking. Wilf Who?

I had found it hard to accept the marginalization of the men who had made Everton Football Club what it is. Therefore, I conceived the idea of Gwladys Street's Hall of Fame. Flattered by a rush of imitators, it was the first of its kind in the country and proceeded the English Football Hall of Fame by four years. Or so I'm told. Mindful that the recognition of noteworthy achievements is often skewed towards modern-day stars, I designed the selection criteria to embrace men who had played meaningful roles during the dozen decades of our history. After consulting with baseball's counterpart in Cooperstown, I recruited a panel of Blues consisting of ex-players, journalists, shareholders and season-ticket holders to painstakingly assess the qualifications of the 900 or so eligible candidates that stretched back to the pioneers of St Domingo.

That task was much easier said than done. Membership of Gwladys Street's Hall of Fame is based on an individual's record, ability, sportsmanship and overall positive impact on the club and only those who have made indelible contributions have been inducted. After a year of impassioned discussions, we concluded that the compilation of the required short-list was a thankless task. How can you compare the claims of a resolute defender from say 1880 with a speedy striker from 1980?

In the end, we reached a consensus on 75 Hall of Famers. Invariably, some Blues disagreed with certain selections and even more with certain omissions. Therefore, to remedy any oversights, new members were added via annual postal and internet ballots. Today its ranks have swollen to 126 members, which is still less than one per year of the grand old club's history. I remain confident that Gwladys Street's high standards are reflected in the qualifications of stars such as Gary Lineker and unsung men such as Wilf Chadwick who have yet to be inducted.

In mid-1998, I pondered long and hard about how to induct these men into the independent Everton Hall of Fame. More than anything, I wanted to organize the type of rollicking - make that raucous - celebrations that would be talked about for decades - for all of the right reasons. Given my limited experience in organizing such a royal blue orgy, most of which was gained amid firework smoke and rodeo manure in Houston, I enlisted the help of the enthusiastic folks at Merseyside Football Programmes and Bluenose Promotions who had put on a couple of successful sportsman's evenings in local pubs.

In the absence of meaningful support from the then Johnson-controlled club, they were responsible for aggressive advertising of the event and subsequent ticket sales. I recall that our ambitious plans to paper the city with colourful posters were abandoned after the 'Liverpool Echo' made a fleeting reference to the date of the 'Everton's Oscars'. Consequently, all 600 tickets were sold within 48 hours and possibly some were re-sold by touts within 72 hours. Without question, the demand far outstripped the supply.

My first of many challenge was to overcome the absence of a comprehensive database of old Everton players. With the aid of Brian Labone's little black book, disguised as a compilation of telephone numbers written on scraps of paper, old envelopes and beer mats, I spent months tracking down lost heroes.

Many from the Eighties had stayed in the game. The older generations, however, had entered the mainstream after hanging up their boots and were more difficult to find. The vast majority were enthusiastic. A few were skeptical. In one or two cases, I feared that I may have blown their cover in some witness protection scheme. My next task was to reserve a venue big enough for the Everton family to let its hair down. I opted for the Adelphi. Why? Well, it has much in common with Goodison. Both are faded dowagers in need of loving care. Built in the age of Atlantic liners, the once-opulent hotel reflected the luxury reserved for those travelling in style across the ocean. At the time of our inaugural dinner, it was managed by Eileen Downey and Brian Birchill, two diehard Blues, and was infamous as the setting for a fly-on-the-wall documentary named 'Hotel'. Unlike some of the hotel guests highlighted by the BBC, we were treated like family.

Remember the so-called learning experiences associated with livestock manure and flaming fireworks? Well, they came in handy by underpinning a real celebration in 1999 - the inaugural Gwladys Street's Hall of Fame Gala. The extravaganza was a family effort and could not have happened without the small army of volunteers. Many were local. Others travelled hundreds of miles to pitch in. I recall that during the morning of the event there was a dozen helpers folding 1,400 napkins into blue and white shirts, another twelve decorating the hotel's ballroom with giant banners radiating all sorts of propaganda. The most popular one was 50 feet long. At the end of the evening, it was auctioned for charity and netted £3,000. It made reference to our off-shoot across the park. You can imagine what it said. Again, it was just a bit of amiable repartee. Friendly teasing. Honest.

On the night, the cavernous and windowless ballroom crackled with anticipation. Behind the scenes it was hard to ignore the nervous laughter, shuffling feet and superstitious rituals of men who had been used to performing regularly in front of 60,000. They appeared intimidated by the 600 star-struck Blues waiting for them. More than 100 old players came from near and far to revel in all things royal blue. They included Jimmy Gabriel from the USA, Howard Kendall from Greece, Tommy Eglington from Ireland and Mike Lyons from somewhere in the Far East.

When the players finally entered to the sounds of Z Cars, the ballroom exploded with near delirium. The deafening roars didn't bounce off the walls. It shook the paint off them, both inside and out. The inductees were introduced individually by Derek Hatton, the master of ceremony, and greeted with standing ovations. All attendees rose to their feet to greet each individual in-ductee. Many stood on their chairs to welcome their heroes with chants and songs from the past. Surprisingly, the female fans were the rowdiest. One group became my reliable benchmark that future evenings were a success. I would ask the stewards: 'Are the Toffee girls dancing on their tables yet?'

The pandemonium was louder than any rock concert or football match I had ever attended. According to the Guinness Book of World Records, the loudest football crowd was at the 2011 clash between Galatasaray and Fenerbahce. It generated 132 decibels - equivalent to standing next to a jet engine at full throttle. Respected for its ability to impact the playing fortunes of the Seattle Seahawks, the Twelfth Man at Century Link Field set a new record of 137 decibels against the San Francisco 49ers in 2013. I don't know about the actual noise level at the Adelphi except that it caused a peculiar ringing in my ears and buzzing inside my wife's head.

More than anything, I recall being alongside grown men with tears in their eyes. Some of them were former-players. I'll never forget the fans and their expressions of belonging, unity and pride. Never before had their heroes been so accessible. As they mingled with players who had won the World Cup, European silverware, FA Cups and League titles, many thought they had gone to royal blue heaven.

Some images come to mind. I remember Wee Bobby Collins - the diminutive villain at the Battle of Goodison - in tears: 'I've never been kissed so passionately or been hugged so hard. It's 40 years since I donned the famous blue shirt but tonight I've been treated like football royalty.' Vividly I remember the public confession of Dave Hickson: 'I'd have broken every bone in my body for my other clubs including Villa, Huddersfield, Tranmere and the other lot, I would have died for Everton.' Then there was the famous observation of Brian Labone. He proclaimed: 'You know it. I know it. One Blue is worth 20 Reds!'

And who could forget Blue Bill, standing behind the top table and conducting the thunderous chants of 'We want Johnson out!' Near him sat Walter Smith. Throughout the evening, the then Everton manager smiled and clapped politely as if he was at the opera. Given the incredible reception for Howard Kendall, I had felt a tad embarrassed for him. That was until I asked him, with my tongue firmly in my cheek, if his beloved Glasgow Rangers had 600 similarly passionate fans. He responded: 'What? We've got 600 effing passionate supporters' clubs.'

As you would expect, not everything went to plan that evening. Given the dearth of tickets, we had to deal with a few uninvited guests. My approach was painless. I encouraged them to join in the fun. That was until we were confronted by a belligerent Cockney Red. This hotel guest not only gate-crashed our event, he started to sing that Rodgers and Hammerstein dirge. For his own safety, the Adelphi security staff ejected him and made sure that he remained on the wrong-side of the hotel's famous revolving doors until daylight. The last time I saw him, he was walking alone in the February frost.

How do you bring down the curtain? It was impossible. At 1.30 am, I announced from the stage: 'Good night. See you next year'. The fans and the players took no notice and continued to make whoopee. After I tried again at 2.00 am with similar results, I retired to bed where my slumbers were disturbed by frantic banging on the door of my hotel room. Through the peep-hole I could see the duty manager. It was 4:15 am. He looked exhausted: 'I've closed the bar. I've turned off the heat. Your friends refuse to retire.' He pleaded for my help downstairs.

Subsequently, we entered the massive ballroom to discover that the celebrations were still in full swing. There were about 100 fans and a dozen old-timers enjoying the time of their lives. My old pals Tommy Eglington, Brian Labone, Brian Harris, Ray Wilson and Bobby Collins were holding court. Wally Fielding, another of my favourites, was surrounded by admirers of all ages. His audience, most of whom had never seen him play, appeared enthralled by his tales of the post-war boom, our relegation season, our promotion campaign and some very odd training regimes which included skipping down County Road. I paused to listen to the 80-year-old, who had made a 10-hour train journey from Bude in Cornwall to attend the function, remind his new admirers that he had been something of a football trendsetter. Apparently, youngsters in the late-Forties mimicked his trademark style of holding his shirt cuffs as he ran.

Because they were entrenched, I asked the duty manager to provide blankets, pillows and hot chocolate to allow the Blues without rooms to bivouac in the world-famous Sefton Room. When I returned three hours later, the pile of bedding remained untouched and the laughter and singing continued to reverberate around the Adelphi.

I felt sorry for the hotel manager and his staff. They wanted to clean the ballroom, finish their night shift and go home. Instead they were treated to rousing renditions of the royal blue anthem which brags about lynching our loveable neighbours in the vicinity of the Three Graces. The merrymakers appeared immovable until Brian Birchill and I hatched a plan. No make that a cunning plan which involved the science of the Maillard reaction in which sugars jostle with amino acids. Yes, the wafting smell of freshly cooked bacon and sausages lured both players and their fans towards the hotel's breakfast buffet.

Many of the older attendees claimed that the inaugural event was better than sex - with their wives. The press reviews were almost as orgasmic. My favourite write-up was penned by Len Capeling: 'If heartfelt adoration was Premier League points then Everton would be so far ahead in the title race that the rest would've given up by now. That much was clear from the intoxicating act of worship that saw 80 greats being ushered up the royal blue carpet into Gwladys Street's fabled Hall of Fame. It was a memorable night with due honour accorded to a pantheon of gods. Tears were unashamedly shed. It was a trip to Wonderland - a field of blue stretching forever, lined with silver trophies. Drugged by past glories, you could believe in miracles. Put it down to the mind-bending properties of Collins, Kendall, Labone, Royle, Reid, Ratcliffe and all. Put it down to love and remembrance.'

The sports editor at the Daily Post had a wonderful way with words. He was spot-on. Gwladys Street's Hall of Fame was a beacon in the Stygian gloom which had enveloped the club in 1999. It lifted the spirits of all attendees and reassured us that - as Evertonians - we had so much to be thankful for.

Ray Wilson ... Ray Wilson ... I distinctly said Ray Wilson!

81. Nuremberg Rallies

The most notable absentee at the inaugural event enthralled me. TG Jones had walked away from Merseyside in late-1949 to manage a football club as well as a hotel in Pwllheli. Yes, Pwllheli – the home of Butlins and Plaid Cymru. I had been warned that he had declined invitations to events celebrating title and Cups. He seemed to take pleasure in avoiding Everton functions. Even so, I sought to lure him to the Hall of Fame Gala in 2000. To do so, I met 'The Uncrowned Prince of Wales' on several occasions.

Naively, I had assumed that old footballers were sweet-natured. I think it is fair to say that TG, who addressed himself regularly in the third person, didn't have a good word to say about Everton Football Club. Players rarely criticize their old team-mates. TG was an exception. He wasn't impressed with many of their inclusions in the Hall of Fame. His unkind evaluations included references to 'snails ... donkeys ... cowards with intellects usually associated with wooden goal-posts.' Worse, he was criticizing men who thought the world of him.

The 80-year-old treated me with a level of suspicion reserved usually for the VAT man. Then one day he invited me for a brisk walk through the streets of Bangor, his hometown. At the tearoom at the end of Garth Pier, I asked about his initials. 'Thomas Gwyner,' he lied. With his eyes focused on Telford's Menai Suspension Bridge, Thomas George Jones ranted about his aborted move to Italy. It had been 50 years ago but he had not forgiven those involved. For the record, he had agreed to join Roma before the £15,000 transfer negotiations had broken down. His personal terms were astronomical for that time - signing-on bonus of £5,000, weekly wages of £25, sun-drenched villa, brand new Lancia car and first-class air travel to and from Italy. With his bubble burst, the world-class defender had to settle for earning £8 per week. He was not embarrassed to enlighten me that he had bolted to Pwllheli to earn more money, enjoy more respect and dodge playing in a poor Everton side destined for relegation.

After months of assuring him that he should be ranked above John Charles as Wales's finest defender and, if he had gone to Italy, would be hailed as Britain's finest export, I agreed to his eye-opening list of demands for attending the second event. In addition to the type of items usually associated with a pop prima donna, he wanted a door-to-door taxi and a hefty appearance fee. TG was well received by the fans. Of course, I'm referring to those that actually saw him at the Adelphi. Shortly after he had taken his seat at the top table, I handed over a cheque for £1,000. The next time I glanced in his direction, he had vanished to North Wales. TG hadn't even tasted his soup.

The first men to be elected by the fans were inducted also in 2000. One special memory of the second Hall of Fame evening was the presence of Paul Bracewell. He had been sacked by Mohamed Al-Fayed and replaced by Jean Tigana as Fulham's manager the previous day but fulfilled his promise to join our celebrations. What a gentleman! Another inductee was Gordon Watson. Our ex-player, ex-coach and ex-trainer was the first man to enter the Hall of Fame in a wheelchair. The hairs on the back of my neck stood up as he was carried onto the stage by Dave Watson. When he took the microphone, Gordon captivated everyone with his pre-war tales of Dixie Dean and Tommy Lawton. At the end of his speech he vowed: 'This time next year I'm going to walk into the Hall of Fame'. My old friend was a man of his word and the following year, after the other players had entered the banqueting hall to the sounds of 'Z-Cars', the doors were swung open for Gordon to march down the aisle holding the FA Cup. I still find it hard to believe that so many men could get something in their eyes at the same time. Weeks later, he passed away quietly without any fuss.

I had anticipated a noisy but structured event. The Hall of Fame Gala, however, became exactly what the fans wanted - an Everton love-fest and the greatest night in the royal blue calendar.

All of the annual events sold out and tickets were as sought after as those for Merseyside derbies. Nonetheless, I strove to provide the attendees with value for money and included an Everton book which doubled as an autographed souvenir as a part of the package. One year we ran out of books. Eight heavy boxes had vanished. We searched high and low for them before eventually discovering them hiding in two of the commercial ovens in the kitchen. There were red faces all round until Billy Butler broke the tension: 'Don't worry, this isn't the first time that someone's cooked the books at the Adelphi.'

Everyone has his or her own favourite Hall of Fame dinner. I have fond memories of the heartfelt feelings of Gordon West, the leadership of Brian Labone, the majesty of Alex Young, the enthusiasm of Blue Bill, the humility of Neville Southall, the youth of Bob Latchford and the rebirth of Tony Kay. Then there were the spine-tingling remarks by Peter Reid as he described his immense pride in capturing so many trophies in the name of Everton and Alan Ball as he talked about his wife. From the hospital where she battled ovarian cancer, Lesley had insisted that he leave her bedside to be among his fellow Blues. Emotionally, he recalled her words: 'Your people will help you through the pain.'

Besides raising funds for the Everton Former-Players' Foundation, Alder Hey Children's Hospital and other local charities, the annual trip down memory lane gave our spirits a lift, especially when the club was struggling on the pitch. Throughout the years, the Hall of Fame events remained a mix of excitement, noise and unbridled passion and are as famous as many of the men they have celebrated. They confirmed that Blues are more than able to spread the mood like a benevolent virus for a full decade.

The 2009 and final dinner was another love-in with the new inductees overwhelmed by the atmosphere. It was the eleventh Hall of Fame Dinner - coincidentally there were the same number of Nuremberg Rallies. That year's poll was conducted via postal votes and web ballots. In my opinion, all of the additions were worthy. Tony Kay was a truly magnificent footballer whose introduction sealed the 1963 title. Graham Stuart saved our bacon in 1994. David Unsworth would charge through brick walls for Everton. I was criticized for including Bill Kenwright on the ballot but it turns out that he was a popular choice. The final addition, Duncan Ferguson travelled from Majorca to attend the bash. He made an emotional speech: 'It's very hard to tell people what it's like to put on that blue jersey. It's something special. Nothing, absolutely nothing compares to Everton Football Club. When you play for Everton, you forget the rest!' His words had the Toffee girls dancing on their tables.

Perhaps there is a link between nostalgia and happiness? Whenever I'm in Liverpool, Blues wax lyrical about their euphoria in meeting Big Joe and Big Bob. Some manipulate their mobile phones to reveal old photos of them hugging Big Nev and Big Dunc. The royal blue orgies confirmed that happiness never decreases by being shared. My only regret is that I didn't add a Hall of Fame of Everton Fans. In terms of courage alone, those who attended all 11 of the Adelphi dinners would be in the first wave of inductees.

I know that you are too polite to ask but need an answer to the question: 'What happened to the shivering Red?' I understand that he disappeared under mysterious circumstances. Probably, that giant hand housed inside the biodegradable dog poop bag descended from the heavens again. Most likely, the hand of God picked up the Kopite, turned the bag inside out and disposed of it on the red heap.

82. Pleasure of strangers

The more I encountered former-players, the more football came across as a mundane job involving lots of tedious travel to boring places. I noted that after hanging up their boots, a huge void opened up in their lives which many found desperately hard to fill.

I had met a handful of old pros during my gas-fitting days. Some had graced Goodison, others Anfield, one or two Wembley. Many had been left bewildered after their adulation had flickered and died. No-one had clarified the rules of fame to them - when the legs go, the back-slapping follows. One of these down-to-earth men claimed to have much in common with old prostitutes. He had ruined his body for the pleasure of strangers. I remember working at the home of Jimmy Hoey. Like you, no doubt, I didn't know who he was. The hobbling pensioner wasn't shy to volunteer that he had played Rugby League for Widnes and England. He felt like the game had moved on and he and his chronic pain had been forgotten. Even worse, no-one clamoured for his autograph anymore. Chemical Harry knew all about 'Jimmy - the man who scored in every match - Hoey'. Apparently, he had been an ever-present and point-scorer in all 40 games during the 1932/33 season and that his incredible achievement had remained unequalled for decades.

Hoey was even more famous for his outrageous dummies. True or false, it's a part of local lore that the Widnes centre set off on a mazy run during the closing minutes at Leeds. At the half-way line, he sold a prodigious dummy to evade two would-be tacklers. At the 25-yard line he deceived another player. Penned in by three more, he sprinted towards the corner flag. Watching from the touchline was a policeman wearing a white raincoat. As the defender closed in on Hoey, he sold his final dummy and the defenders pummelled the constable to the ground.

The old Rugby League star planted the seeds, however the motivation for establishing the Former-Players' Foundation came decades later after I had met old footballers who for one reason or another were struggling with their day-to-day lives. Like Hoey, most limped and complained about arthritic pain in their knees and hips. Some suffered from dementia. A few grumbled about being down on their luck. Then there were the more alarming cases. One old timer had been spotted in public with no laces in his shoes. Another washed down his breakfast with a litre bottle of strong cider. Intoxicated by White Lightning, he told me tales that Baron von Munchausen would have been proud of. Something had to be done.

After all, the modern-day Everton brand is indebted to generations of men like them that played for little reward. I sought advice on how best to proceed from Tommy Eglington, who at the time was one of our oldest living stars. At Goodison, a venue he had illuminated for both his club and his country, we sat in the front of an otherwise empty Main Stand and talked for an hour about the hardships of some of his team-mates. Tommy cautioned me that many of the older players would be too proud to accept charity. When the conversation dried up, we stared at the pitch. It didn't feel uncomfortable. Silent companionship is fine with Blues.

Next, I reviewed my ideas in some detail with Brian Labone. He echoed the words of Tommy and advised me to progress carefully. Very carefully. To do so, I enlisted the help of two prominent local lawyers – Laurence Lee and Norman Jones. Next I met with Liverpool's Ian Callaghan, who represents everything that's good about the game, to determine what our neighbours were doing. It transpired that they had an informal set-up which met their needs. I sought a far more formal entity in which every penny would have to be accounted for. Weeks later, with the benefit of expert council from Norman Jones, I applied to register a charitable organization with the Charity Commission of England & Wales - without success. The paperwork was rejected on three separate occasions because I had failed to provide compelling evidence that taking care of old footballers was a worthy cause. Other people would have taken the hint. Instead, I redoubled my efforts after receiving a reminder of the gap between football's haves and have-nots.

I recall that I had visited an old player who was down on his luck. At every meal-time he dined on a bowl of lentil soup and white bread. On the way home, my car radio reported that 55,000 fans had packed into Old Trafford to pay tribute to the most successful manager in United's history. It claimed that Alex Ferguson would rake in £1 million from his testimonial match. Given that his teams eventually won 12 Premier League titles, five FA Cups, four League Cups and three European trophies, I can't think of anyone more deserving the recognition but in less need of the money. As I stared at the car radio, I realized that this could be my route to change the lives of strangers, something I had sought since my retirement. My persistence paid off in late 1999 when I registered the Everton Former-Players' Foundation to alleviate the medical and other hardships of old footballers. I'm proud to say that it was the first of its kind in the world. From the beginning, I made sure that controls were introduced in order that the charity was operated in a professional and transparent manner.

To do so, I enlisted a handful of businessmen as trustees and former-players as patrons. Next, I panhandled for funds. Bill Kenwright, Walter Smith and my better half made significant donations and years later David Moyes donated the undisclosed damages from the libel suit related to Wayne Rooney's autobiography. As expected, most of the funds were provided by the fans. It never ceases to amaze me that the most generous people are those who can least afford it. They give because they want to, not because they expect something in return. The Everton family is the type of community that people advocate but rarely experience.

During the past 18 years we have arranged for scores of surgeries to treat chronic injuries. Nothing compares to our first beneficiary. Enter Gordon Watson, an old-timer whose name had been on the NHS waiting list for years. Unable to put his weight onto his feet, he was confined to a wheel-chair. Gordon showed me several x-rays of his ball and socket joint. It didn't take a doctor to notice that his hip joint had disintegrated and there was just jagged bone rubbing against jagged bone. Immediately, I searched for a surgeon who was willing to perform the medical procedure on an 80-odd year old. The risks were significant. I remember comforting Gordon before he was wheeled into the theatre at Lourdes Hospital. I squeezed his hand and whispered: 'You are my poster boy, don't you dare die on me!' The operation was a great success and seeing Gordon walk again pain-free was inspiring.

Other initiatives were more cosmetic. I've fond memories of the 2001 Foundation Day which featured the first official reunion of the 1969/70 championship-winning side. It was a special event for one player in particular. Sandy Brown had been extremely ill and needed a couple of walking sticks to get around. I had visited his home in Blackpool and promised to arrange for him to 'tread the bonnie turf one last time.' When he arrived at the ground for the pre-match lunch, I noticed that Sandy didn't have a warm coat. To redress the situation, I popped down to the Megastore and acquired a dozen or so Puma overcoats, identical to that worn by Walter Smith in the dugout, for Sandy and every other member of the 1969/70 squad to make sure that they looked like a team and that no-one appeared out of place.

As expected, the defender received a hero's welcome as he hobbled onto the pitch. By the time Sandy joined his team-mates in the centre-circle, he had tears streaming down his face. I gather that he wasn't alone. He was followed by Brian Labone. The captain had been injured towards the end of the season and Alan Ball had received the silverware in his absence. More than anything, I wanted Brian to stride onto the pitch holding the famous trophy high above his head. It's an iconic piece of silverware. I know because I ogled it throughout the pre-match meal. I was entranced by the beautiful relief work of its Victorian silversmiths. Everton was the first club to be awarded the trophy and I searched through the inscriptions to show our name to Brian. He retorted: 'It's something that I hope we never win again.'

83. Fifty-eight regular

After the removal of the comfort blanket of professional football, life hadn't been kind to Gordon West. His loyal friend Brian Labone and I vowed to get him onto his feet. There was one obvious problem; the keeper had ballooned to a massive 20-odd stones and needed new togs. I recall that we had to drag the proud Yorkshireman to a big man's shop. As the salesman prepared to take the necessary measurements, I asked: 'What size are you Gordon?' The man with the tape-measure responded '58 Regular.' As quick as a flash Brian retorted: 'There is nothing regular about being 58 Regular.'

Gordon was discombobulated. Reluctantly, he selected a suit plus a few white shirts, a couple of ties and handfuls of socks. I took care of the transaction: 'How much do I owe you?' The salesman smiled: 'Would you believe it? You're in luck. Today is our Football Legends' Sale and there's an 80% discount on every item. I'm a Red but my dad will be dead chuffed that I've taken care of the most expensive keeper in the world. By the way, does he need a new handbag?' Anyone privileged to hear Gordon open his heart to his fellow Blues at the 2001 Hall of Fame dinner will testify to his appreciation of the work of the Foundation. It changed his life.

Then there is Tony Kay. He reinforced his reputation as a genuine man of steel during his knee replacement operation. The orthopedic surgeons broke three different blades trying to saw his kneecap and had to suspend the procedure. I understand that they commandeered a Makita chainsaw to complete the job. A man of very few words off the pitch, he wrote to me afterwards: 'Your Foundation is the finest organization on God's earth. The unpaid volunteers work so hard looking after old players that they don't have time to blow their own trumpets.'

Then there was Mick Buckley. Because he had gone public with his problems, I'm comfortable talking about one of my favourites from the Seventies. I had invited him to the first five or six Hall of Fame dinners but he declined graciously. Finally, Mick admitted that he struggled with alcohol and had lost his job, his home, his marriage, wore an ankle tag to comply with a police curfew and - in his words - was approaching rock bottom. Cue the Everton Former-Players' Foundation and a couple of his loyal team-mates. Within days, Gary Jones and Terry Darracott had tracked him down to a bed & breakfast hotel and Harry Ross and Laurence Lee had sorted out his legal woes and enrolled him at the Sporting Chance Clinic in Hampshire - the brainchild of ex-England captain Tony Adams.

Though brief, my subsequent interactions with Mick were uplifting. He looked both happy and healthy - a slightly wrinkled version of the midfielder who had captured the 1972 UEFA Under-18 Championship for England in Barcelona. The last time we met was at a Foundation get-together at Goodison. With tears in his eyes, he embraced me: 'Thank you for turning my life round.' My response was predictable: 'There's no need to thank me. Being a Blue is my reward.' In return, he kissed me on the cheek – several times. Common in the Middle East, Latin America and apparently parts of Manchester, I had never been greeted like that before. Sadly, there was to be no fairy tale ending. Mick experienced cycles of rehab, sobriety and relapse during the next half-dozen years before his death at age 59.

The charity has raised and also spent a small fortune. All grants are confidential but anyone who has made one first-team appearance for Everton is eligible for support. To date, we've improved the lives of 140 men who were unable to help themselves and arranged for 100-plus surgical procedures. Many recipients aren't household names and made only a few outings at Goodison before taking part in football's Iditarod across the icy wilderness of the lower League grounds. Title winners, Cup heroes or simple journeymen, they are all Blues who made the club what it is. From her interactions with scores of ex-players, Elizabeth noticed a direct relationship between age and humility.

Lancashire Lass is an advocate of providing medical assistance to get old-timers back on their feet as well as a proponent of people taking personal responsibility. Yes, my wife thinks that the Foundation has been far too generous. I disagree. In her eyes, regular first-teamers who enjoyed meaningful careers in the professional game should have looked after their rewards. Again, I disagree. She would declare: 'The only helping hand so and so needs is at the end of his own arm. He needs a hand-up rather than a hand-out. Where are his family members? Don't they care?' I would tell her that the Everton Former-Players' Foundation was his family and we did care.

People claim that my modest initiative has polished the image of English football. Believe me, it - like most success stories - was a team effort. Thanks to the steadfast stewardship of Reverend Harry Ross and Laurence Lee and the support of the PFA, Everton Football Club and many thousands of Evertonians, the charity is lauded widely as the UEFA model. Subsequently, Barcelona, Real Madrid, Olympiacos, Hamburg, Anderlecht and Rangers established similar organizations which in turn have assisted several hundred individuals throughout Europe.

Some clubs have raised the bar by a notch or two. Back in 2010, at the 10th anniversary dinner of the Foundation, Barcelona's Ramon Alfonseda announced that 0.5% of every senior player's salary at the Nou Camp would be donated into the coffers of its veterans' organization. A trivial amount? Hardly. If Everton followed Barca's example, the Foundation would receive £275,000 per year from the current squad. It's like Zakat, the voluntary giving of a fixed portion of your wealth to charity, which is one of the Five Pillars of Islam.

Like Barcelona, Everton is more than a club. We are a family that not only supports the men on the pitch. - we support one another. Again, it makes me proud to say that. Personally, I'm gratified by the ongoing compassion shown towards our old players. Whenever I'm in the environs of Mama Blue they often stop me, not necessarily out of politeness but to show off their surgical scars. As important, the Foundation has provided pastoral care and inspired others to do so. I remain in awe of its ability to strengthen people's resilience to cope with pain, loss and anxiety.

Irrespective of the era in which they played, many footballers have lived outside the real world and crashed upon returning to it. Therefore, the charity's work is far from done. Different types of support will be required in the future such as home repairs, counselling and long-term nursing care. No doubt there will be new medical challenges. Research indicates that some suffered from neuropsychological consequences and trauma to the brain from heading a football. The Foundation won't continue forever. It wasn't designed to do so. I'm confident that it will help in tackling such challenges. Even though there should be no need to provide financial aid to footballers from the Premier League era, I've discovered that everybody needs emotional and spiritual support at some time in life. The sympathetic shoulder of the Foundation may be appreciated by even the richest star.

84. Compassionate club

I had sought to improve the health and welfare of old footballers who were unable to help themselves. To what extent I had succeeded was for others to judge. I didn't expect anything in return. The Big Blue Upstairs is the only one who needs to know the results of my initiatives. Therefore in late 2011, I was more than a little shocked to receive a telephone call from the British Consulate-General in San Francisco. A rather eloquent gentleman asked: 'If offered to you in the New Year's Honours List, would you accept the Most Excellent Order of the British Empire for services to football in the United Kingdom and Europe?' At first, I thought that it was some joker from Radio Merseyside. Then I sensed that no-one there, not even my old pal Billy Butler, could fake such a posh accent. I became lost for words, put the caller on hold and attempted to discuss the pros and cons of the potential offer with my wife.

In truth, I was going to decline respectfully and reiterate that being an Evertonian is my reward. Up to that precise moment in my life, I had felt that the UK Honours System was somewhat arbitrary, increasingly meaningless and a slightly dishonourable charade. Her Majesty Queen Elizabeth II aside, I had never been a big fan of the House of Windsor. Its reign had caused as many raised voices at Sycamore Avenue as the Dean-Lawton conundrum. Provoked by his patriotic flag waving - especially on St George's Day, I could hear myself telling Chemical Harry that the monarchy was an affront to the concept of fairness.

Also some of the people I admired and whose artworks paper the walls of our homes, such as Francis Bacon, David Hockney and LS Lowry, had declined similar gongs. Surely, I need not remind you that they didn't have to live with Lancashire Lass after doing so. A minute later, during which time she had thrown a couple of filthy looks in my direction, I informed the extremely patient gentleman with the increasingly cut-glass voice that, despite being more of a Roundhead than a Royalist, I'm not immune to the lure of prestige and would be delighted to accept an OBE on behalf of the Everton Former-Players' Foundation and the rest of the Everton family. While I felt like a cross between a turn-coat and a hypocrite, he seemed relieved and, so for that matter, was my better-half.

Nominees are sworn to secrecy until the official list is published in the London Gazette on New Year's Eve. That morning, at the crack of dawn, Elizabeth and I scrutinized the Gazette's website to no avail. We couldn't find my name. We doubled checked. No success. My wife feared that my telephone manner had offended the man from the British Consulate and he had changed his mind. Eventually she screamed: 'Found it hiding among the diplomatic service and overseas honours! Congratulations, you're an OBE - One Big Evertonian!'

I was more than a tad wary of visiting Buckingham Palace for my investiture but on the day was truly humbled, not by the surroundings - which were even grander than those at Spencer House - but by the accomplishments of many of my fellow recipients. Some had been gallant, others had been selfless. All had brought distinction to the old country. Meeting them reminded me that the United Kingdom is made up of some remarkable people. My day out was enhanced by the observation that, to the best of my knowledge, no pop singers, television celebrities or other publicity seekers were in attendance.

The ceremony took place in the magnificent ballroom where no expense had been spared on attention to aristocratic excess. With the Royal Household Orchestra playing in the background, I approached the Sergeant at Arms and waited until my commendation was announced. During the rehearsal, I had been instructed to take three strides forward, turn left, bow and advance another three strides before halting in front of the dais. Prince Charles was attired in an immaculate uniform covered with more medals than in the Everton Collection. He was attended by Gurkhas and Yeomen of the Guard.

As I waited for a Beefeater to tap my shoulder and inform me there had been royal cock-up, I noticed an equerry providing him my personal details and was ready to clarify that I was the former-university student from Widnes that his father may have told him about. That's right, the one with a bookcase wider than his television set.

Earlier that day, I had been instructed by the Palace staff to look at Prince Charles's face throughout our interactions. I didn't. My eyes followed his regal fingers as he pinned the medal on the lapel of my jacket with military precision. It had a bright red ribbon. Instinctively, I glared at him: 'Don't you have a blue one?' My words were flowed by a moment of absolute silence, like the one at Wembley that followed Graham Stuart hitting the bar and Paul Rideout nodding in the rebound? He cleared his throat and uttered: 'Everton ... a compassionate football club supported by very compassionate people.'

The Prince of Wales had been well-briefed. He asked me about our former-players and what can happen when the comfort blanket of professional football is removed. I mentioned proudly: 'Through the support of the Everton family, we've arranged 110 surgical procedures to date; 50 hips and 50 knees.' When he asked about the remainder, the heir to the British throne and I talked in some detail about the toes of Fred Pickering.

It was Pickering who had the last word about my modest initiatives. Years earlier, when the Former-Players' Foundation was helping the old centre-forward get back on his feet, he had told me: 'People will forget the details of what you did for them. But they will never forget how you made them feel.'

Here's the medal my mother says you deserve for supporting Everton

85. Dignity and integrity

Football fans are inclined to think that if we've watched a match then we've taken part in it. Obviously, we haven't. Nonetheless, we believe that after watching hundreds of contests we know the game inside and out. Embarrassingly, we don't. Permit me to take a minute or two to salute a very special man who did.

Brian Labone lived his life as he played his football, with dignity and integrity. He was a genuine gentleman. No, that's an understatement. He was a genuine Corinthian. Respected as a lifelong Blue and a loyal Merseysider throughout the football world, much of his charm was derived from his fundamental human decency. There was something extra-ordinary about his nature. It reflected his deep consideration of the people around him. He was kind, benevolent, courteous and more. I feel lucky to have ever met someone like him.

Some fans will be surprised to discover that his sportsmanship wasn't to the liking of all of his team-mates. It's no secret that he didn't see eye to eye with Alan Ball who demanded a more ruthless approach to the game. Alan liked to refer to Brian as 'Mister Softy', whereas Brian called him 'Bawly'. Sadly, it wasn't good-natured jesting. For some reason, I had expected old team-mates to be the best of friends. While 'Bawly' was a big Blue, I've never met a bigger one than 'Mr Softy'. In fact, the name of Brian Labone has been synonymous with that of Everton Football Club for as long as I can remember. Upon hanging up his No 5 shirt after playing over 500 times for his one-and-only club, he confessed that the sight of royal blue shirts made him feel proud. Make that Everton proud.

In private, however, Brian often referred to Everton as an ailing and confused loved one and experienced the ups and downs of supporting the club along with the match-going fans. There was one glaring exception. In May 1998, my friend disappeared during the closing minutes of our final game of the season. You may recall that we were clinging to a 1-1 draw and another Coventry goal would send us down to the Nationwide Football League. Brian couldn't stand the emotional strain and was photographed pacing nervously up and down Goodison Road. He was smoking one of the King Edward cigars I had given him to celebrate our anticipated triumph. When I bumped into him afterwards, he appeared overwhelmed by psychological trauma. Nonetheless, he reassured me: 'I told you God was an Evertonian. But I've grave doubts about that Nick Barmby.'

One of my fondest memories is of him entering the Albany in Old Hall Street. I had been invited to write an article on international caps for the Echo and had asked him to bring one from his collection to be photographed alongside those from different eras. You may recall that Brian was the first Everton player to be picked by England at senior level after World War 2 and would have received scores more than his 26 caps had he not withdrawn from Alf Ramsey's 1966 World Cup squad. I arrived early. Brian despised tardiness and wasn't shy to advise latecomers that they had showed disrespect to him. That lunchtime, he made a dramatic entrance by tossing his cap in my direction before picking up his favourite drink at the bar. As he approached me I realized that he had represented his country against Brazil, Uruguay and Mexico prior to the 1970 World Cup tournament. Instead of being the old friend who I was about to dine with, he reverted to The Last of the Corinthians - Labone of Everton and England. In my hands, I had evidence that he had competed against the world's best. Nervously, I enquired: 'What was it like to play against Pele at the Maracana? Was he the greatest?' Brian grinned at me: 'To be honest, I didn't see much of him except for the green No 10 on his yellow shirt.'

Widely acknowledged as our greatest captain - though Kevin Ratcliffe isn't far behind, Brian had been my conscience in establishing the Former-Players' Foundation, my sounding-board in selecting the Hall of Fame candidates and my telephone directory for organizing the Hall of Fame Galas. In addition, he was a terrific font of knowledge about the club and a tremendous conduit to others in the game. His little black book, which was a compilation of scraps of paper and beer mats bearing scribbled names and telephone numbers, detailed the whereabouts of his former team-mates and older players. He also knew about their health and, most important, if they wanted to be left alone. Together we tracked down hundreds of men. When you mentioned his name, people didn't just talk to you - they invited you into their lives.

Many people have played professional football on Merseyside. Some people are football on Merseyside. Brian was one of them. He represented values that have been discarded by English football. He was loyal to one club. He competed with impeccable fairness. Off the pitch, he was courteous with his fellow Blues. Indeed, his love affair with Everton never abated. A typical afternoon with the Blue Ambassador involved him buying drinks for strangers, inserting coins into expired parking meters, toting someone's heavy bags and talking to the homeless. Labone didn't expect anything in return. He would say: 'Give the gift of your smile. Kindness has its own rewards.'

Brian carried a light that attracted other people. There were one or two exceptions. I recall him popping into a newsagents on Old Hall Street where he noticed a pensioner struggling to find the necessary coppers for her cigarettes. His offer to buy them was rejected: 'Mind your own bloody business. I don't accept charity from people like you. You know, people who are as bitter as wormwood and twisted as barbed wire.' I was taken aback but Brian countered: 'Yes, I'm an Evertonian but I think you've me got confused with my friend David. He's the one who is bitter, twisted and proud.'

Revered by all football enthusiasts on Merseyside for his unassuming manner, keen intellect and eloquence, Brian was afforded immunity in all parts of the city and should have been recognized formally as the club's Ambassador at Large. The old skipper was devoted to Everton Football Club and wasn't reluctant to chide Alex Young and Alan Ball about them not spending more time on Merseyside. I regret that the club missed a tremendous opportunity to engage him to disseminate information to the fans, keep the peace among the Everton family and establish goodwill with other clubs. I was aware that he was disappointed not to have been appointed to the position of Fans' Liaison Officer. After Joe Parkinson got the assignment, I reassured Brian that it was a job for a young whippersnapper and that it would interfere with his work promoting the club in city centre pubs. Sadly, there lay the problem. Brian suspected that certain people behind the scenes at Goodison were of the opinion that he drank too much.

While my good friend thought the world of Ian Callaghan, he merely tolerated other Reds. After a couple of double vodkas, he wasn't reluctant to tell them what he thought of their ever-lasting shame. He was so articulate that rarely did anyone get the better of him in an argument. That was until the sportsman's dinner when the subject of the 1970 World Cup arose. A Kopite asked about the role of the England defence in protecting keeper Peter Bonetti prior to West Germany's third and winning goal. As intended, the subject offended him. So much so that Brian confronted his interrogator. 'Listen, I know what I'm talking about. I was there in Leon, Mexico. Where were you son?' The Kopite responded: 'Mr Labone, I was in Huyton at the time and was closer to Gerd Muller than you!' My friend accepted the retort with typical good humour.

86. Labby & Westie

Given my Methodist roots, I was never a good drinker. Like onions, alcohol never agreed with me. My aversion wasn't such a bad thing because, for one reason or another, someone strolling he corridors of power at Texas Eastern feared that cheap booze would decimate the backbone of American society and demanded that all employees keep a clear head and a sharp mind at all times. As a consequence, the consumption of alcohol was banned during lunchtimes and strongly discouraged after work.

Because business and alcohol didn't mix, I rarely consumed the stuff until the mid-Nineties. I turned to Draught Bass brewed in Burton upon Trent, to help cope with the dark days of Mike Walker. I drank moderately, or so I thought. Permit me to explain. After a Radio Merseyside phone-in show in late 1999, Brian Labone and I sought refuge at the Bee Hive pub in Paradise Street. When I think about it, we always met in one pub or another. Anyway, the cask-conditioned elixir was my tipple. Vodka, only Absolut Blue Label or Smirnoff Blue Label, was his. After five minutes Brian turned to me: 'If only young Danny Cadamarteri could run as fast as you can drink!' I thought about his words during the walk to my hotel. If the man revered by the lunchtime regulars at The Exchange Bar thinks that I'm a guzzler then I had better do something about it. Subsequently, I've discovered that Slimline Tonic Water, taken in moderation, enhanced my ability to reach contentment prior to capacity and remain upright. To this day, some friends struggle with the notion that not drinking is a personality flaw.

My final pint coincided with the debut of that famous vaudeville act - Labby & Westie. What a duo! Brian's wonderful charm and natural warmth blended magnificently with Gordon's biting sarcasm and exquisite timing. Well that's what Jackie Hamilton - the Dixie Dean of Comedy - told me. I remember the veteran funnyman waiting to entertain a room full of Blues at the Orange Lodge near Mere Lane. Surrounded by walls covered with Union Jacks and Boyne Standards plus photos of triumphant Liverpool and Rangers sides, the Merseyside comic admitted to me that he suffered from nerves: 'I've told gags for 40 years and am aware that I've got three chances to earn my corn. My first gag must let the audience know that I'm on the effing stage. My second must get their effing attention. And hopefully my third will make them effing laugh. Then they are like Plasticine effing putty in my hand. I'll tell one gag after another and finish with the one about Jimmy and Judy Kopite. It's easy to make Blues laugh. They have been conditioned to see the funny side of life and to poke fun at themselves. Tonight I'll get things going with a quickie: 'What do Paul Gerrard and Billy Graham have in common? They both can make 40,000 people stand up and scream Jesus Christ.' Then I'll move on to one that requires them to listen more closely: 'What do you call 20 multi-millionaires huddled around an ultra high-definition 84 inch television watching the Champions League final? Liverpool Football Club.'

In his playing days, Westie was renowned for the butterflies in his stomach. That night he waited patiently as Jackie Hamilton nailed one punch-line after another: 'I was walking across Stanley Park when I saw a Liverpool shirt nailed to a tree. I took it because you never know when you might need a nail.' The audience was rocking. Jackie was toying with them, so much so that he felt confident to mock his own: 'Walter Smith and Archie Knox offered to send the first-team on an all-expenses paid holiday to the sun-kissed island of Mauritius in the Indian Ocean but they preferred to visit Blackpool Promenade - so they could see what it's like to ride on an open-top bus.' In contrast, it was Westie's old team-mate who had grown nervous. Brian stood in a state of unfolding dismay and seemed to be questioning if improvisation was his strength when the MC warned him: 'One minute to show time. Break an effing leg, Labby.'

As we waited in the wings, Jackie coasted into his next gag: 'Heard about the new competition in the Echo? It's called Spot the Scouser in the Kop.' Then seamlessly into another: 'Heard about the Liverpool fan who threw a coin at an opposing player? He cracked his television screen.'

And then into his infamous gag: 'Married for 10 years, Jimmy and Judy Kopite are childless. So they went to a fertility doctor in Rodney Street. Mrs K sees him first. She undresses. The doctor examines her: Smoke? No. Drink? Only socially. The doctor scratches his head: I can't see anything wrong with you. Send in your husband. The husband takes off his brand-new Carlsberg shirt. The doctor examines him: Smoke? No. Drink? Only socially. The doctor smiles: Fill this bottle up to the brim with sperm and bring it back tomorrow. The next morning the Kopite enters the doctor's office. He bangs the empty bottle on the wooden desk. He looks distressed: I tried right handed. No luck. I tried left handed. Again no luck. My missus tried right handed. No luck. She tried left handed. Yet again no luck. Even my mother-in-law got involved. She tried right handed. No Luck. She tried left handed. No luck. My mother-in-law even took out her false teeth and tried. Again no luck. Embarrassingly he cried: We can't get the effing top off the effing bottle.'

Labby & Westie had nothing to fear. The crowd at the Orange Lodge rose to its collective feet to welcome them: 'La-bone, La-bone … Labone, Labone, Labone' was sung to that melodic tune from Snow White and the Seven Dwarfs. Neither Labby nor Westie needed a trio of warm-up jokes, an inventory of tried and tested one-liners or needless profanity. They were simply themselves - two great friends with great memories about their great times together. Their recollections - in which Gordon used sarcasm like a machete - of playing for both Everton and England didn't produce cackles or chortles. It generated howls of the belly-bursting variety.

Sadly, their famous vaudeville act died young - Brian at age 66 and Gordon at age 69. I miss their laughter but no more than their friendship.

I was the best in the Sixties … you were the best in the Eighties …
but nowadays we're about equal - just two fat buggers

87. The Blue Hope

I don't remember the specifics of their banter except for Brian Labone's tale about Dixie Dean's funeral in 1980. Along with Bob Latchford and Mike Lyons, Brian and Gordon were pall-bearers. As they lifted the coffin from the hearse, Brian spoke solemnly: 'Steady on, I've got the heavy corner.' It was only when the coffin was balanced on their shoulders that the other three started to giggle like shoolgirls. In what Brian claimed was the slowest time taken by a new penny to drop since decimalization, his colleagues had realized that the deceased had had his right-leg amputated four years earlier.

The entire Everton family was grief-stricken - make that heartbroken - by Brian's own death in 2006. I'll never forget the morning that I heard the news. After having a tumour removed successfully at Mount Vernon Hospital near Seattle, I had joined my wife at a nearby hotel. We had planned to rest for a couple of days before returning home. As usual, I needed to get my early morning fix from ToffeeWeb at the hotel's business centre. That late-April morning, the grapevine was dry. The season was drifting into mid-table mediocrity. Then I checked my emails. I opened one from my UK lawyer and had difficulty accepting what I was reading. His message that Brian had passed away after collapsing outside his house hit me like an emotional shockwave.

My old friend had been my strength throughout my own medical battles. By the time I reached my hotel room, tears were streaming down my face. Shortly afterwards they had co-mingled with those of my wife. I'm not sure that Brian would have approved of our sobbing. We had spoken to him only a week earlier. He had become frustrated with the ongoing efforts to acquire my memorabilia and sent me a box containing another medal to aid the decision-making process. Actually, it was a polished metal disc about the size of a florin - the old 10p coin. One side was engraved with the name of Christie's. The other side read Sotheby's.

I tried to call Dave Prentice to confirm the sad news. I hit the number 9 key for an outside line, the UK country code 1144 and the Echo's number. My hands were shaking uncontrollably. I got as far as 151 before hitting the wrong key. I tried again, only to fail again. At this point the hotel operator called me. In response to her enquiry, I confirmed that everything was all right. She must not have believed me because 10 minutes later my wife opened the door to discover a burly police officer standing in front of his even bigger colleague.

They were graduates with first-class honours from the good cop-bad cop school and were easy to differentiate. The bigger and badder one wanted to know why we were in tears and why someone had tried to dial the emergency services at 911. The good cop invited my wife to step out into the hotel corridor in order to quiz her in private. I think he was looking for signs of domestic abuse. At the same time, his side-kick - remember the bigger and badder cop - emptied my pockets and patted me down before interrogating me in a manner typical of Dirty Harry Callahan. To this day, I remain unconvinced that he believed there had been an unexpected death in our family. Nonetheless, Brian will be laughing at the thought of me being restrained - albeit temporarily and for reasons known only to the big, badass and increasingly testy cop - in the tight-fitting handcuffs of the Seattle Police Department.

I had shared my deepest feelings with my mother before her death. In the same way, I was extremely fortunate to tell Brian what I thought of him. The last time we spoke, I reviewed my proposed reference to him in my 'Everton Treasures' book: 'His name catches the eye in more than 500 programmes - No 5 Labone. Their pen-pictures hint at his rare abilities ... a cultured pivot ... dominant in the air ... strong in the tackle ... comfortable on the ball ... constructive in his distribution ... respected universally for his sportsmanship ... blessed with a character that made him deservedly popular with team-mates and opponents alike.'

I took a deep breath and continued: 'Brian Labone was the backbone of his one-and-only club for 15 years and deserved greater recognition outside of Merseyside. Often, I'm asked: What's the greatest Everton treasure you've ever come across? My standard response is Brian Leslie Labone - the Blue Hope, one of the finest diamonds in the world. His essence is woven into the fabric of my post-war memorabilia. Surely, no single player has done more or Everton Football Club after hanging up his boots. Possibly because he has always lived locally and was so accessible, fans have tended to overlook him in favour of the fleeting visits by other stars of yesteryear. Notwithstanding, Labone has continued to promote the royal blue cause not just as part of his official matchday responsibilities but on every single day of the week, every week of the year to football fans of all persuasions.' Brian listened patiently to my words before responding: 'Can't you stop at cultured pivot?'

More than a little piece of my Everton died on April 26, 2006. To tell you the truth, I've found that going to the match hasn't been the same. Often, I think of 'The Last of the Corinthians'. My favourite image? It's not of him towering over Bobby Collins as the Everton and Leeds teams were ordered to the dressing rooms during the Battle of Goodison in 1964; nor of him glaring at Peter Bonetti after the England goalkeeper had fluffed Franz Beckenbauer's shot in 1970. Of course, it's the black and white photograph of him downing a pinta in the Wembley dressing room after receiving the FA Cup from Princess Margaret.

The sight of Brian Labone drinking from a bottle of fresh milk always brings a smile to my face. Especially after The Corinthian - who knew about much trivia - told me that a cow must pump 600 pints of blood through her udder to produce that pinta.

Like putting carbon-fibre spoilers on a Reliant Robin

88. Modern-day football

It has been brought to my attention that on more than one occasion that old Blues like to moan about modern-day football. Where to start? When I was a teenager the concept of replacing injured players because they could no longer run or kick the ball was an abomination. It was nobler to play with 10 men. Since then we've had three-points-for-a-win, red and yellow cards, fourth officials, added time, penalty shoot-outs and the possibility of goal-line technology. I complain so much that my better-half often asks: 'How can there be so much wrong with a game that lasts for only 90 minutes and has fewer than 20 laws?' Well for starters, transfer fees are ridiculous and wages are simply out of control. The amount of money involved is difficult to comprehend. Also, ticket prices are too high and kick-off times are inconvenient. In my eyes, the lack of respect for match-going supporters is shameful. Irrevocably, football is about money. It appears that anything else is a bonus.

Most recently, she claimed that I'm guilty of bitching about footy bling. I suppose from the moment that Alan Ball pulled on his famous pair of Hummel boots, even though they were soon replaced by his more comfy Adidas ones painted white, it was only a matter of time before bootmakers exhausted the rainbow. Forty years ago, only the most gifted player would dare to wear white boots. Nowadays brightly-coloured boots are favoured by every show-off in the Premier League.

Such footwear isn't the silliest thing to happen to our national game. Not even close. The top spot is reserved for WAGs. I don't know about you but, I detest the way in which modern society thrusts attention on people who have no claim to it. A hybrid of gold diggers and parasites that live off the generosity of their partners, these women flaunt their newfound wealth without guilt and flash their silicone enhancements without dignity. Worse still, they encourage young girls to think that owning an expensive designer handbag is some sort of achievement. Now that I've started I might as well tick off other irritations:

I detest the way that Premier League greed has ripped the heart out of English football

I detest football agents

I detest the re-writing of football history by television

I detest Cockney football and its inflated sense of self-importance

I detest the fact that Alan Ball was never knighted

I detest that the goals of Dixie Dean are ignored nationally

I detest that the skills of Alex Young were not recorded for posterity

I detest Kopites working at Goodison - unless they're the best qualified for their jobs

I detest DVDs produced to celebrate successful battles against relegation

I detest badge-slobbering

I detest Mr Clive Thomas ... I hate Signor Pierluigi Collina

I detest Gary Lineker on the television ... I hate Alan Green on the radio

I detest drunks like George Best ... I hate drunks like Paul Gascoigne

I detest Roy Keane's lunge at Alf-Inge Haaland ... I hate Dave Mackay's tackle on Jimmy Husband

I detest hoofball ... I hate tippy-tappy

I detest players who dive ... I hate players who spit ... I despise El-Hadji Diouf

I detest the failure of the Kings Dock project

I detest the media patting our heads and tickling our stomachs for punching above our weight.

Wait, there's more. Now to the couple of things that I hate most about football. One is a certain musical composition by Rodgers and Hammerstein. The other is the Merseyside derby. Some people consider such local skirmishes to be the essence of football; others, like me, dread them. There is so much at stake during the build-up - never mind the match - that I tend to spend the week before the derby shuffling around Arizona with my collar raised and my head sunk into my shoulders. Recent clashes have been so draining emotionally that a small part of me wants the Reds to score in the first five minutes so that I can relax, knowing that it's all over. Of course, the rest of me wants the Blues to rip them to pieces.

It wasn't always so. Some 50 years ago, I was excited at the prospect of attending my first League derby. Like most Blues in the crowd of 73,000 at Goodison, I thought it was going to be a cakewalk against opponents that had spent eight years in the wilderness outside the top flight. I recall that Everton dominated the proceedings but Ron Yeats and his lumbering team-mates - who wore red shirts with badges the size of dinner plates and white shorts complete with a go-faster stripe - never gave up. After Johnny Morrissey made it 2-1, I was convinced that we would run out comfortable winners. Bill Shankly, who had yet to discover that wearing all red is associated with a higher probability of winning, had other ideas. Roger Hunt equalized in the final minute and set the tone for the next 100-plus clashes.

I know that most Blues are tired of the national media harping on about the old days when opposing fans walked arm-in-arm to the ground and mingled shoulder-to-shoulder on the terraces. That said, I do remember standing on the Kop wrapped in my blue and white scarf and not being hassled. Be that as it may, derbies were never cordial. But surely only Margaret Thatcher would enjoy the way in which they have soured. After all, the success of the city's two clubs in the Eighties flew in the face of her policies that brought Merseyside to its knees.

Back then, it was unimaginable that the bonds between Blues and Reds would turn so hostile. It's difficult to pinpoint exactly when things changed. Certainly, segregation policies have made the atmosphere more antagonistic. But, perhaps, it has more to do with the demise of Liverpool's status. I've detected that Reds struggle to accept that their club is no longer considered a major force to be reckoned with. After feasting spectacularly for decades, they haven't captured the title in over 25 years and don't look likely to win it any time soon. In my opinion, fans who hold up five fingers to denote their European Cup victories have become detached from reality. They mirror the Victorian followers of The Wanderers, a club that won the FA Cup on five occasions in another by-gone era and refuse to accept that all dynasties come to an end.

Sadly, some encounters have been tainted by chants of 'mur-der-ers' and stained by weapons of mass revulsion. I witnessed both shortly after Joleon Lescott had opened the scoring in the 2009 FA Cup tie. Oral fluids such as saliva and bile, probably from devotees of a certain El-Hadji Diouf, rained down from the upper tier of the Anfield Road stand onto the visitors gathered below. Other objects possessed a distinctive smell. Someone nearby claimed it was dog faeces, which apparently are reserved for visitors from Manchester. I wasn't so sure. As those around me expressed their anger, I tried to picture the guilty Kopite and his bull terrier parting the crowds along Breck Road on the morning of the match. With Shankly in a red harness and his owner in a matching tracksuit, their swaggers would ensure that shoppers recoiled in fear. The longer I thought about it, the more I realized that I had never ever seen a track-suited owner pick up after his status dog. Upon closer inspection, the missiles were determined to be even more repulsive. You guessed it, half-eaten meat & potato pies.

Actually, something struck me that evening. I hope I'm not alone in believing that an important measure of the quality of a football club is the way it treats both home and away fans.

89. A Bovril-stained start

You know it. I know it. We Blues know our history. It's so important that it has formed the words of an enduring anthem. History has always been important to us. And why not? As a founder of both the Football League and the Premier League, we have enjoyed a peerless tenure in the top flight. Even the most cynical football enthusiast would agree that no other club enjoys such a rich heritage. And if they need evidence, then it's in my collection of football memorabilia.

I'm convinced that it had been determined in some cosmically pre-ordained way - although I'm still waiting for hand-written instructions from the football gods - that I should protect the more meaningful souvenirs from our past against the destructiveness of time and unforgiving alien hands. As the chosen one, I collated anything and everything of significance for 20 years. Believe me, it was a lot of stuff - roughly 10,000 paper artefacts. To be honest there were far too many to count. Some pre-date the formation of the Football League and stretched to our days at Stanley Park, Priory Road and Anfield, but each item is special in its own right.

Unlike most collectors, I wasn't excited by shiny or bulky objects. Information and knowledge were my priorities. I was more interested in football's history than Premier League's hysteria. The real significance of my paper-chase is the unbroken sequences of memorabilia which tell the week-by-week story of Everton and Merseyside football.

As you know, my archives started with a Bovril-stained programme from the 1953 FA Cup clash with United. A few years later, I added the one from my first visit to Goodison. I stored them along with the subsequent programmes from the games I attended in a safe place - an old Bata shoe box. Now, fast-forward 20-odd years. I must confess to having forgotten about these keepsakes until my mother warned me of her plans to empty her attic of junk. My knee-jerk reaction was to beg her to airmail them to me, much to the bemusement of my wife. As I browsed through these childhood mementos I became intoxicated by the copiousness of our history and thought about donating the programmes, bubble-gum cards and tickets to Everton Football Club. Discreet enquiries, however, revealed that the club had no meaningful archives of its own and had no plans for establishing any. As a direct result, I decided to augment my modest collection with other Everton programmes. This far-reaching decision was made during the stressful time that my wife and I waited for an act of God. More specifically, it was a hurricane.

Houston's meteorologists had known about Alicia for a couple of days. The trouble with weather forecasts is that they are right too often to ignore and dead wrong too often to rely on. At Texas Eastern, we had evacuated the off-shore platforms and battened down the hatches elsewhere. At home, Elizabeth and I had bought sheets of plywood to cover the lower windows and other emergency supplies. As she searched for the cheque books, passports, insurance policies, first-aid kits, prescription medicines, credit cards and cash - especially quarters for the pay-phone, I demonstrated my GCE woodwork skills. I was so pleased with my handy-work that I painted 'EFC' in bold letters on the plywood over one window. On another I scrawled 'BLUE HOUse'. Yes, my letters started strong then tapered off.

We watched the television bulletins of the Category 3 storm battering the Gulf Coast. It had been 83 years since similar 115 mph winds had struck the Galveston-Houston corridor and destroyed everything in their path. We hunkered down in the smallest room in the house, the closet where I stored my football memorabilia. Around that time, Alicia elected to take the contra-flow lane up Interstate 45 towards us. When I think about the events in August 1983, there was something unsettling about my wife and me, equipped with two torches, three gallons of water and four buckets of Cracker Jack caramel coated popcorn, waiting for the eye of a hurricane. We weren't well prepared mainly because our fellow Texans had cleaned the shelves of the local supermarkets and convenience stores of the best goodies.

With no little irony, Elizabeth started to make a list of the other items we should have had at hand. These included canned food and a can-opener, plates and cutlery, blankets and pillows, towels and toiletries, rain-coats and sturdy boots, a list of important telephone numbers and an album containing pictures of the house contents for insurance as well as nostalgia purposes. Also, she identified an out-of-town friend to contact if we got separated. My suggestions were pooh-poohed but deserve a belated mention. I proposed that she add plastic bin bags to protect my treasures and extra pens and paper for her to make more lists.

People have different approaches to tackling Mother Nature when she has got her knickers in a twist. The local weirdo, who happened to reside four doors away, saw out Hurricane Alicia holding his gun in one hand and flicking through the glossy pages of 'Hustler' with the other. That's not a sexual innuendo. Apparently, he was perched on an Igloo cooler, packed with bottles of Budweiser, caressing his Glock for eight hours waiting patiently for someone named Looter. We had one big advantage over him - an endless supply of quality reading material. It was the first time that my better half had opened the shoe boxes to inspect the paraphernalia from my childhood. It may have been the fearsome winds but Elizabeth claimed to feel football's history vibrating through their pages. She appeared fascinated by the fact that as a youngster I had jotted down the team changes as well as the scores at half-time and full-time. My printing hadn't changed. That's right, my letters started strong then tapered off.

More than anything, she was amazed by my ability to remember the details of games by simply looking at pieces of paper; the incidents on the pitch and my adventures off it. With so much history at our finger-tips, we followed the careers of unsung champions like Mick Meagan and Dennis Stevens. Also, there were the fleeting involvements of teenagers who didn't quite make the grade such as Frank Darcy and Barry Rees in the Sixties and Steve Melledew and Martin Murray in the Seventies. The publications provided a week-by-week diary of my time following the club. Every high and every low was documented. Buoyed by nostalgia, I thought about my father and grandfather and their visits to Mama Blue. So there and then, I decided to track down every home programme issued during their lifetimes.

I kept quiet about my ambitious plans as the skies darkened and the winds strengthened. The noise was more fearsome than the feet of young Blues stamping in the Park End Stand. The wind didn't whistle, howl or make the noise of an angry vuvuzela. It roared like a jet engine at full -throttle. Adding to the cacophony were the sounds of relentless rain pounding the roof-tiles and items being tossed around outside; someone's tree crashing in one direction, someone's dreams in another. Then there was the sound of silence; an eerie quiet as the eye of the storm hung over us. The wind and rain stopped for an hour or so. I peered through the front door to discover 60 feet tall pine trees lying across the lawns with their roots kicking in the air. Others had collided with houses and parked cars. Several dwellings across the road had been decapitated. Given my new plans, I feared that if something similar had happened to our house, I would be compelled to spend weeks searching through the debris for my Everton memorabilia.

Far from finished, Alicia's eye moved north. The bedlam continued until day-break when the sound of chain-saws announced the all-clear. We wandered outside to inspect the fallen trees that blocked the flooded roads and the power and telephone lines that dangled everywhere. I've read somewhere that the hurricane shattered thousands of windows in the downtown skyscrapers, destroyed 2,500 houses, caused the equivalent of $6 billion in damage and killed 20 people. This leads me to my advice for riding out a Category 3 storm. Hit the supermarkets early to acquire the items on your wife's list, as well as a variety of munchies more exciting than popcorn, and don't be embarrassed to get down on your knees and pray to a very angry God for preferential treatment.

90. Take that stuff back

After a brief honeymoon experimenting with the thrill of haphazard scavenging, I embarked on a business-like approach to collecting memorabilia. It involved a little strategic planning, a small fortune and endless patience. Experts assert that the resulting archives were assembled with a single-minded sense of purpose and the type of intellectual rigour to which many museums aspire. I don't know about that but I did succeed in unearthing hundreds of rare items including football programmes dating back to 1886, gold medals to 1890, minute-books to 1886, season-tickets to 1881, match tickets to 1890, club documents to 1886, correspondence to 1888, team photos to 1881, cigarette cards to 1897 and postcards to 1902. Like the original owners, who had lovingly cared for these treasures, I treated them as my spoilt children.

Many onlookers thought that I had lost my mind. Others were fascinated by the effort put into locating rare memorabilia, especially from the Nineteenth Century. In truth, it wasn't too difficult. I discovered that if you post an attractive bounty, especially during the time when football rarities were unfashionable, they will turn themselves in. Shortly after I had informed the principal UK dealers of my appetite for items in tip-top condition, word spread that there was a madman prepared to pay silly-money for old Everton stuff and people approached me with extremely rare treasures. Well aware that I would never come across them again, I vowed never to let them pass me by for the sake of money. In my eyes, the club's history was priceless.

With knowledge as my principal objective, I targetted matchday programmes. In the pre-eBay era, I dedicated one evening per month scouring catalogues and dispatching orders to dealers. My third-Thursday-in-the-month routine paid dividends. In no time at all, I acquired thousands of programmes. Then by chance I was offered a bound volume from the early Fifties which contained every home programme from that season - every first-team, every second-team and every friendly. I was astounded that the contents were in such immaculate condition. After discovering that the club presented a volume to each director at the conclusion of each season, I concentrated my energies on tracking down these volumes. My timing was perfect. Nowadays, many of them are broken up by unscrupulous dealers because more lucrative markets exist for the individual publications. The act of splitting up volumes is the cardinal sin of collecting.

Looking back, I can identify the exact moment I became a serious collector and changed from cataloguing archives to hunting down elusive items. It was the evening I returned from home an auction in Scotland and revealed that a mad-man had paid £3,500 for a couple of programmes to the gasps of the attendees. I didn't want to upset my wife by revealing that the nutcase was me or that I considered the outlay to be a small price for securing Everton's past.

Lancashire Lass never uttered a word of disapproval until 1995. Convinced that we were doomed to relegation, she accompanied me to the final League game at Highfield Road and was thrilled that Joe Royle masterminded our survival. Upon leaving Coventry, we picked up some items of memorabilia I had acquired after some trans-Atlantic haggling. Clearly, I can remember my better-half's facial expression when I appeared with a cardboard box crammed with treasures. As I drove south, she rummaged through my swag. Her smile evaporated as she examined a white England shirt which had been worn by Tommy Lawton. The bottom third had changed to pale blue, evidence that the navy blue cotton shorts were not colour-fast during torrential rain. She was far from impressed by the fact that these sacred relics had been worn only once. I even reminded her that her mother had been a school-friend of the Everton legend. Then she turned to the dozen or so ledgers and proffered the niggling question: 'How much this time?' I glanced towards her, took a deep breath and announced proudly: 'They were a real bargain, only £78,000.' I still have nightmares about her screams: 'Stop the car and take them back!' Thankfully, the journey to London was mute.

Known passionately as 'The Everton Scriptures', the club's official minute-books chronicle the weekly meetings of the early management committees and later boards of directors. They contain 10,000 handwritten pages crammed with the decisions made at 5,000 meetings and document the unvarnished history of the club as seen through the eyes and the hands of John Houlding, George Mahon, Will Cuff and John Moores. After receiving a tip that some football rarities had been spotted there, I discovered my first ledger in a second-hand shop. It was hiding between a battered violin case and pristine copies of the Encyclopedia Britannica. Hand on heart; I'm sure it groaned: 'What took you so effing long?' I bent down and cradled it in my arms to keep it away from danger. Actually, it took me a minute or so to digest the historical importance of what I was holding. Then reality struck. It must have been ditched possibly along with other volumes by someone at the club, surely someone ignorant of our history.

After skimming the contents, I decided to rescue any and all other volumes. With the resolve of Dog and Beth Chapman, I offered rewards for the apprehension of the fugitives. Slowly they surrendered via a network of dealers until I completed an unbroken sequence dating from 1887 to 1964. Where did they come from? The provenance of such memorabilia is often vague. Most likely they were thrown out amid the re-construction of the Park End. Others claim that they were discarded during the preparations for the 1966 World Cup. Either way, it was no small task. The weight of the 29 ledgers exceeds 120 pounds. Rather than pointing my finger in the direction of the likely suspects responsible for such blatant carelessness, I consider it far more productive to rejoice in the knowledge that the ledgers are now safe.

For 25 years I was absorbed in an unquenchable quest to seek out the treasures of our past. You may find it difficult to believe that I did so from a sterile environment. There were no signs of the club or its history in either of my Houston homes. Both were void of stained glass windows celebrating the Golden Vision, shrines dedicated to the Holy Trinity and ceiling murals featuring Big Bob or Big Nev. There wasn't even a wayward programme. Following an edict from my better half, everything was kept out of sight. Confined to a closet - a tad cozier than a 6 feet by 8 feet prison cell, my children were restricted to short stints of exercise and supervised visitations.

Parenthood is one of the most fulfilling experiences in life and that the most important thing a guardian can give his child is a sense of being loved. Therefore the walk-in closet was organized with an assigned place for everything and everyone. Programmes were kept in chronological order with the home editions bound in volumes. Cigarette cards, postcards and other ephemera were kept in acid-free sleeves within museum-quality binders to protect against the evil forces of sunlight and humidity. Special wooden cases were commissioned to house the medals. The books boasted pristine dust-jackets and were stored in alphabetical order. I know what you are thinking: 'He exhibits an obsessive-compulsive personality disorder.' I understand that this condition is characterized by ritualized behavior and is often used to describe someone who is meticulous or committed to symmetry and organization. I may be in denial. That wasn't me, was it? Surely, I was simply a vigilant guardian.

People have questioned me about the immense amounts of time, money and energy consumed to compile, organize and maintain the world's finest collection of football memorabilia and, more important, what I learnt from my crusade. Well, I discovered that collecting stuff to save it from the tyranny of misuse is imbedded in my psychological make-up. I've met similar enthusiasts who rave about their Coca-Cola bottles, Superman comics and political campaign buttons. Possibly the private act of preserving objects satisfies the craving for parental affection that I never had in my childhood, Or probably, I'm just Everton crazy. So was I insane to spend so many years collecting football memorabilia? Surely not. I accept, however, that my quest straddles the blurred line between obsession and Class A addiction.

91. Blue gold

Because all rare items of memorabilia provide portals into the history of our national game, I travelled hundreds of thousands of miles to secure medals from old players and their families. I know what you are thinking: 'Why own the hard-earned symbol of someone else's accomplishment?' Far from it, I simply wanted to protect them.

Footballers selling medals is not uncommon. Even so, you might wonder how they can part with them. A popular reason offered by sellers: 'I don't need them to remember that I'm a winner. But I do need the funds.' Another justification: 'I've more children than medals and want to avoid conflict after I'm gone.' At the last count, four medals from 1962/63, six from 1969/70 and another four from 1984/85 have been auctioned. The FA Cup is no different. Seven winners from 1966 and seven runners-up from 1968 have cashed in. Even three winners' medals from 1983 have come under the hammer.

After Brian Harris informed me that he no longer needed his 1966 medal, I visited him in Chepstow but was horrified to discover the treasured item attached to a gold chain around his neck. Lost for words, I couldn't separate the medal from its owner. The following week we met in Chester. This time the medal was in a box. He smiled: 'Don't worry I've still got one around my neck.' Apparently, he asked the Football Association for a duplicate after his home had been burgled. Then some years later the thief posted the original medal to him.

Then there is the skipper of that team. Brian Labone was generous to a fault. He never turned down a chance to raise funds to help others yet refused to take anything for himself - not even his taxi fare. Therefore, I was shocked to receive a late-night telephone call in which he spilled the beans about a bit of bother with the Inland Revenue. Brian asked me to buy his treasured medals. He declined my offer of a loan to help in tiding things over and insisted on selling his memorabilia to me - or someone else. The next morning, we met in the Pig and Whistle pub in Chapel Street. Initially, he refused my offer. In his eyes, it was too much and didn't want charity. Subsequently, we spent a couple of hours arm-wrestling until he accepted my offer.

More often than not, medals are sold by the descendants of players who seek to cash in their inheritance. Unlike my interaction with my old friends, I've seen pound signs roll in their eyes like the windows on a one arm bandit - especially at auctions. The tone of these gatherings changed dramatically with the increased popularity of football memorabilia. And so did the prices. Traditionally, the sales-rooms at Christie's, Sotheby's and Bonhams were places for football enthusiasts. Nowadays, they attract mostly dealers, investors and syndicates, the type of people who speculate in vintage whisky and bloodstock.

While there weren't too many tug-of-wars over medals, antique publications were a different matter. Because an Everton programme is a part of the opponent's history, I was required to battle against United and Chelsea fans who, complete with their Stock Exchange bonuses, simply raised their paddles at the introduction of the lot and left it to the survival of the richest. The last erect paddle is declared the winner. My bidding tactics were more subtle. I would decide how much something was worth, double that figure, and plan to go one extra bid for luck. Other bidders adopted different approaches. One auction regular, a part-time manager of bare-knuckle fighters and a full-time supporter of Walter Smith and Rangers, would make intimidating circuits of the salesroom to discourage competing bids. After emanating vibes that suggested he should be approached with extreme caution, the Glaswegian glared at the other attendees throughout the proceedings. Being naive, I happened to stand next to him at one Christie's auction. To my amazement, I picked up the two items without a single bid from the floor. In addition to being guilty by association, I detected that I was also in his debt when he growled: 'You effing owe me.'

As a veteran of 50 or so auctions, I was convinced that successful bidding requires experience. Apparently not. Hospitalized in the USA, I read about the imminent disposal of the gems belonging to the leading United collector who was going through an unpleasant divorce. I coerced my wife to attend the two-day sale at Old Trafford. Although I warned her to steer clear of the Ibrox muscle, she sat next to him. As a result, very few people bid against her and she nabbed every single item on her list for a fraction of what I was prepared to pay. That afternoon, Old Trafford created a monster deluded into thinking that it was an expert worthy of a stint or two on the Antiques Roadshow. Cutting to the chase, I've never encouraged her to attend other sales on her own, simply because other attendees know that her talisman had been in prison for the last few years.

Despite my vow that no items would escape me, I avoided two or three items which can only be classified as religious relics. These included empty bottles of Everton Beacon Ale from the Houlding Brewery, wooden seats from the 1908 Stand and Tommy Lawton's jock strap. I kid you not. In addition, there were numerous items signed by Dixie Dean - some with a blue felt-tip pen. Later, the seller admitted that he had also perfected Duncan Ferguson's autograph.

On rare occasions I unearthed treasures which, for one reason or another, I failed to secure. The biggest one to get away was Ray Wilson's medal from the 1966 World Cup final. That was in 2002. My version of events is that I had been told that the club planned to bid on all of Wilson's items listed in Christie's catalogue. I was asked not to bid. After conceding that Goodison was the rightful place for the only World Cup winner's medal awarded to an Everton player, I conceded not to compete against the club's representative. As agreed, I kept my paddle under wraps throughout the hectic bidding and thought that the club had secured the lot via a series of telephone bids for £81,000, a price far below my budget ceiling. Later, I was disappointed to discover that it had been purchased by an investor. It gets worse.

The medal, like Wilson himself, is a genuine treasure and was at the top of the target list provided to Lord Grantchester when I transferred my archives to the Everton Collection Charitable Trust. Therefore, I urged his lordship and the club hierarchy to make every reasonable effort to acquire the item when it reappeared in a Sotheby's catalogue in 2014. I reminded them that the Trust had been established to make this type of expensive acquisition and that it would be a step backwards if this significant item was not featured in a future Everton Museum. After all, United had purchased the medal awarded to Nobby Stiles for £188,000 in 2010.

Aware that Wilson's gold would require people to work together towards a common goal, I suggested that they adopt the Barca model in which the members of the first-team squad and staff donate 0.5% of their annual salaries to charitable causes. Think about the resulting goodwill that would be associated with Everton Football Club, Everton Collection and current players and management in securing an important part of the club's heritage for the benefit of future generations. Sadly, my suggestion was dismissed and the medal was sold to an alien for £136,000. It was a reasonable price. Other medals from that game have come under the hammer. Alan Ball received £165,000 for his medal in 2005.

Fingers crossed, Wilson's gold will re-surface one day at another auction.

92. Heritage over money

Deep down inside, I regretted that my children had spent so many years confined to closet shelves in Houston. On the other hand, my wife looked forward to the day when they were grown up enough to find a less claustrophobic home for themselves, preferably in a different country. At some point, every collector must address the disposal of his labour of love. The alternatives are simple. One is to sell it lot by lot at auction. Another is to place it in a museum to keep it intact and perpetuate his vision. As a last resort, the collector can dodge the bullet and delay any decision until the disposition of his estate after he has turned up his toes.

Once upon a time, I thought that illness served no real purpose. Not so. In my case, poor health influenced my decision to find a new home for my collection. My goals were noble. I yearned for the football world to have access to my archives on Merseyside as well as the Internet. In order to showcase them, I searched for a building suitable for an Everton museum or a Temple of Blue History where all football fans could research, browse serendipitously and dream. Topping my short-list in 2000 was the Particular Baptist Chapel on Shaw Street not far from the famous bridewell. It was a bargain. Unfortunately, I was pipped by developers who subsequently converted it into luxury apartments. After similar set-backs, I accepted that finding a suitable home for my archives would be as taxing as compiling them.

Having made the decision to transfer my collection to new hands, I was able to comply with the spirit of the Malta Protocol and revise the pecking order to 1 Lancashire Lass - 2 Everton. To prepare for the adoption process, I brought my children to the United Kingdom in style. They travelled first-class in 42 steel storage boxes, the reinforced type employed on construction sites, complete with padlocks to resist forced entry. To accommodate them in the old country, Elizabeth and I renovated a townhouse in Chester. Technically, this was to enable her to spend time with her aging parents and for me to spend more time with my Everton family. From the outside it looked like a modest house on a quiet cobbled street within the medieval city walls. On the inside it mirrored Dr Who's Tardis.

I had shown the contents of the top layer of one box to a few Blues. I recall that Blue Bill was in awe. He reacted like a Bedouin Blue discovering the Dead Sea Scrolls. Whereas Brian Labone was simply lost for words and sat silently fondling one treasure then another. His breathing became shallow. Similarly, Dave Prentice couldn't believe his eyes. Above the sounds of his hands trembling, I could hear waves of adrenaline being released. He was so impressed that his newspaper, the Liverpool Echo, embraced the transfer of the collection to public ownership and encouraged all local football enthusiasts to 'Save Our Scriptures'. Also the independent Everton websites and fanzines stirred sentiments by promoting the importance of the collection to future generations of Blues.

Then there was the radio - the deceptively powerful medium. As you can imagine it's challenging to describe my treasures in written words - let alone in front of a microphone. Somehow Alan Jackson helped me to grab the attention of the audience of his evening phone-in show. It's even harder to describe what happened after I left the studios of Radio Merseyside. I remember walking to my car laden with boxes of rarities when two vehicles pulled up in front of me. There were six heads in the cars – all shaved. I feared that I was going to be mugged there and then in Paradise Street. Thankfully, these burly Blues had been listening to the show and wanted to make sure that I got home safely. I guess that's what makes us so very special. We look out for one another.

Word must have spread about the contents of the Tardis because we were visited by burglars. Somewhat fortunately they ignored the artwork on the walls, which was worth more than the house, and pilfered a few knick-knacks including a slim volume of war-time programmes.

During the investigation of the crime scene, one of Chester's more astute detectives ruled out Kopites because, in his words: 'They think football started in 1962.' After the burglary, the penny dropped that it would be impossible to recreate my labor of royal blue love, the items were transferred to the vaults of Nat West Bank. It was no easy task because they weighed a ton. I apologize for the exaggeration; they tipped the scales at 800 kilograms.

Also I sought insurance coverage. To do so, I invited valuations from Christie's, Sotheby's and others. As a result, a small army of experts examined my archives and salivated about getting their hands on the most complete collection of memorabilia relating to one club in the world. They estimated its market value at £1.5 million to £2.0 million. It was impossible for them to put a value on the ledgers, except to say that they were priceless. Upon learning that my bits and bobs had no equal, I underwent a paradigm shift in my way of thinking about them. Over-night, my children became a world-class archive worthy of the lofty galleries of the British Museum in London and the Smithsonian in Washington, DC.

After years of indifference, the club bowed to pressure from the supporters and took an interest in my archives. Knowing that it was short of cash, I suggested mechanisms in which no money would be diverted from David Moyes's war-chest. I felt sure that most season-ticket holders pay a £4 per season surcharge for four seasons with the club matching those funds. I remained patient and felt confident that something could be worked out. During the many months in which the club dithered with a series of empty promises, I was inundated with requests from Blues who wanted to inspect the ledgers. They included the son of the man who signed Dixie Dean, the relatives of John Moores' ex-partner at the embryonic Littlewoods and the film-makers who were creating a documentary about John Brodie, the Blue who conceived the idea of goal-nets. Sure enough, a minute-book entry detailed one of the very first purchases of his invention.

My long-suffering lawyer recommended that I should let the experts at Christie's take care of matters. He felt that if the club wanted my collection they should be prepared to pay top dollar at a well publicized auction. Not for the first or last time I ignored his counsel. Why? I had become obsessed with transferring my treasures to a secure royal blue home. The reward for my bloody-mindedness was exposure to the Walton waltz - that's right, forwards sideways, backwards sideways — for four years. I wasn't too surprised. After all, the club had its hands full with more important things than the past.

Some Blues claimed that if they had to choose between dodging relegation and avoiding the collection being broken up, they would take the latter. They recognized that the pain would be unbearable either way. Once the collection was dispersed, it would be forever. Therefore I wasn't too alarmed to find Mark Denny, a driving force behind the Goodison for Ever-ton campaign, and Lord John Grantchester at my front-door. Word of my dilemma had spread to Westminster and his lordship - let's call him Lord Toffee - wanted to inspect my treasure trove - or rather the ledgers which told the story of John Moores, his grandfather, at Goodison. It was ironic that they may have been discarded during his lordship's term on the club's board. To cut a long story short, I spurned his very generous offer of £250,000 for the ledgers. I wasn't prepared to sell the club's history to private ownership.

Rumours that the club's hierarchy was stalling served to attract well-heeled collectors and many more dealers from across the country, syndicates from Europe and investors from farther afield. Some were drawn by the fact that I had inadvertently compiled the finest accumulation of Liverpool stuff including 1,000 of their joint programmes with Everton. One dealer held a rare Liverpool-Everton collaboration from 1904 between his finger and thumb like a chorister. I noticed that he ran his other fingers over the publication like it was a braille 'Hustler' magazine.

He claimed to be able to feel the history. Another dealer made a very flattering comparison with the completeness of the Royal Philatelic Collection. Apparently, King George V strove to obtain the rarest postage stamps and spent three afternoons a week cataloguing them. This priceless collection, which remains the personal property of the Sovereign, is lauded as the world's most comprehensive with enough material to fill 2,000 albums. Sounds familiar? Possibly. I doubt, however, that his early items were kept in an old Bata shoe-box. Then there was the silver-tongued get-rich-quick entrepreneur who wanted to split up the ledgers and retail the 5,000 double-sided pages as framed one-of-a-kind pieces of artwork. In theory, his proposal would have netted me about £500,000 for the ledgers alone. I told them that I wasn't interested. Actually, that's an understatement. I said that I wouldn't be interested even if their offer had more zeroes than a season with Walter Smith. To this day, I don't think that they comprehended that I valued heritage over money.

Finally, we invited factions of the Everton family and representatives of both Everton and Liverpool to Chester. I picture my children in every nook and cranny on all four floors. They had never enjoyed so much freedom. The ledgers overwhelmed the dining room. The away publications were displayed in the study on the ground-floor. The medals lit up the living room. The letters and other documents were spread out across the kitchen and breakfast room. The assorted ephemera could be found in the guest's bedroom, where they were joined by 80 bound volumes. The shirts and caps were in the office in the basement. It was an impressive sight.

Armed with 60-page catalogues, each visitor was allowed to spend just two hours among the treasures. Many confessed that they felt like Howard Carter looking into Tutankhamen's tomb. I recall the curator of the Anfield Museum making extensive notes to brief his chairman. Eventually, we had to smuggle him out through the back-door. Everton were represented by Sir Philip Carter who appeared enthusiastic. Others with access to funds were more forceful. Shortly after the viewings we received huge offers - no, make that obscene offers - for individual items associated with the early histories of Chelsea and United. I concluded that the people making the offers, like their clubs, are used to getting their own way and struggle with rejection.

Next, we received substantial cash offers from overseas investors for the whole shebang. One was from the Middle East, the other from the Far East was attached to a huge bouquet. Both were for £1,250,000. Whereas my better half was tempted by these opening bids, I dismissed them. After all, it had taken some 25 years of single-minded dedication to assemble my archives and there was still a slight chance that something could be worked out with Everton.

I was determined that my memorabilia would never fall into alien hands. By now you will have detected that I was headstrong and excelled at royal blue sufferance - the ability to endure real pain without succumbing. Not surprisingly, I can remember feeling abandoned at a meeting involving Brian Labone, Norman Jones and my wife. It started with Brian announcing that he was tired of the shenanigans at Goodison. Always, Brian had wanted to see my archives showcased in a world-class museum. But that afternoon, he had changed his mind: 'You'll be the first fool - perhaps the only fool - to donate $1.0 million to Everton. Everyone else brags about how much they take out of the club.' Gently, my wife concurred with him: 'People are stringing you along. They're not really interested in heritage. You're pressurizing them to doing something they don't want to do. Anyone at Goodison who promises to meet you halfway is likely to be a poor judge of distance.'

My lawyer had always been an advocate on selling the collection at auction or rather, because there were so many rare items, at three or more sales to avoid market saturation. Norman kept his thoughts to himself until he suggested a vote. At 3-1 down, I adjourned the meeting.

I remained determined that my collection would be kept intact, especially after reading about Barry Halper - the baseball collector mentioned by Mickey Mantle. His holy vestiges were featured in both 'The Smithsonian' and 'Sports Illustrated' before being auctioned at Sotheby's in New York. I suppose the price tag of $12 million compensated him for the fact that baseball's history is now scattered across the globe. I refused to consider such a fate for Everton's heritage. Just in case you are wondering about Ty Cobb's dentures, they sold for $4,000.

With my health ailing, I met with Blue Bill and made no secret of my desire that all Blues should have easy access to their heritage. He promised to do everything possible to secure the history of our beloved club and would sort out the details with the new Chief Executive. His verbal commitment was good enough for me. Shortly afterwards Keith Wyness replaced Trevor Birch who had replaced Michael Dunford weeks earlier. While I remained positive, I concluded that, given its uncertain ownership and likely disposal of assets, the club wasn't the ideal home for my treasures. I favoured the formation of a charity, with the independence of the Former-Players' Foundation, as part of a strategic heritage management plan.

To their immense credit, Keith Wyness and Tony Tighe, part of Blue Bill's original consortium, joined Lord Toffee to register the Everton Collection Charitable Trust in 2005. For the record, I would like to clarify that I really liked Keith. He was smarter and more receptive to other people's ideas than his immediate predecessors. Also I admired Tony, who was the driving force behind the scenes. He impressed me with his indefatigable enthusiasm to get things done and would have been a tremendous addition to the club's board in 1994. Without their leadership and the support of many others, we would not be able to enjoy what is now the Everton Collection.

I'm neither a hoarder nor a pack-rat ... I am a collector

93. Desert Island memorabilia

Often, I'm asked to select my favourite pieces of memorabilia. However, I prefer to regard them as a collection boasting unbroken sequences of rarities which provides a 138-year chronology of life as well as football on Merseyside. As such, it illustrates the Everton story from amateur enthusiasts playing in public parks to multi-millionaire stars in the Premier League. But if I were to be cast away on the BBC's mythical island, I would insist on trading the permitted records, book and luxury item for some of my old swag. My selections would start with:

Pick #10: 1909 England Cap ... I was never interested in old kit. The exceptions were England caps. Of the ones in the collection, I would pick the red velvet headwear awarded to Bert Freeman for his appearance against Wales in 1909. The cap is embroidered with an English rose and is plain compared to modern counterparts with their fancy braiding and tassels. More important, it's pint-sized - proof that professional footballers had much smaller heads in his day.

Pick #9: 1914/15 Championship Medal ... When it comes to medals, I would opt for the beauty awarded to Harry Makepeace, who was capped by England at cricket and football. I remember bidding for it by telephone from my home in Texas. Time and again, I was encouraged by the Christie's rep to increase my bid because he had never seen a work of art quite like it. And neither had I. The gold and enamel medal was sculptured by the Football League to reflect the identity of the recipients. It contains the British coat of arms, the Lancashire rose and the Liver Bird.

Pick #8: Harold Hardman Letters ... My next pick is the bundle of love letters sent to the last amateur star to grace the top flight. Etiquette required Will Cuff to invite Harold Hardman, to take part in competitive fixtures between 1904-1907. Afterwards, the winger wound down his career closer to his law practice in Manchester and then served as a director at Old Trafford. I've often wondered why someone who was married to United for 50 years would preserve letters from his dalliance with his first love in such pristine condition.

Pick #7: 1891 Team Photograph ... Photos reflect the changing face of football. Though I nabbed a Sepia snapshot taken in 1881 shortly after we had changed our name, my favourite is one of the 1890/91 title-winning side in their ruby kit. In the absence of a club crest, the international players wore their country badges on their new shirts. As we were the first club to receive the famous silverware, I understand that this may be the first image of the trophy.

Few parents love one child more than another. Yet on occasions partiality is unavoidable. Perhaps, a clear indication of my favourites was the fact that the following items were kept in a special vault at the local branch of the Nat West Bank, just in case my house in Chester ever caught fire.

Pick #6: 1886 Construction Tender ... I unearthed the original plan of Mere Green and Archibald Leitch's quotations for his trademark stands but a more sacred piece of ephemera relates to Walton Breck Road. In order to secure an elusive programme, the vendor required me to purchase a box of seemingly worthless memorabilia. Further scrutiny revealed handwritten quotations prepared by the local builders Armstrong & Dobson to construct a wooden grandstand for £75. Not surprisingly, I received unsolicited overtures from agents aligned with the present owners of Anfield. One head-turning offer was in excess of £60,000.

Pick #5: 1888 Villa Invitation ... Dated March 6, 1888, this letter invites Everton to play in Birmingham for the first time and, because we weren't included on the original short-list, legitimizes our candidacy for membership of the Football League. Since then, we've spent more time in the top flight than any rival - the 2016/17 campaign is our 114th season. And it all started with beautifully hand-crafted correspondence from William McGregor.

Pick #4: 1881/82 Season-Ticket ... I compiled 17 early season-tickets. They reflect the birth of the Blues and chronicle our progress from Stanley Park, Priory Road and Anfield to Goodison. My favourite from 1881 details fixtures played under the rules of the Lancashire Association against the likes of Northwich Victoria, Bootle St John's and Halliwell Jubilee. I acquired it from a collector in Southport. On the drive home, I stopped under a street-light to pinch myself and reflect on its magic.

Pick #3: 1888/89 Home Programmes ... I compiled 4,000 home editions, containing more than 100,000 pages of football information but, contrary to rumour, my collection was far from complete. It included every home programme from the last 80-odd League campaigns and hundreds that are much older. To the envy of all founder members, I secured all our publications from the inaugural 1888/89 season. They are astonishing. The one from our first League fixture against Accrington is truly historic yet no more important than those against Villa, Blackburn, Bolton, Stoke, West Brom or Wolverhampton. I declined an offer of £115,000 for this volume.

Pick #2: Everton-Liverpool Collaborations ... Nothing captures the story of Merseyside football like the joint publications issued between 1904 -1935. The contents featured Everton first-team and Liverpool reserves one week and vice versa the next. In addition to tittle-tattle from Goodison and Anfield, these collaborations provide a unique week-by-week account of the social history of Merseyside. Their contents cover theatrical and cultural events as well as advertisements for the latest forms of transportation and ubiquitous promotions for tobacco and alcohol. After marveling at the 800 programmes, all in pristine condition, a renowned Red reflected on the irony that I had amassed the greatest archives pertaining to his club.

Pick #1: The Everton Scriptures ... Technically, these 29 minute-books cover a 75-year window in our history. Emotionally, they represent the DNA of Everton Football Club and Merseyside football. It took the best part of five years and huge ransom payments to retrieve them. I'll say it again and again, they are priceless. I rejected offers in excess of £110,000 for the volumes dated 1887-1891 and 1891-1892 which detail the split to form Liverpool Football Club. One lawyer hinted that I was discriminating against his overseas clients. He was right. They weren't blue enough. All significant events are meticulously documented, including the founding of the League, specification of club colours, selection of team line-ups, buildup to the acrimonious departure from our Sandon HQ and Anfield ground, development of the Grand Old Lady, escalation of players' wages, movement of stars through Goodison's revolving doors as well as details of scouting reports, transfers, ownership transactions and so much more.

Of course, all of my picks belong to future generations of Blues. So instead of the memorabilia, I would take a modest sheet of A4 paper which reflects that I did my bit for a football family that has provided the vibrant backdrop and sound-track to my life. Dated April 2008, it reads: 'To Whom It May Concern - The Everton Collection Charitable Trust was set up to raise funds to purchase The David France Collection of memorabilia regarding Everton Football Club. The collection has been valued by Sotheby's at £1,400,000. Dr David and Elizabeth France agreed to sell the collection for £800,000 representing a considerable discount to its value as an in-hand donation to the Trust equivalent to $1,200,000. The purchase was completed in December 2007... signed Grantchester.'

Heritage is a part of the fabric of every English club. This may sound incongruous but I fear that we're prisoners of our history. Modern-day football covets a selective memory. Its accent is on what has been achieved in the Premier League era only. As a consequence, our younger supporters have never tasted success. It has winked suggestively but always rebuffed their advances. They deserve to celebrate a magnificent future as well as a glorious past.

94. Do you love Everton more than me?

During my years in the US oil & gas industry I developed a sixth sense, the instinctive knack of recognizing what is happening around me - especially petty infighting. Initially, I had assumed that everyone was pursuing the same objective until it became apparent to me that Lord Toffee and the Everton board had competing agendas. I was disheartened. At night I would dream of a royal blue world where there was harmony. You can imagine my disappointment when I woke up. The feuding escalated so much that Keith Wyness cautioned that he was the only director still committed to securing the club's heritage. I thought he was winding me up, then realized that it was one of those moments in life when the universe, in the shape of the club's Chief Executive, was telling me - as politely as possible - that I was a martyr.

The most crucial of those celestial hints came in late-2005. I had crossed the Atlantic a dozen times to meet with his lordship before we shook hands on the terms. To expedite matters, I instructed my UK lawyer to draft the purchase and sales agreement. Relieved that the deal was done, I returned home. Then a few weeks later - on Christmas Eve - Lord Toffee left an apology on my answering machine. There were problems with the club's hierarchy and reluctantly he could no longer live with the agreed terms. To this day, my better half is convinced that certain people tried to take advantage of my poor health. I can recall the haunted look of anguish on her face as she replayed the message over and over.

I thought of it as another seemingly insurmountable obstacle to be overcome. She didn't. Calmly, Elizabeth asked: 'Do you love Everton more than me?' My wife wasn't nagging or joking. She likes to pick her moments and this was one of them. I knew the answer but it was hard to confess. My problem wasn't Everton; it was my own selfishness in putting my obsession ahead of her. Anaesthetized emotionally, I ploughed on. Why? I had a hunch that my recovery and subsequent possession of the minute-books had stalled progress. One or two directors didn't want to be seen to acquire items that had been discarded during their terms. So despite the significant expenditures involved in rescuing them, my wife and I donated these priceless treasures and agreed to transfer everything else at the low-end of Sotheby's valuation.

Finally, an exclusivity document was inked to provide the Trust with three years to raise the funds. There were conditions to the sale. Every item in my collection must be preserved by experts, catalogued and secured in a vault. None can be disposed of and, when available, rare memorabilia should be acquired. Equally as important, the artefacts should be displayed physically on Merseyside and all printed materials scanned and incorporated into a website to allow worldwide access. There was one final prerequisite. And it's a cracker. No items can be loaned to Liverpool Football Club. For posterity, I can be seen to pontificate on YouTube: 'If Kopites want to see their birth certificate, they're more than welcome to come over to our place and look at it.' I've been told that my words upset our loveable neighbours.

With Alan Ball installed as patron, the Trust launched its appeal to raise the necessary money. To get the campaign rolling, the club pledged £250,000 and Lord Toffee donated £100,000. It's none of my business but I heard complaints that a very long list of other well-heeled Evertonians who proclaim their love for all things royal blue failed to make donations of any size. Nevertheless from my sunny corner of the Great American Experiment, I remained confident. Tony Tighe and Keith Wyness had no shortage of good ideas for raising the balance. I thought that the most productive route was to do what the club did best - organize a football match - and understand that a proposal was made to UEFA to play the Lost Super Cup final against Juventus. An alternative was to pit our old boys against the former-Reds. Therefore, you can imagine my confusion when begging envelopes were distributed at the first home game of the season against United. It was akin to squatting on a street corner with a scruffy dog on a length of washing-line rattling a battered tin cup.

While the Trust had expected to rake in £100,000 from the full-house, the initiative grossed £350. That's right £350. Everyone involved was dumbfounded. A post-mortem showed that many fans believed that the club had secured the collection already. This setback stimulated 'Everton Heritage Week' - a massive fund-raising drive. The exhibition of 100 or so items of memorabilia at Goodison was a resounding success. I recall grandfathers, fathers and their children gazing in wonder at the royal blue treasures on show. Their feedback strengthened my resolve to transfer my archives to a public body based on Merseyside. The week's highlight was a fixture between Everton's Former-Players and Barcelona's Veterans. In advance of the encounter, a formal dinner was held at the Crowne Plaza Hotel. It was a night of mostly kind words from old friends such as Alex Young, Duncan McKenzie, Dave Hickson, Joe Royle and Alan Ball as well as new acquaintances from Barcelona.

During a break in the proceedings I joined Alan who was chatting with a group of friendly Catalans. The subject of intra-city animosity was raised. One visitor compared our loyal fans with those of Espanyol. Another brought up the subject of the Liver Birds on the nearby building. He asked: 'I understand that one bird supports the Blues and the other supports the Reds. How can you tell them part?' Alan retorted: 'The one bowing its head in shame belongs to LFC.' The guests chuckled. Neither I nor the World Cup winner did. At the end of the evening, I met with them in the hotel lobby. They expressed their pleasure at seeing the Barcelona Cup, both the trophy and medals, awarded by their club to Everton in 1924. Both voiced their admiration for the souvenir shirts produced for the match against Everton's Former-Players. They featured half an Everton shirt stitched to half a Barcelona shirt. Worthy of inclusion in the Everton Collection, they boasted the badges of both clubs and were embroidered with the match details. One Catalan added: 'I can't image us sharing a shirt with the likes of Liverpool Football Club.'

Inexplicably, fewer than 7,000 fans attended the Wednesday night game. As a result, people who claim to know about these things have alleged that the Trust spent as much money as it raised. I suspect that none of these cynics bothered to turn up at Goodison. Personally, I know first-hand that Lord Toffee and the Trust was diligent in everything that it did. With the Premier League seemingly awash with cash, I think that many people associated with these initiatives felt let down and understandably angry. Given that the Football Association gave generous assistance to the construction of the £1 billion national stadium, I'm amazed that it never offered to help secure a big piece of the history of our national game. From all accounts, it was saving its coppers for the 2018 World Cup bid. Besides Sebastian Coe, David Beckham and some dodgy character from Trinidad and Tobago, most football fans would concur that the FA's expenditures in excess of £20 million could have been put to better use.

Closer to home, some people alleged that the club manager could have been more supportive. As an example, they cited his protracted recruitment of Anderson Silva de Franca from National Montevideo which coincided with their fund-raising efforts. The mid-fielder was a flop and for one reason or another was loaned out to Malaga for 18 months and to Barnsley for another 6 months. At Goodison, he played a few games for Everton Reserves plus two minutes as a late substitute in a League game. I don't know how much we paid for him or how much we wasted on his wages but more shrewd and strategic use of these precious funds come to mind.

The Trust's last hope was an application for lottery money. It was a long shot especially after his lordship had been warned that the demands of the 2012 Olympic Games had reduced the funds available to other projects. Nonetheless, Lord Toffee, Keith Wyness, Tony Tighe and others redoubled their efforts and, to everyone's relief, the government recognized finally that football is an essential part of the nation's culture and came to the rescue with a £954,000 grant from the UK Heritage Lottery Fund to help acquire and preserve my collection.

95. Separation anxiety

I don't need to be reminded that the dogged determination and the ardent clinging to my goal of transferring my bits and bobs to public ownership is further proof that I'm Everton crazy. Quite definitely, I demonstrated abnormal mental and behavioral patterns throughout the ordeal. I could have sold them for more money but would have been poorer. In my eyes, my children always belonged to the Everton family. I was only ever their guardian.

Handing over the keys to my collection was like giving up my children for adoption. Comforted by promises they were going to a safe home, I hadn't expected to grieve over the separation. That was before I met their new guardians. Brace yourself. The Liverpool Record Office couldn't find room for a single Blue in the experts recruited to look after the collection. I met with them to explain the significance of the priceless items and tour the important sites in our past. Their need for a royal blue education became evident when I pointed to an advertising hoarding on Walton Lane featuring Mike Lyons. No-one could put a name to his face. Worse still, they didn't know who he was or that he had played nearly 500 times for the club. I could hear my mother shaking her head: 'Son, what have you done?'

The expert archivists took 15 months to catalogue the already-listed artefacts. My wife had expected to be kept up to date on developments. She wasn't. Via the grapevine, she heard complaints that the collection had been transferred in no particular order. Elizabeth was disillusioned. She knew that everything had been stored and delivered in chronological order. What could have happened? Her requests for information were ignored. She had every reason to be concerned because someone had attempted to break the locks of my crates during their brief time in storage at the Record Office prior to the sale. It would be unforgivable if any item, especially one in an unbroken sequence, was misplaced.

Almost two years after the transfer, a website was launched to profile the collection. By then my wife predicted that the experts would use the components of a Rolls Royce to build - wait for it - a Lotus Europa. She wasn't far off target. The Trust spent a fortune on something that makes a very good first impression but is littered with errors. Worse still - and believe me it's a doozy - it became evident that the bound volumes had been broken up into individual programmes which had been damaged in the process. Plain and simple, this was child abuse. Shame on them. I trust that the few Everton volumes in the care of the British Library have been shown more respect.

On the other hand and to its credit, the Trust used 8% of the items in the collection to organize an exhibition at the city's Central Library which turned our neighbours green with envy. Personally, I was impressed that 'Everlution - the Everton Collection' had replaced John James Audubon's monumental 'Birds of America' on display in the Picton Reading Room of the Central Library. Whenever I visited the exhibition, it was packed with Blues - both young and old. Unfortunately, some wounds hadn't healed. I had hoped that the Grantchester-Carter feud had been resolved and that all parties would attend the official launch and even volunteered to escort the club's hierarchy around the exhibition. No director showed up.

The Trust no longer receives a government handout and has struggled to stand on its own feet. With zero revenues, the experts were disbanded and, in the absence of a curator, the collection remains in storage. I've encouraged Lord Toffee to take a huge drag on the peace pipe and work closely with the club and the fans on initiatives to raise the fresh funds to ensure the protection and expansion of the collection. To me, it's important that additions are made to reinforce its standing as the foremost collection in the world. In recent years, I've tracked down Alan Ball's League winners' medal, Arthur Berry's Olympic gold medal and other football treasures for Lord Toffee and also donated another 2,000 minor items to the Trust.

Some nights I lay awake wondering what treasures from the past decade should be secured before they are shredded. For example, I believe that somewhere on Merseyside is a file cabinet containing detailed evidence of Sheikh Mansour's negotiations with the club's owners before he diverted his attention to City in 2008.

In the absence of a Goodison showcase, I'm confident that the shiny medals will enhance future football exhibitions planned for the new Museum of Liverpool. I pray that the paper items are not left to attract humidity, dust or, heaven forbid, roaches. After all, no club in the world has archives as old or as complete. It's vital that supporters across the globe understand and cherish our history as well as draw inspiration from it. It's something for all Blues to be proud of - both now and for generations to come. Players, managers, directors and trustees will come and go. The treasures of the past will provide eternal optimism.

I live in hope that one day Mama Blue or her replacement will be decorated with treasures from our illustrious past. They should coat its walls like a second skin. Also the Everton Collection should be exploited to strengthen the club's domestic and international marketing initiatives. The Everton Time Line is a constructive start even though someone had a bit of fun half-way down Goodison Road by including images of Nick Barmby and Mike Walker. Honestly, I'm not making it up. I regret that the powers-that-be didn't seek inputs from the EFC Heritage Society. I established this well-respected organization in 2008 to verify details of the club's past and also to drive important heritage initiatives. It's composed of enthusiastic Blues who don't just sing about our history. They are committed to sharing their know-how with others. I must add that there is only a dash of truth in the rumours that we meet in a bus shelter and wear matching anoraks.

As for the former-guardians, we celebrated the launch of the collection by inviting 20 Blues who had supported our efforts to 'Gwladys Street's Last Supper Encore'. It was a follow-up to the 'Last Supper' organized eight years earlier, shortly after my illness had been diagnosed. The warmth generated in the room epitomized the Everton family. I was taken aback when one attendee presented me with 'The True Blue Award, Second Place'. It was the outcome of a ballot by an independent website which had asked: 'Who do Evertonians trust?' The presenter reported: 'Over 400 votes were cast during a 24-hour period. Despite a late surge in votes for Bill Kenwright, he failed to catch David Moyes and David France. The League Cup win at Hull helped the manager in the neck-and-neck finish.' On hearing the news that my margin of defeat was two votes, I turned to my better half: 'Did you know about this?' 'Yes,' she replied, 'I voted for Moyes.'

I'm lucky. Not all wives fully appreciate what distraught Blues go through on matchdays. After a disappointment or even a humiliation, mine has never said: 'Get over it, football is only a game.' Blessed with the patience of an Everton widow - her term not mine, Elizabeth rarely complained about the amount of time or questioned me about the hundreds of thousands of pounds spent on securing our history. She never moaned about the phone calls from fellow Blues, memorabilia dealers and ex-players. Again, I'm lucky. Extremely lucky. Her support for the royal blue cause has equalled mine,especially as she watched my health tumble. Elizabeth often joked about writing a country song about her ordeal. Accompanied by banjos, fiddles and steel guitars, it would have encouraged women-folk to stand by their crazy men when finding a new home for our spoilt children.

Other long-suffering wives would have embraced our lawyer's advice and telephoned Christie's. Instead, she insisted: 'We can't guarantee a sparkling future for the younger supporters. We can give them a sparkling past. It's the least we can do.'

96. Euphoria of liberation

Let me tell you a secret, I've been energized by the euphoria of liberation that de-cluttering brings. Every now and then I receive an auction catalogue and linger over the images like an addict longing to chase the dragon. To date, I've avoided the temptation because I retained a handful of souvenirs. These include Alex Young's FA Cup winner's medal, Brian Labone's England cap versus Brazil, my World Cup ticket stubs including the final ticket signed 'Ray Wilson, Everton & England' and also an album crammed with the autographs of the men I've met over the years.

They are kept in a safe place on a deserted island in the Pacific North West. Of the few thousand inhabitants, I'm the only Blue by birth except for Walter and Martha - two English Cocker Spaniels. I refer to them as Walter and Archie so that I don't feel guilty when I yell at them after an unexpected defeat. I look for signs of Everton everywhere and have discovered that the substructure of the ferry dock mirrors the iron-work of Archibald Leitch. At the farmers' market, I unearthed an organic potato exhibiting a striking resemblance to Phil Neville and a handsome green pepper that was a dead ringer for Tim Howard. I'm not kidding. We kept them on the kitchen counter for weeks until they turned into withered incarnations of Wayne Rooney.

There is a connection between San Juan Island and the old country. A bit of confusion over the international boundary resulted in a 12-year military occupation of the island by the Royal Marines, including some from Merseyside, before it was awarded to the USA in 1872. Since then, our village of 25 dwellings and six times as many luxury boats has conducted a formal Colors Ceremony at every sunset. Slowly and respectfully, the Maple Leaf flag is lowered to the sounds of 'O Canada', the Union Jack to 'God Save the Queen' and finally Old Glory to 'Stars and Stripes Forever'. With its crashing cymbals, booming brass and perky piccolos, the official march of the USA never fails to motivate locals and visitors alike.

With hand on heart, I sing along to the music of John Philip Sousa: 'Here we go … here we go … here we go … Everton are the best we all know ... we're the team, we're supreme number one and we love you Everton ...' Because my words are drowned out by the horns of the boats moored in the picturesque harbour, people revere me as an American patriot. They don't know that I've embarked on the painstaking process of teaching the words of 'Everton Forever' to the dogs. Without much success at present. To his credit, Walter has learnt to howl aggressively at the sight or sound of anyone named Beckham on the television.

Like many immigrants, I thrived in a fertile business climate that promotes opportunity and remain convinced that there is a better tomorrow for those who want it badly enough. The USA is many things – a seducer, a stabilizer and a scapegoat. While there have been the dramatic decline in US standards during the past 40 years, I don't believe that plunges in social behaviour, gun violence, rudimentary education and family life have anything to do with my presence. In truth, there's never been a shortage of gripes about my adopted land. In addition to morbidly obese and loud-mouthed Yanks, look at its political debates, urban crime statistics and, if you must, television programmes. But ignore them for a minute. Think about rock & roll music and the NFL and NBA in which all teams have a chance of winning. Forget about the inexcusable indifference to the consequences of its foreign policies. Think about Apple iPhones and the MLB and MLS in which all teams have a chance of glory. Try to forget about the mind-boggling debts owed to China. Dream about an EPL in which all teams have an equal chance of winning.

If you've visited the USA, you'll have noticed that all offices of the Department of Homeland Security display a framed official portrait of the titular head of the free world. Possibly you've clocked the facial expressions of Presidents Carter, Reagan, Bush senior and Bush junior. They shared a hint of nervous caution. In Clinton's case it was embarrassment. In Obama's case it's unmistakable arrogance.

I propose that they should have been augmented by a neon sign declaring 'Welcome to the USA' coupled with the words of author Tom Robbins: 'It's never too late to have a happy childhood.' I'm sure you're aware that the US Declaration of Independence, drafted by Thomas Jefferson, includes a sweeping statement on the human rights of individual: 'We hold these truths to be self-evident … that all men are created equal, that they are endowed by their creator with certain unalienable rights, that among these are life, liberty and the pursuit of happiness.' Between you and me, the search for happiness is a chief source of unhappiness. Therefore I would modify the LED display to read: 'It's never too late to support Everton Football Club.'

I continue to encourage the more culturally advanced Americans to root for the Toffees. My mantra is simple: 'If you want to win something, support Manchester United or Liverpool or both. If you want to experience something, then support Everton.' The ambitious venture by the NBC television network to broadcast EPL games has given birth to a new generation of soccer fans. Even with the advent of New York/Manchester City, no European club has made the USA its own.

In my eyes, Americans seeking an English team with heritage and packed with super-heroes have two choices. The first is Tim Howard's club. Arguably the best US keeper since Sylvester Stallone - another American Blue - in 'Escape to Victory', Howard's form in the 2014 World Cup solidified his standing as an American legend and the biggest name in soccer. The other is Landon Donovan's club, who is widely regarded as the best US-born player in history. When you add the likes of Joe-Max Moore, Brian McBride and let's not forget Preki, you realize that there is something oddly American about Everton.

Could this American chap have saved your parent's marriage?

97. Smell of defeat in the morning

What can I say about watching the blue boys live on television while wearing my comfy pyjamas and eating a big bowl of my favourite cereal? Modern American life doesn't get much better. The clash between the Blues and the Reds in April 2012 was an opportunity to show American viewers that Everton Football Club was the true pride of Merseyside. I had attended all of the previous derbies held at Wembley but, with my better-half recovering from a bit of a stroke and uneasy on her feet - she referred to it as the Suarez Syndrome, decided to stay on San Juan Island and donate my ticket to a young fan who had never been to North London.

Like Blues everywhere, I went through a range of emotions during the 24 hours preceding the match. Excited one minute, anxious the next. My fear of losing another semi-final to Liverpool out-weighed my optimism. So, rather than watch the match live on the Fox Soccer Channel, I followed the action via the BBC's commentary on the internet. My plan was simple. I would turn on my computer every 15 minutes to determine the latest score. I hate early kick offs scheduled for 4.45 am Pacific Coast Time. At that ungodly hour I glanced at the line-ups, which contained no surprises, and settled down in the privacy of my office to kill time. How did I spend the next 900 seconds? Well, I scrutinized the entries in my little black book and prepared a list of Blues and Reds to telephone at full-time. It was similar to the list drafted after AC Milan had surged into a 3-0 lead in the Champions League final on that eventful night in Istanbul.

Next, I appealed to the gods of football. Specifically, I prayed that David Moyes understood how much derbies meant to Blues like me and that his Everton side would perform as well as the Everton fans. I envied their blue noses and war paint and reminisced about the FA Cup derbies I had been fortunate to attend in the past. The first to flash through my mind was the 1-0 win in 1967. You may recall that giant closed circuit television screens were erected at Anfield to satisfy the local demand. In excess of 105,000 fans saw a thrilling contest decided by Alan Ball. His acute angled volley brought deafening roars from the Blues assembled at the club's former and present homes. I knew that we didn't have a Ball of Fire in our 2012 line-up but hoped for one of his extra-special goals - the earlier the better.

My alarm clock rang at 5.00 am. Immediately, I examined the BBC website to discover that we had gained an early foothold. Encouraged, I resisted following the minute-by-minute text and frittered away the next 900 seconds in the carefree manner of someone who thinks he's going to live forever. Yes, I watched one of the many compilations of Everton goals posted on YouTube. It included Daniel Amokachi's second against Tottenham in 1995, the last goal we had scored during the 90 minutes of a semi-final. I returned to the BBC at the half-hour mark to learn we had taken the lead thanks to woeful defending in which Daniel Agger and Jamie Carragher had hesitated over a routine clearance, forcing the latter to lash the ball against Tim Cahill and into the path of Nikica Jelavic. At seeing the score-line Art 1 Porn 0, I let out the type of high-pitched sound usually associated with a distressed animal. No doubt my squeals woke up the island. For an intense moment, I was floating in air. Somewhat prematurely, I considered writing a short to-do list about how to waste the next 15 minutes but settled for a one of the things to do in London before the FA Cup final. For the record, it included seeing Blood Brothers yet again.

At half-time, my primary concern was that Sylvain Distin had been booked and that, given the opposition's passion for simulation, we would not be able to keep him and the other 10 men on the pitch. The Merseyside derby has seen packs of red cards, more than any other fixture in Premier League history, and I feared that the outcome would be influenced by another dismissal. Another concern was my disturbing hallucination that Jan Molby would turn out for Liverpool in the second-half. With such thoughts bombarding my mind, I tried to stay calm. It was too early for comfort food or self-medication. I needed a diversion.

Unlike me, many people can crack their knuckles. For some it's a nervous habit; for others the sensation brings relief. I researched the internet to discover that the joint capsule covering the knuckle holds a lubricant which also contains dissolved oxygen, nitrogen and carbon dioxide. When the knuckle is pressed in a certain way it reduces the pressure inside the joint capsule and the sudden escape of gases creates a popping sound. Some people pull the tip of each finger one at a time until they hear a crack. Others bend their fingers backwards, cracking the lot at once. Unable to crack my knuckles, I went outside to stretch my legs. Walter joined me. The dog was distracted by the bald eagles soaring and circling above the house. They must have mistaken my screams of joy with those of bloodshed. In my youth, I hadn't considered pre-dawn to be an attractive experience unless I was making my way home after an away win. Nowadays, I enjoy the delicate auroral glow of daybreak. Walter and I walked quietly. We longed for someone to come to their bedroom window and ask about the half-time score.

I reset my alarm clock for the second-half and checked for team changes. There were none. The opposition continued to field youngsters like Jordan Henderson and Jay Spearing, expensive under-performers like Stewart Downing and Andy Carroll as well as a third-choice keeper named Brad Jones. None of them would have made it into any of the great Liverpool sides fielded during my lifetime. Surely, Moyes would reinforce this fact during his half-time team-talk and make it crystal clear that there would be no greater chance to defeat our rivals at Wembley.

After another dip into the royal blue nostalgia on YouTube, I consulted the BBC website at the hour mark and questioned the Moyesiah's plan of protecting what we had. I knew, however, that such cautious football - keeping it tight and nicking one - had been rewarding in the past. Though his tactics, which revolved around a rigid shape in which everyone was saddled with defensive responsibilities, appeared to have succeeded in weathering the red storm - I was fearful and waited for the inevitable. My thoughts returned to another derby when we had sat on a 1-0 lead - the 1986 FA Cup final between two of the best sides in Europe. It had plenty of memorable moments including a row between Liverpool's Bruce Grobbelaar and Liverpool's Jim Beglin. Before that spat, Gary Lineker had put us into the lead and his team-mates had the game well under control at half-time. The second 45-minute period was a different story. Jan Molby was allowed to run the show and Liverpool scored three times. Some 26 years later, I feared history would repeat itself. To clear my mind I thought about calculating Pi but counted the pricks on Matta's infamous artwork instead. There were still 32 of them. Though I'm no expert on these things, some appeared to suffer from a hint of erectile dysfunction.

I returned to my computer at the 75-minute bell to discover that it was Art 1 Porn 1. Distin's wretched back-pass - I'm a grandmaster of understatement - had fallen short of Howard and Suarez had netted. I prayed that the equalizer would serve as a wake-up call and we would abandon our turgid defensive approach. My mind wandered to the three clashes in the fifth round of the 1991 FA Cup competition. In the first replay, Liverpool took the lead four times only to see us fight back each time and force a second replay which we won. That same kind of spirit would be required by Moyes's men at Wembley. The stress was getting to me. My nervous energy had turned into nausea. I felt like butterflies were fluttering in my stomach. I'm not sure of the collective noun for these creatures. There was a swarm or perhaps a kaleidescope of them inside me. My heart-rate was so rapid that I closed my eyes, took deep breaths and listened to some music. It didn't work. Unable to relax, I tried to crack my knuckles again before deciding to bite my finger-nails. I know, it's a disgusting habit for a young child never mind a 60 odd-year-old. The last thing that you want to be seen doing is chewing your bacteria traps. Walter, my early morning companion, didn't care. He was busy gnawing a plastic effigy of First Lady Michele Obama. I thought about joining him. In truth, I was prepared to do anything to relieve the tension.

Cautiously, I returned to my computer to read the score at 90 minutes. My heart sank. Andy Carroll, yes Andy Carroll, had scored to make it Art 1 Porn 2 with only five minutes to go. My worst fears had been realized. A miracle was required.

Fondly, I recalled that one had occurred when the clubs met in a fourth-round replay in 2009. It was the game made famous by the fact that half of the television audience missed the winning goal when the live broadcast cut to an advertisement for Tic-Tac mints two minutes from the end of extra-time. When the pictures of the action returned, viewers were shocked to see most of our players rolling around on the Goodison turf. For those who missed that winner, Phil Jagielka intercepted a sloppy clearance and passed to Andy van der Meyde who supplied a beautifully-weighted cross from the right-wing. Dan Gosling controlled the ball just outside the 6-yard box. Hemmed in by four defenders, the youngster managed to move the ball onto his preferred foot. Immediately after Gosling's shot went in off the far post, his team-mates buried him under a human pyramid of enthusiasm.

Back at Wembley Stadium, we needed a similar piece of magic from someone - make that anyone in royal blue. Inexplicably, Moyes's men failed to put a previously unknown keeper under any real pressure during the four minutes of added time and there was no royal blue miracle. Again, we had squandered an opportunity to lay some ghosts to rest and exorcize the malignant evil of the Prince of Darkness from Treorchy. We had only our selves to blame. I hate the smell of defeat, especially in the early morning air. Reluctantly, I accepted that I had witnessed a re-enactment of the 1971 semi-final in which the roles of Alun Evans and Brian Hall had been played by Luis Suarez and Andy Carroll respectively. It was a cruel reminder that, by and large, we have lived in the shadow of the Reds since that game. My father and grandfather will never forgive me for saying so but it's painfully true. Blues like me have been systematically brow-beaten into accepting the unacceptable. We understand that our pre-match enthusiasm is often followed by disappointment, fleeting depression and then by renewed optimism as we attempt to journey from a glorious past to a bright future.

After I had put away my little black book of contacts, I returned to the goals of yesteryear on YouTube. The glorious efforts of Temple, Sharp, Gray and Rideout reminded me that little shapes a manager's legacy like glittering silverware. And as the significance of the defeat sank in, I thought about David Moyes. He must have craved a trophy, make that any trophy, to go with his tenth anniversary cake. The Everton manager had participated in many competitions during his decade at Goodison yet remained empty-handed except for the MLS All-Star trophy and the Everton Friendship Cup. And I understand that the club paid for the latter.

Confronted by the images of Suarez celebrating on the shoulders of Carroll, I became engulfed by the heavy clouds of failure and pained by the gut-wrenching stench of disappointment. I was well aware that things often don't go to plan. Things often go wrong. Life is like that. People must learn from their losses and move on. That said, I remain perplexed by our inability to defeat Liverpool in the really important games.

My Wembley disappointments were tempered by an invitation to attend Everton's Annual Awards Banquet a few days after my investiture at the Palace. I had received word from two independent sources that I would receive official recognition of my initiatives from the club's hierarchy. Norman Jones accompanied me to the black-tie event at St George's Hall in Liverpool. Surely, there are few more magnificent venues in the land. We received VIP treatment and were seated at the table alongside the other recipients. There must have been a dozen individual trophies. Norman, who claims to have a nose for these things, predicted that I would receive the Howard Kendall Award.

During the proceedings I structured my acceptance speech in my head. There were many people to thank. I started with my wife, my lawyer, Lord Toffee, my good friends at the Former-Players' Foundation, Blue Bill, Robert Elstone and his staff at Goodison as well as the Everton family. After these kind words, I proposed to encourage the current squad to partly atone for their semi-final performance by finishing above Liverpool in the League table. Afire with idealism, I planned to share a dash of wisdom with them. That's right, you've heard it before: Blues versus Reds is humility versus arrogance; loyalty versus entitlement; and art versus pornography.

Patiently, I waited for my moment in the royal blue spotlight. There were only two awards left and it was unlikely that I would pip Johnny Heitinga for the Player of the Year trophy. So with my speech fixed in my head, I was amost out of my seat on my way to the stage when Robert Elstone made the formal announcement: 'The winner of the Howard Kendall Award for 2012 is ... Bill Kenwright.' I looked at the giant screen above the stage and saw the club chairman accepting the trophy. It was like a scene from a propaganda film made in the Democratic People's Republic of Korea - a poverty-stricken state ruled by an oppressive regime. I glanced at Norman and we burst out laughing. He claimed that I had been misinformed and my guffaws of embarrassment echoed those of Peter O'Toole at the Oscars. Apparently, the great thespian has been nominated and gone home empty-handed on eight occasions.

Far more important, Everton drew at Anfield and defeated West Ham at Goodison to finish four points and one place above Liverpool. It was only the second time we had done so in 24 seasons. For old Blues like me, the satisfaction of spending the summer looking down on the Reds beats any personal award.

I'm convinced you can make Kroldrup look more skillful

98. Dr Everton's Toffeemen

If you've embraced my collection of memorabilia as a labour of love, then let me tell you about Dr Everton's Toffeemen. In the dark days of 1997, I began the massive undertaking of capturing the likeness of every man who had played since our foundation in 1878. Yes I know, I'm Everton crazy. To do so, I commissioned the award-winning artist Peter King to supply two illustrations per week for 950 weeks. That's right, 18 years. Today, my portfolio includes an A-4 size colour caricature of just about every man who has played for St Domingo and Everton, both first-team, reserves and trials, during the past 138 years. I know what you are thinking. Why?

The project was conceived during a cursory review of the Hall of Fame candidates with Brian Labone, Tommy Eglington, Wally Fielding and Tom Jones - that's TE, not the cantankerous TG. We hadn't got far down the preliminary short-list before Tommy smiled: 'Remember what's his name - yes, Julie?' Brian laughed. Wally snorted. I was a spectator to four veterans, with around 2,000 first-team appearances between them, giggling like schoolboys. Tom turned to me and explained: 'Albert Juliussen was the prototype for Brett Angell - a non-scoring forward. I know because as a young defender I had to mark him in training. Julie made me look good.' Tommy volunteered: 'I know because I played alongside him.' Wally added: 'I remember him as Theo Kelly's record signing in 1948 who couldn't finish his dinner.' Brian laughed: 'You three are lucky, I spent my pocket money watching him.'

Tom added: 'I've always felt sorry for Juliussen and Angell. Both scored lots of goals in the lower Leagues. Neither was sharp enough for the top flight. It wasn't their fault. They tried their best but should not have been signed by Everton.' Their chatter moved to how quickly footballers are forgotten. Tom continued: 'The club should build a wall of remembrance, crafted from the finest marble and fastened to the walls of the brickwork on all sides of the stadium, listing the names of everyone who has played first-team football. The great ones, good ones, unsung ones and not so good ones.' I interjected: 'What about a gallery of paintings inside the ground?' And everyone nodded their approval.

It has been a formidable and never-ending challenge. To date, we have drawn 1,800 men who account for 99.9% of all League appearances, 99.2% war-time games and 95.5% of known pre-League outings. The artwork reminds me of a tin of Mackintosh's Quality Street. There are the purple ones - the inordinately charismatic men who fit the heroic mould like Dixie Dean. Then there are the toffee fingers in their gold wrappers - the top-class pros like Graeme Sharp who never received the national acclaim they deserved. Also there are the green triangles and yellow frustums - the journeymen like Barry Horne who roamed from club to club searching for a home. At the bottom, there are the chocolates that have been rejected by even the stickiest of fingers. More precisely, they are ones that nobody wants even after the ones no one wanted have been eaten. I'm sure you have your own list of strawberry delight players. Mine includes the men who failed to offer any measurable returns on the supporters' faith. Blues have never been reluctant to deride players who show a lack of honest toil. The most caustic words are reserved for the ball-dodgers who prefer the comfort of the Main Stand to the pitch. You know who I mean. Players who are sidelined by a combination of niggling injuries, frequent suspensions and mysterious illnesses.

The process of recording them for posterity hasn't changed since the draft of Harry Makepeace, our test subject. Typically, I supply two photographic references of each man, specifications for his kit and suggestions for appropriate poses. Next, Peter draws a pencil sketch. Then we exchange emails across the Atlantic until we agree that I'm right. For one reason or another, some drawings mirror super-heroes. Others resemble fugitives from Easter Island. Many are unflattering. It's not the artist's fault that we've fielded men with noses shaped like penises and the types of ears sported by Vulcans.

Each colour caricature takes four hours to draw. That commitment is the tip of the iceberg. Because of the paucity of material for men who played a handful of games, I scoured London's British Library, Oxford's Bodleian Library and the archives of other clubs. Then Phil Martin came to my rescue. This bibliophile, born on the very same day as yours truly, has assembled a library of 9,000 football books - the most extensive database in the land. The search for some men requires significant diligence. I recall the pursuit of William Hodge who made fleeting appearances in 1913, apparently on the afternoons when no cameras were present. Hodge had vanished until Phil spotted him in the pages of 'Amongst the Ruffs and Tuffs'. Only a bibliomaniac would own such an obscure book about Kilwinning Rangers. His searches have been so successful that I've speculated that the CIA should enlist him to verify the fate of skyjacker DB Cooper. Who knows, perhaps they have.

Blue is synonymous with Everton Football Club. However, it wasn't always so and much research was required to verify the specifications of the club's early colours. Steve Flanagan and Billy Smith, the lauded Blue Correspondent, scrutinized the pre-League match reports at the Liverpool Record Office. They discovered several unusual kits. Some were worn only once. For example, a navy blue shirt with a broad white panel was introduced at Notts County in November 1890. Also a natty blue and yellow striped shirt was favoured the following month at Wolverhampton. To date, the club has adopted 138 different kits along with an infinite permutation of those shirts and shorts.

At the same time, Steve Johnson, the renowned royal blue stato and author, studied the yellowing pages of the Liverpool Courier, Liverpool Echo and Liverpool Mercury to verify the details of appearances and goals. Statistics can be a minefield for errors. Through his diligence I can report with great confidence that prior to the start of the 2016/17 campaign, some 877 players have represented the club in League and knock-out competitions and another 162 men - including a few few ringers from the Bolton area - took part in pre-League action only. Also 184 men turned out in the regional games played during the two world wars.

Five Toffeemen made the ultimate sacrifice for their country. Thomas Gracie (Royal Scots), Leigh Roose (Royal Fusiliers) and Wilf Toman (King's Regiment (Liverpool)) perished during World War 1 and Brian Atkins (RAF) and William Sumner (RAF) died during World War 2. Obviously, they deserved recognition. To remedy the situation, my wife commissioned and paid for the magnificent marble plaque erected in the name of the Everton FC Shareholders' Association in 2011. Since then I've discovered that David Murray was killed in action in 1915 and Dan Sloane suffered the same fate in 1917. There may be one or two others. A few years later, Elizabeth insisted on providing a matching plaque to commemorate the supporters, shareholders and staff who perished during the world wars. While we owe these Blues a debt we can never ever repay, I like to think that these Park End memorials will encourage football supporters, irrespective of their allegiances, to bow their heads in silence and pay their respects to these brave Blues during the month of November and at other times of the year.

No other club has such comprehensive illustrations. If placed side-by-side, they would extend twice around a football pitch. While the artwork is not to the liking of all Blues, ornithological experts claim that the project mirrors Audubon's initiative which took a dozen years of field observations to complete. There are, however, a couple of significant differences. First, a copy of the 'Birds of America' book was sold recently at Sotheby's for £7.3 million. Second, neither Peter King nor I killed any of the subjects before he drew them.

99. Evertoons

Often, cartoonists find a way to tell a story when words alone fail. I discovered that they provide a valuable approach to highlighting the irony or absurdity in everyday situations as well as offering political commentary.

Like Jackie Hamilton - the Dixie Dean of Comedians, you may have observed that Blues are the only football supporters in the Second City of the Empire who don't take themselves too seriously. In truth, we have many reasons to laugh at ourselves. With so much fuel readily at hand, Peter King and I took a flight of fancy into the unforgiving world of single-panel cartoons coupled with single-line captions - better known as Evertoons - to lighten the Toffeemen project. Celebrated by his peers as the British Gag Cartoonist of the Year back in 2007, Peter is a professional cartoonist and a long-time contributor to Private Eye, Punch and The Spectator. While he complained about my interference in the creative process and his lack of artistic freedom, the cartoons and captions are collaborative efforts and evidence that Reds and Blues can laugh together ... at least about the happenings in the royal blue world.

To date, we've produced 200 plus Evertoons and as a portfolio they capture the history of my beloved club. Some of the wittier ones have been accepted for publication in national magazines but remain stored in the Toffeemen vault. Why? They are considered too cruel in the eyes of people - with gossamer thin skin - who claim to know about such things. Others have proposed that the Evertoons are worthy of a book of their own. Perhaps, one day.

In the interim, I trust that you concur that the cartoons selected to illustrate this book are simply good natured fun and inoffensive.

Are you telling me that Mr Cahill threw the first punch?

I had a feeling Tony Hibbert would score today

The manager asked me to get him an old fashioned centre-forward ...

So what makes you think Everton is a selling club?

That'll be one hundred for speeding and another two hundred
for offending the Merseyside public with that number plate

Number 21 ... Leon Osman

The players can have any colour they like ... as long as it's wood

100. Defender of the Royal Blue Faith

To shine a light on contemporary Everton, the beam must focus on the Defender of the Royal Blue Faith. In recent years, it's not been fashionable to appreciate the dedication and hard work of Bill Kenwright. In fact, resentment has been rife in some quarters. But in my eyes, his place in our post-war history compares favourably with those of Brian Labone, Colin Harvey and Mike Lyons. Is there a greater compliment for someone who hasn't worn the club's colours - at least not in public?

Given his decade-long struggles to attract suitably rich and honourable investors to propel the club back into the elite, it's one of life's mysteries why seasoned Blues like me are so fond of Blue Bill. Well, my support has much to do with the belief that no life-long Blue could have done a better job of promoting Everton as an authentic and compassionate football club plus the fact that the charming raconteur combines the showmanship of Michael Barrymore with the kindness of the Dalai Lama to make me feel like I'm on a non-stop elevator to royal blue heaven. With the seismic impacts on football's landscape of roubles in 2003 and petro-dollars in 2009, I wouldn't swap him for any of the ultra-rich but ultra-drab Americans, namely Stan Kroenke at Arsenal, John Henry at Liverpool, Malcolm Glazer at United and Ellis Short at Sunderland. Or, hand on heart, Roman Abramovich at Chelsea, the young Sheikh at City and that chubby chap at Newcastle. Ask yourself, do any of them care for their clubs in the way that our chairman loves Everton?

Blue Bill is no different than the traditional chairman – he's a self-made impresario who invested in his boyhood club as a celebration of his tremendous successes on Broadway and the West End. At Goodison, he overcame a false start, a few hiccups, some unhelpful spin and modest support from his fellow directors, to halt Everton's slide towards administration and possible oblivion. Seriously, things were desperate. You may recall that Blue Bill joined the Goodison board shortly after the club had enjoyed two titles, four FA Cup finals and European success and made a play for control when the Moores family announced its plans to sever its ties with the club in 1994. Out-maneuvered by Peter Johnson, he waited five years to snag the shares of the Birkenhead businessman. Undeterred by the knowledge that far more affluent Blues kept their heads down and hands firmly in their deeper pockets as the storm clouds gathered, he assembled True Blue Holdings - a syndicate that saw these heavy skies as merely a different shade of blue.

I must confess to being a tad wary when it took control. From my experience in buying and selling companies such consortia are usually under-funded and riddled with infighting. My concerns were summarized in the 'Speke from the Harbour' fanzine. They rankled a few people: 'At the start of this decade, Everton and Liverpool were on equal standing. Both had enjoyed a period of tremendous success on the pitch, owned decent stadiums and training grounds and had armies of loyal supporters. Both were in good financial health and, all things considered, worth about the same. Today, Liverpool's value exceeds £220 million. Based on Bill Kenwright's proposal to buy Peter Johnson's 68% stake for £20 million, Everton are valued at £30 million. Given that Bill was a director throughout the decade in question, is it fair to claim that he has overseen Everton's value shrink to 15% of Liverpool's and plans to acquire it on the cheap? Surely, he should have stepped down from the board and eliminated any perceptions of conflict of interest? His advisers claim that the club isn't worth much. How can that be? After the disposal of a few players in the summer, much of the £19 million overdraft will have been eliminated and the outstanding balance could be cleared readily with the sale of Michael Ball. Further sales of say Simonsen, Unsworth and Jeffers could raise £12 million and along with the divestment of Bellefield for another £8 million, this would leave the new owner with two-thirds of an all-seater stadium, a first-team squad including eight internationals, the funds from 22,000 season-tickets and Sky TV sponsorship for the 1999/2000 season, plus one of the strongest brand names in British football – all for nothing. Not a bad bit of business.'

Based on his intimate knowledge of its health, I expected his syndicate to stabilize, re-package and, after a couple of years, off-load the club at a reasonable mark-up to a well-heeled investor with a spend-spend-spend philosophy qualified to shower us with golden visions and silver trophies. While that didn't happen, I've no doubts that Blue Bill started with noble intentions until he counted his NTL chickens before they had hatched. Cognizant that external funds were required to move the club forward in the short-term, he negotiated a much publicized £30 million injection from cable television operators NTL and sanctioned a spending spree. Regrettably, the deal collapsed shortly after these phantom funds had been used to sign Alexandersson, Hughes, Nyarko, Pistone and Watson in the summer of 2000.

This unprecedented spending plunged the club into debt from which it struggled to escape. At the time, I was disappointed by the business acumen of some directors. Under no obligation to inject their own money into the Goodison coffers, they appeared to adopt the relaxed optimism of Wilkins Micawber, the Dickens character convinced that 'something will turn up'. As the club's financial health deteriorated, their actions were predictable. You guessed it. They disposed of our top youngsters - Michael Ball for £6.5 million, Francis Jeffers for £8 million and Richard Dunne for £3 million - and listed the Bellefield training ground for sale at £10 million.

To alleviate our plight, the board claimed to have found investment via Fortress Sports Fund. Embarrassingly, to nobody's surprise except the gullible, it was a mirage. I'll never forget the anguish as the proposal unravelled at the 2004 EGM. This flashback resides so deeply within my psychological system that no amount of digging has removed it. Christopher Samuelson of Fortress Sports Fund proposed to invest £13 million in return for 30% of the club which he claimed to have supported all of his life. His deceit was exposed when a suspicious shareholder asked: 'Who scored the winning goal in the 1966 Cup Final?' Not surprisingly, we never heard of Samuelson again.

Afterwards, Blue Bill arranged for an alternative source of funding. Sir Philip Green provided a £15 million loan and allegedly played a role in the transfer of Paul Gregg's stake to his friend Robert Earl, via a mysterious vehicle based in the British Virgin Islands named BCR Sports. As a result, our ownership was shrouded in question marks. Was Green the de facto owner? Who knew? While his involvement was never clarified, the retail tycoon showed significant interest in all things to do with the club. So much so that Chief Executive Keith Wyness resigned in 2008 citing outside influences behind the scenes. To their credit, Green and Earl - businessmen interested purely in making money - stabilized our finances during some of our darkest days. Though the associated costs are unclear, the arrangement provided time for the chairman to attract a top-class owner with long-term commitment.

Because success can no longer be achieved with a managerial partnership of alchemic genius like Howard Kendall and Colin Harvey, Blue Bill's pushed the boat out time and again to provide his managers with transfer kitties. Though he never complained publicly, just imagine you've sold everything that wasn't screwed down, mortgaged everything else and gone from door-to-door begging from everyone you know? You trust David Moyes's judgment, then have to bite your lip as he unveils Per Kroldrup. The chairman never criticized his manager for buying the not-so-great Dane - recognized as one of the worst deals in the history of football, or Diniyar Bilyaletdinov or even Richard Wright. Nevertheless, few Blues praise the chairman's determined efforts to keep Moyes happy and our beloved club in the top-half of the table. In their eyes, win a game or two and the manager was The Moyesiah. Lose one at Goodison and Blue Bill was at fault for not being a billionaire. I hope I'm not alone in believing that the manager was fortunate to have access to financial resources to smash the club's transfer record and stretch the pay structure. Yes, Blue Bill deserves significian praise for our stability.

During his search for a rich and noble successor, some Blues were amazed that Blue Bill didn't looked over his shoulder in the Main Stand. A couple of rows back sat John Suenson-Taylor, Third Baron Grantchester known for his seemingly bottomless pockets, gentlemanly manners and flexible approach to timekeeping. 'The Sunday Times' reported that after the sales of their interests in football pools, mail-order operations and department stores, he and the Moores family were worth £1.2 billion. So why didn't his lordship - who loves Everton and still owns 8% of the club - step forward with his cheque book? Beats me. But there again, why would any man of real wealth invest in a football club? Until recently it hasn't been a profit-making business. Money has been made only when a club is sold on to someone with a bigger ego.

Also there is the fact that it's a thankless job. All Goodison chairmen - both the good and not so good - have been vilified at some point. I recall that fans protested loudly after John Moores sacked Johnny Carey in a London taxi. Home-made leaflets demanded the beheadings of both Philip Carter and Howard Kendall before they embarked on their period of success. And Peter Johnson was vilified and, even worse, branded a Kopite.

I haven't endorsed all of the decisions made by Blue Bill, especially the amendment of the club's Articles of Association to stifle structured discussions. In my official capacity as the Life President of the Everton Shareholders' Association - founded back in1938 as a watchdog over the important matters concerning the club - I can confirm that there is no representation for minority shareholders in the boardroom. Even though collectively we own around 16% of all shares, our voices are no longer heard.

The elimination of AGMs was a PR disaster. Uncomfortable with democracy, the club mirrored a private company in which the board of directors and its advisors did what they believe is best without worrying how others might react. Sadly, the chairman forgot that the combination of transparency and debate is the route to creating robust solutions for a robust future. Personally, I was schooled by Chemical Harry and encouraged by many elders to be civil to those with whom I disagree and to listen to them if I expect them to listen to me. After all, there is the chance that I may be ill-informed or, God forbid, wrong. Predictably, as the club hierarchy went farther and demonized the more independent-minded shareholders, the lonely voices of dissent grew into a chorus of criticism. So much so that people-power rattled the gates of Goodison. Calling yourself the People's Club yet removing lines of communication wasn't very smart.

Personally, I don't look forward to the day in the not too distant future when all of his shares are transferred to someone with no previous connection to the club. That said, Everton Football Club will survive, hopefully flourish. It continued without John Houlding, George Mahon, Will Cuff and John Moores and will do so without the Defender of the Royal Blue Faith. In the interim, however, we must prepare ourselves for a different world. Our new owners won't see Everton as a vanity investment. They'll expect attractive financial dividends. In my eyes, they are welcome to the latter if they have earned them.

So how will I remember Blue Bill? First and foremost, he was a great Evertonian, a saviour and a stabilizer. Perhaps a victim of circumstances - he is a member of the crew who missed the boat it had helped to launch. After eliminating any lingering fears of relegation, I had expected him and his fellow directors to exploit the fertility of the Premier League. As others flourished, they failed to drum up commercial deals befitting our traditional membership of the Big Five or relocate to a state-of-the-art stadium. While our beloved club trails behind its traditional rivals — on and off the pitch — we are in much better nick today than when he grasped control. The same can't be said for his predecessor who may have captured gleaming silverware but dumped his shares like hot potatoes without too much thought for the consequences.

Chairmen don't get to choose how they are remembered. Blue Bill is no exception. Some Blues think he stayed too long without capturing a major trophy or securing timely investment. Whereas I appreciate that he didn't rush into selling the club to the first well-heeled party or US venture capitalist to come along. Far from it, he chose to protect the future of Everton over easy and ready money. I like to think that he mirrored my desire to protect the past of our beloved club over immediate financial gain. Of course, some fans will remember him as the man who sold the greatest-ever Merseyside-born footballer. Like Blue Bill, I've no doubts that Wayne Rooney was sent from royal blue heaven to lead us from stagnation. That said, his transfer at age 18 saved us from administration. To his immense credit, the Everton chairman squeezed every penny out of the deal. He's a savvy negotiator and did the same with the sales of Jeffers, Rodwell, Big Vic and resales of Johnson, Lescott and Fellaini.

Let's forget about the losses of Rooney and the Kings Dock stadium for a minute, I believe that Blue Bill should be judged on his ability to pass the royal blue baton - sometimes referred to as a poisoned chalice to new owners possessing the right qualifications, integrity and strategy for returning us to the elite of English football. Subsequently in early-2016, the club announced the arrival of the elusive billionaire - Farhad Moshiri. It may have taken a tad longer than we all hoped but Blue Bill delivered on his promise of attracting investment to push the club forward and, from all accounts, appears to have passed the baton to a man with real financial clout, profound business nous, and, above all, uncommon ambition. So thanks to William of Wavertree - Defender of the Royal Blue Faith, I look forward to a bright future in which the differences within the fan-base are repaired and forgotten, the Everton family is re-united in total harmony and Goodison is declared a no-fly zone.

That's it ... shoes polished, shirt ironed and speech updated

101. God in her corner

Now and then, opportunity knocks. Occasionally, it pounds on the doors at Goodison. Too often its demands to be let in are ignored. No error of judgment was bigger than the decision not to move to a modern home with better views and quieter neighbours in 2002. The error mirrored Decca Records' rejection of a certain quartet of local musicians and will haunt Blues for decades. Located on a UNESCO World Heritage site near the city centre, the Kings Dock project was the chance of a lifetime to own a half share in a state-of-the-art venue for a pittance. Like most Blues, I was impressed by the grandeur of the 55,000 capacity facility. The roof could be closed and the pitch, built on a giant concrete tray, rolled to the side to accommodate events like concerts and the hanging of Kopites. Of course, it would be opened to allow God to watch his team in action. Given that the Merseyside public had been informed that the required £30 million was ring-fenced, it remains a mystery why the club didn't pursue it. Most likely, it had to do with increased construction costs. Just think if Blue Bill had concluded the deal at the Kings Dock, concluded a sale to the young Sheikh - before he turned his attention towards City and its new stadium, we would be marvelling at a masive bronze statue of Saviour Bill near the Gower Street.

Whatever the reasons, older fans say that if you place your ear to the pavement near The Three Graces you can pick up the sounds of Will Cuff and John Moores turning in their graves. I've tried it and can confirm that they are spinning at the same number of revolutions per minute as Grandad France. The Echo Arena was constructed as a long-term memorial to the biggest misjudgement in our history. Whenever I pass the new facility, I stifle my tears. In the absence of an autopsy, the mystery has deepened. You may recall that Paul Gregg, more of a business man than a football fan, had joined the board in anticipation of such an investment, offered to rescue the project. His proposal, which modified the club's role from owners to tenants, was rejected. To be honest, I've always believed that football clubs should not be in the real estate business. There is no need to own such a specialized facility. At the time, I was convinced that if we had employed a more resourceful executive team, Blue Bill and Paul Gregg could have finessed a workable deal and the club would be playing football on the banks of the Royal Blue Mersey. That's right, Keith Wyness and Robert Elstone were handed the wrong relocation project.

Impatient estate agents would say that we exhibit the traits of lookie loos - time wasters who masquerade as potential buyers with no real intention of moving. The Kings Dock project was one of umpteen times that the club's plans have come to an expensive nothing. The desire to relocate started with Peter Johnson's desire for greener pastures. At first, he outlined his plans for Kirkby golf course. Then failed to crayon them in. Not long afterwards, he wanted to move to Burtonwood and then to Cronton. I almost forgot about Speke and the fact that he was circling the town of my birth. Because most of these proposals eroded our standing as a top club, I whole-heartedly backed the efforts of the Goodison For Ever-ton group. A decade later, Blue Bill proposed a new home at the end of a rainbow in the Metropolitan Borough of Knowsley. Destination Kirkby polarized the Everton family with a boastful campaign which was at best inaccurate and at worst offensive. Most of the Blues that I know opposed the move to Kirkby. Unlike them, I wasn't interested in whether the new digs were inside the city's boundary. No matter how hard I tried, I failed to see how the move would enhance our net revenues. Perhaps I mix with the wrong crowd. We all supported the Keep Everton In Our City campaign.

Younger Blues may be surprised to learn that we ranked alongside Arsenal and United in status, facilities and trophies at the dawn of the Premier League. Today our matchday revenues are only 20% of those clubs. While a bigger stadium was one route to catching them, the economics of Destination Kirkby were flawed. They assumed that moving a few miles north we would increase our gates by 30%. I understand that if people concentrated on the really important things in life, there would be no empty seats at our home games but the planners overlooked the reality that - with David Moyes's infatuation with hoofball - we rarely filled Mama Blue.

My concern was the anticipated quality of the £100 million home. After occupying a mansion for more than a century, albeit conspicuously worse for wear, Blues like me found it hard to embrace a medium quality facility which would undermine our membership of 'The English Elite'. These are the 10 clubs that have enjoyed the biggest attendances and longest tenures in the top flight. The rankings have changed over time. In no particular order, they are: Arsenal, Villa, Chelsea, Everton, Liverpool, City, United, Newcastle, Sunderland and Tottenham. It seemed to me that the board failed to ask: Would the new stadium be good enough for any of these clubs? Or more specifically: Would Kirkby be good enough for Liverpool Football Club?

While I would like to watch Everton dominate opponents at a home on the banks of the royal blue Mersey, I don't care passionately about where we play as long as we have a city presence. I've always favoured the concept of an Everton Centre in the heart of the city. After beating that drum for more than a decade, I've come to terms with the reality that it will never happen. Over the years I've nurtured a vision of revamping somewhere like the old ABC Cinema with a massive neon sign announcing 'Everton Football Club' in 12 feet or even taller letters which would illuminate Lime Street for 24 hours per day. The building could house the administrative staff, press and communications studio, dining facilities, museum and exhibitions space, ticket office, retail shops, meeting rooms, sponsors' rooms, etc. and free-up floor space for the immediate expansion of restaurant and retail facilities at Goodison. After modest outlays for renovations, 'The Everton Centre' would remind both locals and visitors that there are two foot-ball institutions in the city.

I've mentioned the concept to Blue Bill on a couple of occasions. The first time, he stared at me as if I was a statue weeping blood in a Latin American church before switching topics to the seductive twanging guitars and soft harmonizing voices of the Everly Brothers and his favourite tear-soaked ballad, namely 'Let It Be Me.' The second time, he rolled his eyes like a horse that had completed the Grand National course without its jockey. I had noted that reaction before. Shortly after he gained control of the club, I mentioned tactfully that some of the existing directors were a bit long in the tooth and out of touch with the fans. By the time I mentioned the immediate need for the injections of dynamism and innovation, he had implemented the type of Nimzo-Indian Defence used by chess masters.

I'm extremely fond of Mama Blue, Harridan Blue or whatever name you give to our current abode. She has been a constant throughout my life. I've spent the equivalent of 50 full days at the Grand Old Lady plus another 300 days getting there. She may be irregular and tired but oozes character and, like every other cathedral, has God in her corner. Whereas I've never advocated a major refurbishment of our old home, we can regain some of our swagger in the short term by emphasizing our incomparable heritage and celebrating Goodison as the last of the traditional football stadiums. As for the obstructed views? They are part of the matchday experience. The same can't be said of the monument to mediocrity. When archaeologists rake over the ashes of the stadium they'll discover a shocking waste of space, figuratively and literally, known as the Park End Stand. which some claim was backwash from Peter Johnson's pact with Lucifer which traded Premier League survival in exchange for the rape of Mama Blue.

Others claim that the stand and the excess land, from the demolition of the houses in Goodison Avenue which has been used as a car park and a campsite, are cursed. Yes that's right, by Nana Mouskouri. Apparently, the available footprint could have accommodated a stand with a capacity of 12,000 and by adding a second tier of seats, executive boxes, modern changing rooms plus a breath-taking museum and a Walk of Fame with statues of Dixie Dean and other heroes of yesteryear. If correct, the club could have avoided the pain associated with so many ground move proposals.

102. Big hoof and bigger prayer

You'll have deduced that I'm crazy about a football club that no longer exists. In the Sixties, to suggest that we would finish in the Top 4 once in 24 years would have prompted ridicule. Our recent history has revolved around Blue Bill and the Moyesiah. What did we have to show for their 11-year union? Well, if silverware is the benchmark then the answer is nothing. In fairness, they did provide a level of much-needed stability as well as a dash or two of heroic failure. The manager's track record isn't something to be dismissed. Far from it. Despite having to sell his best players such as Arteta, Gravesen, Lescott, Rodwell and, of course, Rooney, his sides finished in the top-half of the Premier League table nine times during his lengthy tenure - 7th, 17th, 4th, 11th, 6th, 5th, 5th, 8th, 7th, 7th and 6th - a feat achieved only once in the decade prior to his arrival.

Aware that he didn't have much money to spend, the manager painstakingly put together a small squad of talented professionals and raised our ambitions with the terrific additions from the bargain basement like Cahill, Coleman, Donovan, Lescott, Martyn and Stones as well as Arteta, Baines, Jagielka and Neville. While many Blues claim that such stability was as much as the club could expect without major investment, I expected a little bit more. For starters, he failed to beat United, Chelsea and Arsenal away from home. His record against the Reds was as embarrassing. In total, Moyes contested 25 clashes with the old enemy. Victories were so rare that we gave them names. We won the Carsley derby in 2004, the Johnson derby in 2006, the Gosling derby in 2009 and the one in 2010 in which both Cahill and Arteta netted beauties.

David Moyes was a good Everton manager, one of the best though not quite as good as he thought he was. I admired him and was a big fan of his dignity, industry and commitment to his club - which set him apart from many contemporaries - but never his tactics. In my eyes, football should be about silverware and entertainment. Not necessarily in that order. Achieve these and fans will have fond memories to share with future generations. I don't know about you but I can't imagine many Blues waxing lyrical about any of his sides that emphasized organization and graft at the expense of flair. His preference for hoofball - a professional derivative of Tennessee skyball - wasn't to the liking of those of us raised on the skills of The Golden Vision, The Holy Trinity and The Rolling Blue Thunder - my epithet for the quartet of Steven, Bracewell, Reid & Sheedy. Matchdays should be a joy. Sadly towards the end of his tenure, I didn't want to feel happy after watching his side in action - I simply wanted not to feel so utterly miserable.

Though Everton Football Club is no longer the trail-blazer that my father and grandfather worshipped, the club has taken such a powerful grip of me that it's hard to fall out of love with it. However, it's possible to reassess the relationship and ask if you're getting what you want? This question must have been going through my mind in late-2010. I had flown overnight from Victoria, BC and was chatting with pals outside the Winslow Hotel when I decided not to go to the match. Even more disillusioned than jet lagged, I suggestion that Evertonians had become battered wives who keep going back to the same abusers that continue to slap them around. I added that sometimes in life you must walk away.

My friends shook their heads in disbelief as I retreated sheepishly to observe the faces on the tide of match-going Blues. Both the young and old fans appeared depressed. Smiles of optimism had been replaced by frowns of duty. For one little girl, I just wish I could have rewound the clock to when Chemical Harry carried the milk crate for me to stand on. Dressed from head to toe in royal blue courtesy of the Megastore, she was being dragged to the match: 'Dad, you promised to take me to McDonald's. I want a Happy Meal for my birthday!' I may be wrong but remain convinced that she knew the game against the club holding up the table would end Everton nil, Wigan nil, Entertainment nil.

Despite his concept of plucky Everton punching above its weight, I'm convinced that David Moyes did his very best with the resources at his disposal. Alongside Blue Bill, he eliminated any fears of relegation and administration. Therefore, I disagree with those who allege that he was more interested in self-promotion than the competitiveness of his club. However, he did himself no favours in the eyes of many Blues by stringing along the chairman and other diehard fans for about 12 months while he flirted on e-Harmony with suitors in London, Manchester and Europe.

Apparently, Sir Alex Ferguson spent six of those months encouraging him not to sign a new Everton contract. Ironically, from my seat in the Main Stand, I'd been urging him to do the very same thing for six years. In the end, he jumped at the once-in-a-lifetime chance to take charge at Old Trafford. I wished him success but wasn't sorry to see him move on to supposedly greener pastures. In truth, I had wanted Moyes to depart immediately after the semi-final loss to Liverpool. His attempt to hold out for a 1-0 win against lacklustre opponents was extremely disappointed - possibly shameful. .

Worse managers have left Goodison but none of them departed under such a dark cloud of their own making. Evertonians deserved better. Certainly, Blue Bill deserved much better. I met him briefly before Moyes's final against West Ham. The chairman looked like he had been kicked in the stomach and stabbed between the shoulder blades. That Sunday afternoon, for some unknown reason, the club's hierarchy afforded a guard of honour to a football visionary who was so good that he was able to manage Everton Football Club and Manchester United Football Club at the very same time.

Started as a search for the Arteta money ... turned into an escape tunnel

103. Tippy-tappy

Enter the come-to-bed eyes and sweet talking lips of Roberto Martinez Montoliu – who had guided Wigan to FA Cup joy and relegation tears in the same week. To welcome his love of tiki-taka, as it's known in the country of his birth, my wife hosted 'A Grand Old Evening' in San Francisco. Like her, I had never met most of the guests. They weren't strangers - simply a dozen ToffeeWeb patrons from around the globe. Most of all, she was impressed by Robert Elstone who showed no nerves as the deadline came and went for United to trigger the buyout clause in Marouane Fellaini's contract. Now we know that our former manager had hoped for a bargain but was required to return, with no little ignominy, and pay a whopping £27.5 million.

The next day, we caught our first sight of tippy-tappy, as it's called on Merseyside, at AT&T Park - the modern home of the San Francisco Giants of MLB. I swear that after goalkeeper Tim Howard picked up the ball, it took 22 passes - I know because my wife counted them - for his team-mates to get out of their own half, much to the confusion of Andrea Pirlo and Carlos Tevez. As the match progressed, it became clear that possession was a big part of our new game-plan, not a happy accident. Martinez's approach requires players with touch, vision and flair to exhaust opponents and strike when the chance arises. The preference for relentless short-passes is easy on the eye at first but eventually torments the mind like an idiot ring-tone. The match against Juventus - the reigning champions of Italy - saw the debut of John Stones. He had enjoyed an uneventful outing until the International Champions Cup tie went to penalties. Elizabeth and I stood among the Juve faithful and cheered bravely as Pirlo slashed his spot-kick wide. You can picture our reactions as the sublime penalty dispatched by Stones found the top right corner and Howard saved from Federico Peluso.

Little did they know that the Panenka chip coincided with the re-opening of the School of Science. After the addition of attacking sparkle to the defensive foundations laid by his predecessor, Everton finished fifth at the end of his first season and the new man was hailed as another football visionary. To celebrate his accomplishment, the club erected a massive mural. It proved to be premature and a curse. His second and third seasons featured more tippy-tappy but this time at the expense of defending. It was such an anti-climax that dark clouds hovered over the France household throughout the campaign. My wife stopped asking: 'How did the blue boys get on?' She could detect the outcome by the behaviour of our dogs. Walter and Martha spent too many Pacific mornings hiding under the dining table fearful of relegation. Never before had I noticed their disgust with team selections and substitutions.

With the manager's unruffled philosophy and relentless - bordering on comical - positivity in front of television cameras, Elizabeth feared that Martinez showed less than a complete understanding of the soul of an institution like Everton Football Club. She claimed he had exhausted the goodwill created in his first season and lost the backing of many fans. In her eyes, he would achieve nothing, not even the League Cup, without them. What does she know? Not much. But enough to detect that Howard and Alcaraz were too old for first-team duty. In her words: 'You can't blame them for aging but can blame the manager for picking them. What do you expect from a charmer whose reputation is built on a fortuitous FA Cup triumph during which Wigan beat two championship sides - Huddersfield and Millwall, a League One team - Bournemouth and a non-League outfit - Macclesfield? His standing is founded on three goals in four minutes against Everton and a last-minute winner against a 10-man City side.'

The young manager adhered to his tippy-tappy tactics throughout his third season at Mama Blue during which his defensive unit - including Europe's most sought-after youngster, England's most respected pivot, and two of the best full-backs in the land - trembled at the mere thought of crosses and fell apart like a clown's car at a circus when balls were floated into their penalty box.

There had been such a dramatic decline in results since his first season when royal blue optimism was sky-high. Back then, many team performances were spectacular and produced a club record haul of Premier League points. I was impressed but feared that the deep-rooted preference for tippy-tappy was flawed, especially after the 2-3 home defeat to a physical Palace side in April 2014. My suspicions were confirmed beyond all reasonable doubt after the ignominious 2-5 implosion in Kiev. Therefore, by the time of the Capital One Cup loss to City some 12 months later – despite leading by 3-1 on aggregate - my hopes had turned into anxieties that Everton had become nothing more than his relegated Wigan side.

Emotion aside, team performances should be measured by where we finish in relation to our wage bills. Given that Everton pay the 10th highest wages, any League position below half-way is failure. On the pitch, the decline was attributed to unresolved defensive failings, unbalanced formations, Tim Howard's form and the ostracization of both Sylvain Distin and Kevin Mirallas. As for the fans, we were worn down by two seasons of woe and the manager's infuriating desire to take positives from every defeat. Many of us were at the end of our tether. Some felt robbed but weren't sure how. They sought retribution but didn't know from whom. However, they did know one thing. Evertonians were sick and tired of tippy-tappy and phenomenal throw-ins.

On paper, the club had assembled its best squad in decades and even though it reached the semi-finals of two domestic cup competitions, the general consensus was that the Catalan would fail to fulfill his promise of bringing Champions League football to Goodison and his players would not realize their immense potential. So with the club in the bottom half, he was sacked before the final game of his third season. Most likely, history will be a cruel judge of his efforts.

That's right ... put the 'phenomenals' in the recycling bin for next time

104. Sleeping giant

I hope I'm not alone in deploring the vast divide between the people who earn a living from the game and those who pay for that living. Motivated by pure greed, the behaviour of some directors, administrators, managers, agents and players is symptomatic of what is wrong with football and modern-day society. Worse still, my beloved club is partly responsible.

As one of the architects of the Premier League, I had expected Everton to consolidate its place alongside Arsenal, Liverpool, United and Tottenham. As we know, the club preferred to rest on its laurels before experiencing a Shakespearean fall from grace. So much so that throughout most of the past 24 seasons, I've speculated that if you stood outside the Winslow pub in Goodison Road you could detect the unedifying rattle of a famous institution crumbling under the weight of maxed-out credit cards and pay-day loans coupled with the silence of destiny falling into place. A bit harsh? Possibly.

If we forget about the recent heroics by Leicester for just one minute, there are four tiers to the rich moist chocolate gateau with buttercream icing - known as the Premier League. The first is reserved for the obscene wealth of Chelsea and City. The second is limited to Arsenal, Liverpool and United. Therefore the real purpose of most Premier League seasons is to determine which club from the top tier club will be crowned champions and which two from the second warrant spots in the Champions League. Just in case you were wondering, we're languishing in the third tier.

It's the same sad story off the pitch where we are stuck in the third tier of the commercial cake. The absence of domestic trophies and regular involvement in European combined with our parochial sponsorships, humdrum retail operations and, until recently, lack of success in attracting a benevolent sugar daddy has resulted in royal blue purgatory and anxiety of sliding deeper into the darkness of the fourth level.

For most of the Premier League era, our strategy - for want of a better term - has been to run the club at a manageable loss in anticipation that success on the pitch will contain the debt. Unfortunately and unfairly, our progress was halted during our fleeting romance with the Champions League. More precisely, it was derailed by a baffling decision to disallow Duncan Ferguson's header at Villarreal - a goal that would have sent the second-leg into extra-time and Everton into who knows where. As for the other parties involved, the referee retired immediately after the game and our other opponents progressed to the semi-finals.

Conspiracy theorists argue that because the rules had been massaged to allow the holders of the trophy – a certain Liverpool Football Club – to participate in the 2005 competition, UEFA didn't want five English clubs to progress to the group stages. So thanks to that dodgy decision by referee Pierluigi Collina, we were required to return to our faithful contingency plan of biting off the hand of any club prepared to offer silly money for one of our shining young stars. Personally, I find no stigma attached to unearthing gems, grooming them, off-loading them in their prime as long as the proceeds are re-invested in the club. After all, every club has sold its best player at one time or another.

Perhaps it's the American in me but I'm convinced that the times they are a-changing and, in the near future, the business of English football will resemble that of the popular professional sports in the USA. In my adopted homeland, cable television rules and loyal match-going fans lose out to their armchair counterparts in Waco, Wagga Wagga and Widnes, relegation fears don't exist, franchises move to more lucrative geographic markets - sometimes overnight, stadiums are modern and family-friendly, salaries are capped, owners earn attractive returns on their investments and all teams have a decent chance of being crowned champions.

In contrast, Premier League clubs participate in an annual procession rather than a closely contested competition. In the last decade only United, City, Chelsea, Arsenal and, of course, Leicester have won the League. Whereas nine different teams have triumphed in the MLB World Series and seven have been crowned NFL Super Bowl champions. Also there have been at least seven different NBA winners and nine sides have lifted the NHL's Stanley Cup.

While a broader distribution of silverware would improve our domestic game, I have a fear - and it's a really big one. A football revolution is on the horizon - namely a pan European League or even a pan-global League. My fear? Everton - the fourth most successful club in England and the eighteenth most valuable in the Deloitte Money League - could lose out during this revolution. I don't mean to be a harbinger of doom but a few years ago I looked through my crystal ball and saw Everton dominating the Premier League. I'm a novice at psychic readings but had no doubts about it. My only problem was that the top English clubs had progressed to enjoy the massive financial rewards from playing in a pan-European League.

I worry about the future of Everton Football Club. As you know I'm a master of understatement. In reality, the candidates for the new League are the two repulsively rich clubs plus four others. Most likely, the aspirants for the remaining spots will be evaluated in terms of achievements, fan-base and facilities. Our rivals are United - with their huge stadium, impressive sponsorship deals, name recognition and domination of Premier League era, Liverpool - with their European pedigree, global support and knack for getting their own way, and Arsenal - with their state of the art stadium, unbroken run of 91 seasons in the top flight and history of preferential treatment. Therefore the most likely contenders for our spot are Tottenham, West Ham and another Cockney club yet to be determined.

Re-engineering a business with few fixed assets is a daunting prospect and, even with fresh investment, nothing about the way ahead will be easy. There is so much work to do and so many challenges to overcome for us to surpass these clubs. That said, we have made major advances. Let's start at the top. Robert Elstone has been a breath of fresh air. He has established a robust and vibrant organization, engaged enthusiastic staff and nurtured a far more professional culture. I like Robert and have been impressed by his efforts - even though I've not always agreed with them. At our very first meeting, I told him that he was destined for greatness - like running the Super League or more likely the Premier League - and we'll be lucky to keep hold of him. I don't say this about many people but he's good enough for Liverpool Football Club. Strike that. He's too good for them. So for that matter is Denise Barrett-Baxendale. While her professionalism is admirable, her compassion for vulnerable members of our Everton family is heroic. To borrow a term from US oil & gas industry, they're 'corporate rock stars' whose performances have been aided by the support of some very talented musicians and back-up singers at Goodison.

Years ago, after Robert had inherited a somewhat lacklustre organization, I cautioned him to be wary of a couple of bruised apples hiding among the deadwood. They were the type of antagonists who bully their colleagues, stalk the independent websites seeking conflict and rain cynicism across Merseyside and beyond. Personally, I never understood their problems with the objective and often eloquent opinions expressed via these platforms. I agree with some and disagree with others but they are what football is all about. I must confess to enduring one frustrating experience at their hands. It occurred at the book signing for 'Alex Young - The Golden Vision' in aid of the former-players' charity. I still find it hard to accept that senior staff - no longer employed by the club - wanted to prohibit certain season-ticket holders from attending an independent function in the lounge that proudly bears the name of Alex Young. And because they didn't get their way, they threatened to stop the present-day stars from receiving their awards at an upcoming Hall of Fame dinner. I know you couldn't make it up.

While I encouraged all parties to work through their conflicts for the common good, Alex was less amenable and asked: 'Nasty vindictive numpties. Whatever happened to singing All Together Now for Everton?' Because these influential toxins discouraged dialogue between the club and the fans, the former played its cards with the deftness of a latter-day Machiavelli to reinforce an increasingly autocratic relationship with the latter. It appeared not to trust them. The feelings became mutual. The fans deserved better. Robert and his loyal staff deserved much better. I advised him to dispense blindfolds and cigarettes to the antagonists. Too nice or perhaps powerless to clean house, he delayed adopting my Houston approach until the ToffeeLeaks gaffe signalled a new dawn for communications between the club and its followers.

With relationships smoothed, where do we go from here? Surely, we must make the club unique. The task is complicated by the fact that we misplaced our identity for many years. Actually, it may be a case of erosion rather than theft. I'm not sure who we are any more. I like to think of us as a compassionate football club with loyal and enthusiastic fans capable of turning the Mama Blue into Harridan Blue - an emotionally charged cauldron credited with as many goals as Dixie Dean. Nevertheless, the concept of identity must be at the core of the required deep introspection about our future. From even a fleeting glance into the mirror we'll discover we're no longer the Merseyside Millionaires or, because the club failed to register the trademark, the People's Club. Coined by David Moyes at his first press conference, I liked media references to that label because it rankled every Red that I know. It still does.

If you ask the supporters of rival clubs, many admire our community initiatives and respect us as an old club with a big heart. Others define us as not being guess who - that's right Liverpool Football Club. This - as you are well aware - isn't a bad thing. During the past couple of decades, few football supporters outside of Merseyside have shown animosity towards us. Most likely because we were neither good enough nor controversial enough to be disliked. Nevertheless, one young West Ham supporter - no doubt heartened by the move to the Olympic Stadium and re-branding as 'London's Club' - advised me: 'Everton is an old piece of fecal matter floating in the Premier League toilet bowl waiting to be flushed into Sky Bet Championship football.'

Whereas one of my American neighbours - who you won't be too surprised to learn supports Man U - perceives Everton as the cash-poor second fiddle in a distressed city. That's right, he claims that we are the New York Mets of English football. I don't disagree but ask yourself, do we really want to be the Yankees? Worse still, other US soccer fans treat Everton in the way that they dismiss Stoke and Swansea. Recently I argued with one on the flight back to Arizona. He had a polyamorous relationship with City and United. Even though it was a battle of wits with an unarmed man, I contested: 'Shame on you! Everton versus Stoke and Swansea is 114 seasons in the top flight, nine League titles, seven second places and seven third places versus a combined total of 60 or 70 seasons and diddly-squat. Our contribution to world football is immeasurable. We were the first club to use football nets, issue matchday programmes, wear shirts numbered 1 to 11, construct a triple-decker stand, install under-soil heating, win a penalty shoot-out, appear in a live televised match and play 100 seasons in the top flight.' My rant rolled off my boastful tongue. I realized that it had hit a nerve when the passenger moved to a distant seat next to a woman holding a crying baby.

The Toffees, as some people - especially those footie-loving Cockneys - like to refer to us, are respected for authenticity, compassion, humility and heritage - not necessarily in that order. Of course, we are lauded as a pioneering club with a rich history of success and football firsts. For me, a peek at our accomplishments can be uplifting but you may be surprised to learn that I feel somewhat strongly that dwelling on the truly magnificent exploits of Dixie,

The Golden Vision, The Holy Trinity, The Rolling Thunder, The Bin Man and The Dogs of War isn't. No longer must we look forward to the past. Everyone associated with Everton Football Club must focus on the future.

So who are we? Or more important, who do we want to be? How do we proceed? And where do we start in order to get there? Well, how about converting my grandfather's Blue Beliefs into the Ten Pillars of Evertonia? We can add that Blues appreciate their heritage and Blues care for one another to his manifesto of royal blue and white kit … entertaining and cultured football … leaders and innovators not followers … top-class facilities … high moral code … youth development … soul of the local community … run by Blues for the benefit of fellow Blues. I think that many of these dusty pillars are as valid as they were six decades ago. Possibly, we can be special again by rediscovering Will Cuff's commitment to entertaining and productive football and imposing a distinctive style of play from the first-team to the youth teams.

Cue Ardavan Farhad Moshiri. In March 2016, the Premier League approved his acquisition of 49.9% of the shares of Everton Football Club Company Limited. Given his reported personal wealth - estimated by Forbes magazine at some £1.3 billion - Moshiri's arrival ended Blue Bill's decade-long search for investment which for too many years had attracted only fantasists and criticism. Fed up of the trophyless years and false dawns, my immediate reaction was predictable: 'What kept you? Where have you been?'

I'll miss having an Evertonian as our leader. In the distant past, my wife joked with Philip Carter that every prospective director should be a life-long Blue with a tasteful EFC tattoo and subjected to the Z-Cars Test. She professed that a reputable US research institute can detect shivers down a human's spine and proposed that all members of the club's hierarchy be tested to the sounds of John Keating's Orchestra. She added that the exercise would be augmented by a grilling involving a spotlight, a black leather chair and a Magnus Magnusson look-alike at an AGM. The sole topic would be 'The Early History of St Domingo Football Club'. She concluded: 'Of course the Z-Cars Test is impractical. We rarely have AGMs.' He laughed loudly then volunteered: 'Which arm?'

Three decades ago, the Everton Football Club of my childhood and adolescence went to sleep as a colossus. With the arrival of the Second Blue Billionaire - who holds his stake through an Isle of Man company named poetically Blue Heaven Holdings - it has awakened to discover that football has moved on. More than likely, the next four seasons will be the most important in my royal blue lifetime. During this window, we must win one or two meaningful domestic trophies, progress in European competitions, establish a popular international brand and move to a home consistent with a leading club. If we fail - and believe me this is difficult for me to accept - we'll join the ranks of Stoke and Swansea except, of course, that both of these mid-table clubs have modern stadiums and their names engraved on the League Cup.

Without a doubt, exciting times are ahead for Evertonians. We have an ambitious owner, a younger board of directors and a light at the end of the tunnel. Make no mistake, this is our last opportunity to rejoin the elite clubs and qualify for the pan-European League. The challenges throughout the next four years will be truly monumental. The club made a positive start. I was impressed by the methodical vetting process adopted to recruit both Ronald Koeman as manager and Steve Walsh as director of football. In particular, the vigorous pursuit of The Man from Zaandam - whose accomplishments as a manager include Dutch titles with PSV and Ajax - reaffirmed our standing as a member of football's aristocracy. While he has yet to taste success in one of Europe's top leagues, I pray that his management skills mirror his truly world-class playing abilities.

Unlike his immediate predecessors, the new manager won't be required to hunt for bargains, loans or free transfers. He'll have the funds to rebuild the side to embrace his style of play and, most important, get results and capture silverware. I understand that, founded on solid defending, he likes his teams to move the ball quickly. What a relief! No more tippy-tappy.

To date, we've appointed 14 men to the Goodison hot-seat - including Howard Kendall on three different occasions. Unlike them, our most ambitious recruit must hit the hallowed turf running. My expectations? During his first season, I expect the smooth and painless bedding in of his squad, a Top 8 finish and a derby win. The following season, I seek entertaining football, a Top 6 finish, a domestic cup - preferably the League Cup and another derby win. Then, if he hasn't replaced Arsene Wenger at Arsenal or Luis Enrique at Barcelona, I pray for a Top 4 finish and two derby triumphs. Remember, without hope and patience - there is nothing.

Can you imagine a victory at Anfield? People say that winning means nothing without the pain of losing at our old home. Well, Evertonians should know. We've experienced a sequence of eight defeats and a similar number of draws since that eventful evening way back in 1999 when Kevin Campbell scored and Francis Jeffers slapped goalkeeper Sander Westerweld. As part of Walter Smith's royal blue army, I remember the wild celebrations in the packed Anfield Road End and during the boisterous return journey along Walton Lane to the Blue House pub. Our joy converted into unadulterated bliss when we encountered a bunch of Reds with their tails between their legs who, in typical good humour, were complaining about young Steven Gerrard's unjust dismissal for a reckless waist-high challenge on Campbell.

While no longer impoverished, we'll need every penny to attract and keep top players. Therefore, our commercial activities will come under the billionaire's microscope. Capturing meaningful trophies will increase many revenues streams and muffle the most strident voices of dissent. But as we know too well, our beloved club has been a product of sociology rather than marketing and, as a consequence, has lagged behind its traditional rivals in generating income from sponsorship, advertising and merchandising. This must change. In the immediate future, we must fully exploit the attractive opportunities available to the world's twentieth most valuable brand in football to provide the funds to sustain our increased expenditures and ambitions. For example, our current shirt sponsorship deal is the ninth most lucrative in the Premier League but valued at 10% of that negotiated by United. At the expiration of the existing deal in 2017, our shirt sponsor must be a global household name prepared to pay a hefty fee for adding its name and logo to the kit of a legitimate candidate for pan-European football.

After all the doom and gloom of recent times, it's an exciting time to be an Evertonian. Even from my sunny corner of the Great American Experiment, I can feel a vortex of positive energy and believe that the club and its success-starved supporters are poised at the beginning of another era of great success. Within months of his arrival, Blue Farhad — given his previous stake in Arsenal, it's possible that he's more lavender than royal blue at present - replaced the under-performing manager and his side-kicks. And with the likes of Pep Guardiola at City, Jurgen Klopp at Liverpool and Jose Mourinho at United, he understood the need to lure a similar big name to Goodison. After he had identified Ronald Koeman as his primary target, he made sure that - like a member of the Royal Canadian Mounted Police - he got his man. It was a genuine statement of his intent and his immense ambition.

As always, some Blues remain skeptical. They're aware that the new manager inherited a bit of a mess - as you know, I'm a master of understatement - and wish him well in upgrading the playing squad, coaching staff and scouting system. If rumours are to be believed, Koeman has a war-chest of £100 million - which sounds extremely impressive but won't go very far in the merry-go-round of inflated transfer fees and salaries of 2016 - to paint the skies over Mama Blue with instant rainbows. At the same time, I hope someone has one eye on our compliance with the financial regulations agreed by all Premier League clubs when we were skint and the other eye on the long term. After all, we don't want a team of veterans in three years time.

I'm thrilled that we are at the verge of a new beginning with fresh ambitions, new ideas, clear vision and solid resources plus a dash of patience to tackle these challenges. Let's hope that our billionaire's financial clout and Ronald Koeman's drive will transform Everton into a robust candidate for the pan-European League. It's going to take hard work and possibly a miracle. While every new season starts with hope, the harsh reality is that if we don't make a great leap forward in 2016/17, then it might never happen.

Now, all that remains is for Blue Farhad to shower us with golden visions, silver trophies and, as a bonus, free scouse. I know not to expect too much too soon but, with the recruitment of a top-class manager and an acclaimed director of football, the application of a bit of lipstick to Mama Blue and the rumours of a waterfront stadium, I'm optimistic about the future. These advances remind me of the dawn of the Moores era. While we wait for our Second Blue Billionaire to lead us towards royal blue heaven, young Blues must draw strength from the fact that they support one of the oldest and greatest football clubs in the world. It's an institution that must be made special again. Better late than never, we are behaving like the football club of my youth. I'm so excited that tonight I'm going to allow myself to dream about a world-class museum for the world-class Everton Collection and, of course, the name of Everton Football Club engraved on the League Cup trophy. Be positive. It's there to be won!

Not a big fan ... but Distin does keep the kids away from the fire

105. Dinner party

Just like the club that I love, I've struggled with poor health throughout the past decade. If it wasn't my dodgy prostate then it was my dodgy colon or something else. I discourage friends from visiting my sick-bed. It minimizes remarks like 'Don't worry, you've got the strength of character to fight this thing'. Survival is based on a whole range of advanced technologies. Personality isn't one of them. Because I don't want to be defined by it, I've put on a good public face. Notwithstanding, darkness has been a companion. It's too easy to entertain pessimistic vibes. Experts advise you to simplify your life. They suggest spending time with friends and laughing out loud. I've turned to Mama Blue. You're always guaranteed a good chuckle and the odd cackle watching Everton.

I've become a poster-boy for colonoscopy, the procedure which allows the doctor to search the large intestine for abnormal growths. To do so, he inserts a 60 inch long probe into your rectum. Uncomfortable? You betcha but not as much as the preparation involving magnesium citrate to evacuate the colon. Remember that phrase. One day, if you're unlucky, it'll bring tears to your eyes. The evacuation procedure involves the use of an industrial strength laxative which should come with a rope for you to tie around the toilet bowl and weave through the fingers of your left hand. Tremors in the stomach and uncontrollable leg movements start after a mere sip. They escalate until seismic measurements reach those often associated with an erupting volcano. The secret is to sit upright rather than squat and to hold on to the rope for grim death.

I don't wish to sound morose but the only good thing about illness is it reminds you that life is perishable. I bade farewell to the Everton family for the first time at 'Gwladys Street's Last Supper' in 2003. The guests included fanzine editors, website masters and shareholders and season-ticket holders. At the last minute the organizers invited Alex Young. Consistent with my mother's final wishes, I presented EFC shares to the men who had helped run the Hall of Fame Galas. My initiative was trumped by Alex who pressed something extra-special into my hand. It was his FA Cup winner's medal from 1966. I've learnt more about our beloved club from chin wagging with him and other ex-players than from pouring over my crates of memorabilia. I regret not meeting more of them, especially those from the pre-war era.

There are a dozen ancient Blues I would love to chat with at a fantasy dinner party to better understand the nagging questions of today. My choice of venue would be the Adelphi's Sefton Suite, which was the White Star Line's template for the first-class dining room on RMS Titanic. In bygone days, the hotel was a landmark that most Merseysiders walked by. My father wasn't alone in believing that admission through its famous revolving doors was reserved for bankers, lawyers, doctors and other toffs.

Lore claims that Hitler worked there and was a regular at Goodison. The myth gained momentum after the publication of 'Young Adolf'. Beryl Bainbridge's novel alleges that he had lived in Upper Stanhope Street with his step-brother Alois between 1912-1913. Was Adolph Hitler really a Blue? Given that we were the city's top side and he wasn't the type of Nazi to waste his time on our neighbours who had just avoided relegation, it's possible that the Fuhrer of the Third Reich stood on Gwladys Street's terraces. His allegiance may account for Everton being hailed as 'The English Masters' when we played four games against the German FA in 1932. More likely, there isn't a grain of truth in the story. There may be more weight, however, in the rumour that Muammar Gaddafi was a bit of a Blue. While I never bumped into him at Goodison, some say that he had been a supporter since the club visited Libya in 1979.

Returning to my dinner party and the pursuit of old-fashioned wisdom; Will Cuff would be my guest of honour. All Blues are indebted to him. He built the club into a football institution and converted the football ground into a cathedral. Sadly he fell out with the other directors towards the end of his life over the refinements to the by-laws which allocated one vote per share rather than one vote per shareholder. These changes encouraged John Moores to buy out the small shareholders in the Fifties and allowed for the transfer of the majority ownership to Messrs Johnson, Kenwright and Moshiri. I would welcome his opinions on the financial health of the club and the small matter that we have had four chief executives during the past decade and none of them were Blues.

Another guest would be Frank Brettell - a sports reporter and a football administrator - who played for St Domingo Football Club before serving on Everton's committee. His initiatives have been airbrushed from our history yet Brettell is lauded for developing the professional game in the South. I would welcome his opinion on the growing domination of the London clubs and the London media. Is it because the streets of the Smoke are paved with gold while those in the North are covered with discarded chewing gum? Also why does the local newspaper inexorably ease from editorial to advertorial when describing the stewardship of the club?

Next would be George Mahon, the founding father with the courage to walk away from Anfield. My questions relate to ground moves. Should the Merseyside giants have met half-way to share new digs - a shrine to their collective passion - befitting the most successful football city in the land? As one of the region's top accountants, I would ask Mahon to take a gander at our financial reports to unearth the Arteta money - sorry, I couldn't resist it. He could employ his forensic skills to tackle other taboo subjects such as Yakubu Aiyegbeni's real age and Steve Simonsen's actual transfer fee.

Sixty seasons and two-million miles ... ever thought about
writing a book about your condition?

106. Other guests

Who next? I would invite John Bell, the brains behind the Association Footballers' Union formed to oppose the introduction of the maximum wage at the turn of the century. My questions would address player-power. Does he approve average Premier League wages in excess of 100 times those of typical fans? Also what does he think about flash - my politer epithet - young players. Should they and their entourages be forced to clean the muddy boots of the senior pros?

Hoping that he had forgotten about our encounter at the Dublin Packet, I would like to chat with Dixie. In particular, I would love to call him Bill. I've known his family for years and always stop to admire his Goodison statue. It's magnificent. Surely, his contributions to our national game are worthy of two more statues located at the northern exits of the Mersey Tunnels. While Dean would be embarrassed by such suggestions; I would welcome his views on the subject of the next Goodison statue – The Holy Trinity or The Golden Vision? I regret that I would be unable to resist asking him how many goals he would have scored as the lone striker in a 4-5-1 formation.

I've heard fewer kind words about Theo Kelly. His son, who lives in New Jersey, has told me that our first manager received unfair criticism related to his role in the sales of Dean, Lawton and Mercer. I remain open-minded but would like to know what Kelly was thinking when he designed the club's badge. Some years ago, I tracked down his original rendition. Why didn't he incorporate the Liver Bird? Given that we've won only four titles in the 70 years since its introduction, does he think that the Latin motto is a burden? Also, I've never understood the need to include the club's name in the design. Personally, I would introduce a new shirt and revised badge every summer to emphasize one of the things that make us special - our unparalleled tenure in the top flight. I would highlight the following numbers under the crest: '2016/17 - 114th.'

To please Chemical Harry, I would include Tommy Lawton who I've met. Sort of. Chemical Harry and I spotted him in a motorway cafe near Nottingham. He signed my father's AA handbook. No footballer's career suffered as much as that of Lawton. Because we've never been relentless, ruthless or recurrent champions, I would welcome his slant on the missed opportunity to create a royal blue dynasty in the Forties. Also I would welcome his opinions of simulation - the curse of the modern game. Today's players are notorious for their tendency to trip, fall and cry more often than toddlers learning to walk. Whereas Chemical Harry bragged that despite being kicked black and blue, his hero rarely went to ground.

Joe Mercer, an England team-mate of Lawton, also forfeited his best years but went on to enjoy post-war success by earning two titles and the FA Cup at Arsenal. I've had the pleasure of meeting his widow several times and inspecting the bracelet made from his medals. It's truly magnificent. Mercer was an Everton shareholder throughout his adult life and, after his spell in charge of the England national side in 1974, I thought that his knowledge and wisdom would have been of no little value to Billy Bingham and Gordon Lee as well as the board. Personally, I would welcome Mercer's opinion on how his School of Science team of 1938/39 compared with the all-conquering champions of 1969/70. More than anything, I need to know if his assistant manager learnt anything of value from crossing paths with a scruffy hitchhiker in 1968.

I'm fascinated by Jack Taylor. Few fans appreciate that Taylor recorded the highest number of first-team appearances during the pre-World War 1 era, 400 League games and 56 FA Cup games in 14 seasons. He competed in a total of eight semi-finals, including replays, and three finals and is the only survivor of the team that lost to Villa in the 1897 final to be included in the side that triumphed over Newcastle in 1906. As a result, he was the first Everton captain to parade the trophy around the city's streets. My questions would be simple: Why have we won the silverware only four times in the past 100 years? Are we unlucky or are we damned?

Then there is Edgar Chadwick, who took part in our inaugural League game and was a regular international when England was lauded as the best side in the world. I would ask which gave him most pride – his first international cap or his first medal. While I had assumed that nothing compares with being driven around the streets of Liverpool in an open-top bus, the stars that I've polled from the Thirties, Sixties, Eighties and Nineties didn't confirm my expectations. A half-dozen voted for club and six voted for country. My other question would relate to him beating the path across Stanley Park for the likes of Hickson, Barmby and Xavier. It's a simple question: 'Why Edgar? Why?'

Last would be the Victorian goal-machine who scored 27 times in only 22 games in his one full season at Everton as well as 97 times in 108 outings with his previous club - Blackburn Rovers. Jack Southworth, like Gary Lineker, finished his Everton career as the League's top scorer but trophyless. Given his pedigree, I would like him to tackle the old chestnut: Who would be his first pick at centre-forward – Dixie Dean or Tommy Lawton? And, though he didn't see either in action, who would be his last pick – Albert Juliessen or Brett Angell? As you may know, Southworth was a violinist with the Halle symphony orchestra. Nevertheless, I would resist temptation to ask him to play 'Z Cars' for his supper. Even though Bob Dylan recorded the song for the album 'The Bootleg Series Volume 11: The Basement Tapes', the music at my fantasy dinner would be provided by the battered acoustic guitar and tattered baritone voice of Leonard Cohen.

Now to the menu. Given that we've had the same tried and tested items at every bash I've organized at the Adelphi , Messrs Cuff, Mahon and friends would dine on the hotel's finest chicken dinner washed down with Chang beer. Yes, I know. I've taken this fantasy too far.

Madam, I can assure you that we're not a couple of Kopites

107. Iya love

Now permit me to recall a real-life dinner - let's call it my 'Final Ta-ra'. It started with a plain white envelope postmarked 'City of Liverpool' in my PO Box. I assumed that it was a parking fine from a recent excursion to the old country. Therefore, it was with no little apprehension that I read the contents: 'The Freedom of the City Panel has voted unanimously to award you the prestigious title of Citizen of Honour.' The letter explained that the award recognized inspirational people who had made significant contributions to enriching the life and image of the city. Open mouthed, I shared the news with wife: 'I'm going to have my name added to the walls of Liverpool Town Hall.'

As you may know, the Grade 1 listed building has stood at the junctions of Dale Street, Castle Street and Water Street for more than 250 years. One of the finest Georgian buildings in the land, its magnificent exterior is surpassed only by its interior. Interestingly, the building is no stranger to Americans. I understand that the last act of the American Civil War occurred there in 1865 when Captain Waddell surrendered the CSS Shenandoah to the British government. Again I shared my good news with Elizabeth: 'I'm going to have my name added to the walls of Liverpool Town Hall.' She responded: 'What in spray paint?'

Six months later, Lancashire Lass and I attended the civic ceremony and accepted my award for services to football on behalf of the Everton family. Its significance only became apparent after I was informed that the last person to receive it for services to football was Bill Shankly. The award is entirely ceremonial and confers no special privileges. That said, I fib occasionally that as a Citizen of Honour I'm allowed to herd Kopites from the airport to Anfield at weekends and to park on double yellow lines in the city centre during the week.

As for my first visit to Liverpool Town Hall? I wasn't disappointed. Indeed, I was impressed by the panelled council chamber, grand staircase, Eisteddfod thrones and breath-taking dome. Of course, som of my friends reenacted the Beatles clowning about on the balcony during their famous civic reception in mid-1964 as the Liverpool Police Band performed 'Can't Buy Me Love' to the vast crowds gathered in Dale Street. As for the official ceremony? The best part wasn't the grandeur of the setting or the formal procession behind the footman carrying the silver mace. It wasn't the presentation by the Lord Mayor or the kind words of Joe Anderson, then the Leader of the City Council. It was the genuine friendship of everyone involved. This was best demonstrated by the Lady Mayoress. As we shook hands firmly and exchanged warm smiles, she proclaimed: 'Iya love'.

Later that evening Elizabeth hosted an 'Everton Family Gathering' in the Town Hall. The guests included 32 representatives from 25 different branches of the Everton tree - from the Chief Executive of Everton Football Club to the leader of the Blue Union. It was a shining endorsement that people known to have significant disagreements put them to one side. It was a night for fans so starved yet so deserving of success on the pitch. While the atmosphere crackled with the pride and humour associated with being Blues, she also invited three well-behaved Kopites - so that they could witness real and unconditional love for a proper football club. I had an ulterior motive and halted the proceedings shortly after the first course. During the time-out, the attentive staff served plates of scouse, without even a hint of laxative, to the Kopites. It was intended as a welcome to our great city and was accompanied by maps of the area with directions written in Norwegian. Born out of poverty, this nourishing mush of lamb and vegetables, slow cooked to make the cheap cuts of meat more palatable, is the traditional dish of the people of Merseyside. Predictably, the response to my gesture was somewhat mixed. It was well received by one or two of the Reds and all of the on-looking Blues.

When it comes to our neighbours at the other end of Stanley Park, I must make it crystal clear that not all of them possess an overblown sense of entitlement that fuels delusional beliefs. Not all are gobshites either. It's just simple rhyme. A bit of friendly jesting. Some of the most generous and compassionate people I've encountered on Merseyside or anywhere else for that matter support Liverpool Football Club. They know that I'm in awe of their club's tremendous successes in Europe, especially the incredible comeback in Istanbul.

In addition, they know that I admire Kenny Dalglish as a world-class player and support the good deeds of the Marina Dalglish Appeal to raise funds for the treatment of breast cancer. They are well aware that I was as distraught as them to learn about the tragic deaths and injustice at Hillsborough. Most understand why I've never bought - and never will buy - 'The Sun' newspaper and share their confusion related to the former-Liverpool players who happily pocket money from Rupert Murdoch's News Corporation. I trust that they understand that my words are simply friendly joshing designed to get under their thin skins.

Where was I? Yes, the plain white envelope which boasted the Liver Bird. Our neighbours would have the world believe that the bird is red. Positively nothing could be farther from the truth. The Liver Bird is neither blue, red or even lavender. Like scouse, it belongs to the people of the Second City of the Empire. There are colonies of the feathered, winged, bipedal, warm-blooded, egg-laying vertebrates beyond the boundaries of Anfield. In addition to famous examples which adorn the skyline at the city's famous waterfront, there are in excess of 100 different versions decorating local museums, libraries, hospitals, cemeteries, banks, hotels, shops, pubs, bridges and, of course, tunnels. They all stand proud.

I must clarify that I'm not a passionate advocate of incorporating the fierce guardian of the tides of the River Mersey complete with its mouthful of seaweed into our official badge. But because the followers of the People's Club are proud of their roots and citizenship, I would like to see at least one royal blue example of the Liver Bird grace Goodison or, perhaps more appropriately, a new state-of-the-art waterfront stadium. After all, no respectable building in the City of Liverpool is totally complete without one.

The bad news is that your condition has deteriorated ...
the good news is that you'll never see Everton play in Kirkby

108. Sick Blue

You may have noticed that I've hinted at the conflicts between the demands of a career in the oil & gas industry, the responsibilities of marriage to a saint and my devotion to the royal blue cause. Clearly, Everton won hands down. The rewards for my unswerving loyalty have changed dramatically over time. Even though we never realized our full potential, I enjoyed the excitement of the Sixties, Seventies and Eighties. Since then I've endured almost three decades of frustrated optimism. In recent times the buzz associated with a run of a few good results is often dampened by shivers of pessimism. As I've moved from middle age into - there is no getting around it - old age, I no longer worry that my modest expectations have been well and truly managed.

This undercurrent of despondency has made me stronger. I know because I've followed the exploits of Everton Football Club in sickness and in health. That applies to both its condition and my own. My specialist is aware of my craziness. He jokes that I'll never see the club's name on one of his prescriptions - not even for a transdermal patch - because there is no safe dose. Previous doctors have claimed also that watching the blueboys hasn't been good for me. I've few doubts their diagnosis and second opinions are valid. Certainly, I've exited Goodison in a poor state of mental health on more occasions than I care to remember yet can think of only two occasions when I've entered the ground in poor physical condition.

The first time was after I had been discharged from Battle Hospital in Reading where I had been treated for a heart-attack. Still groggy, I ignored the doctor's advice to take things easy and drove 200 miles to Merseyside on a bitterly cold night to see the encounter with Newcastle Reserves. Why? It was the home-coming of Duncan Ferguson who had been incarcerated for an assault on John McStay during a match between Rangers and Raith. I wasn't a big fan of the Big Man. I liked the fact that he thumped opponents rather than defenseless corner flags but didn't enjoy the way his team-mates bypassed midfield and lobbed the ball up to him. That aside, I thought it was unjust that he had been punished twice for the same crime. Horrified by my irresponsibility, my doctor deduced it was the reckless act of one Everton nutter paying homage to another Everton nutter.

The second occurrence was more capricious and downright stupid. A few days after surviving an emergency operation at the Countess of Chester Hospital - which left me with a stomach wound requiring 38 staples - I attended the UEFA Cup tie against Brann at Goodison. To do so, I wore a catheter strapped to my right leg. This foolhardy behaviour was stimulated by an out-of-body experience. Aware of the fact that you may not believe in ghoulies, long-legged beasties and things that go bump in the night, I must confess to meeting one in the High Dependency Unit at Chester. My recollections are somewhat hazy because I was attached to a morphine drip at the time but my ghostie had a mop of white wavy hair that belonged on the front row of the Main Stand or the threshold of the Pearly Gates. His black cloak made a rustling sound as he checked the identities of the occupants of the beds, some of whom had lost limbs, before he approached me: 'You must be the Blue, right? I've only seen such miserable faces as yours in the Park End.' I wasn't spirit-friendly and hoped that he would leave me to my Class A pain-killers.

Undaunted, he speculated that my best memories were linked to football: 'Remember the first time someone called you a good Evertonian? And how special it made you feel?' Then he asked me to pin-point where I learnt about the deaths of President Jack Kennedy, John Lennon and Princess Diana. I couldn't. But in answer to his next question, I knew exactly where I was when I heard of the defection of Alan Ball to London - Marks & Spencer in Manchester; the exit of Howard Kendall to Bilbao - Sardi's Restaurant in New York; and the sale of Wayne Rooney to United - Charles De Gaulle Airport.

He reminded me that listening - or even keeping tabs via the internet - to royal blue action churns the emotions but there was no better pick-me-up than being there. Vividly, I recall him leaning over my bed and whispering: 'You're not on this earth for long - visit the Old Lady whenever you can!' I believed him because he resembled the Grim Reaper, albeit without the scythe-wielding personification of death. Subsequently, I slept for the rest of the afternoon and woke to discover an absence of self-pity. I was ready for Goodison and the visitors from Norway. I suspect that I'm not the first man to have urinated watching Everton in action and, from the facial expressions of the Norwegian defenders, I doubt that I was the only man to piss himself that evening.

Whenever I visit Merseyside, I'm humbled by the warm smiles and kind words of my fellow Blues. I've been stopped by hundreds of fans who wanted to express their gratitude to me. I'm flattered and embarrassed by the attention. One extreme example involved two stalkers. I had sensed that these intoxicated brutes were following me along Church Street before they eventually confronted me outside Liverpool Central Station. While a firm handshake may be universal greetings, they refrained from such practice and threw their muscular and tattooed arms around me. Immobilized in a hearty embrace, one of them looked me straight in the eyes and mumbled: 'Thanks for everything you've done for our club'. He grabbed my lapels, shook me hard and repeated: 'Thanks for every effing thing you've done for our effing club.' The other must have had Maori origins because he pressed his nose and forehead against mine. As our breaths intermingled, all I could say was: 'Don't thank me. Being a Blue is my reward.' It was one of those very rare occasions in life when you find the right words to say exactly how you feel.

Three home defeats on the bounce and now this ...

109. Everton family

Our neighbours enjoy a well-earned international profile but the streets of the city are teeming with Blues. Make that match-going Blues. None are more dedicated than those at Bluekipper, who invited me to accept the 'Brian Labone – True Evertonian Award for 2008' at their annual presentation night. The old Olympia Ballroom was jam-packed. The stage was crowded with stars from the Eighties and Nineties and I remember thinking what am I doing alongside these great Blues in front of these other great Blues? I agreed to say a few words. Slowly, I reached into my jacket to extract my glasses and a sheet of A4 paper. The latter contained three words. I held it at arm's length and in my best RADA voice pronounced: 'Kopites are Gobshites'. Without uttering another sound, I left the stage. Stunned for a second or two, the audience erupted into the spine-tingling chant: 'Kop-ites are Gob-shites … Kop-ites are Gob-shites'. The 500 voices grew louder as I made my way to the green room where I bumped into Joleon Lescott who was to receive the Star Man Award for 2008. I whispered to him: 'Follow that big guy!' With fear in his eyes, he looked at me as if I was a Black Hawk helicopter.

Believe me, I regret making that vulgar speech. It seemed like a good idea at the time - similar to indulging in a late-night chicken vindaloo curry or spending your life savings on a Lotus Europa. I prefer to keep a low profile but am flattered when Blues put a name to my face. Of course, that's not always the case. I recall minding my own business outside the Adelphi on the evening of a home defeat when I noticed a Blue walking towards me. Sad-faced, he was wearing a blue t-shirt displaying the profound message: 'Blues versus Reds is art versus porn … Dr Everton.' The fact that I couldn't take my eyes off the shirt seemed to irritate the owner: 'What you looking at old man?' I retorted: 'Rare wisdom'. He glared: 'Fuck off you old Kopite'. I wasn't pleased by his reference to my aging appearance. It was his use of the K-word that upset me. I'd never been called one before. It made me feel dirty.

No experience compares with the company of Blues. I enjoy their memories, moans and gossip as much as their passion. Such encounters confirm that we're fugitives from the law of averages. What makes our bonds so extra special? For starters, we exhibit an inherent strength of character developed from supporting Everton. This manifests as an independence of spirit and lack of deference. We are blood brothers - loyal to one another rather than a commercial brand - who radiate collective warmth that puts more conventional families to shame.

Our devotion is passed from generation to generation by word of mouth. Examples abound. Last year, I recall pondering how to negotiate the mass of litter swirling around the entrance to the Megastore. I noticed that the cyclone contained discarded bags of every flavour of Walkers' Crisps known to mankind - even mint sauce. After side-stepping Gary Lineker's most enduring gift to Merseyside, I held open the door for an anxious-looking mother pushing her youngest in his stroller ahead of the rest of her family. The father recognized me. His face lit up: 'Dr Everton, you got a minute or two? I'd like my eldest to sing for you.' So against a backdrop of discounted third kits, the 5-year-old gave a jaw-dropping performance: 'We don't care what the red shite say … what the fuck do you care … because we all know that there's gonna be a show … and the Everton boys will be there …' I smiled at the boy. To be honest, I was lost for words. His father wasn't: 'I've told you before, it's 'what the heck do you care' when you're outside of effing Garston!'

While some friendships have fizzled out or fallen by the wayside during the past six decades, my devotion to Everton has endured. Always, I've wanted to hammer the Reds at home, away and Wembley, win silverware every season, play cultured football like the Holy Trinity and smash transfer fee records like we did in the days of old. But nowadays, my expectations are modest. I continue to love Everton Football Club dearly but am pleased if we finish in the top-half, beat the Reds especially against the run of play at Goodison, put in gallant performances against the rest of the Premier League elite and enjoy a good cup run - above all in the League Cup.

That said, I encourage all Blues - young and old - to never be afraid to love Everton even when there's little chance that you'll be loved in return. Nowadays I tell young Blues, that they have the advantage of early exposure to life's unfairness and don't have a God-given right to expect anything except an equal opportunity. I can attest that supporting Everton builds character.

You'll have detected that I'm indebted to a wife who claims that behind every good Blue is a great woman rolling her eyes. My Everton addiction is her addiction. My journey is her journey. I don't think that she would have wanted it any other way. Elizabeth rarely complains but is irritated by my abuse of technology. Trawling the internet for Everton news is acceptable whereas employing iPhones to gossip about the goings-on at Goodison is prohibited. The ban has something to do with not needing a silicon-enhanced seducer to take away the face-time she has with me. Elizabeth believes that such electronic devices turn people into ill-mannered zombies. Actually, it has more to do with the fact that my muscular right thumb developed during my hitchhiking days has made me a clumsy texter. Lancashire Lass remains bemused by the hold that the club has over me but her support for the royal blue cause has expanded over the decades. She has hosted many get-togethers including 'Gwladys Street's Tex-Mex Feast' in 2004 for the Blues visiting Houston from different parts of North America. Held at Ninfa's, the Tex-Mex restaurant on Navigation Boulevard in the city's barrio, the attendees came from Boston, Chicago, Los Angeles, Miami and Seattle. They had never met before. One Wall Street wizard drove from New York to taste the fajitas and enjoy the sizzling chat about Everton. Talk about being Everton Crazy? The investment banker drove a Ferrari to the match.

His commitment was no greater than the thousands that travelled from Merseyside. To see the shopping malls, bars and restaurants in my adopted hometown heaving with Blues was a dream come true. My wife was so impressed that she deposited a wad of Benjamin Franklins behind the bar at the Home Plate Grill to ensure no Blues went without liquid refreshments during their brief stay in Houston. An hour later, she secretly added another wad. Apparently, a bar packed with Blues consumes Mexican beer at the rate of $850 per hour plus gratuity. I told her that it was a small price for an evening of hugs and for being accepted as a Blue.

My journey has chronicled what football does to rational individuals. In my case the first club of Merseyside has been the single constant throughout my life. As a schoolboy, an apprentice gas fitter, a part-time university student, a rocket scientist, an oil & gas executive and a management consultant, my heart never strayed from Everton. The list is endless so I'll continue as a do-gooder, an author, a collector, a football historian and - in the words of Wikipedia - a philanthropist, I've always been able to rely on the Everton family. It kept me out of trouble during my childhood in Widnes. Also it kept me grounded in my adult childhood worldwide. For 60 match-going seasons and counting - more than half of the club's tenure in the top flight - it has provided me a rare sense of belonging. The Everton family has never let me down. Of course, such lasting relationships involve lots of compromise. Some family members are better known than others - namely Judy Dench, Mark Carney, Andy Burnham and possibly Paul McCartney. Some are diehards. Some lapsed. Some transient. All are welcome, even Sylvester Stallone and Justin Beiber.

Though my connections with my beloved club no longer sizzle like they did in my youth - today they are more about pragmatism than idealism - my bonds with the Everton family are stronger than ever. My Everton is still about people. Not the players and managers who only acknowledge the existence of the fans with a few seconds of applause at full-time. No, my Everton is about special people - my fellow Blues. I'm delighted to be accepted as one of them and feel comfortable in repeating my deepest held belief that the Everton family is one of life's masterpieces.

110. What do you call a life dedicated to Everton?

Some Americans question the age at which you choose their club. Because the decision affects your whole life, these soccer fans, who happen to follow United or City or both, believe that an amnesty should be offered at age 18 and again at age 60, whereby fans could opt for a change of allegiance with impunity. They see no purpose in the sufferance associated with supporting a club with no promise of silverware.

If you need guaranteed success to brighten your day-to-day existence then Everton Football Club isn't for you. On the other hand, if you want to be a part of something extra special and enjoy an uncommon sense of belonging that is increasingly rare in life, then welcome to the family. We are more than a tribe, we are kin. Whenever I've come across my blue-blooded relatives, even in the most remote and unexpected places, we've plunged into spontaneously intimate conversations, mixing the present with the past, as if the club's history has been our personal history too. I've always been aware of the special bonds between family members but hadn't appreciated until a dozen years ago just how much this camaraderie had enhanced my life. More than anything, it taught me to value fidelity.

To rationalize a journey that has involved in excess of two million miles and 800 matches, I like to claim that Everton Football Club is a part of my DNA. When it comes to the nature versus nurture debate I don't know how much of my craziness is determined by genetic predisposition and how much by my life experiences with the Everton family. Either way, There's no escaping the fact that I'm crazy. Always have been and no doubt always will be. I wish I was more ashamed of my own condition. I'm not.

At this point it may be timely to determine if you suffer from this mental condition. Because the symptoms are complex, please ask yourself the following questions:

1 Have you ever felt heart palpitations at hearing the first strains of 'Z Cars'?

2 Do you attend League Cup games, season after season, expecting a different outcome?

3 Do you refuse to acknowledge anything scarlet, crimson or flame? Even traffic lights?

4 During the summer, do you trawl the internet for transfer gossip? More than once a day?

5 Are you guilty of withdrawing from social interactions after the most predictable defeat?

Obviously, there is a theme developing here. By now, you may be starting to see yourself as others have seen you for years.

6 Do you own a range of Everton replica shirts - home, away and third - that stretch from size M to size XL and beyond?

7 Are you willing to fork out your hard-earned money to watch tippy-tappy football?

8 Do you check the Internet for news of earth-shaking expenditures during transfer windows?

9 Have you trained your children or dog to growl at Gary Lineker throughout 'Match of the Day'?

10 Hand on heart; do you have lucky blue socks? Or perhaps lucky blue underwear?

11 When you go to the toilet at 3:00 am, do you check ToffeeWeb on your way back to bed?

12 Do you know someone with a voodoo doll that boasts a resemblance to Mr Clive Thomas?

13 Do you think that Bob Latchford can still walk on water?

14 And finally, do you own an item of clothing that boasts 'Blues versus Reds is humility versus
   arrogance; loyalty versus entitlement; and art versus pornography?'

So how did you do? Be honest, did you answer 'yes' to half of these questions? If so, then your
appetite for all things royal blue is insatiable and in my eyes - wait for it - you are Everton crazy.
Is that such a bad thing? Certainly not. I must caution you, however, there are no known
anti-psychotic medications available from the National Health Service or natural remedies from
holistic practitioners to treat your condition. Personally, I don't suffer from being crazy - I enjoy
every single minute of it! As you know, our beloved club demands a great deal from you. The more
your mind tries to discard it, the more your heart holds on to it. This leads me to the most
important question of them all: What do you call a life dedicated to Everton Football Club?

Answer: Time well spent.

Forget about Wembley ... set the sat-nav to Europe

Postscript - David France

While this book is done - my royal blue odyssey continues.

I trust that it has succeeded in capturing the impact that football has had and continues to have on me and those around me. While the manuscript was finalized after Farhad Moshiri bought his near 50% stake in the club in mid-2016, most of the words were crafted towards the end of the David Moyes era in 2012 and, like a good pan of good scouse, were left on the door-step to cool down. Because - as we know - Blues are the only supporters in the city who laugh at themselves, I detoured into the world of chuckles and, aided by Peter King, peppered the text with gag cartoons better known as Evertoons.

As for my tales, I've honed them with other captive audiences, including rabbis in a New Jersey synagogue, tool-pushers on an off-shore platform, US Senators after giving testimony at the Capitol Building and Native Americans in an Arizona long-house. Perhaps like you, many listeners to my royal blue anecdotes concluded that if Everton Football Club was a pharmaceutical then selling it would be illegal in the USA. Whereas, an American neighbour who practices as a clinical psychologist, has advised me that my daily routine of a brisk half-hour walk with Walter and Martha followed by a similar stint on ToffeeWeb - let's call it Medical Everton - is a valid defence against age-related dementia and the temporary misplacement of house keys. So believe it or not, supporting Everton Football Club is good for you.

While producing this autobiography, I developed a much better understanding of the role of Everton Football Club in my life. The process validated many of my fears. At the top of that list is the private revelation that I'm mad about a football club that no longer exists and hasn't done so for some years. Perhaps decades. Also I've discovered that all of the dates in my personal timeline are defined by memorable football fixtures. And that as you get older, you remember things that never happened quite as you describe them and forget things that are really important to other people.

Please permit me to elaborate. I was driving home along the freeway from Flagstaff to Sedona at about 22 mph above the speed limit. Well that's what the officer of the Arizona Highway Patrol claimed before demanding to see my driving license, insurance certificate and proof of ownership of the vehicle. After inspecting the paperwork, he asked: 'Is this your Land Rover? How long have you owned it?' I answered: 'Yes sir. Going on 10 years. It was manufactured in the old country and has never let me down.' Unimpressed, he enquired: 'So what's your plate number?' I thought for two or three seconds before responding: 'No idea.' The officer didn't smile as he presented me with a speeding ticket for $198. Neither did my wife.

As expected, I endured some world-class nagging from Lancashire Lass during the remainder of the journey but thought that was the end of the matter. Four weeks later, however, I was in the process of parking the car in the garage when my wife asked: 'What's the registration number on this Land Rover?' Again, I thought for a few seconds before responding: 'Not the foggiest idea.' She smiled: 'How can you remember so much about Everton yet so little about everyday things? Why don't you check the plate and learn the random collection of letters and numbers?' Dutifully, I went to the back of the vehicle and read the shiny new plate: 'EFC 1878.' I laughed: 'That's one problem solved, now where did I leave the house keys?'

We've all misplaced keys and forgotten names When you're young, you don't worry about such short-term memory loss. When you get older, fatter and balder, you agonize over cognitive problems. That said, what I do remember is that I've enjoyed a monogamous relationship with Everton Football Club for 60 years during which time it has graduated from my faithful crutch to my life-long companion.

Clearly, I've struggled to support my beloved football club in moderation - and remain hopelessly captivated by the mere sight of royal blue. I realize, however, that my Everton is different than that of younger Blues but can assure them that while supporting Everton Football Club has never been easy - and most likely never ever will be - it will provide some of the best times of their lives. I believe strongly that our Everton family is extra-ordinary and a fundamental building block of Merseyside society. Furthermore, I'm convinced our inherent strength of character - developed from being raised as Blues - radiates a collective warmth that puts more conventional families to shame.

My Everton journey has been both long , enlightening and fulfilling. I've been extremely fortunate to have met every chairman since John Moores, every manager since Harry Catterick and every secretary since Jim Greenwood. While some appeared more committed to the cause than others, I reminded them all that we - the Everton Family - will be around long after they had moved on to greener pastures or made an ignominious exit into obscurity. With this in mind, I would like to share one of my most strongly held beliefs - which I must add has been critically examined, evaluated and validated - let's call it Dr France's Second Law: Everton Football Club is nothing without Evertonians.

It's acknowledged universally that the opening line sells a book while the closing line sells the author's next one. So please permit me to leave you with a refinement of the sound advice that my father gave to me as a youngster: 'You're not on this earth for long. Work less, live more. Watch Everton whenever you can.'

Dedication

An autobiography is no more than a diary of intimate confessions,
long-held feelings, well-honed opinions and a dash of transparency.
Hopefully after reading my words, readers will feel like they know me.

This book is dedicated to the person that understands me ...

Elizabeth France